GHOSTLAND

ALSO BY COLIN DICKEY

Cranioklepty: Grave Robbing and the Search for Genius
Afterlives of the Saints: Stories from the Ends of Faith

GHOSTLAND

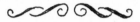

An American History in
Haunted Places

Colin Dickey

VIKING

VIKING
An imprint of Penguin Random House LLC
375 Hudson Street
New York, New York 10014
penguin.com

ISBN 9781101980194 (Hardcover)
ISBN 9781101980217 (eBook)

Printed in the United States of America
1 3 5 7 9 10 8 6 4 2

Set in LTC Cloister
Designed by Nancy Resnick
Illustrations © Jon Contino

For Nicole

The main work of haunting is done by the living.

—JUDITH RICHARDSON

Ghostland lies beyond the jurisdiction of veracity.

—NATHANIEL HAWTHORNE

CONTENTS

AUTHOR'S NOTE

This book is not about the truth or falsity of any claims of ghosts. There are questions there—fascinating to some, problematic or uninteresting to others—about physics and metaphysics, theology and superstition, the natural and the supernatural, but all those questions ultimately end up circling back on themselves. As Samuel Johnson mentioned to James Boswell more than two hundred years ago, "It is wonderful that five thousand years have now elapsed since the creation of the world, and still it is undecided whether or not there has ever been an instance of the spirit of any person appearing after death." There is no amount of proof that will convince a skeptic of spirits, just as no amount of skeptical debunking will disabuse a believer. As Johnson remarked regarding the paranormal, "All argument is against it; but all belief is for it."

This book instead focuses on questions of the living: how do we deal with stories about the dead and their ghosts, and how do we inhabit and move through spaces that have been deemed haunted? These are questions that remain whether or not you believe in ghosts. Even if you don't believe in the paranormal, ghost stories and legends of haunted places are a vital, dynamic means of confronting the past and those who have gone before us. Ultimately, this book is about the relationship between place and story: how the two depend on each other and how they bring each other alive.

GHOSTLAND

ANATOMY OF A HAUNTING

New York, NY

A ugust 1933, a summer's day in Manhattan's Lower East Side. There are children playing outside on East Fourth Street; they are wild, they are shouting and running through the street, trying to gather up the last of the season before the fall sets in. There is nothing unusual about any of this. Then the door swings open at 29 East Fourth Street, and an old woman emerges onto the stoop overlooking the street, waving her arms wildly and shouting to the children to be quiet. The children and the adults all recognize her: Gertrude Tredwell, who's lived in the house for more than ninety years, born there in 1840, five years after her father purchased it. She is enraged; she tells them they are being far too noisy, they must calm down. The children quiet, turning toward the high staircase that leads to Gertrude's front door, looking up with fear at the old woman, who, satisfied, returns indoors and shuts the door.

There's nothing unusual about any of this—except that Gertrude Tredwell has been dead now for several weeks.

It is not the last time Gertrude Tredwell will be seen at the house on East Fourth Street. In the months after her death, the house falls into the hands of a distant cousin; since by now most of the old merchant houses of lower Manhattan are gone, he decides to preserve the house as a museum, first opening it to the public in 1936. Over the years there are dozens of sightings of odd and inexplicable things happening *in the house. In the early 1980s tourists come across the house and ring the bell. A woman in period costume tells them politely that the museum is closed for the day, and could they please come back at another time. Later, when they call the house to get the hours, they are told that the museum was in fact open when they came by and that, furthermore, none of the staff ever dresses in period costume. Gertrude has also been seen inside the house, sometimes humming, sometimes playing the piano— always appearing as a frail, petite woman in period costume.*

Nor is she alone. A visitor to the house in the summer of 1995 claimed that while upstairs she had a lengthy conversation with an older gentleman in a tattered suit and a heavy wool jacket smelling of mothballs, who talked to her of what the house was like to live in. After listening to him for a few minutes, she turned away for a moment, and when she looked back, he was gone. Later she identified the man she'd seen from photographs: Samuel Lenox Tredwell, Gertrude's brother, who'd died in 1921.

⌁

Ghost stories like these mean more than we are usually prepared to admit. If you want to understand a place, ignore the boastful monuments and landmarks, and go straight to the haunted houses. Look for the darkened graveyards, the derelict hotels, the emptied and decaying old hospitals. Wait past midnight, and see what appears. Tune out the patriotic speeches and sanctioned narratives, and listen instead for the bumps in the night. You won't need an electronic device to capture the voices of the dead; a patient ear and an open mind will do. Once you start looking, you'll find them everywhere.

"We tell ourselves stories in order to live," Joan Didion once wrote, and that is just as true of ghost stories: we tell stories of the dead as a way of making sense of the living. More than just simple urban legends and camp-fire tales, ghost stories reveal the contours of our anxieties, the nature of our collective fears and desires, the things we can't talk about in any other way. The past we're most afraid to speak aloud of in the bright light of day is the same past that tends to linger in the ghost stories we whisper in the dark.

Ghost stories are as old as human civilization, appearing in the earliest written epics and throughout the ancient world. In one of his letters the Roman writer Pliny the Younger describes a house haunted by a ghost "in the form of an old man, of extremely emaciated and squalid appearance, with a long beard and disheveled hair, rattling the chains on his feet and hands." The house remained vacant until the philosopher Athenodorus rented it; his first night he waited up for the ghost, writing in his study, until the apparition appeared.

Athenodorus, according to Pliny, was not in a hurry and, when confronted by the ghost, "made a sign with his hand that he should wait a little, and threw his eyes again upon his papers." Eventually the philosopher allowed the ghost to lead him out of the house into the yard, where the ghost vanished. The next morning Athenodorus dug up the spot where the ghost had disappeared and found the remains of a skeleton in chains. He gave the long-neglected corpse a proper burial, and the haunting ceased.

Ghosts bridge the past to the present; they speak across the seemingly insurmountable barriers of death and time, connecting us to what we thought was lost. They give us hope for a life beyond death and because of this help us to cope with loss and grief. Their presence is the promise that we don't have to say goodbye to our loved ones right away and that— as with Athendorus's haunting—what was left undone in one's life might yet be finished by one's ghost.

Perhaps this is why, even without centuries-old castles or ruined abbeys, the United States is as ghost-haunted as anywhere else in the world—perhaps even more so. You'll find ghosts in the stately plantations of the South, in the wilds of the Plains states, in the ornate hotels of California, in the wooden colonials in the Northeast. They roam the streets of rust-belt cities like Detroit and Buffalo, and they haunt the gothic cities of the South. You'll find them in abandoned mining towns and in the bustling metropolis of New York City.

According to one poll, 45 percent of Americans say they believe in ghosts, and almost 30 percent say they've witnessed them firsthand. Though this belief lies outside the ways we normally explain the world—contradicting science and complicating religion—it's a difficult belief to shake. That we continue believing in ghosts despite our rational mind's skepticism suggests that in these stories lies something crucial to the way we understand the world around us. We cannot look away, because we know something important is there.

∽◦◯◦∽

The Merchant's House Museum in lower Manhattan has stood alone against the din and rush of the city; it has stood for one hundred eighty years and might stand for that many more. Within, walls continue upright, bricks meet neatly, wood floors give gently underfoot, and spirits gather.

The house was bought by Seabury Tredwell in 1835, when he retired. Owner of a large hardware firm, he had eight children altogether, the last of whom, Gertrude, was born there in 1840, when Tredwell was sixty. Gertrude never married—she had one suitor, but her father disapproved of his Catholicism—and so she lived out her life in the house on Fourth Street, her siblings dying one by one until only she remained. Over time she focused her energies on keeping the house exactly as Seabury had intended it, maintaining its nineteenth-century charm until she died, at the age of ninety-three, in 1933. Her cousin turned the house into a museum, and the ghosts, they say, came quickly thereafter.

The Merchant's House is a prime example of a grand old American haunted house. Its exterior is stately, refined, with a touch of frayed elegance. Its front door welcomes even as it seems to be hiding something. Inside the floors creak without warning, without any sense of someone there. The old wood is thick with the humidity, as if the walls and floors still breathe. It is the oldest brownstone in New York with the furniture of its original owners still intact. All around it are gleaming glass-and-steel towers of the modern age, bustling with life still being lived.

It is easy to feel as though you're stepping back in time as you walk in

4

the steps of those long gone. And it's easy, in such a well-worn house, to feel that something is not quite right: an invisible presence, a trace of something that doesn't belong. Through the years guests have reported feeling cold spots or seeing strange, wispy streaks of light, some of which have been captured on film. Paranormal researchers have conducted EVP (electronic voice phenomena) sessions in the house, turning on a tape recorder and asking questions to an empty room, playing back the tape later in hopes that the ghosts will have answered back. Several EVPs from the house have recorded bits of faint, muddled noise that some claim are voices speaking from the beyond.

But these events alone are easy for a skeptic to brush aside and discount. A paranormal event without a story is tenuous, fragile. What makes it "real," at least in a sense, is the story, the tale that grounds the event. That sense of the uncanny, of something not-quite-right, of things ever-so-slightly off, cries out for an explanation, and often we turn to ghosts for that explanation. Just as an oyster turns a speck of dirt into a pearl, the ghost story doesn't make the feeling disappear, but can transform it into something more stable, less unsettling.

Long before the word "haunting" became associated with ghosts, it meant simply "to frequent," in the way teenage kids haunt a park or drunks haunt a bar. A house like the Merchant's House Museum is haunted, then, by use and by habitude, by grooves worn into the floors and walls—as though you could map out the daily patterns of the people who lived here by analyzing these signs of wear.*

The ghosts at the Merchant's House emerge not only out of the uncanny feeling we get from creaking wood and antiquated architecture but also from the stories about its onetime inhabitants that are told and retold over the years and embellished where necessary to heighten the drama. Tales of Gertrude emphasize that she never married; that after her father

---

*This usage of the word "haunting" predates its associations with ghosts by several centuries, according to the *Oxford English Dictionary*, and it's not until Shakespeare that ghosts also begin to haunt.

disapproved of her only suitor, she promised him she'd stay single and live in his home. The spinster who honored her father's wishes even after his death, Gertrude seems tragic, bordering on the pathological. Even before her death, she haunted this house—an emotionally stunted recluse, unable to let go of her attachment to her father.

Her brother Samuel, by contrast, is described as a "black sheep," someone who never amounted to much and was disinherited by the family. This is a tad unfair; Samuel followed in his father's footsteps as a merchant, specializing in china and crockery, though he was not the success his father had been. He was indeed written out of Seabury's final will, mainly due to debts Samuel had incurred in the wake of the Civil War. (Seabury instead left a trust in Samuel's daughter's name.) But the legends of the Merchant's House exaggerate the tensions and family drama, relying on melodramatic caricatures. The sight of Samuel's ghost is far more exciting and menacing, after all, if he has come back from the grave to claim his rightful inheritance.

A spinster and one who seemed to resist time in a place as restless as New York City, Gertrude Tredwell embodies a set of ideas—and anxieties—about women, domesticity, and modernity. Likewise, in the ghost of threadbare Samuel Tredwell we have a story of disinheritance and filial failure that reflects how we as a culture treat men who don't live up to certain concepts of masculinity. Add to this the overbearing portrait of Seabury himself, and what the Merchant's House offers is an uncanny portrait of the American family, one that frustrates our basic assumptions about how a father and his children should act.

Instead of, or perhaps in addition to, the supernatural, old buildings are haunted by their memories: memories of those who once inhabited them, and the memories we bring to them. We're conditioned, after all, to conflate memory and physical space. At the same time that Pliny was writing his tale of Athenodorus's haunted house, Cicero and Quintilian were developing a technique for remembering great quantities of information, known as a "memory palace." Rather than memorizing information directly, one imagines a house and "places" different parts of it in different rooms. With a speech, for example, one's first point is placed in the entryway to the home, the second point in the first room, and so on. To remember the speech, the orator simply has to "walk" through the house in her or his mind, picking up each aspect of the speech as she or he moves through the building. The technique suggests the degree to which memory is spatial or at least primed to work spatially: our brains are hardwired to think in terms of place and to associate psychic value or meaning to the places we inhabit.

Just as imaginary houses may be used to help us remember things, real physical houses may have their own memories—or at least memories we project onto them. A haunted house is a memory palace made real: a physical space that retains memories that might otherwise be forgotten or that might remain only in fragments. Under the invisible weight of these memories, the habits of those who once haunted these places, we feel the shudder of the ghost.

∼◦◦∼

Ghosts, historian Thomas W. Laqueur writes, are "a representation of the unrepresentable: the dead who were somewhere." In a world where nearly every moment of our lives is photographed, recorded, and documented, the gaps in the past still beckon us. Searching for ghosts can be an attempt to reconstruct what is lost. By sifting through time for stories that have been misplaced or forgotten, we listen to the voices that call out to be remembered. Our ghost stories center on unfinished endings, broken relationships, things left unexplained. They offer an alternative kind of history, foregrounding what might otherwise be ignored.

Ghost stories are a way of talking about things we're not otherwise allowed to discuss: a forbidden history we thought bricked up safely in the walls. They cover over the gaps and in the process help us assuage our anxieties, providing a rationale after the fact. Just as Gertrude Tredwell's life has informed the ghost stories that now circulate around her, so, too, does the legend of her ghost make meaning out of her life. Those aspects of a life that are discontinuous, fragmented, or unexpected, are made whole through the ghost story.

In her study of the ghost stories of the Hudson Valley in New York, Judith Richardson describes how one ghost in particular has changed shape through the decades to suit different needs of different eras. For more than two centuries residents of the village of Leeds have reported seeing a spectral apparition of a ghostly horse galloping down the main road, dragging behind it a young woman. The story, in its most basic form, has to do with a cruel master who wickedly killed a young servant girl as punishment for some minor transgression. When she was invoked by writer Miriam Coles Harris in her 1862 novel, *The Sutherlands*, the ghostly victim is a slave of African and Native American descent; Harris used her as a parable in the vein of *Uncle Tom's Cabin*, castigating not only the institution of slavery but Northern whites for their complicity. In 1896 the same ghost appears in Charles M. Skinner's *Myths and Legends of Our Own Land*, but now she is a white European immigrant, reflecting Skinner's interest in class differences and labor warfare. Contemporary retellings of the story, though, lack these politically charged details; in a 2002 book containing the Leeds legend, for example, the slave's ethnic heritage is unmentioned and the class divide is downplayed. Her master is indeed cruel and callous, but he's portrayed nowadays as a singular figure of evil rather than a representative of a corrupt ruling class.

Paying attention to the way ghost stories change through the years—and why those changes are made—can tell us a great deal about how we face our fears and our anxieties. Even when these stories have a basis in fact and history, there's often significant embellishment and fabrication before they catch on in our imagination, and teasing out these alterations is key to understanding how ghosts shape our relationship to the past.

We like to view this country as a unified, cohesive whole based on progress, a perpetual refinement of values, and an arc of history bending toward justice—but the prevalence of ghosts suggests otherwise. The ghosts who haunt our woods, our cemeteries, our houses, and our cities appear at moments of anxiety and point to instability in our national and local identities. A ghost story is what Freud called "the return of the repressed," when something we'd rather forget returns in another form—such as the famous "Freudian slip" (what he himself called a parapraxis), revealing what we've hidden deep in our subconscious.

Our country's ghost stories are themselves the dreams (or nightmares) of a nation, the Freudian slips of whole communities: uncomfortable and unbidden expressions of things we'd assumed were long past and no longer important. If American history is taught to schoolchildren as a series of great, striding benchmarks, the history of America's ghost stories is one of crimes left unsolved or transgressions we now feel guilty about. They offer explanations for the seemingly inexplicable, address injustices after the fact, and give expression to our unstated desires and fears. They can also, just as easily, mold reality to our preconceived notions and cover over a messy reality in favor of well-worn clichés and urban legends. Ours is a forward-looking country that can have trouble sometimes reckoning with the past and the actions of our ancestors, and the spirit world has become yet another arena in which the shameful chapters in America's history, including slavery and the genocide of the American Indians, are addressed and relitigated. Uncomfortable truths, buried secrets, disputed accounts: ghost stories arise out of the shadowlands, a response to the ambiguous and the poorly understood.

∽◦◠

I spent several years traveling the country, listening for ghosts. There was no shortage of stories to choose from: there is not a city, town, or village in this country that isn't crammed with spirits. I started with places that were renowned for their ghosts, places that had caught on in the popular imagination, whose legends seemed particularly resonant. I looked for ghosts whose stories spoke to some larger facet of American consciousness while still being rooted in a specific building.

In some cases it wasn't always clear to me at first why I was drawn to a particular place. Sometimes simply being in a strange building—spending the night in a haunted hotel, for example—was enough to leave me with a feeling that I wanted to know more. Much of this book involves not just listening to ghost stories but listening also to architecture: how a building can feel alive and unsettling due to its age or a quirk in its construction. Any building whose construction is a little bit off, as often as not, has spirits swirling about it. The language of ghosts, it seems, has become an important (if abstract) way of talking about architecture and place.

Cities and historic sites across the United States clamor to have the most ghosts per cubic inch, the most frenetic paranormal activity, so they can earn the label "most haunted." Any major city in this country offers some kind of ghost tour in which you can hunt for cold spots or EMF vibrations or otherwise find proof of the supernatural. The phenomenon has come to be known as dark tourism, a vibrant industry in its own right. Ghost tours are popular with tourists, explains geographer Glenn Gentry, because they "allow access to dissonant knowledge, dirty laundry, back stage." They are the celebrity gossip of history, the salacious underbelly of the past, and we're drawn to them because the standard history often obscures as much as it reveals.

In a quest to find this other history—the one obscured, forgotten, and ignored—I've interviewed ghost hunters and psychics, local historians and preservationists. I've read academic treatises and cheesy guidebooks, compared the legends to the historical record, trying to unearth the genealogy of the specific ghosts and how we came to love telling the specific stories. What makes a place haunted? When is a creaking floorboard more than just a creaking floorboard? And what is behind the ghost stories that we tell? A spinster locked in a decaying mansion, a slave on a plantation whose soul won't rest—what are they trying to say to us from beyond the grave?

The answers aren't confined to houses but cower in hotels and prisons, on bridges and in graveyards. Though houses are more likely to be haunted than any other place, other kinds of buildings have their own stories to tell. This book moves from the private space of the home to progressively more public spaces—to businesses, to civic spaces, and finally to whole cities. What secrets do towns harbor? Why do ghosts linger when buildings empty of living people?

Examining our country's local ghost stories—where they came from, how they've evolved, how they're recounted—may tell us a great deal about things we thought were long settled and in the past.

I

THE
UNHOMELY

houses and mansions

M y wife and I began searching for a house in 2008, precisely when the real estate market was crashing, just as
those first waves of foreclosures and short sales were
hitting the market. We were finally able to afford
houses whose prices had been ridiculously inflated only six months earlier.
Occasionally we went to those open houses with smiling real estate agents
and bowls of candy, where owners had recently landscaped or repainted,
but we could never seriously consider any of these homes. The ones that
mattered had lockboxes, were abandoned or in the process of being
abandoned—houses that reeked of disrepair and despair.

We spent the summer touring nearly every distressed property in the
neighborhoods east of Hollywood—Los Feliz, Silverlake, Echo Park, At-
water Village—looking for a home. There were, of course, the hoarding
houses: homes we couldn't enter because of the high stacks of magazines and
newspapers or other safety hazards, where we could only peer in through
the windows. Far more common, though, were the malformed do-it-yourself
homes. Los Angeles is a zoning no-man's-land, host to thousands of unper-
mitted additions and modifications, which means each house on a block of
once-identical residences will look different. Dozens of bungalows in East

Hollywood were built as seven-hundred-square-foot cottages, and, over time, extra bedrooms were added, garages converted, crawl spaces enlarged into dens—often without rhyme or reason or any real sense of purpose. Living rooms were constructed behind existing bedrooms, so an exterior window would look from one room to the next; thousand-square-foot homes somehow contained four or five bedrooms, each one barely more than a closet cut from some once-sane layout; bathrooms sat in the middle of kitchens; bedrooms without windows were built into the sides of hills; doors on a second floor opened into empty air. The effect was vertiginous: you walked into a room and felt a sense of unease before you could say why.

Throughout that stifling summer, we walked into home after home that had been closed against the light but bristled with claustrophobic air. We took to nicknaming these places: the Flea House, after whatever it was that bit our agent; the Burn House, with its charred patches of wall and blackened carpets; Tony's House, after the name on the novelty license plate stuck to a bedroom door, a detail particularly creepy amid the otherwise empty gloom of the house, as though Danny Torrance would big-wheel down the hall at any moment.

It seemed impossible that anyone had called these places home. I found myself thinking of Shirley Jackson's *The Haunting of Hill House* and her description of the eponymous haunted mansion:

> This house, which seemed somehow to have formed itself, flying together into its own powerful pattern under the hands of its builders, fitting itself into its own construction of lines and angles, reared its great head back against the sky without concession to humanity. It was a house without kindness, never meant to be lived in, not a place fit for people or for love or for hope.

These homes, too, seemed without concession to humanity, but in a sense they were just the opposite. These were not the caprices of strange, wealthy men whose hubris unleashed a holy terror. Instead, they were the products of dozens of lower-class families trying to make their homes a little bigger, a little more livable, creating unworkable labyrinths out of necessity.

The feeling of moving through these spaces—particularly as we were visiting seven or eight of them in an afternoon—was indescribable. A sense of wrongness pervaded so many of these homes. In the end, the only word that seems useful for talking about the houses is one made famous by Sigmund Freud: *unheimlich.* A German word, it means literally "unhomely" or "not of the home," "unfamiliar," "eerie and ghostly"—more idiomatically translated into English simply as "uncanny."

Freud's 1919 essay "The Uncanny" is among the stranger of his well-known works. He doesn't really know where to begin with the uncanny—when it comes to the feeling, he admits, "the present writer must plead guilty to exceptional obtuseness." One wonders why he's bothering with the subject at all. Mostly he wants to contradict another psychoanalyst, Ernst Jentsch, who first attempted to define the uncanny in 1906, thirteen years before Freud's essay. Jentsch posits the sensation of the uncanny as stemming from a kind of cognitive uncertainty, where one is unclear as to whether an object or figure or person is inanimate or somehow alive.

Freud, unconvinced by Jentsch, begins by surveying dictionaries, copying out as many different definitions of "uncanny" as he can. What finally catches his attention is the fact that *heimlich,* in addition to meaning "homey" or "familiar," can also mean "hidden, locked away." He finally seizes on Friedrich Schelling's definition of *unheimlich:* "Uncanny is what one calls everything that was meant to remain secret and hidden, and has come into the open." This formulation works for Freud—he is, of course, interested in repression—but it doesn't work as well for haunted houses. What, after all, is being repressed? Jentsch's notion, of a confusion between the living and the inanimate, might work better—think of the anthropomorphized façade of *The Amityville Horror*'s house. With a haunted house, the question is: to what extent is the house itself alive, and to what extent is it inanimate?

But, really, it's the most basic definition of "uncanny"—"unhomely"—that matters. The haunted house is precisely that which should be homey, should be welcoming—the place one lives inside—but which has somehow become emptied out of its true function. It is terrifying because it has lost its purpose yet stubbornly persists. Neither alive nor dead but undead, the haunted house is the thing in between.

～◦∂ ○～～

There are haunted structures of all kinds: churches, hotels, toy stores. There are haunted bridges and haunted alleyways, haunted parks and haunted parking lots. But in the United States, the most common—the most primal—haunted place is a house. Home ownership has always been intertwined with the American dream; we have magnified this simple property decision in part because it represents safety and security. The haunted house is a violation of this comfort, the American dream gone horribly wrong.

Even if its very construction isn't distorted, as with the homes in East Hollywood, a house can still attract ghosts, still attract stories. The French philosopher Gaston Bachelard offers a succinct and plausible nonsupernatural explanation for why the structure in which we live can itself feel alive. Our houses are the places where we spend the most time, and they are, as he suggests, the places where we do the most dreaming. More than just a place of shelter, a place of comfort, or a place of privacy, the house for Bachelard "shelters daydreaming" and "allows one to dream in peace." The more elaborate a house, the more spaces it has, the more evocative it is for our dream life: "If it has a cellar and a garret, nooks and corridors, our memories have refuges that are all the more clearly delineated." It is in the corners and crevices—the places just off the main traffic corridors—that our dreams, like dust bunnies and forgotten toys, accumulate and our imagination begins to run wild. "Every corner in a house, every angle in a room, every inch of secluded space in which to hide ourselves," Bachelard notes, "is a symbol of solitude for the imagination; that is to say, it is the germ of a room, or of a house." Live in a house for any length of time, and you make it your own memory palace.

Such places in which we're actively dreaming, he suggests, become so associated with those dreams that the building itself seems to vibrate psychically: "The places in which we have *experienced daydreaming* reconstitute themselves in a new daydream, and it is because our memories of former dwelling-places are relived as daydreams that these dwelling-places of the past remain in us for all time." As Vladimir Nabokov once put it, "When we concentrate on a material object, whatever its situation, the very act of attention may lead to our involuntarily sinking into the history of that object." Just by lingering in a house, you could say you end up sinking into its history.

Houses seem to live, in other words, because we spend so much time living in them. Buried inside the word "inhabit" is *habit*: a way of being, the patterns and repetitions of life. One's habits and one's surroundings are engaged in a constantly changing, ever subtle dance. Houses are designed with certain patterns of behavior in mind, even though those patterns sometimes change faster than architecture can keep up. And of course everyone will use a house differently, leave different patterns of wear. I spent my childhood in homes that were built as part of subdivisions—my house replicated four or five times over on the same street. Visiting one of these doppelgängers was always a vertiginous experience: everything the same and yet totally different. Cool blue walls instead of white, a nook that held a flower vase instead of a bookshelf, a room used as a library instead of a bedroom—an utterly unfamiliar landscape that I could, nonetheless, walk through blindfolded.

This is another way to make sense of that haunting sensation: to walk into a home and recognize, even if you can't name the feeling, that someone else not only lived here but adopted patterns of life completely alien to your own, whose daily ritual and marks of wear will never match your own. Haunted houses are the repository of the dreams dreamt inside them—both our dreams and those of previous occupants. This can make even the most simple of houses feel, at times, alive.

꙳꙳꙳

Houses outlast us; they contain more than one generation's worth of stories. They can become, in turn, repositories of family histories, for both good and ill. And though ghosts may be specific to the places they haunt, they can reflect larger preoccupations and concerns of their time and place, echoing the anxieties of a community and its people. One can treat an old house like a geologist's core sample—a physical representation of time—accruing meaning and history through the years of successive owners. To own an old home means inhabiting not just your own imagination but the imaginations of all those who've lived there before you.

The houses in this section have earned their reputations in no small part by combining all these various aspects: an odd construction, an unnamable feeling, and an anxiety made physical through a building whose past isn't entirely known or understood. Like the Merchant's House Museum in New York City, they've inverted not only the notion of what a home represents but also the very architecture of the house. In the process, they've become puzzles that seem to demand some kind of response, riddles for which there is no obvious answer.

CHAPTER ONE

THE SECRET STAIRCASE

Salem, MA

Houses of any antiquity in New England," Nathaniel Hawthorne once wrote, "are so invariably possessed with spirits, that the matter seems hardly worth alluding to." It's true: you could spend a good portion of your life cataloging the haunted houses of New England: the Captain Fairfield Inn of Kennebunkport, Maine, whose original owner, Captain James Fairfield, wanders the basement; Captain Grant's, a B&B in Prescott, Connecticut, haunted by colonial spirits; the Sylvester Knowlton Pierce mansion in Gardner, Massachusetts, haunted by Pierce, his family, and a murdered prostitute from the years when the house was used as a brothel; and of course the house Lizzie Borden occupied in Fall River, Massachusetts. The countless ghosts that linger in the stately mansions up and down New England only multiply.

Despite this glut of spirits, no place in New England has a greater reputation for being haunted than Salem, Massachusetts. Home to the most famous miscarriages of justice in America's early history, Salem hosts the spirits of the nineteen men and women executed during the witchcraft trials of 1692. Strange fax machine messages come through in the office building that now stands on the old courthouse grounds. In the apartment complex built on the old Salem jail, toasters jump up and down without warning. And in the alleyway behind the Turner Seafood Restaurant—on land that many believe once belonged to Bridget Bishop, the first person executed during the witch trials—a tree drips blood.

Here in Salem, amid all these ghosts stands the House of the Seven Gables, one of the most well-known haunted houses in the country—a first among equals. Set at the end of Turner Street, looking out over Salem Bay, the house doesn't stand out; it's no taller than its neighbors, and without the signage and the parking lot you might miss it altogether. Its distinguishing feature is its color: it's painted entirely in matte black, as though it wants to suck all the available light into itself. Its name, curiously, is a bit of a misnomer. The house does not actually have seven gables; it has nine, though not all of them are original. This architectural confusion, you could say, is just one of the many strange aspects of the house—a house that defies description down to its very name.

The house started small, built by John Turner, a wealthy sea captain and merchant, in 1668. Through the years and generations, the building was enlarged several times, then pared back, as it passed to Turner's son and then his grandson John Turner III. Bankruptcy forced John III to sell the property, and it came into the hands of Susanna Ingersoll, who, among other things, was the aunt of Nathaniel Hawthorne. By the time Ingersoll bought it, the house had apparently already been nicknamed the House of Seven Gables, though by then it had, at best, four gables. The house, during the years, has gone through so many various additions and renovations, such that its shape, at least up until the early twentieth century, was never truly stable.

It was Ingersoll who first encouraged a young Hawthorne to write about Salem when he complained to her about a lack of subject matter. "Oh there are subjects enough," she replied and, gesturing to an old piece of furniture by the fireplace, went on: "Write about that old chair. You can make a biographical sketch of each old Puritan who became in succession an owner of the chair." Ingersoll's prompting led Hawthorne to one of his first writing projects, a children's book in 1840 called *Grandfather's*

Chair. A decade later, riding high on the sudden success of his novel *The Scarlet Letter*, Hawthorne returned to Ingersoll for further inspiration. This time he turned to her house.

At the center of Hawthorne's gothic romance *The House of the Seven Gables* is a house with a buried past that continues to affect its modern-day inhabitants, a house that seems somehow evil in ways we're hard-pressed to define. Its construction isn't quite right: it's "a rusty wooden house," its seven gables facing toward various points of the compass, with a "huge, clustered chimney in the midst." What's more, the book's narrator tells us, it's curiously anthropomorphic: "The aspect of the venerable mansion has always affected me like a human countenance, bearing the traces not merely of outward storm and sunshine, but expressive also, of the long lapse of mortal life, and accompanying vicissitudes that have passed within."

It's true that the house, which still offers regular tours, can feel unsettling. Walking through its rooms you feel the discomfiting effects of its low roofs, its tight rooms, and its misshapen layout. The centuries-old wood timbers seem, perhaps, to bow and breathe. Convincing yourself the house is alive is not terribly difficult.

For his novel, Hawthorne concocted a backstory to explain his fictional house's unsettling presence. The house's origins are tainted. It was built on fertile land owned by a man named Matthew Maule. The avaricious Colonel Pyncheon, desiring the property, fabricates an accusation of witchcraft against Maule, which results in Maule's execution and allows Pyncheon to easily acquire the land, on which he builds his massive, sprawling mansion.

But Pyncheon's house, despite its splendor, is cursed, and the night the colonel hosts a gala to celebrate its completion, he's found dead at his desk, blood dripping from his mouth. Nor is the colonel the only ghost of the mansion; his great-granddaughter Alice, who had "grown thin and white, and gradually faded out of the world," has come to haunt the House of the Seven Gables: "a great many times,—especially when one of the

Pyncheons was to die,—she had been heard playing sadly and beautifully on the harpsichord." In this landscape of greed and calamity, ancestral curses and mournful ghosts, Hawthorne turned the oddly built house on Turner Street into a rival of the abandoned castles of Europe's gothic novels.

Though Ingersoll's own house lacked the melodramatic origins of Hawthorne's invention, ghost stories have become so firmly associated with the house that, as one historian suggests, they "form a patina, a part of the thing itself." While the management doesn't go to great lengths to play up its haunted past—there are no ghost tours, and the tour guides seem uneasy if you press them for stories—its odd construction and subsequent reputation have nonetheless attracted numerous stories, usually involving Susan Ingersoll or Hawthorne. One former visitor to the house sent a photo to the Web site graveaddiction.com, which collects paranormal testimonies, where supposedly in one of the upper windows you can see "what appears to be a teenage girl peering back out! No, the closer you magnify it the more it becomes apparent that it is an older woman complete with sunken eyes and hair!" (I've looked and can't see anything myself.) There is another photo that has become particularly famous, of the house's exterior fence, in which supposedly the ghost of Hawthorne's son, Julian, can be seen—though everyone I've shown the image to agrees it's a shadow or, at best, a raccoon.

Many of the ghost sightings and other mysterious incidents revolve around the house's bizarre hidden staircase, its most enduring architectural feature. Just to the left of the main fireplace is a small door, one that could perhaps lead to a wood closet but in fact opens onto a strange, winding, claustrophobic staircase. Twenty steps that haphazardly curl around the house's main chimney ascend to an attic—a short but oddly perilous journey.

It is here, on this staircase, that many guests to the house have reported feeling the presence of ghosts. Visitors describe feelings of vertigo, an inability to breathe, and a pressing need to flee the house. "I began to feel . . .

as if I was on a high mountain top where the oxygen becomes less. I felt sort of dizzy and off balance in all directions," one visitor wrote on Grave Addiction. Another tourist reported that while he was climbing the hidden staircase, "I heard a woman's voice RIGHT next to my ear whisper a 'Shhh, Shhh' type of sound. I thought it was my girlfriend trying to spook me, so as I turned my head to say 'knock it off,' I saw she was still 3 to 4 feet behind me." Another writer later recounted in detail how

> as we moved through the house, I suddenly became aware of a disquieting "presence" around me. I felt it at first when we went to a dining area, and it grew stronger once we went up a cramped brick-lined stairway into the attic. Later, after we stood outside, I mentioned to my sister that I felt odd—"displaced," if that makes sense. . . . Something touched me when I was in that house—plugged into my subconscious somehow. I don't know what or who . . . but I've come to believe that a piece of "it" attached itself to me.

How long has this spectral presence haunted this mysterious staircase? Does it date from 1692, during the town's infamous witch trials, or perhaps even earlier? Did a young Nathaniel Hawthorne feel it, and did this presence haunt him when he set out to immortalize his aunt's home as the most famously haunted house in American literature?

✺

The nation was still young when Hawthorne began writing, but he could already draw inspiration from Puritan New England's buried past and hidden legacy. Salem has long embodied a contradiction in the bedrock of American consciousness: upright piety mixed with hypocrisy, sober religion mixed with violent hysteria. Hawthorne's own great-great-grandfather John Hathorne was one of the judges who presided over the Salem witch trials of 1692, and Nathaniel had grown up knowing about the family legend—that one of Hathorne's victims had cursed him and his descendants.

Certainly Salem was a place ripe for haunting, and Hawthorne would repeatedly return to wrongs unavenged in his hometown to propel the more gothic aspects of his fiction. This is the recurring structure of a classic ghost story, after all: the ghost remains because it cannot believe the perverse normality of a world that has gone on living, that has forgotten whatever personal tragedy happened here. The carpets are cleaned, the furniture is sold, and the house continues with new inhabitants, the ghost alone keeping vigil over whatever once took place.

With *The House of the Seven Gables*, Hawthorne took a house that, by accident of haphazard and evolving construction, had acquired a gothic patina and imbued it with the history of Salem—transforming the house into a microcosm of not only the town's rise and fall but also its hidden secrets and unrighted wrongs. The goal of the novel, as Hawthorne writes in his preface, is to "convince mankind—or, indeed, any one man—of the folly of tumbling down an avalanche of ill-gotten gold, or real estate, on the heads of an unfortunate posterity, thereby to maim and crush them, until the accumulated mass shall be scattered abroad in its original atoms."

And in Hawthorne's novel, it is precisely because the house is the physical spoils of this injustice that it becomes haunted. The book pushes and pulls against the stain of the past, straining under the effort of breaking free of it. There is only one way to escape this curse, according to Holgrave, the novel's young hero: we must tear down old houses altogether. Holgrave, a daguerreotypist (the technology was brand new then, suggesting a cutting-edge man of the future), opines that we shall soon live to see the day "when no man shall build his house for posterity." He instead imagines a country in which "each generation were allowed and expected to build its own houses," a simple change that would ameliorate most of society's ills. "I doubt whether even our public edifices," he concludes, meaning capitols, courthouses, and other government buildings, "ought to be built of such permanent materials as stone or brick. It were better that they should crumble to ruin once in twenty years, or there-abouts, as a hint to the people to examine into and reform the institutions which they symbolize." As the ill-gotten remnants of the past, the build-ings that have borne witness to the sins of the fathers, the houses we in-herit must be destroyed. If we want to truly be free of the past, we must first start by destroying our ancestral homes.

Holgrave's proposal is seductive, and certainly each generation dreams of remaking itself anew without the baggage of the ones that have come before. But even though architecture embodies the past, the past is more than the buildings we leave behind, and even cities that are famous for demolishing old buildings in favor of the new—Los Angeles, New York, Las Vegas among them—have not escaped their pasts.

Holgrave's dream of a world free of property inheritance stands in stark contrast to the actual context of the witchcraft crisis, which was far more about real estate and land acquisition than we normally assume. While we mainly associate the Salem witch trials with hysteria, religious fervor, and scapegoating, scratch the surface some and one finds property disputes and shady transfers of property and money.

One of the first girls who claimed to be afflicted, twelve-year-old Ann Putnam, initially accused the servant Tituba, as well as two other women, Sarah Good and Sarah Osborne. At the time Osborne was involved in a property dispute with Putnam's parents. Osborne's first husband had died owning a fair amount of property; he wanted to leave some of it to his sons, who were second cousins to Putnam. Osborne and her second hus-band wanted to keep all her first husband's property for themselves. This dispute was ongoing when Putnam accused Osborne of visiting her as an apparition and "pinching and pricking" her "dreadfully."

Ann Putnam would a few weeks later also name Rebecca Nurse as a tormentor. Like Osborne, Nurse was involved in land disputes with the Putnams. While some of the women accused during the crisis were marginalized—servants, widows, or otherwise impoverished women with-out community support—Nurse was a well-respected figure in the community, pious and well liked by many. What was happening in Salem was no longer the traditional model of witchcraft persecution, in which primarily the defenseless were targeted. It was now clear there was money to be made and land to be gained.

Among the most rapacious players in this drama was the Essex County sheriff, George Corwin, who'd quietly begun seizing property and assets of those convicted of witchcraft. One of the richest citizens to be accused of witchcraft, Philip English, managed to flee Salem to avoid trial, but after he disappeared, Corwin seized his house and other assets, roughly 1,500 pounds' worth. In the case of John and Elizabeth Proctor, Corwin didn't even wait until they were convicted and began removing their property while they were still awaiting trial, leaving nothing for their children. On December 12, 1692, a new law—meant explicitly to protect Corwin—allowing the seizure of property and land of those convicted of witchcraft was passed. The situation got so out of hand that the governor of Massachusetts, Sir William Phips, finally complained to William Stoughton, lieutenant governor and chief justice of the Court of Oyer and Terminer (the body empowered to try the Salem witches), that Stoughton "by his warrant hath caused the estates, goods and chattles of the executed to be seized and disposed of without my knowledge or consent." (After Corwin's death, supposedly, Philip English put a lien on his corpse, seizing the sheriff's body and refusing to relinquish it until Corwin's relatives paid him what little was left of his estate.)

In Hawthorne's novel, at least there is the possibility of justice, as Pyncheon's avarice leads in short order to his death. Hawthorne attempted to blend what he called "romance" and the "novel": despite his general adherence to realism, supernatural elements creep in. For one, Hawthorne implies that the accused wizard Matthew Maule is, in fact, capable of damning Pyncheon. As Maule faces his accuser from the gallows, he turns to Pyncheon, "with a ghastly look, at the undismayed countenance of his enemy," crying, " 'God will give him blood to drink!' " before he dies—a phrase that haunts the novel when Pyncheon is found dead of unknown causes, blood spilling from his mouth.

In this Hawthorne borrowed a bit from history: while Sarah Good awaited execution on the gallows, she defiantly told one of her accusers, the Reverend Nicholas Noyes, "you are a lyer; I am no more a Witch than you are a Wizard, and if you take away my Life, God will give you Blood to drink." According to the nineteenth-century historian Thomas Hutchinson, Noyes did ultimately die, in 1717, of a hemorrhage, which was seen by some as Good's prophecy fulfilled. The popular narrative of Salem, perhaps, also partakes of a blend of fact and fiction and a sneaking suspicion that the ghosts of Salem are in fact capable of supernatural vengeance. Perhaps it's true that ghost stories arise from an injustice unavenged, but perhaps it's also true that part of what keeps such injustices alive in our consciousness is the titillating possibility that they were not entirely unjust.

This may explain why we have returned so many times in the past three hundred years to Salem, trying again and again to make sense of what happened there. Numerous theories have been advanced as to what happened in Salem: everything from actual witchcraft to petty juvenile delinquency, from hallucinations induced by ergot poisoning to an outbreak of encephalitis. Some of these theories fit better than others, but the theories—and the books—keep coming, as though the question itself can never be fully answered, as though the itch can never fully be scratched.

~∽⁐∾~

The House of the Seven Gables was in bad shape when Caroline Emmerton bought it in 1908, for the measly sum of $1,000. Emmerton, a philanthropist from a wealthy Salem family, had long been involved with the settlement house movement—a program that helped provide education and other social services to impoverished and immigrant children—and in the old house on Turner Street, she saw a unique opportunity. By restoring the ruined house to its former glory, she could revitalize a piece of Salem's past and use revenue from tours to fund the town's Settlement chapter.

Emmerton had first seen the house when it was owned by Henry and Elizabeth Upton. "My first visit to the House of Seven Gables was in 1879 or 1880, when I was still a young girl," she later recalled. "I went there with a party of young people and I will remember the thrill that the gaunt old house gave me when I first caught sight of it." She and architect Joseph Everett Chandler went to work, ultimately spending more than ten times what she'd paid for the house on its restoration.

By then the house no longer had anything close to seven gables; what's more, it wasn't even clear where those seven gables had once been. When Emmerton bought the property, the house was T-shaped, with only three gables, though remnants of another set on the south wing were visible. Emmerton and Chandler quickly found traces of another by studying the beams in the attic. In her account of the restoration, Emmerton speaks of reconstructing the seven gables as something of a puzzle and a mystery—tracking down old plans of the house in stacks of probate court records, divining the shape of the old house through traces left in the woodwork. She decided that the seventh and final gable must have been over the back portion of the house, which had been torn down long ago and thus could give no clues.

Only after she'd rebuilt this back portion with its gable did Emmerton discover court records showing the seventh gable over the kitchen instead. Subsequent restoration work further revealed that the house at one point had an eighth gable, over a second-story porch. She couldn't find evidence that the house had ever had just seven gables, and it certainly didn't by the time she got done with her restoration. "To console me my friends suggested that Hawthorne called his novel 'The House of Seven Gables' because that title was more pleasing and prosaic than the 'House of Eight Gables' would have been."

Though Emmerton stressed that she was careful to not let the book influence her restoration, Hawthorne's novel persisted as a shadow about the building, she claimed, forcing her and Chandler to second-guess every move, to seek clues where none existed, to add restorations that might not have been true to the house itself.

And then there is its crooked spine: the curling, amorphous, and anomalous staircase that curls around the central chimney, snaking skyward as if it might draw out the bad spirits from the house. Emmerton claimed that the secret staircase was rediscovered by Upton, who found on it a "pine-tree sixpence and a book" in 1888 while he was renovating the chimney. She writes that, while she was still a young girl, he showed her the staircase and the book: "It was a religious book, a prayer book or a hymn book, and very ancient." When the secret staircase was built and why, Emmerton didn't know for sure, but in her narrative she weighs—and dismisses—several possibilities, including that it was built for smuggling ("Of what use for smuggling is a secret stairway unless it leads to a secret room where goods could be stored . . . ?") or that it was used as a hiding place against Indian raids ("Hiding places would hardly avail against Indians whose practice it was to set the house on fire").

Her best guess was that it had been built by John Turner II, in the fateful year of 1692. Five minutes away was the house of Philip English, who fled after he was accused of witchcraft. When he finally returned, he found his house ransacked, and Emmerton suggested that he built a safe room of sorts in case of future incidents and that this gave Turner the idea to build his own secret hiding place. "Can there be any doubt that the arrest of Mrs. English would make John Turner anxious for the safety of his sisters?" Emmerton asks. "Can there be any doubt that he began to plan to protect them, and whatever plan he hit upon a temporary hiding place in the house would probably be needed. I believe that he built the secret staircase for that purpose—a recent addition to the house giving him the opportunity."

If Emmerton is correct, then the House of the Seven Gables preserves traces of the witchcraft crisis in its very DNA. Hawthorne's use of this house was no accident, for no other building remains as haunted by those terrifying months. And yet the seemingly most important detail—the staircase itself—appears nowhere in the novel.

Why doesn't the novel mention the staircase? If it was so central to the house's construction and well known by its inhabitants, and if it influenced Hawthorne's conception of his own gabled house, why does it never appear in the book? There does not appear at first to be any clear answers for such a pressing question. "Thinking it over," Emmerton writes, "I have been wondering if Hawthorne did not come across in some way, in an old letter, perhaps, some allusion to the secret staircase which he made use of in the first draft or outline of his romance, but on showing it to Miss Ingersoll encountered her strong objection to anything which should arouse the interest of the curious in her house." Perhaps the hidden staircase was meant to stay hidden, a feature known only to the house's inhabitants, like some family secret bricked up in the walls.

And yet, Emmerton insists, it exists, it influences the novel, it exerts its force on both readers and those who move through the house. "For it seems to me that we feel the absence of the secret staircase in the story just as we feel the absence of a bit of a picture-puzzle that has been lost and has left an unfilled place in the picture."

A few years ago the management of the House of the Seven Gables admitted the truth: the staircase was built not by Turner or Ingersoll, nor by smugglers or freedom fighters or witches, but by Emmerton and Chandler themselves when they first restored the house in preparation for giving tours. Hawthorne made no mention of it because in his day it didn't exist; the door on the first floor that opens to the staircase did, in fact, originally lead to the wood closet.

Reading Emmerton's explanations for the staircase in light of this information reveals a remarkable bit of mythmaking in which she suggested that the staircase deeply inspired the novel while at the same time offering a reason why Hawthorne didn't mention it. Hers is also a remarkable effort of literary criticism, turning the staircase into a hidden presence that works on the novel—an absent presence, an architectural ghost haunting a novel about a haunted house.

And she ensured that the house would remain an enduring attraction, above the other colonial revivals and period museums dotting New England. Over the years the tour script has changed every so often regarding the origin and meaning of the staircase, and it remains adaptable to any number of plausible explanations. What Emmerton and Chandler seem to have understood is that the simple addition of an anomalous element to a house's construction immediately opens up vertiginous possibilities. The secret staircase, simply by virtue of not being immediately self-explanatory, renders the entire house even more uncanny. Its meaning, then, can shift with the times. The Underground Railroad, the witch trials, smugglers, the Indian wars—it can evoke and encompass all these aspects of history simply because it has no real apparent meaning.

~~~

The ghosts of Salem linger in strange ways. Most of the nineteen men and women executed in 1692 were pardoned in the early eighteenth century, but six women—Bridget Bishop, Susannah Martin, Alice Parker, Ann Pudeator, Wilmot Redd, and Margaret Scott—went without exoneration for more than two centuries. Not until 1946 was a bill to clear their names introduced in the Massachusetts legislature, and it failed. It failed again when reintroduced in 1950, and in 1953, and in 1954. It took a change in the bill to get it finally passed, in 1957: the six women would be pardoned, but the legislation would also absolve the state of Massachusetts of any legal or financial obligation to the victims' descendants. Which is to say, whatever gains had been gotten by Sheriff George Corwin and his ilk, no matter how ill gotten, they would not be righted.

The town seems caught between past and present, like a doubly exposed negative. By the end of the nineteenth century, various Salem businesses (including a fish company, a popcorn factory, and a bicycle company) had begun using the nickname "Witch City" to sell their wares, and by the 1930s the town itself had begun to see itself as a tourist destination. In 1971 the TV series *Bewitched* filmed a few episodes in Salem and shortly thereafter a Wiccan named Laurie Cabot arrived in Salem. She opened a "Witch Shop" selling witchcraft supplies and trinkets and quickly attracted a following. Dubbed the "official witch of Salem" by Massachusetts governor Michael Dukakis in 1977, Cabot more than anyone changed the modern face of Salem, turning it into a mecca for those interested in both the pagan practice of Wicca and the Disneyfied image of witches with their black conical hats and broomsticks.

But what does any of this have to do with 1692? The people executed by the Court of Oyer and Terminer, no matter what else they were, almost certainly were not witches, neither pagan witches nor supernatural servants of Satan. They were devout Christians, wrongly accused; if anything, the condemned would have the same antipathy toward the modern Wiccans as their accusers. Hawthorne's confusing blend of romance and novel, fact and fantasy, has come to embody how we treated the victims of Salem's executions. We see them as innocent victims, and yet throughout pop culture we have repeatedly returned to the idea that they were also, paradoxically, somehow supernatural, actual witches. Twentieth- and twenty-first-century pop-culture depictions of Salem—not just *Bewitched,* but the recent TV series *American Horror Story,* with its coven descended from Salem, J. K. Rowling's *History of Magic in North America,* which asserts that a "number of the dead were indeed witches, though utterly innocent of the crimes for which they had been arrested," and of course the show *Salem,* in which the town is the scene of an actual metaphysical battle between witches and Puritans—treat the victims of 1692 as actual witches capable of working spells and magic.

These confusions lie at the heart of Salem, and they're what keeps the town going. It is undeniable that these days the Salem witch trials mean, for the city and its inhabitants, money. The town is overrun on Halloween with tourists, despite the fact that neither Wiccans nor Puritans celebrate the holiday. Salem, with its broom-riding-witch logo on its police cars, has turned tragedy into spectacle. The same unresolved questions that drive scholars to understand the town's past also fuel its kitsch popularity.

In a town suffused with kitsch, nonsense, and a few tasteful memorials, the House of the Seven Gables wants none of it; tour guides do not bring up haunting and are encouraged to downplay it if asked. The eponymous house of Hawthorne's novel is presented simply as a historical museum. And yet a big feature of its allure remains the hidden staircase, an architectural feature built originally to beguile tourists.

The ghosts of Salem, and of the House of the Seven Gables, are a product of ambiguous commemoration. We know Salem—we know it to be a tragedy, we hold it up as a cautionary tale about mass hysteria and persecution—and yet we're also confused: we conflate the dead with actual witches, we attribute actual supernatural powers to those killed, we revisit their deaths for comedy and entertainment. Above all, we fail to apply the lessons we've supposedly learned from 1692, for by no means was this the last time in American history when a powerless minority was scapegoated, persecuted, and killed by an ignorant mass. We recall the events of Salem, but we can't quite remember why they matter.

And so the ghosts remain—they walk the streets, haunt the buildings that have been erected over their hanging grounds. They keep alive the events of 1692 without forcing a reckoning. What remains is barely more than a whisper in the dark or a strange presence on the staircase.

CHAPTER TWO

SHIFTING GROUND

St. Francisville, LA

I n her book *In the Devil's Snare,* historian Mary Beth Norton argues that one pressing fact lay behind the witchcraft trials and drove the hysteria: the judges and magistrates overseeing the trials were all military and civil leaders who had failed repeatedly to keep Essex County safe from Native American attacks during King Philip's War and "unable to defeat Satan in the forests and garrisons of the northeastern frontier, they could nonetheless attempt to do so in the Salem courtroom." The witchcraft trials might have begun with a group of teenage girls, but Norton argues that the town's leaders quickly seized on this outbreak as a means of exonerating themselves for past shortcomings: they were the ones on trial, and they acquitted themselves.

Norton's theory reminds us that the Puritans who settled New England were not simply religious zealots but were also actively, constantly engaged in territorial warfare—with the French, with the Wabanaki and other indigenous groups, and with one another. The ghosts haunting Salem must include the casualties of those land wars alongside those falsely accused of witchcraft. As Hawthorne puts it, this curse goes to the very bedrock of the town's foundations: "The pavements of the Main-street," he writes in one sketch, "must be laid over the red man's grave."

Salem, of course, is far from the only place in the United States whose pavements are laid over the graves of indigenous people. There's nowhere in this nation that wasn't already inhabited before Europeans arrived, and there's no town, no house, that doesn't sit atop someone else's former home. More often than not, we've chosen to deal with this fact through the language of ghosts.

⧼⧽

Fifteen hundred miles to the south, just off Louisiana State Route 61, stands the Myrtles Plantation. Hemmed in by giant oaks that drip Spanish moss, the low-slung plantation sits at a remove from the road, the lace ironwork delicately enclosing the portico beneath the row of symmetrical gables along its second floor. It was built in 1796 by David Bradford, a lawyer from Pennsylvania who'd taken a prominent part in the tax revolt known as the Whiskey Rebellion in the early years of the republic. With a warrant out for his arrest, Bradford fled the nascent United States for Spanish-owned territory, establishing his home in what is now St. Francisville, Louisiana. Even though the Myrtles has undergone expansions and renovations over the centuries, it has none of the haphazard feel of a building like the House of the Seven Gables: everything seems neatly ordered and in its place.

Look closely, though. The keyhole to the front door is upside down, a detail added by Ruffin and Mary Catherine Stirling, who bought the house in 1834 and nearly doubled its size. Based on a folk belief that ghosts who lived in the trees would try to enter the house at night via keyholes, an upside-down lock was a means to confuse the ghosts and keep them out.

Over the years, at least ten murders have taken place on the grounds of the Myrtles, including three Union soldiers who were shot while trying to ransack the plantation during the Civil War; and William Drew Winter, the man who married the Stirlings' daughter Sarah—shot in 1871 on the portico, and who still roams the house.

The most well-known ghost is that of a slave named Chloe, whose story is beloved by guests and a highlight of the plantation's tours. When Bradford's son-in-law, Judge Clark Woodruff, lived on the plantation, in the early nineteenth century, he took a shine to a young slave girl—a light-skinned mulatto no more than thirteen or fourteen—whom he brought into the house and made his concubine. As the master's mistress, Chloe had far more freedom than the other slaves on the plantation and was allowed to come and go throughout the house as she wished. She used this freedom to eavesdrop on Woodruff, who caught her one day with her ear pressed against the door while he was doing business. As punishment, Woodruff cut off Chloe's ear—and from then on she wore a green turban to hide her deformity.

Chloe was sent to work in the kitchen but, desperate to win back her lover and owner, concocted a plan to redeem herself. She would secret a mild poison (boiled oleander leaves) into a cake she baked for Woodruff's children, Mary Octavia, James, and Cornelia Gale—just enough to sicken them—then she would swoop in and nurse them back to health, proving her worth and earning her place in the Woodruff household once more. But the plan backfired horribly—the oleander didn't just sicken the children; it killed them outright, along with Woodruff's wife, Sarah, who also ate the cake.

It didn't take long for Woodruff to discover who had murdered his family; Chloe had run to the slave quarters in hopes that she would be safe there, but her fellow slaves turned her in. Woodruff ordered his slaves to hang Chloe and afterward to throw her body in the river. Killed violently and denied a proper burial, Chloe now stalks the grounds of the Myrtles Plantation, talking to guests, wandering the hallways, and appearing in photographs—always wearing her green turban.

Melodramatic and tawdry, Chloe's story is also, depending on whom you talk to, either mostly or wholly fictitious. None of Woodruff's family died from poisoning—his wife, Sarah, and his children James and Cornelia Gale all died of yellow fever just over a year apart from one another in the early 1820s, and Mary Octavia lived until 1889. None of the records of the plantation have turned up a slave named Chloe. This is unsurprising: Chloe's tale plays up several basic stereotypes common to American folklore and reads more as an amalgamation of stock characters than the story of a real person. It has strains of both the Jezebel figure, a sexually precocious slave who disturbs the natural order of the nuclear household, seeking to supplant the white wife; and the "mammy" figure, a motherly slave who earns her spot in the white household by loving and caring for the master's children. Appearing in some versions as notably light-skinned, Chloe, as historian Tiya Miles points out, also conforms to the cliché of the "tragic mulatto": a woman, alluring because of her mixed-race heritage, who seeks entrance into white society but is rebuffed by her white lover. The lack of clear details or historical substantiation means that the legend of Chloe is adaptable: each person who tells her story can borrow from the various stereotypes as needed, emphasizing different aspects over others to suit the telling.

Frances Kermeen had never heard of Chloe or any of the other ghost stories surrounding the plantation when she bought it in 1980, hoping to turn it into a bed and breakfast, but she soon found herself beset by paranormal events of all kinds. During the ten years she owned the plantation, among other things, she saw candelabras float through the air and balls of light hovering about her, smelled inexplicable perfumes whose source could not be found, heard footsteps in the middle of the night and voices that called her by name. Chloe appeared to guests and spoke to them, and the ghost of Clark Woodruff made amorous advances toward young women staying at the plantation. Amid this flurry of activity, a new spirit appeared: a young Native American woman, who would appear naked in the courtyard beneath a weeping willow tree. Reportedly, once spotted, she will turn to face you, holding your gaze for a moment before blurring slightly as she fades away.

This last ghost, Kermeen implied, might hold the key to the Myrtles Plantation and its host of spirits. Writing in 2005, she offered a few different explanations for the surfeit of ghosts at the Myrtles Plantation. One was an Indian burial ground located beneath the parking lot. This land, so her story goes, was sacred to the Tunica, a small Indian band famous throughout the Mississippi River Valley during the Colonial period. Adept at making salt (then a highly prized commodity), the Tunica were sought out by both Spanish and French colonialists as trading partners. According to Kermeen, when Bradford set out to build his plantation, he sought out a hill above the surrounding swamps, inadvertently choosing land sacred to the Tunica, who used hills for their burial sites. It was this ill-fated decision that started all the trouble.

⤙⤚⤛⤜

The Anglo fascination with Indian burial lands stretches back at least to the eighteenth century. The Revolutionary poet Philip Freneau was one of the earliest to approach these sacred lands with a mix of exoticism and foreboding. In his 1787 poem "The Indian Burying Ground," he saw the spirits of vanquished Indians still hunting, feasting, and playing:

> Thou, stranger, that shalt come this way,
> No fraud upon the dead commit—
> Observe the swelling turf, and say
> They do not lie, but here they sit.

Be wary of the Native burial ground, Freneau warns us, for life still moves there.

In the 1970s this idea reappeared in the country's imagination, turning malevolent and becoming the foundation for a series of horror movies and stories of haunted houses. Its popularity stems almost entirely from Jay Anson's 1977 massive best seller, *The Amityville Horror*, and the genre-defining horror film based on it. Anson's book, advertised as a true story, was based on testimony from George and Kathleen Lutz, who claimed to have undergone a harrowing experience in the Long Island, New York,

41

hamlet of Amityville. When the Lutzes bought their dream home, they knew it had been the site of six murders: in October of 1974, twenty-three-year-old Ronald DeFeo, Jr., shot his father, mother, two sisters, and two brothers in the house. Deciding not to let this factor influence their decision, the Lutzes bought the house just over a year later. But a host of unexplained occurrences took place as soon as they moved in: George began waking up every morning at 3:15, the time that the DeFeo murders had happened, and the Lutz children began sleeping on their stomachs, the same pose in which the DeFeo victims had been found dead. The children began acting strangely and claimed to see a pair of red eyes hovering outside their bedroom. In less than a month, the Lutzes abandoned the Amityville home, leaving their possessions behind.

According to Anson, while George and Kathleen Lutz were trying to find out why their new home was so haunted, a member of the Amityville Historical Society revealed to them that the site of their home had once been used by the Shinnecock Indians "as an enclosure for the sick, mad, and dying. These unfortunates were penned up until they died of exposure." Anson further claimed that "the Shinnecock did not use this tract as a consecrated burial mound because they believed it to be infested with demons," but when paranormal researcher Hans Holzer and psychic medium Ethel Johnson-Meyers investigated the Amityville house, Johnson-Meyers channeled the spirit of a Shinnecock Indian chief, who told her the house stood on an ancient Indian burial ground.

None of this has held up under any kind of scrutiny: the Shinnecock lived some fifty miles from Amityville, and according to Ric Osuna (who spent years unearthing the facts about Amityville), the nearest human remains that have been found to date are more than a mile from the house. Nor would the Shinnecock—or any other Native people—have treated their sick and dying in such a callous, brutal fashion. But then, the entire *Amityville Horror* narrative was, it now seems likely, an elaborate hoax: in 1978 the Lutzes sued two clairvoyants and several writers working on alternative histories of the house, alleging invasion of privacy. In the course of the trial, William Weber, Ronald DeFeo's defense attorney, claimed that the entire story had been concocted by him and the Lutzes and that he had provided the couple with salient details of the DeFeo murders to substantiate their account.

This sensationalized portrayal of Native burial rites shouldn't be entirely surprising. What is surprising, then, is how quickly the trope of a haunted Indian burial ground took root and spread throughout the rest of American culture. Haunted Indian burial grounds have appeared in *Poltergeist II*, in Stanley Kubrick's adaptation of Stephen King's *The Shining*, and in countless lesser-known films, novels, and TV episodes. It's a legend that's become so ubiquitous that it's something of a cliché, showing up these days as often as not as a punchline in comedies, appearing everywhere from *South Park* to *Parks and Recreation*.

Stephen King's 1983 novel *Pet Sematary* is a particularly striking version of this narrative, in part because he describes in great detail the nature and function of the burial ground. Louis Creed, the protagonist, has moved his family out to rural Maine to take a job as a doctor at the local university. When his daughter's cat is hit by a car on the nearby highway, his new neighbor Jud Crandall takes him to a Micmac burial ground that has the power to bring the dead back to life. They bury the cat, which returns the next day, alive but changed: mean and smelling of death and foul earth. After Louis's two-year-old son is killed on the same highway, Louis, overcome with grief, attempts to resurrect him in the same manner, with predictably horrific consequences.

At the time the book was published, it was quite topical, as scholar Renée Bergland points out: during the years that King was writing *Pet Sematary*, the state of Maine was involved in a massive legal battle against the Maliseet, Penobscot, and Passamaquoddy bands of the Wabanaki Confederacy. Beginning in 1972, the tribes sued Maine and the federal government over lands to which they were, by federal law, entitled, which amounted to 60 percent of the area of the state. Long inhabited by non–Native Americans in Maine, the land in dispute was home to over 350,000 people who would have needed resettlement had the tribes been successful. Once it became clear that their claim had merit, the government scrambled to find a settlement that wouldn't involve the displacement of large amounts of nonindigenous residents, ultimately awarding the three tribes more than $81 million, much of that earmarked to purchase undeveloped land in Maine, along with other federal guarantees.

All this history lies in the background of King's novel. Early on, Louis is exploring the wilderness that is his backyard with his family and his neighbor Jud, when his wife, Rachel, exclaims, "Honey, do we *own* this?" (a question that will become fraught as the novel progresses). Jud answers Rachel, "It's part of the property, oh yes"—though Louis thinks to himself that this is not "quite the same thing." This tension between holding the deed to a piece of property and true ownership of the land continues throughout the book.

Jud repeatedly invokes the very real land disputes happening in Maine at the time, though in King's book it is the Micmac people fighting for land in Maine (an odd distortion: the Micmac people were never part of the Wabanaki Confederacy and lived primarily in Canada, not Maine). "Now the Micmacs, the state of Maine, and the government of the United States are arguing in court about who owns that land," he says at one point. "Who does own it? No one really knows, Louis. Not anymore. Different people laid claim to it at one time or another, but no claim has ever stuck." Jud stresses that the power of the land predates the former owners: "The Micmacs knew that place, but that doesn't necessarily mean they made it what it was. The Micmacs weren't always here."

In her account of the Myrtles Plantation, Kermeen follows a similar logic. As she discusses the "sacred Indian burial ground" beneath the house's parking lot, she hypothesizes that "the Indians chose that spot because it already possessed mystical qualities. The house was reportedly haunted long before a previous owner paved over the graveyard to make a parking lot." As King does with his pet cemetery, Kermeen attempts to attribute power and mystery to the Tunica burial ground while at the same time downplaying the tribe's agency and ownership—they, too, were simply temporary lodgers on a land with its own autonomous power.

The narrative of the haunted Indian burial ground hides a certain anxiety about the land on which Americans—specifically white, middle-class Americans—live. Embedded deep in the idea of home ownership—the Holy Grail of American middle-class life—is the idea that we don't, in fact, own the land we've just bought. Time and time again in these stories, perfectly average, innocent American families are confronted by ghosts who have persevered for centuries, who remain vengeful for the damage done. Facing these ghosts and expelling them, in many of these horror stories, becomes a means of refighting the Indian Wars of past centuries.

King's novel, like the legend of the Myrtles Plantation, works by playing off a buried, latent anxiety Americans have about the land they "own." If you're willing to see this conflict over land as the basis of many of our ghost stories, then it won't be surprising that so much of America is haunted. There's precious little land in the United States that hasn't been contested, one way or another, through the years. Americans live on haunted land because we have no other choice.

∽∾◦∽∾

The land of lower Louisiana is constantly shifting. A floodplain of the meandering Mississippi, the land has evolved and sometimes disappeared without a trace as the river changed course. The land on which New Orleans stands didn't even exist five thousand years ago. At the end of the last ice age, some eighteen thousand years ago, glaciers that had come down as far as Cairo, Illinois, began to melt and recede, sending a deluge of water down the Mississippi's alluvial plain. The water was loaded with sediment accumulated from farther north, and it carried this sediment down the Mississippi Embayment (the low-lying basin that runs from Illinois south) until it hit the Gulf of Mexico, where the water slowed and deposited its sediment. Over time, this sediment built up and became the Mississippi River delta—a process of accumulation that was still under way until very recently. While Louisiana had mostly reached its current state by the time the French found it in the early 1700s, the topographical changes continued into the nineteenth century. One visitor to New Orleans, Captain Basil Hall, wrote in 1828 of coasting along "past small sandy islands, over shallow banks of mud," and on through Lakes Borgne and Pontchartrain, "whose Deltas are silently pushing themselves into the sea, and raising the bottom to the surface."

The constant evolving of the land around the Mississippi delta is anathema to human habitation, and civilizations that don't make their mark through massive earthworks and geologic engineering—as New Orleans has—are easily erased by the constant flow and flux of the river and its mud. Finding archaeological material is difficult, since geographical clues in missionaries' reports or oral histories often no longer correspond to contemporary landscapes.

But the clues are there, if you look closely enough. In 1968 a guard at the Louisiana Penitentiary in Angola began hunting around at the former Trudeau Plantation, a swath of swampland on the east bank of the Mississippi, near the prison. Leonard J. Charrier was not a trained archaeologist, but he understood the land of Louisiana and, in particular, how the course of the river could change over the years. Using historical documents that he researched in his spare time, and comparing those against the changes in the meander of the river, he was able to make a stunning discovery: a lost burial ground.

Using a metal detector, Charrier located the grave of a Tunica chief, Cahura-Joligo, as well as more than a hundred other graves. He excavated hundreds of objects from the fields of the Trudeau Plantation and, having nowhere else to put them, began stockpiling them in his house. Jeffrey P. Brain, a curator at Harvard's Peabody Museum, was alerted to Charrier's find and in 1970 traveled to visit him and his priceless artifacts. Objects from the burial grounds were on every piece of furniture, in every closet and cupboard, and covering the floor so thoroughly that only small walkways were left. One walk-in closet had been filled with a four-foot-high pile of kettles, muskets, wire, and other ephemera.

Charrier loaned the objects to Harvard while he haggled over the price, but when Harvard asked for some kind of document from the landowner renouncing any claims to the Tunica artifacts, Charrier stonewalled. A series of lawsuits ensued, involving Charrier, Harvard, the state of Louisiana, and the squabbling heirs of the Trudeau Plantation, each claiming a right to a share of the artifacts that had become known as the Tunica Treasure.

The only parties unable to enter into litigation were the Tunica themselves, because the tribe wasn't recognized by the United States. The Tunica-Biloxi Tribe had been fighting since the 1920s for federal recognition, but a continual stumbling block had been a lack of clear evidence that the tribe had a history. In a curious twist of fate, Charrier's discovery remedied this problem, proving beyond doubt that the Tunica had inhabited southern Louisiana; as a direct result, in 1981 the tribe was granted federal recognition. Now it, too, could pursue a claim for the artifacts. After more than a decade of ongoing litigation, the Tunica-Biloxi Tribe was finally granted possession of the Tunica Treasure, now housed in a cultural center in nearby Marksville.

Not everyone, of course, was satisfied by this outcome. "I found the thing," an embittered Charrier told the *New York Times* when it was all over with, "I spent many an hour digging it up, and if I hadn't, the Mississippi River would have taken it from us all."

~~~◦~~~

The land where the Trudeau Plantation once stood is almost twenty miles from the Myrtles Plantation, and the claim that the Myrtles Plantation has anything to do with the Tunica ground that Charrier excavated is demonstrably false. But in the wake of the long-running legal dispute over the Tunica burial ground and the war between the heirs of the Tunica tribe, Harvard, and the federal government, rumors began to circulate that the Myrtles Plantation itself stood atop this contested land, the treasure and its fraught ownership becoming part of the lore of the house.

Over time the Tunica burial ground and the Myrtles Plantation have fused together, one becoming part of the story of the other. Alongside the fictitious story of the slave Chloe and the dozen unsubstantiated murders that supposedly took place on the Myrtles' property, the plantation has accrued these legends and allowed them to settle, like sediment, about its foundations. Today the plantation is a popular spot for tours and ghost hunts and has parlayed its history into a successful destination for seekers of the paranormal. Like the ground beneath the property, over the years these stories have shifted and changed with the tides and with the tastes of tourists, changing subtly with the landscape.

If you listen closely, the ghost stories of the Myrtles Plantation say more about the tellers than they do about the supernatural. A slave abused by her master, who in response turns murderous; the Indian ghosts whose burial lands have been disturbed—all of these stories, in one way or another, respond to history. Ghost stories like this are a way for us to revel in the open wounds of the past while any question of responsibility for that past blurs, then fades away.

CHAPTER THREE

THE ENDLESS HOUSE

San Jose, CA

I t's hard to know where San Jose, California, starts, where it ends, and what distinguishes it from the dozens of adjoining small suburbs that stretch northeast to San Francisco and northwest to Oakland. The city—if you can call it that—is a labyrinth of repetition, a nonspace, a suburban blur that spreads northward from the Santa Clara Valley into two fingers of land: one the San Francisco peninsula, the other the East Bay. Individual hamlets like Santa Clara, Sunnyvale, and Cupertino overlap, their individual downtowns long dried up and replaced by shopping malls and office parks that distort any real sense of geography.

Urban sprawl isn't unique to San Jose, of course, but the city has a miniature allegory of itself in the form of a sprawling, formless Victorian mansion that sits in its very center. If there is a central monument to San Jose now, it is this labyrinthine, inscrutable house in the heart of the city. Tours leave every twenty minutes, lasting roughly two hours, every day but Christmas. During the course of the tour guests walk over a mile, mostly staying inside the house. This is the Winchester Mystery House, just off Interstate 280, facing the major thoroughfare now named for it, Winchester Boulevard, next to a Cineplex and across the street from two massive shopping malls. It is what many have called the most haunted house in the world.

Implacable, anachronistic, unchanging. Holding its secrets within.

❦

The basic facts of how the house got started are clear enough. In 1862 Sarah Pardee married William Wirt Winchester, the son of a successful shirt manufacturer who would go on to found the Winchester Repeating Arms Company. Sarah and William's only daughter died in infancy in 1866, and William died of tuberculosis fifteen years later. In 1885 the wealthy widow moved to the Santa Clara Valley, where she bought an eight-room farmhouse and began work on enlarging it. It grew massively; by the time she died in 1922, it had 160 rooms and sprawled in every direction. At one point it was even larger, but much of it was damaged by the 1906 earthquake, including a seven-story tower, which she never repaired or rebuilt. Many of the rooms remain unfinished, as though the builders simply walked off the job the day Sarah Winchester died.

Opened to the public the year after her death, the house became immediately famous, working its way into American culture in unlikely ways. Author Shirley Jackson grew up not far from San Jose, and the mansion features briefly in *The Haunting of Hill House*: as Dr. John Montague describes the features of Hill House, he claims its builder, Hugh Crain, "expected that someday Hill House might become a showplace, like the Winchester House in California." Ten years later, the Winchester house was used as the inspiration for Disneyland's Haunted Mansion: Walt Disney wanted a haunted mansion but nothing that was derelict or in ruins, so he turned to the immaculate Victorian façade of the Winchester house. Stephen King claims he first heard the story of the house in a *Ripley's Believe It or Not* comic when he was a kid and remembered it for years after. King's *Rose Red*—a television miniseries from 2002 about a team of paranormal researchers who investigate a massive, sprawling maze of a house—was the closest direct work of his to be based on the Winchester house, but one finds traces of it throughout his other work as well, from *'Salem's Lot* to *The Shining*. And then there's the artist Jeremy Blake, who shortly before his suicide produced a trilogy of short films based on the Winchester house. In them, the façade of the house is merged with shifting, kaleidoscopic colors, images from 1950s cartoon westerns, and the suburban landscape of San Jose. The effect of the films is unsettling in the extreme as Blake's work draws out a latent foreboding in the Victorian eaves and gables of the house. "There's the psychological aspect of the place," he said at the time, "the neurosis and mad logic and creativity all flowing together in this crazy quilt of rooms. It gets unbelievably twisted."

❧

The legend of the house, which has been told so many times that most people take its veracity for granted, begins with the death of Sarah Winchester's daughter and husband. Believing her family to be cursed, Winchester went to a famous Boston psychic named Adam Coons. During a séance, Coons told her that her family was being haunted by the ghosts of all those killed by Winchester rifles, particularly the Native Americans who had been killed by the "gun that won the West," and that the only way to keep them at bay would be to begin building a house that was never to be finished, an endless work in progress. And so Winchester came to San Jose, bought an eight-room farmhouse, and hired crews to build onto her house, literally twenty-four hours a day, seven days a week, for the rest of her life. When she died in 1922, all work immediately stopped: rooms were left unfinished, nails were left half driven into walls. This is the story Stephen King remembers: "At one séance, Sarah Winchester asked the medium, 'When will I die?' . . . The medium replied, 'When your house is done.'"

This story of the endlessly deferred completion of construction as a means to stave off death reinforces the notion of a woman whose superstition and gullibility led her to create a house beyond the bounds of sense or competence. Nightly séances were conducted in a blue room in the center of the house, from midnight until 2 a.m., when Winchester would summon ghosts to instruct her on the next day's construction and how to keep herself safe from evil spirits. Among the house's signature features is a staircase that ascends half a flight, makes a ninety-degree turn to the left, then ends directly at a wall, as though to trick ghosts who might be pursuing the solitary heiress. These are the prime selling points of the Winchester Mystery House: the dead-end staircases, the trapdoors and false rooms, the labyrinthine network of traps and detours. All of which were meant to confuse the ghosts haunting Winchester, creating a private maze that only she knew and understood, in which she could feel safe from these forces of malevolence.

Winchester managed this incredible building feat due to her extreme wealth: because of her stock in the Winchester Rifle Company, Sarah Winchester's income, the tour guides explain, was around $1,500 a day, somewhere north of $32,000 in today's dollars. As such, she bought lavishly and could afford to be eccentric. An early stop in the tour is the so-called Million Dollar Storeroom, which holds several priceless works of Tiffany glass that Winchester had specifically commissioned. The room conveys opulent wealth, but the message is clear: these things belong in a palatial mansion, not a madwoman's house. A crazy person should not have had access to them.

Among the Tiffany pieces is one with an intricate, stunning spider-web pattern, made with thirteen semiprecious stones. Winchester's fascination with the number thirteen is a well-established aspect of the lore surrounding her life—there are thirteen bedrooms, thirteen bathrooms, thirteen windows in certain rooms—and her triskaidekaphilia is presented as more proof of her morbid eccentricity. It was, supposedly, in the thirteenth bedroom of her mansion that Winchester died, on

September 5, 1922, attended by her improbably named physician, Dr. Euthanasia Meade.

As compelling as this narrative is, there are several problems with it. People talk of the "staircases" that go nowhere, but there's only one—most likely an uncorrected architectural mistake. The fascination with the number thirteen is also a later concoction. No record of a Boston psychic named Adam Coons exists (though Euthanasia Meade was certainly real), nor is there any definitive evidence that Sarah Winchester ever visited a psychic. The story of the ghosts of the Winchester Rifle's victims is almost certainly invention as well. Nor do most people know that Winchester owned several other spectacularly average homes and that most of her later years were spent in her home in Atherton, some miles away, or that she spent very little of the last seventeen years of her life in the Winchester Mystery House, which she called Llanada Villa ("house on flat land"). The blue room in the center of the house, where she supposedly conducted séances each night at midnight? This was her gardener's bedroom.

Still, questions remain. If this story is mostly, if not entirely, false, then what is the real story—why is the house so large, why did she keep on building, and why doesn't it have any kind of observable order or plan? Why tell this lie instead of the truth, and why did it take such firm root in our psyches? How did it come to obliterate nearly all traces of the true story, and why does it remain so alluring?

～⁓◦⁓～

Sarah Lockwood Pardee was born in 1839 in New Haven, Connecticut, into an upper-middle-class family. (Throughout her life she was called not Sarah but Sallie, after her maternal grandmother.) The third-youngest of six children, all but one of them girls, she grew up amid the Golden Age of New England industrialism. The wizard Eli Whitney had just moved his factory to nearby Hamden, and all around New Haven mill towns like Lowell and Lawrence, Massachusetts, thrummed with life. Sarah's father, Leonard, was a woodworker by trade and established himself as an expert craftsman of the ornamental flourishes that came to define Victorian architecture.

Among those who were rising on the wave of American industrialism was the Pardees' neighbor Oliver Winchester. He had arrived in New Haven from Baltimore in 1845, virtually penniless but determined to make a name for himself. Possessed of an ideal combination of business acumen and mechanical understanding, within ten years he had reversed his fortunes. Using an innovative design for the production of men's shirts, he and his business partner, John Davies, founded the Winchester and Davies Shirt Manufacturing Company, which would in a few short years transform into a juggernaut of industry.

From 1850 to 1860, Leonard Pardee, building homes the barons of industry could now afford, increased his income tenfold, to $15,000 in assets (roughly a million dollars today). But he had a problem: too many daughters in an age when women were mainly thought of as a financial liability. He gave his children a strong education—they learned foreign languages, art, and music—and then set about marrying off his girls. The second to reach the altar, Sarah married her childhood neighbor William Wirt Winchester in 1862. It was a simple ceremony that belied the wealth of the two families: there was a war on, materials were sparse, and it was not a time for ostentation. The week that William and Sarah married, there were battles in Louisiana, Missouri, and Virginia. It had been a year since the first battle of Bull Run had awakened the United States to the horror of battle, and in a few weeks the Second Battle of Bull Run would grind up another eighteen thousand soldiers. By then, death had reached all corners of the North and the South.

Most of the Pardees and Winchesters stayed out of the war, being rich enough to spend the $300 for a deferment. (Sarah's brother served in the first Battle of Bull Run but chose not to reenlist when his initial three-month appointment was up; her brother-in-law Homer Sprague was the only member of her near family to see sustained conflict.) If anything, though, Oliver Winchester wanted more involvement in the war. In 1857 he had bought the failing Volcanic Repeating Arms Company from Horace Smith and Daniel B. Wesson, two designers who had invented a promising but as-yet-unsuccessful rifle that could fire multiple shots without the cumbersome and complicated reloading process of most rifles. (Smith and Wesson, of course, would found another arms company, bearing their names, that would find a great deal more success.) Winchester knew that a repeating rifle, a rifle that one could reload in a matter of seconds rather than minutes, could change the landscape of war forever, and he was convinced that the U.S. Army needed to adopt it. He took one of his most valued mechanics from his shirt factory, Benjamin T.Henry, and worked with him to improve on Smith and Wesson's idea.

Despite its obvious advantages, the resulting Winchester Repeating Rifle, nicknamed "The Henry," failed to make an impact on the war. Some individual soldiers purchased them, but the army never adopted the rifles wholesale; by the end of the Civil War, repeating rifles made up only 1 percent of all weapons used in battle. At the time, William saw his father's venture into weapons as an interesting side project; the real family fortune still lay in shirts. By then William was the secretary of Winchester and Davies, and he and Sarah had built themselves a comfortable life—one ideally suited for a child. On June 15, 1866, Sarah gave birth to a daughter, whom they named Annie, after William's sister, who had recently died in childbirth.

The delivery was fairly uneventful, but almost immediately Annie seemed to deteriorate before their eyes. A doctor diagnosed her condition as marasmus, a deficiency in which the body cannot process calories or manufacture its own protein. Normally marasmus results from severe malnutrition, but Annie was not lacking in food; her body simply could not process it. In an utterly cruel irony in a nation that had recently undergone such deprivation, Annie, born to one of the few families well off enough to provide handsomely for their child, was dying of want.

Annie Winchester died on July 25, a mere forty days old. William returned to his job at Winchester and Davies, but his father's other business was rapidly changing. The Henry rifle had finally begun to take off, and with it, the Winchester Repeating Arms Company. By securing lucrative contracts with foreign militaries, Oliver Winchester was able to keep his company thriving even through a postwar depression. By 1869, with the completion of the transcontinental railroad, the rifle assumed a new purpose: the company began aggressively marketing it as *the* best weapon for frontier self-defense. In time the Winchester rifle would earn the nickname "the gun that won the West," becoming synonymous with America's westward expansion and the Indian wars.

As the West became increasingly important to the company's fortunes, Winchester established offices in San Francisco, and in 1870 he sent William and Sarah to the Bay Area to oversee their installation. In portraits of the couple taken during that trip, William looks haunted, hollowed-out; his eyes hold a haggard allure, fixed deep into the distance. The tuberculosis that plagued him most of his adult life is not quite visible, but he seems fragile. Sarah, on the other hand, seems to face the camera head-on, even from a three-quarters profile. She exudes, if not beauty, then a vitality and a quick-wittedness, an awareness of the world around her and a desire to reshape it.

୦ଽ୦ୈ

When people speak of the deaths in Sarah Winchester's family that drove her to build her house in San Jose, they mostly mean the deaths of her infant daughter and her husband, as if these two events happened coterminously. In fact, they took place sixteen years apart. Annie died in 1866, and Sarah continued to live on in New Haven until the mid-1880s. She and William never had another child, but by the few extant accounts, they lived generally happily and comfortably during that time.

Then in early 1880 Sarah's mother died, and in the winter of that year, her father-in-law, Oliver Winchester, died, followed by her husband less than a year later from tuberculosis. A few years later, she lost another close relative. By the mid-1880s Sarah Winchester found her family life decimated.

But when she moved to San Jose, she didn't come alone: she came with two sisters and their families. Why San Jose? Sarah and her husband had visited San Francisco in the 1870s, and found it quite pleasant, but the real reason has to do with her brother-in-law Homer Sprague, who in 1885 was appointed president of Mills College, in Oakland. When he and Sarah's sister Antoinette (Nettie) moved to the Bay Area, both Sarah and another sister, Isabelle (Belle) Merriman, and her family all moved together. In San Jose they would re-form their family, and Sarah, who had married into money and had the most stable fortune, would build a home to house them all.

In those years after the Gold Rush, the San Francisco Bay Area promised much. San Francisco's population grew at around 8 percent a year during the 1860s and 1870s, from 135,000 people in 1867 to 233,700 in 1880, and they were still coming in droves, thanks to the railroad. Most came seeking not gold but the "life-giving Nature" of the West; as one unnamed physician of the time put it, "Nor is sickness that scourge of humanity here to harass and hinder us in our pursuits. The general salubrity of California has justly become a proverb. The surgeons of San Francisco have remarked that wounds heal here with astonishing rapidity, owing, it is supposed, in a great measure, to the extreme purity of the atmosphere."

People afflicted with all manner of disease came to California, but consumptives most of all; stories were told of tubercular cases, or "lungers," as they were known, miraculously healed simply by breathing the dry, warm air of the West. According to one historian, by 1900 one-fourth of all migrants to California were tuberculosis patients who had come for their health and ended up staying. And so as Sarah Winchester joined the disease train to the San Francisco Bay Area, she was followed by her husband's killer, the White Plague.

She settled in the small but ambitious rural community of San Jose. Always in the shadow of its neighbor to the north, San Francisco, San

Jose by then had begun to try to distinguish itself. It could boast of its great Electric Light Tower, built in 1881 for $5,000. Straddling the intersection of Santa Clara and Market streets, the tower was 207 feet high, topped with six carbon arc lamps that provided 24,000 candelas of light—so bright, one could read by its light over a mile away. "For the first time the citizens of San Jose realized that they had the wonder of the nineteenth century," the *Daily Herald* proclaimed, "that they lived in the only city lighted by electric light, supported by a tower, which like the Colossus at Rhodes, stood astride her two principal streets." Local cops preferred working the beat around the tower, because migrating ducks would often fly into it and fall, electrocuted, dead to the ground, and the cops could pick up the dead ducks and sell them to restaurants.

Despite this welcoming beacon of progress and light, most people reaching the Santa Clara Valley found a city adrift. "California was a hotbed that brought humanity to a rapid, monstrous maturity," the *Annals of California* reported in 1855, "like the mammoth vegetables for which it is so celebrated." People everywhere "lost their brains," which is to say, they went insane. Suicides by strychnine and arsenic were common, including that of a woman named Claude Lorraine, who'd lost a sock containing $500, and a man named Riley, who botched a suicide attempt in January of 1884, told the police he was tired of life and wanted to die, and apologized for not making a "better job of it." Newspapers referred to suicide as "solving the Great Problem," as in the headline that ran in the July 13, 1885, *San Jose Daily News*: "STRYCHNINE: Margaret Risley Solves the Great Problem." The Great Problem was life; the solution was death.

~~~○~~~

Sarah Winchester's original idea was to enlarge her house so that it could comfortably fit her family. But her brother-in-law Homer Sprague's tenure at Mills College ended almost before it had begun, and within a year he and Winchester's sister Nettie moved to North Dakota for a different university job. Meanwhile, her sister Belle Merriman and her family had moved to San Francisco, leaving only their daughter Marion, whom Sarah all but adopted. The goal of building a great house for herself and her siblings' families ended almost immediately.

And yet Winchester kept building. She initially hired at least two architects but quickly dismissed them, preferring to do most of the work herself. Most of what we know about her building methods come from two surviving letters written to her sister-in-law Hannah Jane (Jennie) Bennett in 1898. They speak not of a madwoman beset by spirits but of a woman experimenting with the construction and design of her house. "I am constantly having to make an upheaval for some reason," she writes on June 11. "For instance, my upper hall which leads to the sleeping apartment was rendered so unexpectedly dark by a little addition that after a number of people had missed their footing on the stairs I decided that safety demanded something to be done so, over a year ago, I took out a wall and put in a skylight." Despite what you're told on a tour of the house, she did not employ workers twenty-four hours a day, seven days a week; when she found that the plaster she wanted couldn't be set in the heat of summer, she dismissed her workmen in order to wait for cooler weather, and she writes, "then I became rather worn and tired out and dismissed all the workmen to take such rest as I might through the winter." Her fatigue is a constant refrain. "If I did not get so easily tired out I should hurry up things more than I do," she wrote, "but I think it is better to 'go slow' than to use myself up. Just having the furnace man here and going over all the details with him used me up completely for a day or so."

There's a passive-aggressive quality to Winchester's building: she was nominally getting her house ready to entertain guests, particularly family from New Haven, who were accustomed to houses of a certain size, but then continually begged off guests under the pretense that the house was never quite done. "I hope some day to get so situated that I shall feel that it would not be an imposition on my friends to invite them to visit me," she says, more than ten years after she began improvements on her house.

At some point the perpetual building seems to have become a pretense to keep her family away.

This is one, perhaps uncharitable, way of looking at the house. Another perspective is that at some point the building ceased to be a means to housing her family and became an end unto itself. We are not used to seeing Sarah Winchester as an architectural pioneer, but she was. At the time she began work on her house, most would have seen the phrase "woman architect" as a contradiction in terms. Perhaps the most famous female architect of the early twentieth century, Julia Morgan, had not yet applied to École des Beaux-Arts, in Paris. When she did, in 1897, the school had only recently begun allowing female applicants. Particularly recalcitrant was the architecture school: Morgan had to apply three times before they were willing to admit a woman. The second time she nearly made it, but according to one judge her score was lowered because "they did not want to encourage young girls." Morgan would go on to define the architecture of the San Francisco Bay Area in the first half of the twentieth century before being hired by William Randolph Hearst to design many of his buildings, including, ultimately, Hearst Castle in San Simeon, California.

It's tempting to compare Winchester's house to Morgan's work—two female architects at the dawn of the twentieth century. But the tendency to judge the house by other architectural models or too closely through the lens of its creator is to miss the thing itself. Without any overall or grand design, without any intention of a unified effect, the Winchester mansion sprawls and flops in a dozen different directions, moving like a coral reef. Its aesthetic, its beauty, is precisely in its lawlessness. The house is, in a way, a form of automatic writing, a stream of consciousness made spatial.

For many visitors this is also what makes the house so unsettling. The Winchester house can feel endless, much larger on the inside than it is on the outside. This is something you find in Shirley Jackson's Hill House, and you find it in the disorienting space of Disney's Haunted Mansion (only from an aerial view do you understand that nearly all of the ride happens not in the house itself but in an adjacent warehouse space, giving you the sense that the tiny mansion you enter goes on forever inside). The disturbingly endless house appears repeatedly in horror novels, from Poe's House of Usher to the eponymous structure in Mark Z. Danielewski's *House of Leaves*, built elegantly around the unsettling fact that the house in question is slightly larger inside than it is outside. And this is to say nothing of the numerous gothic novels that feature secret passageways, where the endlessness isn't supernatural, including the estate in H. P. Lovecraft's "The Rats in the Walls." If houses are supposed to be places of security, then most terrifying is the idea that they might go on forever, that they might be labyrinths.

But this isn't the only reason the Winchester house has captured the imagination of so many. Add to this another kind of haunting, the one popularized by Charles Dickens in his 1861 novel *Great Expectations*, a novel involving the spinster Miss Havisham, living alone with a young girl named Estella in a massive mansion. Everything in her house is frozen in time: place settings are covered in cobwebs and dust, but readied as though at any moment the dinner party might begin again. As Pip tells us,

> I began to understand that everything in the room had stopped, like the watch and the clock, a long time ago. I noticed that Miss Havisham put down the jewel exactly on the spot from which she had taken it up. As Estella dealt the cards, I glanced at the dressing-table again, and saw that the shoe upon it, once white, now yellow, had never been worn. I glanced down at the foot from which the shoe was absent, and saw that the silk stocking on it, once white, now yellow, had been trodden ragged. Without this arrest of everything, this standing still of all the pale decayed objects, not even the withered bridal dress on the collapsed form could have looked so like grave-clothes, or the long veil so like a shroud.

Here, too, we find a fictional story ready to be transposed onto Sarah Winchester, complete with the young girl, played by Winchester's niece, Marion Merriman. The spinster in perpetual mourning, time standing still, the perpetual sense of arrested decay—none of this had much to do with Winchester, but from outward appearances it was a perfect fit, and it offered a ready-made explanation of what went on behind closed doors. Ghosts, you could say, flock to women left alone.

❧

On Friday, March 29, 1895, an unsigned article titled "Strange Story: A Woman Who Thinks She'll Die When Her House Is Built" was published in the *San Jose Daily News*, with the subheading "A Magnificent Mansion on the Saratoga Road Near San Jose—A Maze of Turrets and Towers." The legend of Sarah Winchester, widow in perpetual mourning, superstitious kook whose wealth was squandered in a deluded quest to keep the spirits at bay, truly originates here.

"The first view of the house fills one with surprises," the article proclaims. "You mechanically rub your eyes to assure yourself that the number of the turrets is not an illusion, they are so fantastic and dream-like. But nearer approach reveals others and others and still others." With a mixture of wonder and a tinge of horror, the anonymous *Daily News* writer taps directly into the idea that the house may literally be endless:

> How it is possible to build on an already apparently finished house and preserve its artistic appearance through so many changes is a query that nobody can answer, but the fact remains that it has been done. From every point of view new towers appear, and one has to make a circuit of the building to see all of these, for every addition to the many that is made has one or more separate roofs, and every roof is elaborated into a tower or resolved into a dome.

From there, the article gets down to business.

> Ten years ago the handsome residence was apparently ready
> for occupancy, but improvements and additions are constantly
> being made, for the reason, it is said, that the owner of the
> house believes that when it is entirely completed, she will die.
> This superstition has resulted in the construction of a maze of
> domes, turrets, cupolas and towers, covering territory enough
> for a castle. Although no part of the structure is over two
> stories high, the house is large enough to shelter an army.

As the article continues, it lays out the story that has come to be associated
with Sarah Winchester, which has remained almost entirely unchanged in
over a century.

> As fast as new rooms are finished—and they are all made
> with the very latest and most modern of accessories—they are
> furnished with the utmost elegance and closed, to be used
> hardly at all. Mrs. Winchester and her niece live alone in the
> great residence, and its doors are closed to all but a few. The
> tap, tap, tapping of the carpenters' hammers never disturbs
> them in their many and luxurious quarters, which are far re-
> moved from the sound as if it were somebody else's house that
> was being built.

Here one finds, arising almost *ex nihilo*, the entire mythology all at
once: A building somewhat anachronistic, no longer fully in use. A
woman, arrested in time, living in the past, unable to move forward and
rejoin the stream of humanity. A house that never ends, that's built as a
labyrinth, that is uncanny in the way it uses familiar domestic elements
while upending them in a strange, discomfiting way.

One last element that would have been on the minds of readers of that original article might have contributed to the vicious rumors that began to spring up around Sarah Winchester. Two years earlier, on May 5, 1893, the United States suffered its worst economic shock in decades, one that would lead to a depression that would be eclipsed only by the Great Depression of the 1930s. By 1895 unemployment had gone from 4 percent to 14 percent; there were more than 500 bank failures and 1,600 business failures. Henry Adams saw the panic of 1893 as a conspiracy from Wall Street, by that "dark, mysterious, crafty, wicked, rapacious, and tyrannical power to rob and oppress and enslave the people." According to H. P. Robinson, the editor of *Railway Age*, writing in 1895, "It is probably safe to say that in no civilized country in this century, not actually in the throes of war or open insurrection, has society been so disorganized as it was in the United States during the first half of 1894; never was human life held so cheap; never did the constituted authorities appear so incompetent to enforce respect for the law."

In this context of social upheaval, in a city like San Jose, already teetering on the edge, we find Sarah Winchester—a recluse, a woman, someone who gave to charity but did so anonymously, who had no real social circle to stand up for her. She made an easy target, and the slurs of insanity, the echoes of Miss Havisham and her own pathological mourning—these things all clung to Sarah Winchester because she appeared to those around her as a gaudy reminder of the haves versus the have-nots. She was the 1 percent, and the city resented her for it. And so it punished her through gossip and myth.

At any other point in time, in any other place, and with any other person, any other structure, none of these stories would have gelled quite in this way. Sarah Winchester's house is unique not because of its architecture or because of the motivations for its construction but because it was vulnerable to a series of resentments that converged in a singular moment in history.

Defenders were few and far between. Two years later an article titled "Only Gossip: No Truth in the Story of the Winchester Palace" appeared in the *San Jose Evening News*, arguing that the myth was the "result of rural rumors." The article quoted an "acquaintance" of Sarah Winchester's, who said bluntly that the "story about Mrs. Winchester being superstitious, and believing that she is going to die when the house, or rather all additions are completed, is all nonsense. She is not superstitious, but is an unusually sensible woman. She has erected a magnificent home. She has made many improvements on the first plans. It may be that building is a fad with her, and if it is, she is able to satisfy it, for she is a woman of ample means." This acquaintance, not satisfied, went on quite pointedly:

> We are constantly inviting people of wealth to locate in Santa Clara valley. Mrs. Winchester is one of the most desirable settlers we have ever had. If people who come here with fortunes are inclined to spend it, I do not think it is wise to circulate reports that they are "cranks" merely because they do not get "thick" with the neighbors.... Mrs. Winchester is a lady of refinement and culture.... If she wants to build a castle on her premises near Campbell, she should be permitted to do so without ascribing her motives to foolish superstitions. If people of wealth who settle in Santa Clara are to be ridiculed when they spend their money lavishly, we might as well put up the bars.... After awhile the lady might not want to have a nail driven about the place for fear that someone would run off to a newspaper with a cock-and-bull story. This would be the means of preventing the circulation of a large amount of money among builders and furnishers and that is why we encourage people of wealth to locate in Santa Clara valley. We want industries developed, improvements made and this valley beautified.

The article was indeed a corrective to the urban legends of the reclusive Winchester, but it was curiously couched in the language of civic investment, encouraging the wealthy to relocate to the Santa Clara Valley.

The house was either the work of a rich, mentally unstable widow or a potential source for local jobs and investment. The story of Sarah Winchester's house, built on the fortune of the rifle that "won the West," is always, one way or another, the story of money.

⟆⟍⟐⟍⟆⟍⟆

After her death, her numerous real estate assets were sold off one by one. Of all her holdings, including the houses and vast plots of land she owned throughout the valley, the Winchester house itself was, according to her lawyer Samuel Leib, "appraised as of no value." Gargantuan, sprawling, beautiful, as salable real estate the house was worthless: too odd, idiosyncratic, lavish, and useless to be sold to another buyer. At an auction of the property, no one bought it; the only interested party was a man named John H. Brown, who didn't have the money to buy the house but offered to lease it, with an option to buy it later.

Brown had come a long way: from an amusement park called the Crystal Beach Resort on the Canadian side of Lake Erie. There he had invented one of the earliest roller coasters: a ten-mile-an-hour ride called the Backety-Back, which in June 1910 had killed a woman who'd somehow been thrown from its slow-moving car. Brown relocated his family to California, where he heard of the Winchester house and the rumors regarding its construction. Among Crystal Beach's other attractions was a "house of mystery" that Brown had seen draw large crowds. According to historian Mary Jo Ignoffo, who put together a biography of Winchester, it was Brown who took the rumors of the Winchester house and reinvigorated them, building a mythology around it and offering tours. As attitudes toward America's westward expansion and manifest destiny changed, so, too, did the role of the Winchester rifle in the tour, now emphasized as the gun that had killed untold Native Americans, all of whom were now haunting the widow who'd profited from the murder weapon. As with the Myrtles Plantation, vengeful American Indians have loomed large in the script.

Among those who took a tour in those first years was Harry Houdini, who had spent much of his professional career by that point debunking psychics and disproving supernatural phenomena. Yet when he got to the Winchester house, his attitude seemed to change completely. After his visit, he did not speak of the folly of superstition or of Winchester being crazy or duped by disreputable psychics. After repeating the story that by then had been accepted as gospel, Houdini went on: "The whole thing is beautifully inlaid because the woman wants the workmen to take plenty of time. Never was there such a marvelous place."

After the great debunker gave his seal of approval to the tourist attraction that Sarah Winchester's house had become, its business grew steadily. Over the years her former employees and friends made attempts to correct her story; when she died, Leib's son and business partner Roy commented that she was "as sane and clear headed a woman as I have ever known, and she had a better grasp of business and financial affairs than most men." Testimony from her many employees over the years mattered little, though; what mattered, then as now, was the story that taps into those larger social and cultural trends, perfectly embodied by such an architecturally unsettling house.

The legend of Sarah Winchester depends on a cultural uneasiness to which we don't always like to admit. An uneasiness about women living alone, withdrawn from society, for one. An uneasiness about wealth and the way the superrich live among us. And, perhaps largest of all, an uneasiness about the gun that won the West and the violence white Americans carried out in the name of civilization.

These may be unconnected anxieties, but they're brought together in this story of a rich woman alone, haunted by the American Indians killed with her father-in-law's gun. It's a compelling story, perhaps, because it's one in which Sarah Winchester is punished for these transgressions—driven mad by guilt, unable to join society, her money wasted and misspent. Winchester herself had little documented guilt about the role of the rifle in American history, but we've projected shame on her nonetheless, as though we can quarantine such thoughts in the mind of someone long dead so the rest of us can go about our days unburdened, enjoying the California sun.

CHAPTER FOUR

THE RATHOLE REVELATION

Georgetown, NY, and Bull Valley, IL

arah Winchester may not have designed her house with guidance from the spirit world, but if there is a house that *was* indisputably built by someone influenced by the dead, it is Timothy Brown's in Georgetown, New York, about thirty-five miles southeast of Syracuse. Brown had not yet begun building his house when, he later explained, his dead sister, Mary, presented him with a vision one morning. She offered up several types of house and invited him to pick the one that suited him. From that point on, the spirits guided him in its construction. As the Spiritualist journal *Banner of Light* later related, Brown "found that if he put his chisel in the wrong place his arm had no power to use the mallet or strike a blow, but when his chisel was rightly placed the blows were freely dealt."

The house that Brown and his spirits built still stands, a remarkably odd and beautiful structure from the 1860s. It might have been an unremarkable square house but for the fringe of scalloped wood that hangs from its eaves, an ornamental design of wooden lace that drips down as though the roof is melting. The wooden lace adds a richness of detail and a depth of character to the house that begs for closer inspection. Rather than constructing an A-frame roof to keep snow from building up, as was customary, Brown built his roof with a unique funnel that leads to a central drainpipe. (This might have led to the leak that severely damaged the interiors when the house was left vacant in the mid-2000s.)

Ghosts are the quintessential unwanted guests: like pests or dry rot, they do not belong. When homeowners discover ghosts on their property, they will do anything in their power to excise or exorcise them. Usually, that is. For there is a long history of Americans doing exactly the opposite: people who've tried to populate their houses with the paranormal, to *welcome* spirits in and make them feel at home. Timothy Brown saw himself as part of a larger movement—Spiritualism—and his house stands as a monument to the great American passion for communing with the dead that held fast in this country (and elsewhere) for the better part of a century.

America's popular fascination with ghosts began in 1848, in a small house in upstate New York, where two sisters, fifteen-year-old Margaret and twelve-year-old Kate Fox, revealed that they had been communicating with the spirit of a dead man in their basement. The house had been thought haunted before the Foxes moved in, and almost immediately after they arrived, they were tormented by loud, unexplained sounds, doors closing by themselves, and objects that inexplicably moved. Beset by this unexplained activity, the sisters found that they could talk to the resident spirit by rapping on the wall and floor; it would answer questions with knocks, indicating that he knew the girls' ages as well as other pertinent information.

One neighbor recorded his experience with the Fox sisters' ghost:

> I then asked if Mr. ———— [Naming a person who had formerly lived in the house] had injured it [the spirit], and if so, manifest it by rapping, and it made three knocks louder than common, and at the same time the bedstead jarred more than it had done before. I then inquired if it was murdered for money, and the knocking was heard. I then requested it to rap when I mentioned the sum of money for which it was

murdered. I then asked if it was one hundred, two, three, or four, and when I came to five hundred the rapping was heard. All in the room said they heard it distinctly. I then asked the question if it was five hundred dollars, and the rapping was heard. . . . I then asked it to rap my age—the number of years of my age. It rapped thirty times. This is my age, and I do not think anyone about here knew my age except myself and my family.

Soon the Fox sisters were touring the region, displaying their abilities to communicate with the dead while others rushed to get in on the act. Within a year there were more than a hundred spiritual mediums in New York City alone, and in Philadelphia there were another fifty-some "private circles." Popular contacts included not just lost loved ones but historical figures: Thomas Jefferson and Benjamin Franklin, as well as Francis Bacon, Enlightenment-era mystic Emanuel Swedenborg, Daniel Webster, and Shakespeare. The dead communicated through table rappings, by moving objects about the room, and by automatic writing, in which mediums scribbled on paper until words began to emerge. There was no shortage of means of reaching the dead, and the growth of Spiritualism was exponential: by some estimates, there were as many as eleven million Spiritualists in the United States by the end of the 1850s.

At least some of Spiritualism's appeal lay in its social aspect: it was a means of bringing together a community over a shared grief or curiosity, in an intimate and emotionally intense setting. In Georgetown Timothy Brown and his wife held annual gatherings for Spiritualists in the house that became known as Brown's Temple, and, as *Banner of Light* concluded, "his wonderful persistence has well-nigh conquered the prejudices of his doubting neighbors, and the structure stands *a striking edifice of the power of will concentrated on one object, and of the guiding inspiration, as he firmly believes, of spiritual beings in the life beyond.*" It is without a doubt a testament to the power of a self-trained carpenter, a genuinely artistic achievement.

And it is also, based on contemporary reports, a testament to one way in which Spiritualists could ingratiate themselves with a community, which may further explain Spiritualism's widespread appeal.

Which is not to say that the new religion wasn't controversial; the word "Spiritualism" first appeared in print in 1853 in a book by skeptic John Ross Dix, in which he referred to Spiritualism as one more "paroxysm of humbug" afflicting America. In spite of its many detractors, the movement only grew in ensuing decades. When Margaret Fox publicly confessed in 1888 that she and her sister had faked the original rapping incident, many Spiritualists denounced her, and she was forced to recant her confession a year later.

Spiritualism's explosion and massive popularity was never the result of a single event; rather, a confluence of obsessions and cultural needs all came together in the 1850s. Preceding the movement was another home-grown philosophy: Transcendentalism, which caught fire in the American imagination in 1836 with the publication of Ralph Waldo Emerson's essay "Nature." In it Emerson emphasized a personal revelation free from organized religion, in which one could seek direct access to the divine through solitary contemplation of nature. His teachings would inspire some of the seminal works of American literature, including Henry David Thoreau's *Walden* and Walt Whitman's *Leaves of Grass*.

The Transcendentalists often viewed Spiritualism with a skepticism bordering on outright hatred. Emerson called it the "rathole revelation" and claimed that the adepts of Spiritualism "have mistaken flatulence for inspiration." His disdain was shared by, among others, Herman Melville, who parodied Spiritualism and its "table-rapping" sessions in a short story, "The Apple-Tree Table," in which a family believes a table to be possessed by spirits, only to discover that it's infested with bugs. "I hate this shallow Americanism," Emerson proclaimed in an 1859 lecture, "which hopes to get rich by credit, to get knowledge by raps on midnight tables, to learn the economy of the mind by phrenology, or skill without study."

Like it or not, Emerson and his fellow Transcendentalists had laid the groundwork for the kind of personal revelation Spiritualism promised. Emerson himself, after all, wrote in his essay "Nominalist and Realist," "It is the secret of the world that all things subsist and do not die, but only retire a little from sight and afterwards return again," as if agreeing with all those mediums reaching out across the grave into the spirit world. The basic tenet of Transcendentalism was that one need only open up an extra-sensory perception to access the divine all around us. If Emerson could find God in the forest, why couldn't a medium find departed loved ones in a darkened room?

Spiritualism took fast hold of the American consciousness at the same moment our attitudes toward death were changing. The early half of the century had seen a war between religion and science over how to handle the dead body and when dissection was permissible. Burial reformers pushed the importance of sanitary corpse disposal, and so families, many of whom were used to keeping vigil with a loved one's body for several days after death, saw these bodies removed from their care at a rapid rate. Suddenly bereft of this final communion due to medical and sanitation laws, families turned to Spiritualism as a means of continuing that conversation, seeking in séances a closure that had been denied them.

For Spiritualists, there was no hell, and there were no evil spirits; rather, the spirit world existed on a continuum with the world of the living: in the afterlife, the dead were at peace in a place known as Summerland. Spiritualism offered hope and comfort, not just because it put the living in touch with the longed-for dead but because it did so without the intermediaries of organized religion. In the world of Spiritualism there was no vengeful God who damned infants who died before baptism, there was no predestination condemning you to Hell no matter your actions. The harsh Calvinism of the Puritans had given way to an afterlife without pain or judgment, and one that anyone could access. Spiritualists, despite nominally maintaining their Christian faith, began to downplay the role of Jesus himself, since without a judgmental God or Hell, there was no longer a theological need for a savior to die for their sins. Death instead was simply part of a natural process, overseen by a benevolent deity.

This new DIY religion brought with it an additional attraction: since the spirit world was accessible to all, Spiritualists saw little need for the men who traditionally controlled organized religion. In short order Spiritualism became dominated by women: for one thing, they were generally acknowledged to be superior mediums, and many saw in Spiritualism an antidote to the patriarchal misogyny of traditional religion. In volume 3 of *History of Woman Suffrage*, edited by Elizabeth Cady Stanton, Susan B. Anthony, and Matilda Joslyn Gage, Spiritualism was singled out as "the only religious sect in the world . . . that has recognized the equality of woman."

Among the many reasons Transcendentalists like Emerson might have viewed Spiritualism with skepticism may lie in how it took a philosophy authored by men and transformed it into a women's movement. Spiritualism tended to valorize traits that were elsewhere labeled as women's psychiatric diseases, including convulsions, incoherent babbling, open displays of sexuality, and other violations of Victorian decorum. Behavior that would have then been diagnosed as nervous sensitivity and hysteria were exactly the kinds of traits that made for good mediums. In an age when male-dominated religious and medical institutions were working overtime to contain, train, diagnose, and treat all women who didn't fit an established mold, the Spiritualists, Stanton, Anthony, and Gage noted, "have always assumed that woman may be a medium of communication from heaven to earth, [and] that the spirits of the universe may breathe through her lips." Spiritualism offered a radical inversion, according empowerment and respect precisely to those who refused or were unable to toe the line.

Early suffrage meetings were heavily populated with mediums and trance speakers; in some places it was difficult to find suffragists who *weren't* also Spiritualists. Spiritualism had given many of these women practice and confidence in speaking to groups with authority; by allowing others (the dead) to speak through them, American women began to speak for themselves in greater numbers. Spiritualism was only one of many factors and social movements that drove women's suffrage, but it was a vital and important one.

As Spiritualism became associated more and more with a rejection of patriarchal religion and traditional marriage, women's rights, and other subversive agendas, the backlash became increasingly vehement. The contemporary attitude toward Spiritualism as a particularly ridiculous belief stems in no small part from the misogyny with which it was attacked in the second half of the nineteenth century. It has been subsequently consigned to the dustbin of that century's excesses and ridiculous fads, alongside phrenology, animal magnetism, and the temperance movement, but Spiritualism-influenced political agitation led to lasting reform: the Nineteenth Amendment to the U.S. Constitution, passed in 1920. Since women gained the vote, however, Spiritualism's importance as a women's movement has more or less been forgotten or downplayed. Its influence waned as the nineteenth century drew to a close, and after a brief resurgence in the wake of World War I, Spiritualism was absorbed by the broader, more diffuse field of parapsychology. As a movement with clear leaders and well-articulated beliefs, it had mostly died out by the end of the 1920s.

~~~◦✺◦~~~

The movement itself may be gone, but Spiritualism's penchant for using the latest technological advances to communicate with the dead has found a resurgence with modern paranormal enthusiasts and ghost hunters. Ghosts have become a business of gadgets. Amazon.com is filled with gadgets for the paranormal investigator: KII meters, which measure electromagnetic field variations; portable motion sensors; "ghost boxes," which sample FM frequencies randomly in search of voices from the beyond; and all manner of digital recorders rebranded as EVP recorders, claiming to offer superior paranormal recordings ("Get Ready to Converse with Spirits!" boasts one such device, which retails for $119.85).

Ghost hunting is a thriving, growing business, thanks to a glut of reality TV shows that have emerged over the past decade: starting with Syfy's *Ghost Hunters* in 2004, in which a crew of investigators travel to reputedly haunted locations to trot out gadgetry in search of definitive proof of the hereafter. Add to this the popularity of ghost tours in historic downtowns throughout the country and museums like Merchant's House, which have increasingly added ghost tours as part of their public outreach. You could say that Spiritualism, now practiced at Halloween and on reality TV shows, is back from the dead.

∿⊘℗∽

During his speech on the mysteries and virtues of Sarah Winchester's house, Harry Houdini mentioned a curious room without corners, built by a man he claimed to know from "the East": "This fellow had been taught by spiritualists. He built himself a perfectly round, tower-like room, so that when the devil came for his soul he wouldn't be able to find a corner in which to catch it." Houdini went on to claim that Winchester's supposed séance room was similarly built: "There is a séance room without corners, so that the spirits won't hurt themselves coming in and out. Mrs. Winchester has a vast wardrobe of variously colored robes, and she uses a different robe for each spirit."

Houdini was wrong: there are no round rooms in the house, and the one currently claimed to be her séance room is certainly rectangular. But he did not originate the idea that Spiritualists built rooms and houses without corners, and lately this fascination has become attached to one house in particular: the George Stickney House of Bull Valley, Illinois.

Far outside Chicago, a distant suburb barely deserving of the name, Bull Valley was untrampled wilderness when George Stickney went there in 1835. He helped found the nearby town of Nunda, Illinois, building its first school and serving as the town's school director as well as its road commissioner. In 1839 he met and married Sylvia Beckley, ten years his junior, and brought her with him to the hardscrabble wilds of Illinois, where they settled down to raise a family.

They began construction on their home not far from Nunda in 1849, on land that would eventually be incorporated as part of Bull Valley, finally finishing it in 1865. The house's rounded corners—which punctuate its otherwise unremarkable Italianate style—are often held as evidence of the Stickneys' Spiritualist beliefs, though there does not appear to have ever been any kind of codified building regulations, rounded corners or otherwise, for spirits. Certainly Brown's Temple did not feature circular rooms or rounded corners.

The notion of round buildings being built to prevent the devil from catching you in a corner has a longer lineage, one that predates both Spiritualism and George Stickney, and it was used sometimes to account for the curious design of barns built by Quakers and Shakers. While it's not clear where this superstition might have originated, the rounded barn has much more prosaic origins. Scotsman J. C. Loudon's *Encyclopaedia of Cottage, Farm, and Villa Architecture and Furniture*, first published in 1833, notes that cows and horses are approximately half a foot narrower at their heads than they are at their hindquarters, which means that the most economical shape for a stall is a wedge. A circular barn with wedge-shaped stalls can house the same number of animals as a rectangular barn in three-quarters the amount of space, with the added benefit of making it easier for the farmer to feed all the animals from the center.

There is a Chinese folk belief that evil spirits—*kuei*—can travel only in straight lines, a belief that supposedly accounts for the curved eaves on Chinese roofs, and which might have at some point filtered into the American consciousness, leading to the supernatural association with round barns and houses. And so a practical, if unusual, design becomes associated with a foreign folk legend about the devil, which then gets repurposed as part of the narrative of the new, burgeoning Spiritualist movement, and this in turn gets attached to an ordinary house in rural Illinois. The legend stuck, the stories began to accumulate, and over the years the house's reputation made it the target of vandals and bored teenagers. And so the building's current owner, the village of Bull Valley, has been trying its best to downplay the myths associated with the Stickney House. In 1995 the village clerk, Phyllis Keinz, who worked in the building, told the *Chicago Tribune* that the closest thing to ghosts in the house are the birds that sometimes get into the attic. Local politician Virginia Peschke, of the Stickney House Restoration Committee, told the paper, "There's never been anything to those stories, which we believe were just made up by local kids. And we feel the stories have contributed to a lot of the terrible vandalism the house has suffered." Peschke said she'd interviewed several previous residents of the house, and none had ever complained of ghosts. "The house is out in the middle of nowhere," she added, "and they were always bothered a lot more by vandals than any ghosts." One former resident, Devona Edinger, who was born in the Stickney House and lived there for a few years, confirmed this: "It's just something creepy that kids like to say about the place."

More than a century later, the house remains, having been passed down through various owners until it was eventually deeded to the village of Bull Valley. Now it sits by itself, a squat two-story building that houses the Bull Valley Police Department and the village clerk. The Stickney House, like Sarah Winchester's mansion, may have little or nothing to do with Spiritualism, but the fact that we impute a Spiritualist motive to anomalous houses like these attests to the strange grip the movement has on our imaginations. The more unusual the house, the more likely it'll cause unease among its neighbors and the more we seem to require some kind of story to explain its construction. That several of our eeriest, most inexplicable houses are misattributed to Spiritualism suggests how little we know about the movement, aside from Hollywood depictions of wild-eyed mediums and table sessions.

The Stickney House's reputation for ghosts nowhere matches the House of the Seven Gables or the Winchester Mystery House, but among locals it has long been considered haunted. Presumably a house built to welcome good spirits at some point brought in a few bad ones, and since the 1970s stories have circulated about its strange energy. In a 2011 post to the Web site trueghosttales.com, a woman named Carri Williams wrote about an experience with the Stickney House. Her brother had been killed on the highway near the mansion in 1984, and she had thought little of it until a few years later when, driving to school one cold January day, she saw a tall, hooded man dressed in a black robe "walking toward a group of pine trees in the snow. There were no houses around. . . . I did not understand why someone would be walking in the bitter cold like that. I did not think nothing of it until I realized the man dressed in the black robe was headed for Bull Valley and he was walking in the direction toward where my brother had died in a car accident and near the Stickney Mansion." Later, Williams claims, she realized that this was not a man but some kind of spirit, and "an evil one" at that.

Whatever one makes of this story, it's hard to connect it to the house's actual history: no terrible murders were committed within its walls, nor is there any record of a single horrible event that might give rise to an evil spirit. Perhaps this malevolent spirit might account for the fact that only three of the ten Stickney children lived past infancy, but then, child mortality rates in the nineteenth century were high everywhere. It's just another of many stories that imply, more or less, that by dabbling in Spiritualism, the Stickneys invited ghosts to this corner of Illinois—ghosts that haven't ever left.

Meanwhile, Brown's Temple has vanishingly few stories of ghosts attached to it. In 2009 it went up for sale, and money manager turned spiritual healer Madis Senner attempted to buy the house, with hopes of restoring it to its former glory. In a YouTube video, he discussed the floating orbs (mysterious balls of light that sometimes appear floating in videos and photos) that many people find on photographs of the house but went on to say that it "is a divine place that has been a sacred site for thousands of years." Rather than view it as a haunted place that inspires fear, Senner suggested instead that one should "put fear aside, and you may well encounter the divine there."

The walls of Brown's Temple retain the imprint of Spiritualism in its very architecture. And if it is truly haunted, then it is haunted not by ghosts or evil spirits so much as by an idea that has vanished; a building left behind, without the animating spirit that inspired its construction.

Spiritualism, like Transcendentalism, is woven inextricably into the fabric of American consciousness: much of what we now accept as our canonical culture was influenced by Spiritualism—in ways we'd perhaps like to forget. Not only were some of America's great literary masters (including Walt Whitman and Mark Twain) believers in ghosts, but inquiries into the afterlife drove the philosophy and teachings of William James, the founder of American psychology. But Spiritualism ultimately was not an institutional religion by and for "great men" like Whitman and James; it was a messy, homespun set of beliefs that were embraced and spread mainly by women, and so American history has downplayed it as aberrant and foolish rather than accept its place in our national psyche. As a political and social movement, Spiritualism has become a ghost itself, a legacy of feminist liberation and belief without dogma that still haunts the land.

Spiritualism might have lost its influence by the end of the 1920s, but it may be more accurate to say it simply went mainstream. The percentage of Americans who identify as spiritual but not religious has been creeping ever slowly up in recent years as people turn away from organized churches and seek their own spiritual paths. Meanwhile, our belief in ghosts remains high; according to one study, 73 percent of Americans believe in life after death, and 20 percent believe in communication with the dead. While these people may not call themselves Spiritualists or spend their Friday nights clasping hands around a table, it's clear that they have adopted a similar belief system: a focus on personal revelation unmediated by dogma or doctrine, and a belief in the perseverance of the soul beyond death, a spirit that is still somehow apprehensible by the living. Belief in a spiritual realm may now be depoliticized, divorced from the radical social agenda that once went hand in hand with Spiritualism, but it remains vitally alive nonetheless. One can dismiss Spiritualism as unscientific, as wishful thinking, as hucksterism, or as any number of other things, but it was—and continues to be—anything but fringe.

CHAPTER FIVE

THE FAMILY THAT WOULD NOT LIVE

St. Louis, MO

I t is, quite literally, a dark and stormy night. A summer storm has settled over St. Louis: gray-black clouds turning the air yellowish and electric, the rain pulsing down in waves. The sprint from the parking lot to the front door of the Lemp Mansion—no more than fifty feet—leaves you soaked. The thunder is following on the heels of the lightning; it is right above us. In the bar the stained-glass portraits of William Lemp, Jr., and his first wife, Lillian Lemp—the Lavender Lady—flicker to life from the lightning outside with disturbing frequency, the accompanying thunder coming fast afterward. It is the perfect night for a ghost hunt: the air already electric, everyone already a bit on edge. In his portrait, William Lemp looks prematurely old; the glass artist has added shading to his face to give the appearance of three dimensions, but the result instead is that he appears haggard, black pits around his eyes, deep creases in his skin.

As if he knows he's going to die.

Unlike the House of the Seven Gables' management, the owners of the Lemp Mansion seem quite content to capitalize on the building's reputation. Ghost hunters come here regularly to take tours, use KII meters and ghost boxes, and record for EVPs and orbs. I'm here for one such tour, led by a local ghost-hunting group. I'm also here to spend the night, since the Lemp Mansion operates as a bed-and-breakfast—though I won't be able to get into my room until 11 p.m. My room, the Elsa Lemp Suite, is itself part of the tour: the most haunted room in this most haunted house.

The Lemp family story should be remembered as your classic rags-to-riches success story: Johann Adam Lemp emigrated to America from Germany in 1838 and within a short time had grown a prosperous business selling beer. At the time the only beers available in America were strong English ales, and Lemp, along with John Wagner in Philadelphia, is credited with introducing the lighter, German-style lager beer that has since become ubiquitous in the United States. Lemp's beer caught on quickly, particularly in the German immigrant community of St. Louis, and by 1850 he was shipping four thousand barrels of beer annually. Prior to electric refrigeration, Lemp had found that the natural caverns beneath St. Louis provided a stable and year-round cool environment, which allowed him to ramp up production without fear of spoilage. His success was mirrored by constant rivals Eberhard Anheuser and Adolphus Busch, whose Budweiser beer would play second fiddle to Lemp's Falstaff brand well into the early twentieth century. Johann died in 1862, but the company soldiered on under the direction of his son, William, who continued to grow the brewing juggernaut, which, by the dawn of the twentieth century, seem destined to endure forever.

The first suicide in the Lemp Mansion happened in 1904. Three years earlier, William's twenty-eight-year-old son, Frederick, who had been groomed to take over the family business, died suddenly from heart failure, leaving William distraught. When William's closest friend, Frederick Pabst (of the blue-ribboned Pabst Brewing Company), died a few years later, on January 1, 1904, it sent William over the edge: he shot himself in the head just over a month later in the mansion the family had occupied since 1876. William's successor, William Jr. (Billy), lacked his father's head for business; he spent lavishly, and the business floundered. His marriage to Lillian fell apart, and the couple's messy divorce in 1906 made headlines. But the real crippling blow to the Lemp brewing empire came in 1919, with the passage of Prohibition. Billy shuttered the company without notice, and within two years both he and his sister Elsa had killed themselves. The family retired from the public eye, out of the beer business for good, almost forgotten, until another of William Sr.'s eight children, Charles, followed in the footsteps of his father, brother, and sister, killing himself with a revolver on May 10, 1949. (Tradition holds that Charles shot his dog before himself, though this is nowhere mentioned in the police reports of the incident.)

Charles Lemp was the only one to leave a note, which read simply, "In case I am found dead, blame it on no one but me." But most have instead chosen to blame a curse of some kind, a curse under which the Lemp family suffered, unable to shake the fate that awaited each in turn. In the Haunted Lemp Mansion board game, players move through the mansion while collecting various strategy cards; if a player collects both a "revolver" card and a "bullet" card and then happens to land on a "suicide" space, he's out of the game—an oddly tasteless reference to the gruesome series of tragedies that repeatedly befell the House of Lemp.

Unlike the Winchester Mystery House, with its sprawling, formless labyrinth of rooms; the George Stickney House, with its rounded corners; or the House of the Seven Gables, with its secret staircase, there is nothing particularly odd—architecturally speaking—about the Lemp Mansion. It is large, to be sure, and stately, but its outer construction is straightforward, and its rooms are laid out in a fairly sensible order. Its additions over the years increased its size, but its overall shape and appearance don't suggest anything out of the ordinary.

And yet the mansion itself—far more than the neighboring brewery, the caves below the city where the fabled Falstaff beer was once stored, or the other homes the Lemps have owned through the years—remains inextricable from the family and its curse. This is how we tend to think of old, august families that have lasted through the generations: there should be one central, ancestral home, a single estate that embodies the bloodline.

It's an idea ingrained in the very word "house," with its dual meaning as both building and family. And like Edgar Allan Poe's House of Usher, the House of Lemp seems to have failed. In Poe's story "The Fall of the House of Usher," house and House are conjoined so tightly that when Roderick Usher's sister, Madeline, seems to rise from the grave to carry off her brother (the last surviving member of the Usher family) to his own death, the house itself collapses, supernaturally torn asunder, and crumbles into the swamp just as the narrator escapes. But unlike the house of Usher—and despite the tragedies and calamities that have befallen its occupants—the Lemp Mansion still stands.

～～o

The rain is deluging the streets outside, and we gather in one of the dining rooms on the first floor, where there are light snacks and infrared camcorders. My friend Elizabeth has joined me for this tour, and we wait along with the other guests—there are maybe twelve of us total—who range from college age to mid-forties, and altogether we are a fair enough cross section of the general population. It's hard to read the faces of the other people on the tour, or discern their interest in ghosts or this house. As we settle in and munch on our celery sticks and slightly stale cookies, the guide gives us a brief rundown on the history of the house. In our hands are ordinary camcorders to which infrared rigs have been attached, and we're instructed how best to hold them so our arms won't get tired, as well as other basic tips, such as don't pan too fast through a room or the image will blur, and don't look through the viewfinder while going up or down stairs or you'll get vertigo.

After the guide finishes with the instructions, we gather our equipment and head toward the stairs. You feel a bit dizzy, but you tell yourself it's probably because you're looking through the infrared camera's viewfinder too much. Your feet feel a bit unsteady, but that's probably because, after more than a hundred years, the staircase and the floors have begun to slope slightly as the foundation of the house has become uneven. All your hairs are standing on end—probably, you tell yourself, from the storm outside. It's time to go upstairs.

∽∽๑ᕉᕐ∽

Ghost hunts without technological devices these days are almost unheard of; one could almost say that ghosts don't exist without the technology that records them. But though the devices have gotten more complex, the spirit world has long been intertwined with technology. Four years before the Fox sisters' rapping, Samuel F. B. Morse demonstrated the first use of the telegraph; despite its very straightforward technical workings, here was a machine that could send and receive disembodied messages over great distances—as though they'd come from another world. The parallels between Spiritualism and telegraphy were immediately drawn, and early publications, such as the *Spiritual Telegraph*, attested to this very simple analogy: just as the telegraph could send and receive over great distances, the Spiritualist could send and receive across the divide of life and death. The raps of the Fox sisters, after all, were themselves a form of Morse code. Media and medium were two sides of the same coin.

It's not that a belief in ghosts began in 1848, of course, but the Spiritualist revolution reformulated *how* we believed in ghosts. No longer were they purely emanations of terror; now a direct communication with the dead could be established through technology. This has largely continued through all subsequent technological advancements: nearly every major communication technology has sooner or later been appropriated by ghost seekers.

There is photography, of course: pioneered just prior to the telegraph, it came into its own in the second half of the nineteenth century and became one of the prime means of documenting ghosts (though from the very beginning the veracity of spirit photos was questioned by skeptics). Radio and television, too, were seen as receptors for spirit messages from the beginning, with ghosts frequently discerned through static and failed connections. The introduction of consumer magnetic tape recordings in the 1940s and '50s spurred yet another revolution in communicating with ghosts; with recording now significantly cheaper and more portable, ana-log tape (with its added bonus of tape hiss and other audio imperfections) put the voices of the dead in the hands of the masses.

In the late 1950s Swedish painter and documentary filmmaker Fried-rich Jürgenson decided to record birds singing in his garden; while playing back the recording, he unexpectedly heard on the tape the voice of his dead mother calling his name. He spent years making further recordings and researching the technique before publishing *Radio Contact with the Dead* in 1967. Jürgenson's work was followed and greatly expanded by Latvian psychologist Konstantin Raudive, who published his extensive documentation of EVPs in his *Unhörbares wird Hörbar* (The Inaudible Made Audible), published in English in 1971 as *Breakthrough: An Amazing Experiment in Electronic Communication with the Dead*. Raudive reported his lengthy experiments with EVP and transcribed some of the more disturb-ing communications he received. "Here is night brothers, here the birds burn," one voice told him one night. Another came through the wire to tell him: "Secret reports . . . it is bad here."

Raudive claimed that his work would lead "to empirically provable real-ity with a factual background," but skeptics point to the degree of leeway he gave his spirit voices in their attempts to communicate. He explained that spirits talked in multiple languages, even in the same sentence; that they could speak in languages they hadn't known in life; and that they sometimes spoke backward. Considering all these allowances, it's not ter-ribly surprising that Raudive could discern so much chatty conversation from the dead. If you're looking for spirit voices, you can find them in just about any string of gibberish or noise if you listen hard enough.*

Perhaps it's less important *whether* one believes than *why* he believes. Jürgenson used EVP as many Spiritualists did: to contact lost loved ones,

---

*As the media theorist Jeffrey Sconce put it in his *Haunted Media* (p. 87), "Such difficulties testify either to the genuinely mysterious complexity of spiritual communications or to the number of allowances Raudive was willing to make to convince himself of the reality of such communications."

to be reassured that they were okay and in a better place. The search for ghosts often takes this form: of a kind of mourning, a working through of grief and loss. We look for the ghosts of those whose deaths we have not yet gotten over, as though we need their blessings to let them pass on.

⁓ ◦ ⁓

There is no sense of grief or loss—at least nothing outwardly visible—in any of the people climbing the Lemp Mansion's stairs with me. If anything, the vibe is of veiled thrill seeking and vague curiosity. Near the top of the stairs is the Elsa Lemp Suite, where I'll be staying the night in a few short hours. Elsa was the youngest of William Sr. and Julia Lemp's eight children, born in 1883, when Julia was forty-one years old. Elsa married the vice president of a metal company, Thomas Wright, in 1910, but by all accounts the marriage was troubled. After losing their only daughter in childbirth, Elsa filed for divorce in 1919, citing mental anguish and abandonment. After their separation, Elsa, the wealthiest woman in St. Louis, changed her will to write Thomas out of it entirely. But just thirteen months later they were reunited and they remarried on March 8, 1920. Twelve days later Elsa killed herself with a single self-inflicted gunshot wound to the heart.

The unassuming suite that bears her name, hers when she was a child, looks out to the north, with St. Louis spilling out before it. But though Elsa succumbed to the same "curse" as did her brothers and father, you will not find her ghost here. She died in her own home, at 13 Hortense Place, some seven miles from the Lemp Mansion. The ghosts that haunt this room date from a period in the mid-twentieth century when the house was used as overflow housing for a local pediatric hospital. The spirits of terminally ill children, they've been known to engage in mischievous behavior: pulling at the sheets while guests are trying to sleep or tugging at their legs as if they were by their feet.

Nearly every room in the house, it turns out, has a story. In Charles Lemp's bedroom, sometimes small items will move about the room without warning. In another bedroom, a smell of raw sewage sometimes emanates from nowhere, indicating that the spirits of the house don't like you. Through the hallways roams the spirit of a young child whose identity has never been completely verified. A shadowy figure lurks in the basement, and an unknown man has been seen sitting down for a meal in the first-floor dining room, only to vanish when approached. With this many stories, I half expect a scene out of Disneyland's Haunted Mansion, with rooms of translucent figures cavorting and mischief making—but so far, even with the spooky weather outside, we've seen nothing.

Then at some point I find myself alone in the Elsa Lemp Suite while the other guests are investigating other rooms. All the lights on the floor have been shut off, and the only way to see anything is through the infrared camera. I run the camera over the room, pausing on a small window air conditioner that's rumbling slightly under the stress of keeping the room cool. As I hold my camera on the window, a strange light moves across it, a wave of light that holds, then passes by and disappears.

It could have been car headlights passing by outside, except that I'm on the third floor and the light would have to have been coming from behind me, where there are no windows or other sources of light. No one is nearby that I can see, and no other explanation offers itself. I keep the camera focused on the air conditioner, seeing whether the phenomenon will repeat itself. For a minute I watch the machine soldier on stoically, but the light doesn't reappear and nothing else happens.

Viewing a dark mansion through an infrared lens is undeniably eerie, no matter who you are. The realm of otherwise mundane objects takes on a pall. People's irises turn ghostly white, so that the folks standing next to you—living, breathing, and very much alive—look like hollowed-out zombies. Things that are still in normal light pulse faintly in infrared; they seem like they could come alive at any moment.

It's not just the infrared; walking around the mansion, I see how the viewfinder of a camera can change the landscape. The way a camera can single out a specific object for our attention makes us presume that something specific is going to happen. The more ordinary the object and the longer the wait, the more our expectations heighten. You tense up.

Horror movie premises so often involve a perfectly innocuous object turned malevolent—a house, a toy, a child.* I discover that holding the camera for a long five seconds on an object is usually enough to make it unnerving, and I begin to question the light that I saw playing out over the air conditioner. Perhaps it was just my expectation of something, but standing alone in a pitch-black room of an old mansion, with nothing for illumination but an infrared camera, thunder rolling through the distance—it becomes unnerving very quickly.

⁓⦿⦿⁓

We're now on the second floor, in one of the large middle bedrooms. Because houses were taxed based on the number of bedrooms, the Lemp Mansion, as was the custom at the time, has overly large bedrooms separated in the middle by pocket doors (once the doors were fully closed, two bedrooms could be had for the price of one). Supposedly ghost hunters have gotten strong electromagnetic pulse (EMP) readings from the center of this room, supposedly this is significant, supposedly the distant sound of a dog can be heard on some recordings. The infrared cameras, we're told, can pick up organic matter that's otherwise invisible on carpets. And sure enough, panning a camera down to the floor reveals stains in blotches and clumps. This is the room where apparently Charles Lemp shot his dog, and it's strange to look down and see beneath your feet what looks like the poor animal's blood, as though it was killed only yesterday.

But it's probably not blood: without the camera, the stains look more like ground-in dirt than spectral blood. Despite the great legends of the Lemp Mansion, it becomes clear that the terrifying experience always happens on some other tour, some other time.

---

*Among my favorites in this genre is 1983's *De Lift*, a Dutch film about a haunted, murderous elevator, with the tagline "Take the stairs, take the stairs. For God's sake, take the stairs!!!"

It's at this point that my friend Elizabeth reveals a secret: if you toggle your infrared lights on and off while standing near someone else, the interference will cause orbs and shadows to appear on the person's video. You can, in other words, create your own ghosts. The light I saw moving across the air conditioner in the Elsa Lemp Suite may very well have been this. Perhaps someone passed by me in the hallway while I wasn't looking, and some unintended interference on their part was enough to create a momentary play of light—one that I was all too ready to accept as paranormal.

No matter how hard we look, it seems, the ghosts won't materialize on demand. Why should they? Moving through these rooms supposedly haunted by the Lemp family, the other people on the tour are eagerly hunting for orbs and shadows, evidence of the ghostly presence of the Lemps and their supernatural curse. But it seems equally plausible to read their story as a history of family mental illness, perhaps a clinical depression or bipolar condition passed down through William Sr.'s genes to his doomed children, children who lacked the cultural or medical support to combat this neurological condition. The tragedies of the Lemp Mansion might have been entirely a matter of brain chemistry, attributable to nothing other than a lack of timely medical intervention.

❦

In 1901 a man in a black suit entered a downtown jewelry store and identified himself as William Lemp, Jr. He asked for the largest sunburst diamond in the store, then told the owner, "I will take it with me now, and you may send the bill to the brewery." He pawned the diamond and was never heard from again. In 1915, according to historian Davidson Mullgardt, a woman named Mrs. Fannie Zell had herself sent flowers from Billy, Charles, and their brother Edwin Lemp to convince others that she had admirers among the rich and powerful.

And then there's the curious case of Andrew Paulsen, who appeared in St. Louis in 2010 claiming to be one of the last living descendants of the Lemp family. He had a key to the Lemp mausoleum, along with a painting by Louise Lemp (one of Billy's nieces and an established artist) and other assorted memorabilia, including housewares he claimed were from the family, which he began selling on eBay. "Our desire and passion is to let the wonderful people of St. Louis and the world know there is a Lemp descendant who is willing to share never before told stories of the famous Lemp family of St. Louis," his business partner, Cheryl Sochotsky, wrote on their Web site, Lemp Treasures. He began giving tours of sites in St. Louis and attracted admirers among those obsessed with the Lemp family.

But in short order Paulsen's story began to unravel. The woman he claimed was his mother—Anne-Marie Konta, granddaughter of Annie Lemp (Elsa's eldest sister)—died in 1973, thirteen years before Paulsen was born. As people began asking questions, he was unable to provide anything like proof that he actually descended from the Lemp family. When *St. Louis Magazine* reporter Jeannette Cooperman asked him for some kind of confirmation, he stonewalled, then threatened legal action. Why someone would concoct an elaborate fiction solely to hawk some meaningless housewares online for a few bucks is a mystery, but just one more example of someone trying to capitalize on the long, sad history of the Lemp family.

It does speak to the aura surrounding the family, which has not diminished along with their fortunes. In some ways, the dramatic ending of Poe's "Fall of the House of Usher" seems overly optimistic and convenient: with Roderick's death and the end of the family line, the house falls into the swamp and the name vanishes as well. In reality, decline is much messier, and even though the House of Lemp has lost its former glory, the house and the name still linger, drawing an odd breed of revenants along with the ghost seekers.

After the tour one of the dining room servers stops us in the hall. "Did you see anything?" she asks, excited. She has been working here for only three weeks and hasn't experienced any haunted moments, though she's hoping to. She has no doubt in her mind that the house is haunted; after all, she's seen ghosts all her life. She was seven or eight, she says, when she first saw one, on her family's land, which had once been a plantation: a young girl, pale, running, terrified, always returning near her birthday. The server didn't ever try to figure out what the story was: "I figured it wasn't my business. She wasn't hurting anyone." Her face now is full of excitement: how lucky we are to have had the chance to commune with the spirits in such a legendary place. How could we have failed to see at least one?

Spend enough time debunking the legends associated with haunted places, trying to see past it all—the marketing, the dubious electronic devices, and all the other trappings—and you sometimes forget how real, and how persistent, the belief in ghosts is for many of us. A belief that in various ways, and for various people, gives an explanation and a meaning to experiences that can't be explained away easily. A belief that can help us mourn and give us hope.

The hunt finally over, I retrieve my bags from the foyer and head back up to the Elsa Lemp Suite, hoping for a good night's sleep in the most haunted room of the most haunted mansion in the country. By now I've been awake for almost nineteen hours, having woken up at four thirty in the morning to make my flight to St. Louis. I am thoroughly exhausted, and though I toy with the idea of staying up to see what happens through the night, the truth is, I pass out in minutes. If ghosts swarmed about me that night, they did not trouble my sleep.

II

AFTER HOURS

bars, restaurants, hotels,
and brothels

Houses are by no means the only haunted places in America. Hotels, bars, bookstores, restaurants—all manner of businesses, really—also attract the supernatural. If a haunted house is unnerving because homes represent safety and security that's upturned by the presence of a ghost, the haunted business is the inverse of this: the place where *we* are the ones who don't belong—places we pass through, spending a great deal of time in without ever thinking of them as "home."

A hotel room, for example, is meant to mimic your own bedroom: bed, television, nightstand—it's all there. But it's not yours: not your bed, not your chair, not your taste in tasteful art. You're only the latest in a long string of folks who have slept on those sheets and used those towels, a fact hotels (at least the nice ones) take great pains to hide from you. Hotels are *unheimlich* in the truest sense of the word: like a home but stubbornly not.

The ghosts of the Stanley Hotel in Estes Park, Colorado, like to remind you that you're not the first to stay there. If the guidebooks are to be believed, guests have reported spectral figures in tuxedos and 1920s-era gowns moving about the hallways and ballrooms, raising champagne toasts and carousing through the night. Built in 1909 by industrialist

Freelan O. Stanley (creator, with his twin brother, of the Stanley Steamer automobile), his namesake hotel was advertised as the first to "heat, light, and cook meals exclusively with electricity" and offered opulence and mountain air to the well heeled. A four-story Colonial Revival nestled among the mountains just outside Rocky Mountain National Park, the hotel has seen its share of ups and downs over the years but has always been a popular destination for those seeking luxury in the Rockies.

The stories of the hotel's haunting are in themselves unremarkable, and the kind of thing you'd hear about in dozens of hotels across the country: mysterious children running down hallways, the piano playing itself in the dead of night. That anyone cares about the Stanley's ghosts at all is thanks to the imagination of one guest in particular and the novel it spawned: *The Shining*.

Stephen King and his wife, Tabitha, came to the Stanley the night before Halloween, right as the hotel was closing for the season. "We found ourselves the only guests in the place—with all those long, empty corridors," King writes. Alone in an old hotel, he was inspired. "Except for our table all the chairs were up on the tables. So the music is echoing down the hall, and, I mean, it was like God had put me there to hear that and see those things."

That sense of emptiness is key to a good haunting. Few things are more unsettling than being somewhere emptied out, after everyone else has left. If you've ever worked a closing shift, or as a security guard, you know the way a place can change after the doors are locked and the lights are dimmed, when the lighting so carefully designed to spotlight the latest gadgets goes slack, when the mood lighting gets moodier. It's as though you don't belong there. The Moravian Book Shop in Bethlehem, Pennsylvania—the oldest bookstore in the country, founded in 1745—has a ghost that manifests only after closing. A longtime employee, Jane Clugston, told *The Guardian* that she saw a dark figure in a back hallway of the bookstore one night as she was closing up. The figure walked into the kitchen, and Clugston followed her, only to discover that the stove and fan had been left on. "I don't know why this person, ghost, spirit drew us back there, but I guess to turn off those appliances," Clugston said. "I'd never thought of it until I told someone else and they said a ghost led you back there. But in that back hallway a lot of people have said that they've felt things and they've seen things." As with King's story of his time at the Stanley, things get eerie when the lights go down.

Once you start looking for them, you notice that haunted businesses can come in all shapes and sizes—even brightly lit, happy places that sell toys. Though I grew up near the Winchester Mystery House, the haunted spot where I spent far, far more time as a child was down the road in the opposite direction. The Toys "R" Us in Sunnyvale, California, has a long history of haunting, all of which revolves around a former ranch hand who died pining for his true love. Johnny Johnson, as he's known, worked on Martin Murphy's massive wheat plantation, on land that's now the city of Sunnyvale. He was killed in some sort of machinery accident in 1884, when the artery in his leg was severed and he bled to death on the spot where the toy store was eventually built, and now he floats amid the board games and stuffed animals, setting off remote-controlled cars and spilling basketballs.

✂◦◦◦

Reports of Johnson's ghost have fluctuated since the toy store was built in the early 1970s; he was popular in the late '70s and again in the early '90s. As the landscape around it has changed through the years, the store has sat alone, unchanged by time or renovation. A stucco brick of a store, with no windows and only a few sets of doors, it might as well be an Egyptian tomb, sealed to the external world, if not for the iconic, brightly colored letters inviting children of all ages into its darkened doors. A former employee delightfully named Putt-Putt O'Brien told the *Chicago Tribune* in 1991 that she saw Johnson's ghost once. She described him as a young man, likely in his twenties or thirties. Wearing a work shirt, knickers, and a gray tweed snap-brim cap, Johnson walked past her once while she was working. She also told the paper that she'd heard horses galloping through the store.

"He's a classic case of a ghost caught in a time warp," says Sylvia Browne, a world-renowned psychic who has made her name investigating places like my local Toys "R" Us. "He's hard at work at his handyman job, tending to the Martin Murphy ranch that thrived on the same land a hundred years ago. He can't figure out for the life of him (excuse the expression) where all these loud, rambunctious children keep coming from who tear up his freshly planted vegetables, having no clue that the children are actually playing up and down the aisles of the toy store that sits there today." According to Browne, Johnson had fallen in love with his boss's daughter, Elizabeth Murphy, and was heartbroken when she married an East Coast lawyer and left for Boston. A short time later, he gravely injured his leg in the accident that killed him, and now his ghost limps through the toy store's aisles, still tending to work he believes is left undone.

Browne's fame is bound up in Johnson's, since Browne hosted a séance in the Sunnyvale Toys "R" Us in the late '70s specifically to commune with him. She had been giving psychic readings for only a few years at the time, and the ghost of Johnny Johnson—and the subsequent attention the event attracted—helped jump-start her career. In an infrared photo taken during the séance, one can see the cluster of people gathered around in a circle, their bodies colored white and gray, as one would expect of warm bodies caught in infrared. Standing at the edge of the group, a figure leans against the wall; his hands might be in his pockets, or it could be that his thumbs are hooked in his belt loops in stereotypical cowboy fashion. Unlike the warm, light bodies of the people in the foreground, the figure in the distance appears to have no body heat whatsoever—he is an almost completely black silhouette.

In an age when anyone can digitally manipulate a photograph in seconds, it's easy to dismiss how captivating such a photo could be, ostensibly offering definitive "proof" of a spirit. It helps that infrared photography is often misunderstood by the public. One might assume, for example, that the figure in back is black because he's not giving off any body heat, but infrared film isn't the same as thermal imaging and doesn't capture heat. Whoever this figure is, he's likely simply too far from any available light source to be reflecting any infrared waves back at the camera. A simpler explanation, to be sure, if also a lot less fun.

The whole event, including the mysterious photograph, was featured on the 1980s TV show *That's Incredible*, establishing the fame of both Browne and Sunnyvale's Toys "R" Us. Coming at the dawn of the syndicated daytime talk show, Browne came to popularity in a tabloid-hungry era when media outlets were more and more willing to showcase fringe beliefs in order to give their audiences something salacious. The story also gained traction because it suggested that *anywhere* could be haunted—not just creepy old Victorian mansions or derelict graveyards. Even a seemingly anodyne toy store might have a deeper story. (As if to prove the point, in the wake of Sunnyvale's fame, numerous other Toys "R" Us stores, from San Bernardino, California, to North Bergen, New Jersey, have also been known to house spirits.)

Browne went on to become a best-selling author who, by the end of her career, was charging hundreds of dollars for psychic readings and appearing regularly on *The Montel Williams Show* to communicate with the beyond. But paranormal reports involving Browne might best be taken with a grain of salt. Though she often claimed to have helped law enforcement with missing persons cases, independent analyses of her work have determined that her advice was always either too vague to be useful, of no help at all, or an actual hindrance to investigations. She developed a notorious record of being wrong, telling families that their missing loved ones were alive when they were already dead and vice versa.

She never forgot Johnny Johnson, though, and made regular trips to the Toys "R" Us to stay in touch. According to her 2003 book *Visits from the Afterlife*, she repeatedly tried to convince Johnson that he was dead and that if he wanted to be reunited with his lost love, all he had to do was "go to the light of God that was waiting for him." But Johnson had no interest in following her advice: "He got so tired of hearing it that one day he snapped at me and said, 'If you don't stop telling me I'm dead, I'm never going to talk to you again.' I decided that keeping the lines of communication open between us was better than nothing, so I've never mentioned it again."

An informal poll I took of workers at the Toys "R" Us in December of 2015 confirmed that nearly everyone who works there is aware of the ghost of Johnny Johnson, but no one I spoke to claimed to have personally seen anything of him. I myself can't recall any paranormal sightings from my childhood visits. But I would have felt differently, I think, had I stayed the night and participated in a séance, particularly a séance filmed for national television. Primed for something to happen, expectant and a little on edge, in a building you only ever see during business hours that's now darkened and newly unfamiliar—it's natural that noises and lights in the dark would take on new meaning.

Commercial spaces are designed to be navigated in a very specific way, to entice a purchase and then to facilitate customers getting out of there. There are myriad techniques, refined through decades of research, to accomplish this: fast food uses bright colors—mainly red and yellow—which work to activate hunger and grab your attention; furniture showrooms like IKEA use their layouts to guide you through a scripted experience; big-box retailers line the checkout aisles with impulse buys. Perhaps, most obviously, one thinks of casinos, where every detail is managed to create a specific kind of psychological effect once you step inside the doors. Some proponents have long argued for casino layouts that are dark and confusing, that encourage a labyrinthine disorientation so as to keep people gambling and discourage them from leaving. Others favor a bright, airy landscape with high-end decor to give players a sense that they are themselves high rollers and embolden them to spend lavishly. Either way, what's clear is the amount of energy devoted to using a building's architecture, layout, decor, music, even scent, to craft a specific, highly engineered experience.

It's when this script breaks down that we start to see ghosts. They over-run places like the RMS *Queen Mary*, built to embody the grand opulence of an age, now a struggling tourist attraction in the harbor of Long Beach, California. It's operated mostly as a hotel these days, going through a suc-cession of owners who've yet to make a profit on the enterprise. When my wife and I stayed on the *Queen Mary* one summer Sunday night, we found its ornate detail still relatively intact, including the lovely Observation Bar and Art Deco Lounge. There, deep wood fixtures are overseen by a back-lit mural of Jazz Age flappers, and plush red leather chairs offer a glimpse of an age of glamour long past. On a ship from the 1930s, designed for opulence and for more than two thousand passengers, we walked the halls encountering almost no one else except a few who did occasionally material-ize, jarringly out of place in shorts and flip-flops. Like the Stanley Hotel, closed up for the season, the *Queen Mary* seems to be waiting for some-thing, though for her the spring will never arrive.

Ghosts move into places such as these: businesses that have fallen on hard times, places where the façade has started to fall away.

CHAPTER SIX

A DEVILISH PLACE

Richmond, VA

There are ghosts everywhere in the historic Shockoe Bottom neighborhood of Richmond, Virginia. The upscale restaurant Julep's is thought to be haunted by the ghost of a gunsmith's apprentice, Daniel Denoon. His boss, James McNaught, shot Denoon over a disagreement while Denoon was climbing the stairs. The staircase his body fell down was later converted into a storage closet, but employees report hearing the thump of a body falling in it from time to time. Tiki Bob's Cantina, a bar on Eighteenth Street, is now closed, but in its heyday it was home to bikini contests, Jell-O wrestling—and the spirit of a knife-wielding fishmonger.

At the ornate Main Street train station, workmen and security guards have heard footsteps through the empty halls late at night. Next door Rosie Connolly's Pub is haunted by several ghosts: one, a woman in period dress who vanishes when confronted; another, a man often seen in the kitchen, whose past is similarly unknown. Over on East Cary Street the building standing between Fourteenth and Fifteenth streets is supposedly built on the site of a brothel that dates back to the early 1800s; on its upper floors spectral women clad in gauzy dresses wander. Staff are known to hear their names called, only to turn and find no one there.

It's hard to find a building in Shockoe Bottom that *doesn't* have a ghost story attached to it. Local historian and paranormal investigator Pamela Kinney speculates that this is because Virginia was home to the earliest settlements in North America. Which makes sense so long as we all agree that by "settlements" we really mean "settlements of Europeans." Which is to say, the kinds of ghosts you look for, and the kinds of ghosts you see, depend on your frame of reference. For when I began to tally the supernatural records of the area at the heart of Richmond, a simple fact emerged: the ghosts of Shockoe Bottom are overwhelmingly white.

This is curious, because if you walk just a little way away from the haunted bars and shops, down by the freeway you'll find the Devil's Half Acre. For decades black men, women, and children were brought here, imprisoned, and tortured while they waited to be sold to planters and speculators. Dozens of slave traders had offices here, where slave auctions were widely advertised and men came from all over the South to make their fortunes on the backs of those enslaved. Tens of thousands of men's and women's lives changed hands here in the years leading up to the Civil War; all the activity centered on Wall Street, in the heart of Shockoe Bottom. Today Wall Street is gone, replaced by the freeway, though the rest of the area remains mostly unchanged. While it's difficult to estimate how many people lost their lives in the slave pens of Shockoe Bottom, hundreds of sets of human remains have been found in the nearby slave burial ground.

We typically think of ghost stories in terms of the remnants of a terrible tragedy, a past we cannot escape, or a justice unavenged. Why, then, in a place that should be so haunted by the legacy of such a terrible injustice, the scene of countless deaths, should there be nothing but white ghosts?

꿍꿍

Given its low elevation and proximity to the James River, the Bottom became an ideal place for trading, easily facilitating the loading and unloading of cargo. Alongside tobacco, cotton, and other goods, slavers traded men, women, and children. After the transatlantic slave trade was banned, in 1808, traffic in enslaved individuals in Richmond actually increased; after New Orleans, this was the most heavily trafficked slave trading area in the United States.

In the decades leading up to the Civil War, much of the South was sick with "Alabama Fever," the idea that any (white) person could get rich by buying frontier land and putting enslaved people to work with cotton—a fever from which Northern traders, even those who on the surface were fervently opposed to slavery, nonetheless benefited greatly.

The human capital that was lost here in Shockoe Bottom is staggering. Only New Orleans had a larger volume of human beings been bought, sold, or hired out for temporary work. What's more, Richmond was first in the nation for slavery-related price manipulation and futures speculation. It was, in other words, not just where men, women, and children were bought and sold but where the entire economic foundation of the industry of slavery was built.

The cruelty on display in Shockoe Bottom was starkly evident to foreign visitors. In 1842 Charles Dickens came to Richmond on a tour of America, and despite being taken with the city itself, "delightfully situated on eight hills," he was horrified by the barbaric acts he witnessed at Shockoe. In his *American Notes* he excoriated the men and women who profited from Richmond's slave trade, namely

> owners, breeders, users, buyers and sellers of slaves, who will, until the bloody chapter has a bloody end, own, breed, use, buy, and sell them at all hazards: who doggedly deny the horrors of the system in the teeth of such a mass of evidence as never was brought to bear on any other subject, and to which the experience of every day contributes its immense amount; who would at this or any other moment, gladly involve America in a war, civil or foreign, provided that it had for its sole end and object the assertion of their right to perpetuate

slavery, and to whip and work and torture slaves, unquestioned by any human authority, and unassailed by any human power.

As Dickens rightly noted, such people, when they speak of "freedom," "mean the Freedom to oppress their kind, and to be savage, merciless, and cruel."

"The exposure of ordinary goods in a store is not more open to the public than are the sales of slaves in Richmond," remarked Frederick Law Olmsted, the great architect behind New York's Central Park. While touring Richmond in the 1850s, he happened upon a commission agent's office, empty save for

> three negro children, who, as I entered, were playing at auctioneering each other. An intensely black little negro, of four or five years of age, was standing on the bench, or block, as it is called, with an equally black girl, about a year younger, by his side, whom he was pretending to sell by bids to another black child, who was rolling about the floor. My appearance did not interrupt the merriment. The little auctioneer continued his mimic play, and appeared to enjoy the joke of selling the girl, who stood demurely by his side.

Among those unfortunate enough to find themselves imprisoned in such a hell was Solomon Northup, a freed Northerner who was kidnapped and sold into slavery. As he later recounted in *Twelve Years a Slave* (later adapted into an Oscar-winning motion picture), Northup was held in Richmond on his way from Washington, D.C., where he'd been kidnapped, to New Orleans, where he'd later be sold. He described how, on reaching Richmond, he and his fellow captives "were taken from the cars, and driven through the street to a slave pen, between the railroad depot and the river, kept by a Mr. Goodin." Northup describes a surreal scene, one where "there were two small houses standing at opposite corners within the yard. These houses are usually found within slave yards, being used as rooms for the examination of human chattels by purchasers before concluding a bargain."

Northup soon found himself chained to a man named Robert, "a large yellow man, quite stout and fleshy, with a countenance expressive of the utmost melancholy. He was a man of intelligence and information." Robert had been born free, like Northup, but had been "seized at Fredericksburgh, placed in confinement, and beaten until he had learned, as I had, the necessity and the policy of silence. He had been in Goodin's pen about three weeks." Northup did not stay long in Richmond before being moved farther south, to New Orleans. By this point Virginia had less need for slave labor for its own sake, and Richmond functioned more as a market for buying and selling people, like Northup, who would end up in the South and the West.

At the center of this activity was slave trader Robert Lumpkin's jail complex. To reach his half acre of land, you had to either descend a sandy, irregular embankment from Broad Street that descended dangerously down one hundred feet to the floor of the Bottom, or enter via Franklin Avenue, an untidy, crooked lane that worked its way down. Lumpkin's house on the property was bordered by a fence that stretched ten—in some places twelve—feet high. Nearby were several squat brick buildings where he kept enslaved men and women waiting to be sold. In the center of the complex, its focal point—a nightmare of torture and misery—was the low, rough brick building that served as Lumpkin's jail.

As abolitionist minister James B. Simmons would later remember, "In this building Lumpkin was accustomed to imprison the disobedient and punish the refractory. The stout iron bars were still to be seen across one or more of the windows during my repeated visits to this place. In the rough floor, and at about the center of it, was the stout iron staple and whipping ring."

Accounts like this, from foreign observers, from the enslaved men and women who spent time here, and from the wardens themselves, helped cement Lumpkin's jail as a truly horrific place. Among the many who were whipped in it was the Reverend Armstead Mason Newman, who was taken to the jail in 1862, when he was just a child. "On the floor of that room were rings," he later recalled; his hands and feet were stretched out and tied to the rings, leaving him spread-eagled and facedown on the floor, while a "great big man" stood over him and flogged him.

Simmons referred to the complex as a "place of sighs." In its time it was known more generally—throughout the country—as the Devil's Half Acre.

࿊࿊

In their collection of ghost stories, *Haunted Richmond: The Shadows of Shockoe*, Scott and Sandi Bergman write of Shockoe Bottom's rich and complicated history, particularly as "the epicenter of some of the most profound and tragic events in United States, Virginia, and Richmond history." But in their subsequent list of these tragic events, slavery is absent: "The area surrounding the Shockoe Valley has been the backdrop for the destruction of indigenous peoples, a revolution, the birth of a nation, foreign and domestic wars, famine, disease, floods, fires and engineering disasters, to name some of the causes of turmoil, tragedy and trauma experienced in the capital city." After recounting the ghost stories of Rosie Connolly's Pub, the bar housed in the building once known as the Railroad YMCA, the Bergmans confess, "We have been able to find very little in the way of historical details of the Railroad YMCA that might help explain the identity of the reported ghosts." And yet the land where the pub stands is steps from the former site of the Charles Hotel—where many traders, including auctioneers Benjamin and Solomon Davis, had their offices—and mere yards from Lumpkin's Jail.

Rather than explore this complicated history and whether the ghosts of Rosie Connolly's Pub might be related to the tragedy of slavery, the Bergmans tell stories mostly of mass-casualty accidents: the collapse of the Statehouse gallery in 1870 that killed sixty-two people and wounded another two hundred; the fire at the Old Richmond Theatre on December 23, 1811, that killed seventy-two; the Church Hill Tunnel Collapse in 1925 that killed four. "If a premature exit from this world is the primary reason for paranormal activity," they note, "then it is no wonder that there are so many shadows to be found in Shockoe." In Shockoe there is a hierarchy of shadows: those known to ghost hunters, whose stories are told to tourists, and those allowed to slip unseen into the fog of forgetting.

Ghost stories and haunted tales connect us to the past, to family and to our ancestors. The ghost stories of the South, particularly those that reach back to the antebellum era, establish a through line in a property or a place, giving our surroundings a depth and a richness that go beyond the present moment. As supernatural beings, spirits often come to represent some universal truth of the past. They turn space into time and can be a way of making a place stand for some transcendental value or universal ideal.

A good case in point is Thomas Jefferson, whose ghost can be found haunting his home, Monticello. There the president is heard whistling in the corridors or seen seated at his writing desk as the ghosts of his beloved mockingbirds flutter in cages around him. Tourists and workers on the property have spotted him in the entrance hall, eyeing distinguished guests, or beside his wife, Martha, at the dining room table, exuding charm and goodwill. Jefferson's ghost is not in pain, nor is he anguished by some injustice never addressed. He is serene, patriarchal, and benevolent. His reassuring presence, real or imagined, connects us to the past, giving guests a sense of what it was like to live at Monticello two hundred years ago.

Of course, Jefferson did not live there alone; Monticello was populated by slaves. Despite his love of liberty and his eloquence in defending it, and despite the myriad apologists over the years who've attempted to mitigate or downplay his slave owning, Jefferson's treatment of his slaves remains an inexcusable aspect of his legacy. He was never particularly shy or embarrassed about being a slave owner, as many others were; on the contrary, he repeatedly laid out lengthy justifications for the practice. In 1821 Jefferson lamented that "we have the wolf by the ears, and we can neither hold him, nor safely let him go"; if not for the traffic and exchange of slaves throughout the South, he worried, the enslaved would rise up and overthrow their white captors. Diffusing slaves' numbers over as wide an area as possible was the only means of keeping whites alive. "Justice is in one scale," he wrote, "and self-preservation in the other." As Tiya Miles notes in her book *Tales from the Haunted South*, the consuming horror that animated most whites was "not a fear of ghosts but a fear of black rebellion." The only way to keep alive the white world of Southern belles and elegant gentlemen was to deny the humanity of black people: their names, their identities, their families.

An advocate for liberty and equality, and yet a slaveholder, Jefferson embodies the contradiction of early America, particularly of the South. And for all its architectural beauty, Monticello bears the ineradicable stain of its origins in slave labor. Indeed, in 2002 archaeological evidence of a graveyard for Monticello's slaves was discovered at the edge of the south parking lot, some two thousand feet from the main house. Monticello does now offer tours specifically addressing the plantation's slaves, but so far no reports have emerged of any of these Americans reaching out from the afterlife.

If ghost stories depend on an ongoing oral tradition, passed from one anonymous source to another, embellished and refined through the telling, then they can only ever reflect the knowledge and the folklore of the people telling them. Does an absence of these ghost stories suggest that there is still, over a century later, a lacuna in the culture's memory, a taboo about its past, a refusal to discuss certain things? What does it mean to whitewash the spirits of a city? Does Virginia have ghosts that it is still not ready to face?

The absence of black ghosts at Monticello is not unusual; you're not likely to find them in most places in the South. The Myrtles Plantation's Chloe is a rarity, and ghosts like her are vastly outnumbered by whiter shades. There's a kind of effacement here, which in the end is not terribly surprising, since the work of slavery, after all, was to destroy the interior lives of those enslaved, marginalize their humanity, render them nothing but empty bodies. Slavers learned early on that the best way to keep the machinery of slavery in motion, and to make as high a profit as possible, was to break the individual into a series of component parts: height, age, price. In New Orleans one trader advised a new plantation owner, "It is better to <u>buy none in families</u>, but to select <u>only choice, first rate, young hands from 16 to 25 years of age</u> (buying no children or aged negroes)."

The Africans who were kidnapped and brought to the New World had, like every culture, significant ties to their ancestors and their burial grounds and derived no small portion of their identity from these kinships. Families broken apart and moved roughshod throughout the country obliterated connections to the past and to the dead. This was not unintentional; the forced migration of enslaved people, facilitated by the massive slave markets in places like Shockoe Bottom and New Orleans, stripped people of their humanity so as to maximize their profit potential.

Funeral rites, sacred burial sites, and even ghost stories—people of all stripes use these as a means of taking the sting out of death. They're how we remind ourselves that after we're gone we won't be forgotten—a relative who tends to our gravestone and brings flowers to our grave keeps us alive year after year even after we're gone. It was precisely these kinds of rituals and rites that the slaver meant to rob his victims of, stripping them not only of their life but also of their memory in death.

The goal in all these varieties of violence was to create what historian Edward E. Baptist calls "the new zombie body of slavery": the body of the slave that could work but not feel, that would not be slowed down or deterred by such human qualities as memory, longing, despair, or fear. Slavery was designed to create bodies without souls, to exorcise out of men, women, and children their spirits, so that they would function as animate and obedient bodies.

And yet slave owners were never fully invested in completely robbing these men and women of their humanity; there were always aspects of a slave's humanity that were retained for specific political and economic purposes. The most obvious example of this was the Three-Fifths Compromise built into the U.S. Constitution, which determined a state's population by counting each slave as three-fifths of a person so as to increase the South's number of elected officials in the federal government. That slave owners could not have fully dehumanized these men and women, because they were first and foremost people, is important, but it's worth recognizing that slavery's objective was to make them both present and absent simultaneously—to enslave someone was not necessarily to efface that person entirely but to render him or her a ghost.

Here, then, is a central paradox in the way that ghosts work: to turn the living into ghosts is to empty them out, rob them of something vital; to keep the dead alive as ghosts is to fill them up with memory and history, to keep alive a thing that would otherwise be lost.

∽ ⸰ ⸰∾

Once you start looking for ghosts that aren't white, they're easy to find. As Baby Suggs tells Sethe in Toni Morrison's *Beloved*, "Not a house in the country that ain't packed to its rafters with some dead Negro's grief." In the 1930s workers under the Works Progress Administration began collecting stories of former slaves: everything from recollections of their day-to-day lives under slavery to questions about clothing, medicine, and firsthand accounts of slave auctions and mistreatment. The stories were compiled in seventeen states, from Indiana to Florida, and accelerated with urgency once it became clear that these firsthand accounts were quickly disappearing—more than two-thirds of the respondents were in their eighties when they were interviewed between 1936 and 1938. By the twentieth century America's understanding of the history of slavery had become tinged with nostalgia via folklore involving contented slaves and benevolent owners, emphasizing agrarian life—typified by Joel Chandler Harris's Uncle Remus folktales. The slave narratives collected by the

WPA, on the other hand, sought a more neutral approach. Allowed to speak in their own voices, those interviewed as part of this project offered a largely untold version of the antebellum landscape.

Interviewers were given a list of questions to ask, and one of them—number 13—asked specifically about ghosts. Could the respondent remember the songs and stories of their childhood? Had she heard any stories about "Raw Head and Bloody Bones" or any "other 'hants' of ghosts"? Had he personally seen ghosts? Answers to the question vary: some interview subjects didn't believe, some knew rumors of ghosts were just whites intimidating them, some spoke of ghosts as terrifying things, as comforting things, as exhausting things.

Jane Arrington of North Carolina told one WPA worker the story of John May, a slave who had been beaten to death by two white men named Bill Stone and Oliver May. After his death, she reported, "John May come back an' wurried both of 'em." He kept them awake, hollering and groaning all through the night, hounding them relentlessly. According to Arrington, it got so bad that other slaves became afraid of the white men, because the "ghost of John wurried 'em so bad."

Another respondent, George Bollinger, spoke of a haunted Benton Hill in Missouri, telling the interviewer, "One night we was driving through dere and we heard something dat sound like a woman just a screaming. Old man Ousbery was with me and he wanted to stop and see what it was but I says, 'No you don't. Drive on. You don't know what dat might be.'"

In these stories ghosts terrify, but embedded in the terror are cautionary tales. A woman named Florida Clayton recalled how, as a child, she and her peers would often see a covered wagon that would appear in Tallahassee, where she lived, always in some secluded spot. While the kids would be tempted to approach this mysterious wagon and investigate it, they were told by adults that inside was "Dry Head and Bloody Bones," a ghost "who didn't like children." Only as an adult did Clayton learn that the wagon was in fact owned by a slave hunter, who would steal children and take them to Georgia to be sold, and that her parents and other adults had invented the Dry Head and Bloody Bones ghost as a means of protecting them.

A man named Thomas Lewis of Indiana once described a "place where there is a high fence" that was haunted: "If someone gets near, he can hear the cries of the spirits of black people who were beaten to death. It is kept secret so that people won't find it out. Such places are always fenced to keep them secret." He then recounted a story: Two men were out hunting nearby, and their dog began chasing something, running through the fence after it. As one of the men started to follow, his friend asked, "What are you going to do?" The other replied, "I want to see what the dog chased back in there." His friend told him, "You'd better stay out of there. That place is haunted by spirits of black people who were beaten to death." Isabelle Daniel of Missouri recalled one haunted tobacco factory that no slave would go near after nightfall: "When the nights were still and the moon was full," she reported, "you could hear the ting, ting, ting, of the lever all night long and voices of the slaves crying out and complaining, and you knew there wasn't anybody there at all, jest hants."

Throughout, the WPA narratives reference "hags" and "witches" who would visit people at night, inhabit their bodies, and "ride" them all night, returning them in the morning. Silvia Witherspoon of Alabama put it succinctly: "How come I knows dey rides me? Honey, I bees so tired in de mawnin' I kin scarcely git outten my bed, an' its all on account of dem witches ridin' me." Ghosts steal one's capacity to work.

Again and again, these ghost stories revolve around a tenuous and threatened connection to the past. Ghosts will emerge at times through the breakdown of family. One woman in Tennessee saw the ghost of a woman appear before her while she was giving birth. Not recognizing the apparition, she called out, "Who are you?" The ghost replied, "Don't forget the old folks," then vanished. That was when the young woman realized that it was the ghost of her own mother. A man identified only as Uncle Louis spoke of ghosts in terms closer to melancholy than fear. Ghosts, he claimed, are "sociable," and they want to stay near living people. "When folks gets scared it hurts de haunt's feelin's an dey goes somewhere else." If slave owners and traders sought, in a very real way, to obliterate memory and history for those they enslaved, then melancholic ghosts like the ones Uncle Louis saw may themselves be in search of their own pasts.

Folklore always bleeds and blurs, and it would be overly reductive to state a hard and fast distinction between ghost stories told by whites and those told by the black community. There are, of course, stories of black ghosts that serve the same function as white ghosts—marking a location, explaining the unexplainable, commemorating an event. But what is clear is that history is not just written by the victors; it's written by the literate. The prohibition against enslaved Americans learning to read or write had the immediate purpose of denying them agency and keeping them under control, but in the long run it also meant that the stories, lives, and opinions of millions of Americans were lost to time.

Ghost stories, theoretically, should be an antidote to this. Based on oral tradition and handed down through the years, outside the purview of acceptable history, such folklore should—and often does—act as an alternative history, a record of the oppressed and forcibly illiterate, the marginalized.

But Shockoe Bottom's ghosts show that this isn't always the case, that precisely because ghost sightings are so ephemeral, and so vague, they can easily be attached to the dominant narrative and only that narrative.

"The legacy of Wall Street is a difficult history to commemorate, as it involves memories that are painful, controversial and unsettling," Jack Trammell wrote of the Richmond slave trade. "People are interested in battles, campaigns, and military heroics; they are not as interested in what those campaigns were fought over." And while I had assumed that ghost stories are one way to tell those stories that people don't want to hear otherwise, as it happens, they are just as often used to reinforce those blind spots.

❧

Once one of the main economic engines of the South, Shockoe Bottom now feels hollowed out, devoid of life and real commerce. Far from the universities, it doesn't attract much in the way of a nightlife feel, though not for lack of trying. There are half a dozen bars, Thai food and by-the-slice pizza, a couple of vape shops, and a few nightclubs. Which is not to say that there haven't been attempts to revitalize the area. For years the mayor of Richmond had pushed a plan to build a new stadium for the city's minor league baseball team, the Squirrels, downtown on land adjacent to the Devil's Half Acre. Meant to draw new life into a faltering part of town, the plan succeeded mainly in drawing ire from preservationists and those worried that such a massive construction project would obliterate valuable archaeological traces of the city's past.

After the project was announced, an archaeological team largely funded by Richmond's Slave Trail Commission set out to uncover the Devil's Half Acre; through a careful study of old maps, they located the area where Lumpkin's complex had stood, some of it now partially obscured beneath the freeway. But in December 2008 excavation work through the damp and muddy ground by the James River Institute for Archaeology, under the direction of Matthew Laird, unearthed the remnants of the jail. While the team didn't find the expected implements of torture, such as whipping rings or iron chains, what it did find were unexpected hints of lives lived here—bits of tableware, including English china and earthenware and the remnants of a porcelain doll.

How does a city balance commerce with remembrance? The ghost stories that are told about Shockoe Bottom are not only harmless; they add a festive patina to the city's bars and restaurants, an air of mystery and glamour. They invite you to spend an evening with an ephemeral time just out of reach, to add a small bit of wonder to an otherwise average night out. What they don't do is speak to a past whose legacy can still traumatize. They don't ask the patrons of Richmond's nightlife to consider a complicated history; in particular they don't ask the city's white citizens and tourists to face difficult facts. For those who would rather not revisit those days, the city's ghost lore makes it easy, turning our attention to murdered gunsmiths and fabled prostitutes. But that's not to say that these other ghosts are not omnipresent. "I started weeping and couldn't stop," recalled Delores McQuinn, chairwoman of Richmond's Slave Trail Commission, when those bits of china and porcelain doll were discovered. "There was a presence here. I felt a bond. It's a heaviness that I've felt over and over again."

Nor was she the only one to feel the ghosts of those who passed through Shockoe. When Lupita Nyong'o won an Academy Award for Best Supporting Actress for her role as Patsey in *Twelve Years a Slave*, she opened her acceptance speech by invoking ghosts. "It doesn't escape me for one moment that so much joy in my life is thanks to so much pain in someone else's," she told the Los Angeles audience. "And so I want to salute the spirit of Patsey for her guidance." Then, as she thanked the film's director, Steve McQueen, she told him, "I'm certain that the dead are standing about you and watching and they are grateful and so am I."

The dead are watching, whether or not we choose to listen to their stories.

CHAPTER SEVEN

BABY

Reno, NV

Among the great tall tales of the Wild American West is that of Bella Rawhide and Timber Kate, two prostitutes who worked the brothels of Reno, Nevada, in the late nineteenth century, when money and lives ran fast and dried up quickly. Bella was blond-haired and blue-eyed, buxom and sweet, known for a routine she performed called "Eve's Leaves": she would appear onstage wearing nothing but gilt fig leaves; a patron could remove a leaf for a pinch of gold dust, and the man who removed the last leaf could take her off to bed. Timber was tall, muscular, brusque, known as much for her wild haymakers that could knock a man flat as for her talents in bed. The two were always together and claimed to be sisters, though this was a cover for their romantic relationship. In advance of their shows, Timber would plaster the town with posters advertising their act, and in the boom-and-bust towns of the West, both women got rich.

Then a deadbeat grifter named Tug Daniels came to town. Daniels had heard of Bella and Timber's success and set out to use them for all he could get. He seduced Bella first, but soon both women had fallen madly in love with him, and in jealousy they turned on each other. Rather than deal with Timber, Daniels ran away with Bella to nearby Carson City, where he pimped her out in a brothel on North Quincy Street called the Beehive. While Bella continued to rake it in, Timber fell into a depression and hard times. She tried dressing as a man and performing as a weight lifter, but this routine flopped.

After a few years Daniels stole everything Bella had saved and skipped town. Bella was heartbroken and despondent—until, that is, Timber showed up in Carson City and the two reconciled. They continued working the Beehive, and though they were back together again, Timber became increasingly worried that Bella might leave her once more. Then Tug Daniels reappeared.

Seeing the man who'd humiliated her and absconded with her love, Timber set out for revenge. The two squared off in the Beehive's parlor. Timber let loose with one of her trademark haymakers, only to have Daniels sidestep it neatly, produce a knife, and gut her savagely. As Timber Kate lay dying, Daniels fled out a back window. Not long after, Bella Rawhide killed herself by drinking a dose of cleaning fluid.

None of this story is rooted in any real fact, and even the carefully placed details that seem so specific lead only to dead ends; for one, there is no North Quincy Street in Carson City. And yet for much of the early twentieth century, people in northern Nevada claimed to see mysterious posters still advertising Timber Kate and Bella Rawhide. Those who tried to remove the posters would be met by a ghostly haymaker from the spirit of Timber Kate. Others claimed to see Timber's dying, ragged form straggling down moonlit streets, clawing at her stomach where Daniels had fatally cut her open. Bella, for her part, still haunts the building of her once-famous brothel, the Beehive—even if no one knows where it actually stood.

❧

Kate and Bella are far from the only brothel workers who've entered the annals of hauntings in this country. The Red Onion Saloon of Skagway, Alaska, is haunted by a woman from its heyday in the late 1800s, a Lydia, about whom nothing is known but who announces her presence through the scent of strong perfume. The Dumas Brothel of Butte, Montana, claims similar spirits; reports include mirrors falling from the wall, beds that shake by themselves, and visitors touched by ghostly fingers. The Hotel Lincoln in Manns Choice, Pennsylvania, now stands as an antiques store, but ghosts of ill repute still wander its halls, disturbing tchotchkes and trinkets. And of course there is New Orleans, home to so many reputedly haunted brothels that one company gives a tour specifically devoted to them.

Why do brothels and their employees loom so large in collections of ghost stories? Perhaps it has something to do with the fact that a brothel is a secret place: mostly illegal and under the radar, its goings-on are, for the most part, hidden, and often even its location is a mystery, passed through word of mouths that have long since quieted. Any old grand house, any long-standing bar in a former boomtown, seems a likely candidate as a onetime brothel; they seem to hide in plain sight, no different from any standard hotel, bar, or mansion. The haunted building in Richmond on East Cary Street is assumed to be a brothel, but ghost hunters attribute this to rumor rather than any kind of established record. Brothels—despite being real, functioning businesses—belong to a special subterranean oral tradition, one that's highly ephemeral.

The picture of the Wild West whorehouse is one associated not just with illicit sex but also with violence: saloon brawls, depravity and revenge, disfiguring attacks (such as the one that drives the plot of Clint Eastwood's *Unforgiven*), rape and murder. Outside the reach of polite society, the brothel would seem to be a magnet for the kind of intense, violent human experience that often becomes the fodder for ghost stories and hauntings.

The Lincoln House in Manns Choice is reported to be haunted by a woman who worked there, whose enraged husband shot her one night when he discovered that she wasn't bringing in enough money. Then there is what came to be known as the Murder Bordello of Galena,

Kansas, which in the 1890s was operated by a woman known both as Nancy Wilson and as Ma Staffleback, who was convicted, along with her husband and two sons, of murdering a miner named Frank Galbraith and were ultimately implicated in the murders of upward of thirty other men.

Brothels are *liminal* (from the Latin *limins*, "threshold") places, borderland places where the traditional rules of a society are momentarily suspended. Both for good and for ill, the world of the brothel seems a world in extremis. And so perhaps no other business venture is so primed for ghost stories. The brothel, with its mix of tragedy and hiddenness, rowdy violence and erotic allure, seems the perfect place for spirits to take up residence.

In late November 2014 I was sent by a magazine to Reno to interview Lance Gilman, the owner of the most famous legal brothel in the country, the Mustang Ranch. I was there to profile him because of his role in securing a half-billion-dollar deal with the car company Tesla, which had just agreed to build a massive factory to make electric car batteries on Gilman's industrial park outside Reno. For two days I spent time with Gilman and his employees, including several working girls and the Mustang's madam, Tara Atkins. The photographer on assignment with me brought an SUV's worth of equipment, and while he was setting up an elaborate shot featuring a number of the women, I stood idly chatting with Atkins, killing time. It was then that she mentioned that the Mustang Ranch was haunted.

Not just haunted but extremely haunted.

Brothels in rural Nevada have always been tolerated, and while not explicitly illegal, they sometimes ran the risk of being shut down as "public nuisances." Joe Conforte, often described as the godfather of legalized prostitution in Nevada, bought the Mustang Ranch in 1967 from a competitor, and in 1971, after extensive lobbying and legal battles, he finally wrangled from Storey County the first legal brothel ordinance. From the beginning the allure of brothels for most counties was the licensing fees, but there were always the citizens who saw prostitution as a blight on the county. Alexa Albert, who lived at the Mustang Ranch for a month as a researcher and observer in 1993 (and who later wrote a book about her experiences), described the original brothel as "a seedy biker bar, minus only a pool table and a pinball machine."

Just as with those Wild West saloons, trouble was at home in the Mustang Ranch. In 1976 professional heavyweight boxer Oscar Bonavena was killed in the parking lot. He had been brought in by Conforte to help publicize the ranch, but in short order he began an affair with Conforte's wife, Sally. After being banished from the Mustang, he returned on May 22 and demanded to speak to Conforte. While arguing with the guards in the parking lot, Bonavena was shot in the heart; Conforte's bodyguard, Willard Ross Brymer, later pled guilty to voluntary manslaughter and spent fifteen months in prison.

Conforte managed to avoid any implication in Bonavena's death, but he eventually ran afoul of the federal government, which charged him in 1980 with tax evasion. He fled to Brazil to escape extradition, and the Feds subsequently seized the ranch.

By that point Lance Gilman had purchased a monstrous business park on the edge of Reno, the Tahoe Reno Industrial Center. Storey County desperately needed the tax revenue that brothels brought in, and announced a plan to issue new brothel licenses. Realizing that another seedy, lawless brothel could damage the area's reputation and his plan for attracting modern technology firms, Gilman went ahead and bought a license himself and opened the Wild Horse Ranch in 2002. A few years later the federal government auctioned off the Mustang Ranch—its name and copyright, its assets, and the building itself—on eBay. Again seeking to forestall unsavory competition, Gilman bought the Mustang with a winning bid of $145,100, eventually consolidating the two brothels under one name.

⁓⊙⊙⁓

Moving the Mustang Ranch required more than just cutting it up and putting it on trucks; structured as a massive octagon, its frame was too wide and unwieldy to be moved into the narrow canyon where the Wild Horse was built, so Gilman's team ultimately had to bring in much of the building via helicopter. It was reconstructed across the parking lot from the Wild Horse, and today the two buildings have an uneasy relationship.

The layout of the Wild Horse is straightforward. One walks in first to a bar (technically, it's an entirely separate business that has nothing to do with the brothel, since one can't sell liquor on the premises of a brothel in Nevada). Walking through a back door reveals a plush room made up to look like a high-end hunting lodge, with a perpetually roaring fire, overstuffed leather couches, (barely) tasteful nude paintings, and a wall of taxidermy. Under the watchful eye of a moose, a bison, and a bevy of elk are a high-tech security operation, a clinic, and a well-stocked kitchen. The only element not in keeping with this hunting lodge aesthetic is the mirrored wall, used for "lineups," in which all the women working at the moment are summoned to line up so the customer can select a favorite.

The lighting throughout is subdued but clear; there are no dingy corners, no dark passageways. There are smells of recirculated air and baby oil, which no doubt mask a number of other odors, and while it may be a stretch to call the place "cozy," it's certainly pleasant enough. It's laid out symmetrically: from the lodgelike parlor, two wings, which hold the individual bedrooms, extend out to either side; in the back is the pool, flanked by two smaller wings with "party rooms."

The original Mustang Ranch building, set at a slightly lower grade, has none of this openness. One enters into a dark, neon-lit bar, with jarring neoclassical columns wound with fake ivy. From there, hallways branch off in different directions, leading down corridors that fade into darkness.

From the outside you can guess at a vaguely octagonal shape, but what's not evident (the entire building is ringed with hedges) is that from this central octagon radiate five hallways of uneven length. "It's an octopus of a building," Gilman told me, and an aerial view confirms this, with its tentacles spreading out in all directions into the Nevada scrub.

If anything, the Mustang is slightly smaller than the Wild Horse, but it feels like it goes on forever. As with the Winchester Mystery House, the building distorts one's sense of space, inviting mystery and ambiguity. It's not intentional that the overall shape is masked, but the resulting effect is the same: entering the building, one more or less succumbs to it.

~~⁓⊙⊙~~

Atkins has been the Mustang Ranch's madam for a few years; its ghosts have been around much longer. In 2013 investigators from the reality show *Ghost Adventures* came to the Mustang to check out these spirits, bringing with them a bevy of equipment and machismo. During the show, Atkins took them to the original Mustang building and told them that many women refused to go down "B" hall in particular, where they reported being held down by an unseen force, after which they occasionally discovered bruises they could not explain. Women who spent time in Room B1, she said, were prone to wild mood swings. Nor was this restricted to the working girls; housekeepers reported having their hair pulled by invisible hands. At one point the ranch called in a shaman of some kind to purge the building of evil spirits.

The ghost of Oscar Bonavena, naturally, roams the premises, too, though he was shot in the parking lot at the Mustang's original location. One housekeeper told the *Ghost Adventures* crew of a man she'd seen standing outside the building in a white shirt; when she was shown a picture of Bonavena, she affirmed that it was him.

I tend not to put too much stock in reality shows like this. Any paranormal activity on *Ghost Adventures*, or any of the many similar shows, inevitably is presented via highly selective and suggestive editing; re-creations tend toward melodrama and often are presented to the viewer as fact. As most viewers know by now, reality television is anything but real, and this is no less true of supposed paranormal encounters.

But that afternoon, standing with Atkins while we waited for the photo shoot to finish, I heard the story of one girl we'll call Jean, to whom a spirit seemed to have attached itself. Not malevolent but certainly omnipresent, the ghost knocked over trinkets on a dresser and moved objects around. When the ranch brought out a psychic as part of the *Ghost Adventures* shoot, Jean asked about her personal spirit and was told that it had a name: Baby.

"Baby apparently likes water," Atkins relayed to me, and so at some point Jean placed a small fountain in her room, which appears to have quieted the ghost. We talked about other hauntings, and I suggested that usually hauntings were tied to the land as much as the building, and that one would assume that once the Mustang was transplanted from its earlier location, the reports of ghosts might have subsided. But Atkins says that the paranormal activity has, if anything, increased since the ranch was moved to its new site. Whatever is causing the paranormal activity here, it's in the bones of the house.

I listened politely until, almost as if on cue, Jean walked by. Atkins grabbed her by what little clothing she was wearing and said, "Hey, go get your videos—the ones with the ghost." Caught a little off guard, Jean nonetheless complied, returned a few minutes later with her phone, and proceeded to show me two videos.

The first video she shot for her husband; when she's at the Mustang, she's separated from him for weeks, and so she sends him videos from time to time. In this one she dances seductively, apparently unaware of the small ball of light—maybe an inch in diameter—that seems to be floating behind her head. The orb dances throughout the frame, out of sync with her, sometimes flitting across her face, while she carries on. At one point it disappears, then, a few seconds later, it rushes back into the frame, seems to careen straight for her head, and, at the moment it makes "contact," she topples over rather comically.

The second video is shot from her bed, as though she's just woken up. A slightly shaky hand holds the camera toward the window, where Venetian blinds half block the morning sun. Then the camera pans upward, and emblazoned on the ceiling appears to be the number 13. On the video it's clear as day: a white-blue light projected on the ceiling of the room. When she first showed the video to her coworkers, they all tried to figure out what the "13" could possibly mean and what its significance was, until Atkins noticed how close together the 1 and 3 were and suggested that instead of a "13," perhaps it was a "B."

"B" as in "Baby."

⌇⌇◯◯◯⌇⌇

The Mustang doesn't hide from its heritage, but neither does it revel in the lawless days of Joe Conforte. There is a suite named after him (including framed newspaper clippings of the murder trial), but the overall vibe is one of a high-end (if sometimes gaudy) hotel with unusually high security.

When Gilman got into the brothel business, together with his partner, Susan Austin, their goal was to remake legal prostitution as a luxury commodity. No more trailers, no underhanded financial deals—everything strictly by the book. Here the women are classed as independent contractors and paid by check, and there are extensive and constant health checks, redundant security features, and personal security.

They may be selling liminality, but it feels very much like business as usual. No sense of tragedy clings to the women who work here; the Mustang has an extensive waiting list of women looking for work, and Gilman and Atkins say they turn away nine out of ten applicants. It's a good, high-paying job, and the women are treated well; a fair number of the Mustang's independent contractors started at other legal brothels in Nevada but quickly applied at the Mustang because its reputation is so much better.

This doesn't mean the work itself is, by any stretch of the imagination, easy. After I'd spent two days talking to the women at the Mustang Ranch, it became abundantly clear to me how psychologically demanding the work was. In addition to the sex itself, the role of the sex worker has a complicated emotional and intellectual component. To the extent that these women are selling sex as a luxury product, their job involves not just creating a fantasy but being able to read their client: his needs, fears, desires, things he's ashamed of, things he's unable to say, the parts of himself he hasn't worked through. At one point, musing on the emotional labor involved in working at a brothel, I suggested that perhaps 90 percent of the job was psychological.

"No," Gilman corrected me, "more like 100 percent." The women I interviewed agreed completely. "This is the epitome of caregiving," Gilman said.

At one point in our conversation about hauntings, Atkins mentioned to me that the women who are most likely to see ghosts at the Mustang are the most psychologically taxed and worn out, her most nervous and high-strung girls. I thought of the complaints surrounding Room B1, and in particular reports of wild mood swings from women who'd spent too much time there. But when I pointed out that there might be an obvious corollary here, that the sightings may be more a manifestation of burnout and emotional exhaustion, Atkins immediately rejected the idea. After all, she told me, she sees them, too.

❧

In the architecture of the traditional brothel, form will mirror function. In a place designed to be liminal, outside the law, where power relationships are upturned, the building itself will be secretive, strange, distorted. A nameless mansion, a secluded château, an unmarked basement entrance, a distant shack at the edge of civilization—such places play to our sense of mystery, of the wonders of the invisible world, which include not only sex but ghosts, too. The ghosts at the Mustang Ranch may have less to do with the things we traditionally associate with brothels—lawlessness, violence, secrecy—and more to do with the fact that, as a place of business, it's simply a highly stressful place to work.

I still can't shake those two videos. Assuming, of course, that they weren't digital manipulations (and why would they be?), my best guess is that the "B" shining on the ceiling was somehow reflected off the Venetian blinds—a piece of shiny metal hardware that somehow caught the light in a strange way. The orb knocking her over I assume to be just some kind of visual noise in the recording, which happened to coincidentally line up with her losing her balance. But I'll be the first to admit that there are days I don't feel particularly confident about these rationalizations. Of all the places I have visited in search of spirits, the place where a psychological explanation seemed most likely also happened to be the place where I found the strongest evidence of the paranormal.

CHAPTER EIGHT

PASSING THROUGH

Los Angeles, CA

Why does Elizabeth Short—the Black Dahlia—haunt the Biltmore Hotel in downtown Los Angeles? True, it was the last place she was seen alive, but why doesn't she haunt the sad stretch of sidewalk in South Los Angeles where her body was found? Why doesn't she haunt wherever she was actually murdered?

The Biltmore is old Hollywood, classic Hollywood. Opened in 1923, at the time the largest hotel west of Chicago, it displaced the nearby, equally opulent Alexandria as the epicenter of LA glamour. It was here, in the grand Crystal Ballroom, that the Academy of Motion Picture Arts and Sciences was founded, in 1927, and where eight early Academy Awards ceremonies were held, in the hotel's underground banquet room, the Biltmore Bowl.

I understand why people feel the Biltmore is haunted. I've stayed there, heard the heating pipes creak and tick in unpleasant, unfamiliar ways, as though the whole building were alive, breathing. I've stared down the desolate hallways, half assuming that some vague butchery was taking place behind one of those doors, something to be hushed up and forgotten, something whose trace would come to inhabit the walls like a stain—even as its grand ballrooms still speak to the glory and allure of

Hollywood. In October of 2010 a woman named Laura Finley fell six flights down the stairwell to her death; a few hours after her half-naked body was found, her husband auditioned in the lobby in front of Piers Morgan, Sharon Osbourne, and Howie Mandel for the next season of *America's Got Talent*.

As though these things happen all the time. One former employee later claimed, "There are many stories about ghostly presence on the 10th and 11th floor. I know when I used to work there lots of employees, even security, didn't like working the graveyard shift there due to a lot of ghostly presence. My sister used to work the 10th floor VIP lounge . . . , and there have been ghosts touching and moving stuff around there. People might say ghosts don't exist. Try staying there. I know—I have experienced it myself."

Los Angeles has its haunted houses, its haunted bars and haunted restaurants, but its best-known ghost stories involve hotels. Not just the Biltmore: nearby, the Alexandria Hotel, now apartments, supposedly hosts Rudolph Valentino, still dancing under its oval skylight. Valentino also haunts the retirement home that was once the Hotel Knickerbocker, along with the ghosts of Elvis Presley (haunting the perennially cold Room 1016) and William Frawley (who played Fred Mertz on *I Love Lucy* and dropped dead in the Knickerbocker's foyer). Frances Farmer was dragged from the Knickerbocker to be institutionalized against her will, and the Hollywood costume designer Irene Lentz jumped from its roof in 1962, distraught over the death of Gary Cooper. Marilyn Monroe, too, haunts the Knickerbocker, but she also haunts cabana room 246 of the Roosevelt Hotel on Hollywood Boulevard, where she shares duties with the malicious spirit of Montgomery Clift, who plays his trombone all hours of the night. Carole Lombard, Clark Gable, and Harry Lee all have been seen at the Roosevelt. The Culver Hotel hosts the ghostly traces of the dwarf actors who played the Munchkins in *The Wizard of Oz*, filmed across the street at Sony Studios; none of them died here, but it's their voices you hear conspiratorially whisper as you move through its halls. And finally there's the Hollywood Tower, a hotel so famous for its ghosts that Disney built a ride (the Twilight Zone Tower of Terror) based on its haunting.

But, then, all hotels are haunted. You're kidding yourself if you don't see this, if you don't recognize that you sleep with ghosts. Every hotel staff has its stories; any cleaning person or bellhop knows the score. In Wilkie Collins's 1878 gothic novel *The Haunted Hotel*, an Italian villa is converted to a hotel shortly after hosting an unexplained, horrific tragedy. On opening night a guest ("not a superstitious man") takes Suite 14 and leaves hurriedly the following morning. The next night a couple takes the suite; throughout the night the woman has horrifying dreams; awake, "afraid to trust herself again in bed," she, too, makes excuses and leaves.

Assume, then, that every nightmare you've ever had in a hotel was a cry for help, some violence from the past reaching out to you.

∽◦◦∾

You can go searching for Marilyn and Valentino, but, truth be told, these are among the least interesting ghost stories that Hollywood has to offer. The postmortem celebrity sightings have their tragic elements, to be sure, but after a while they feel banal. You can't hope to understand Hollywood, its glory and debauchery, if all you care about is the marquee names. You have to seek out the forgotten stories.

"How many times do you need to hear what's-his-name playing the trombone in the Roosevelt Hotel?" Lisa Strouss asked me. It was August 2012, and we were sitting at an outdoor café in the Hollywood Hills, talking about ghosts. "Why are ghosts only famous people? It's so stupid."

Strouss is a co-founder of the Ghost Hunters of Urban Los Angeles (GHOULA for short), which she and Richard Carradine started in the summer of 2008. She has believed in the paranormal in one form or another since she was a teenager. Carradine, on the other hand, is a skeptic, though by his own account he's had multiple experiences with full manifestations (when a ghost appears not just as an orb or a voice but as a visible, full-bodied translucent specter)—the gold standard of paranormal sightings. For several years GHOULA has been holding monthly meetups, called "Spirits with Spirits," each at a different haunted location in Southern California, always on the thirteenth of the month.

"There are people who came to GHOULA in the early days," Strouss told me, "who I had known for years, never heard a peep from them about ghost stories, and then they come to a meeting and just barf up this story. It's always preempted by 'I totally don't believe in ghosts, I'm totally logical, I'm a scientist, whatever . . . but there was this one time.' That's always the kicker." From there, a story spills forth, one that's been bottled up for who knows how long. "They almost get weepy," Strouss said, and then as soon as it's over, they go back to their shell of logic. "But they feel relieved to get it out there. It gives them reassurance somehow, hope," she added, looking away. "It's a comfort to hear this story, even if it scares you."

It was at a GHOULA meeting in 2009, at the Eden Bar and Grill in Pasadena (a building that had formerly operated as a morgue), that Craig Owens met Bobby Garcia. Owens was working as a still photographer in the film industry when he started carrying around ghost-hunting equipment. He'd been spooked once while working at the Warner Bros. lot, and what started out as a side hobby has gradually taken up more and more of his life. Garcia had been seriously exploring the paranormal for about five years; he'd started out on Yahoo! chat groups, trying to find people in the San Gabriel Valley who might be interested in going on investigations with him. The two hit it off, making for an almost perfectly paired odd couple. Garcia is a large guy, soft-spoken, a stark contrast to Owens's wiry frame and loquaciousness. "We're two different people," Garcia told me, "but our fascination with history and LA history is what we talk about a lot. . . . My connection with Owens is that we both love the history of LA and read into it."

Unlike Owens, Garcia sees the paranormal in terms of science. "It has a lot to do with physics," he explained, "and natural phenomena—as natural as lightning. They have guys that feel that it could be a wormhole, and you have an opening, and it just shuts, and during that moment you have voices or something coming through. And the wormholes open and close all during the day, like right now, they could be doing it right now. It could be something related to the geomagnetic magnetism coming out of our earth or something, I don't know. But it seems like it's more of a science thing than an actual religious or an actual mystical thing."

After that first GHOULA meeting, the two decided to team up, seeking out places in Los Angeles where they could hunt for ghosts. Among the places Garcia suggested as possible venues was the Aztec Hotel.

⁓⊘⧖⁓

Far from downtown Los Angeles, in the tiny hamlet of Monrovia, stands the Aztec Hotel. A Mayan revival designed in the 1920s by Frank Lloyd Wright's contemporary Robert Stacy-Judd, the hotel was one of the many roadside attractions that made Route 66 famous. But with the rise of the interstate freeway system, Route 66 became a footnote to history, along with the Aztec. Forgotten in suburban Monrovia, the hotel struggled financially for much of its history, going through a succession of owners.

Owens earned the trust and friendship of the then owner, Kathie Reece McNeil, who allowed him and Garcia to hunt for ghosts in the hotel after hours. "Craig was the one who pretty much set up everything," Garcia recalled. "He talked to the lady and he was able to get it, which a lot of people couldn't, so I give him credit for that. . . . The management didn't seem too friendly with people walking around there, and when you're asking questions, they didn't seem too forthcoming." (Said Owens: "She took a shine to me.")

They'd spend all night in the basement and unoccupied rooms, sometimes three or four nights a week, sometimes with others, sometimes not. Garcia and Owens found the most psychic activity in the basement. Garcia repeatedly heard the same woman's voice, barely a whisper, and later was able to hear it more audibly on his recorder. Another time, just as he was packing up to go, without any recorder, he heard her say his name, loudly, as if to say, "Where are you going?" "I think she became familiar with me," he said. Owens heard a voice on one of his EVP recordings stating, "My name's Quiggle"—a reference to James Quiggle, Monrovia's chief constable, who used to participate in the raids on the basement when it was a speakeasy. "My guess," Owens told me, "is that some really bad, dark stuff happened in that hotel and he's somehow associated with that. . . . I think he's a corrupt cop." Eventually Quiggle was replaced by a guy named Frank Scott, and one night Owens got the other investigators he was with to ask for Scott—only he screwed up the name and told them to ask for "Frank Little" instead. "When I listened to the audio," he told me, "I get this weird voice going, 'Frank *Scott*' . . . so it's like we were corrected. The mistake actually makes the evidence more compelling."

But it's not the basement that the Aztec is most known for; it's Room 120—haunted, most agree, by a ghost named Razzle Dazzle, a name divined by psychics who've visited the room over the years. According to one version of her story, Razzle Dazzle was a prostitute murdered in Room 120 by her john. Another version casts her as an aspiring actress, newly married, who fell on her wedding night, hit her head on the heater, and died instantly.

Her story, told and retold in so many conflicting versions, is never about celebrity; it's about a no one, such a nobody that no one even knows her actual name. Herein lies the darker side to classic Hollywood: its promise lured so many starlets and other hopefuls to LA throughout the past century, but some instead found fame only in death. Virginia Rappe, dead in 1921 from a ruptured bladder after a wild party involving Roscoe "Fatty" Arbuckle, or perhaps dead from a violent rape, or perhaps from complications of a botched abortion. Peg Entwhistle, a failed star whose 1932 leap from the "H" of the HOLLYWOODLAND (later, HOLLYWOOD) sign began a vogue of thematic suicides. Lou Tellegen, stabbing himself repeatedly in the chest with sewing scissors, his former glory as a matinee idol long faded. One could spend all day listing these tragedies, as Kenneth

Anger did with savage detachment in *Hollywood Babylon*, pillorying those who wagered and lost as so much used-up trash.

Strouss spoke of Los Angeles's turbulence, its reputation as "a violent, exploitive place. . . . LA is really effed up, so we technically should have more ghosts." The world Hollywood manufactures is uncanny; it's a world of strange similarities, repeated without end. Freud describes one aspect of the uncanny as involving unusual repetition, or "involuntary repetition"; a random number may not be particularly striking or noteworthy on its own, but if you see it over and over again in a single day, "or if we begin to notice that everything which has a number—addresses, hotel rooms, compartments in railway trains—invariably has the same one," then it does start to feel uncanny. Add to this aspiring actress Elizabeth Short, brutally dismembered and left as a grotesque calling card, famous now not because of what she accomplished in life but because of the barbarity of her unsolved murder. The haunted hotel manages to record both sides of the great narrative of classic Hollywood, its light side and its dark, kept close within tattered walls in buildings that seem to live on beyond death.

⁓⦿⦿⁓

Stare down a long hotel corridor and you'll feel something like this: there's something uncanny about the very nature of a hotel, its endless, involuntary repetition of home-seeming spaces, rooms that could almost be home but are always somehow slightly off. Cultural critic Wayne Koestenbaum writes, "The uncanny is home defamiliarized—its rule book torn at the seam. The hotel mutates the unhomelike into industry and canned hospitality." And behind each one of those uncanny doors, perhaps, another uncanny aspiring star, each like the next and yet somehow slightly different.

⁓⦿⦿⁓

A short walk from the Biltmore is the Cecil Hotel. Built in 1924 and originally advertised for traveling businessmen, the Cecil fell on hard times immediately. Already by 1935 Raymond Chandler could refer to it as "an old hotel that had once been exclusive and was now steering a shaky course between a receivership and a bad name at Headquarters. It had too much oily dark wood paneling, too many chipped gilt mirrors. Too much smoke hung below its low beamed lobby ceiling and too many grifters bummed around in its worn leather rockers." It's been recently refurbished and renamed Stay on Main, as though a name change might help it escape its past, though its original name is still painted in stories-high letters on the building's side.

After World War II the core of Los Angeles emptied out as people fled to the suburbs that sprawled endlessly in every direction, leaving downtown an increasingly empty space. Smaller hotels were torn down, but the larger hulks, too big to be torn down but not too big to fail, were left behind. The Cecil, with its seven hundred rooms, became a transient hotel, edged against Skid Row. Its reputation took a further nosedive as a result of two particularly notorious guests. Richard Ramirez, a serial killer known as the Night Stalker, lived at the Cecil, as did Jack Unterweger, an Austrian serial killer. Unterweger had been convicted of murdering a prostitute in 1974 and served fifteen years in prison, during which time he established himself as a successful writer. Upon his release in 1990, he came to Los Angeles on a writing assignment, stayed at the Cecil, and killed at least three more prostitutes. While neither man, so far as has been established, committed any murders within the walls of the Cecil, Ramirez and Unterweger nonetheless remain inextricably linked to the hotel as its most famous residents.

Until, that is, the strange death of Elisa Lam captivated the Internet in 2013. A Canadian student vacationing in Los Angeles, Lam had been staying in the Cecil when she disappeared. Her body was found almost three weeks later in the hotel's rooftop water tank, after residents complained about the smell and color of the water coming out of the tap. An elevator security video showed her shortly before her death. She enters the elevator and presses a button, but nothing happens; after a few seconds she goes back into the hall and appears to be engaged in a heated conversation with someone who can't be seen. She returns to the elevator, pressing her body against the wall as if hiding from someone. Even though nothing is obstructing the door, and Lam herself is not pressing any button that could be holding the elevator, the doors never close, not during the entire three-minute video, until the moment she leaves the elevator.

Amateur sleuths became obsessed with the video and Lam's story, convinced that the unknown figure she was talking to was her murderer or that the elevator's odd malfunction was evidence of a malevolent spirit in the hotel. Police later determined that Lam had most likely been experiencing a psychotic episode and at some point had climbed onto the roof and either deliberately or accidentally ended up in the water tank, where she drowned.

What should have been a private tragedy for a family who'd lost their daughter became a circus: an Internet spook story, an urban legend, and the inspiration for the fifth season of the TV series *American Horror Story*. Elisa Lam's story proved irresistible in the modern age: the surveillance video, the inexplicable malfunction of the elevator, her bizarre actions, the hotel's history—it was all too much. This is how ghost stories are born, after all: not from a complete story so much as from bits and pieces that don't quite add up, a kaleidoscope of menace and unease that coalesce in unpredictable ways. And what better breeding ground for such stories than a place like the Cecil?

The Cecil Hotel (or, if you must, Stay on Main) leaves one feeling trapped between spaces, neither here nor there. For years it has operated as an uneasy mix of a residence hotel and a backpacker hostel, and despite being a permanent fixture downtown, it seemed perpetually out of time and out of place.

Almost three years after Lam's death, I spent two nights at the Cecil. Its lobby has rentable computer terminals and pumps techno music at all hours, and every morning the staff rolls out one of the dreariest complimentary hotel breakfasts I've ever had. The furnishings in the room are

IKEA pieces installed on top of a hotel over ninety years old. There's been no visible attempt to scour the rooms of the decades of slow accumulation of grime—though, in full disclosure, it was by no means the worst hotel I've ever stayed at.

But this is what it feels like being in a hotel: attuned to a past that you can't understand and yet can't ignore. Hollywood doesn't do messy, it doesn't do unresolved, and it doesn't do ambiguous. Ghost stories are unresolved, ambiguous. There's a vision, a noise, maybe a voice that speaks a name, offering the tiniest bit of a story. Usually not much else. You have to go digging through the archives; unearth a story of a long-forgotten murder, a jilted lover whose name has been lost to history, local lore that no one bothers with anymore. Even then it's hardly a guarantee you'll be able to put the pieces together.

Many times a ghost story is simply an attempt to account for some scattered tidbits, some disconnected facts, that don't add up. We tell spooky tales and scary stories because the alternative—the open-ended chaos of the unknown—is even more terrifying. That's why ghosts cling to Hollywood, why they whisper underfoot.

It's not the mansion of Norma Desmond from Billy Wilder's *Sunset Boulevard* that best exemplifies old Hollywood's history. It's the Hotel Earle from Joel and Ethan Coen's *Barton Fink*, a building that the directors described as a "ghost ship floating adrift, where you notice signs of the presence of other passengers, without ever laying eyes on any."

One of the strange beauties of *Barton Fink* is how the film eschews standard cinematic practice and avoids establishing shots: we're brought immediately into interior scenes without a sense of what the buildings look like. And so we see the Hotel Earle's lobby, its elevator, its corridors, and its rooms, but never its exterior. We have no sense of its size, its layout, how it appears to the unsuspecting passing by. It could go on forever. If not for the diffused light coming through the windows, the hotel could be miles underground.

When Barton Fink checks in at the Earle, the desk clerk asks him,

"Are you a trans or a res?" meaning transient or resident. Fink doesn't get it, he's confused, as though he's not yet ready to commit to the implications of the question. He stammers out a vague response: "I, uh, I don't know. I mean, I'll be here indefinitely." The clerk finally answers for him.

⌒⌒∅⌒⌒

By the time I started attending GHOULA meetings, they had already exhausted the usual suspects: the Biltmore, the Roosevelt, the Culver, and, of course, the Aztec. Because they try not to repeat a location, after the first few years the meeting spots became more and more unexpected, including Burbank's Pickwick Bowl, the haunted bowling alley, and the haunted *Queen Mary* in Long Beach. Which is how I ended up at a seemingly unlikely candidate for a haunted hotel: the top-floor revolving restaurant at the futuristic Westin Bonaventure in downtown LA.

Designed by architect John Portman in 1976, and still standing as the largest hotel in the city, the Bonaventure's easily recognizable shape of five clustered glass cylinders has made it a landmark of Los Angeles. Inside, a massive atrium dominated by a central concrete pillar is populated with floating plazas, rings, and balconies. A lobby bar circles the central pillar, which in turn is bordered by a gentle moat and escalators and circular staircases lead off in all directions. It has no exterior windows, so you can quickly lose track of what time of day it is. Iconic enough that it's been featured in dozens of films and is visible from two major freeways, it stands out easily against the tepid skyscrapers surrounding it, even those that tower over it.

By the time the Bonaventure was built, much of downtown was a dead zone. Unlike many downtowns, Los Angeles's has had, for much of its history, a curious excess of space. Boosters who tried to sell the city as a tourist destination in the 1920s and '30s built up a massive downtown filled with monstrous hotels like the Biltmore and the Cecil, and much of that real estate was gradually vacated after the war. Unlike in San Francisco or Manhattan, here few geographical barriers stood in the way of suburban sprawl. Many of the old buildings were too big to demolish, so for decades they stood emptied out in an emptied-out city. With little commercial interest to dictate how one experienced the city, downtown Los Angeles became, in its own way, a dream space—free to be colonized by alcoholics and junkies, of course, but also by artists and writers who found cheap living space and no one looking over their shoulders.

The Bonaventure, whose street-level façade is grim and bunkerlike, seemed to want to insulate itself from the dream world around it. Despite (or perhaps because of) its status, the hotel has over the years become almost universally reviled. It was most famously excoriated by literary theorist Frederic Jameson in 1991: "It does not wish to be a part of the city," he wrote, "but rather its equivalent and replacement or substitute." Jameson singled out not just the façade but also the glass cylinders, which achieve "a peculiar and placeless dissociation of the Bonaventure from its neighborhood: it is not even an exterior, inasmuch as when you seek to look at the hotel's outer walls you cannot see the hotel itself but only the distorted images of everything that surrounds it."

Without a doubt, it is a disorienting space. Though it seems symmetrical, not every elevator bank goes to the top floor, and not every stairwell in the atrium leads to every other floor. Though it's wide and airy, sightlines are oddly obscured by the concrete pylons, so it's difficult to see sometimes which stairway will take you to the floor you need to get to. Describing the central core as a "bagel," architect-critic Charles Willard Moore commented, "You are likely to move around and around that bagel with increasing frenzy, since you can't help feeling that you're lost. The place is as frustrating as a Piranesi prison drawing." As open as the atrium is, it feels perpetually claustrophobic.

The Bonaventure's tendency to disorient its visitors, to confound space, and, yes, to turn the simple into the uncanny has no doubt helped attract its fair share of ghosts. There are those of Eli and Esther Ruven, murdered in the Bonaventure in 1979 during a drug deal gone south, their bodies dismembered and carried out in trash bags. In the basement lives another ghost, a young red-haired girl who wanders the tunnels beneath the hotel's parking garage. Those tunnels were once part of LA's original trolley line, the Red Car, already in disuse when they were caved in to form the foundation of the Bonaventure. Even as the hotel looks toward a *Blade Runner*-esque future, in the decades since it first opened, the space has become as haunted as every other hotel in Los Angeles.

Which is to say, even in a place as sprawling as Los Angeles, whose buildings aren't nearly as old as New England's, you can't build anywhere without building on top of some other ruin, on top of some old ghosts. Hawthorne's character Holgrave might be happier here than in Salem, since Southern California has less compunction about demolishing the old to make way for the new, but even here the ghosts remain. The problem with ghosts is that they can never figure out if they're transients or residents—they don't quite stick around, and yet they never really leave.

❦

In Los Angeles, a city of endless dreams and endless dreamers, the old, glamorous buildings—historic yet faded, baroque yet underused—are vulnerable to a different kind of infestation: not ghosts but ghost hunters. At some point a shift happened in the paranormal community in which money and fame began to eclipse earnest, solitary searchers. Around the time GHOULA formed in 2008, more and more shows started appearing on basic cable, shows called *My Ghost Story, Fear, Ghost Hunters, Ghost Hunters International, Ghost Hunters Academy, Most Haunted USA, A Haunting, Paranormal State, The Othersiders, Celebrity Paranormal Project,* and on and on and on. Nearly all these shows follow a basic routine: a "crew," usually in matching T-shirts and usually consisting of three or four guys and one woman, in a default pose of a tough, crossed-arms stance staring straight at the camera, investigating a reputedly haunted locale. They bring with them a variety of devices for locating ghosts:

infrared cameras, audio recorders for EVP sessions, thermometers for locating "cold spots," and the ever-popular KII meter, a handheld device for measuring electromagnetic fields of electrical devices.

Los Angeles's status as the mecca of movies and television has guaranteed an explosion of near-identical outfits imitating the crews on TV: LA Ghost Patrol, LA Paranormal Association, Ghost Interactive Investigations, Paranormal EXP, Darklands Paranormal, California Society for Paranormal Research and Assistance, and so forth. These groups range from the serious to the absurd—at the more absurd end of the spectrum is perhaps the Paranormal Hot Squad, an all-female group of several models and exotic dancers whose motto is "We'll scare you stiff."

All these ghost-hunting groups sell T-shirts and other merchandise on their Web sites, and each of them, more or less explicitly, is gunning for its own show, trying to build up enough street cred and cult following for producers to notice them. People come to LA to get famous for all sorts of reasons; the ghost hunters are only the latest round of starlets who want to make their names in show business.

"I come from the old school," Craig Owens clarified, "where you don't try to capitalize on this. . . . That used to be completely unethical ten, fifteen years ago. . . . I associate hauntings with pain and suffering of somebody; why capitalize on that to make a buck? Something horrible might have happened."

For GHOULA it was never about getting famous. "They want to capture the ghost," Strouss told me. "We want to capture the ghost story." And yet, she admits, GHOULA, with its clever acronym and its ability to bring together so many lone investigators, might have inadvertently birthed many of these groups. "We triggered that," she said after a pause.

This may seem harmless, but the proliferation of guys in T-shirts and event planners hoping to make a buck off of LA's haunted past has had unforeseen effects on the city's fragile historical buildings, and it was the pursuit of the dual succubi, money and fame, that contributed to the downfall of the Aztec. "Some paranormal groups want to hijack a location," Owens scoffed. "They want to be the house band, and charge money, and commercialize it." The *Queen Mary* is one such location. The Aztec was another: groups began charging money for fans to essentially hang out in the bar, and without giving a cut to the hotel, they quickly alienated the owner, who turned to Craig Owens. "She just appointed me to weed through people to see who was legitimate and who was not," he said, still sounding bitter about the whole affair. "Well, I wasn't getting paid, I wasn't earning a dime." He all but gave up, as did the Aztec, which called off all investigations, and what meager income these groups were contributing to the failing hotel dried up.

As Garcia put it, you try to be respectful, do your research, but most of all you try to distinguish yourself from these types of people. "We were on the *Queen Mary*," he recalled. "We were in one of the ballrooms, and it's quiet, and then all of a sudden you see this group of people running through, and then you see security chasing them." Wanting to be entertained is one thing; the larger problem is guilt by association. "It's the people who're wanting to be scared, waiting for Halloween to come—that's the ones who're kinda ruining it. They're looked at as your peers, and when they're there, they're seen as the same as you."

❧

One of the last GHOULA meetings I attended was in the summer of 2012, in downtown Venice, at the Townhouse Bar, which has been around since 1915 and that operated a speakeasy in its basement during Prohibition. According to stories, the former owner still occupies his booth downstairs in the former speakeasy, a basement that currently features local bands on weekends. We were there on a weeknight, so the basement wasn't open, but one of the bartenders told us she was going off shift soon and if we waited, she'd take us down there for a few minutes. So those of us assembled milled around, waiting for something to happen.

Overall, the evening was, as I had been prepped to expect, mostly devoid of the magic that Strouss and Owens described of the early days.

Neither of them was at the Venice meet-up, and while Garcia showed up late, he didn't say much. The paranormal groups, however, were there, and while they weren't wearing T-shirts, for most of the night, people stayed in their little cliques without interacting. I spoke to one ghost-hunting crew, whose name I've forgotten now: it could have been the LA Paranormal Association or the LA Ghost Hunters, the Ghost Busters of LA—they become a bit interchangeable after a while. The leader could've been any generic guy just out of USC or UCLA: short but muscular, close-cropped hair, answering my questions in as few words as possible. The obligatory girl—his girlfriend, naturally—was the bubbly, outgoing member of the group; the third guy didn't say anything at all.

It will be a shame if groups like this become the face of LA's paranormal community. Asked during a local TV affiliate's Halloween coverage one year why they do what they do, the lead investigator of the LA Ghost Patrol said, "We want proof. We want to be the team that proves that this stuff is real. We want to be the ones that capture it and prove to the world that this stuff does exist." It's the kind of fairly pat, unexamined answer that one finds again and again; it's one of the many reasons why the whole enterprise threatens to teeter into nonsense. Contrast that with the work of someone like Craig Owens, obsessed as he is with the history of a place and how that history may imprint itself on one's psyche. Not just the recorded history but also a forgotten history, and a history that will never, ever be known.

Take, for example, the mystery of Room 120 in the Aztec, the supposed home of Razzle Dazzle. Searching the Monrovia city archives, Owens found no mention of any prostitute or actress killed at the Aztec. "The room does appear to be haunted, but her name was never Razzle Dazzle, if in fact someone died there."

He did find something else, though. When the hotel opened, the local Elks Lodge operated a monthly gambling and drinking night in the basement, something unsanctioned by the cops during Prohibition, except perhaps by the few, like James Quiggle and Frank Scott, who might have been bribed or might have taken a cut of the action. Owens believes that some dark aspects of Monrovia's history might have surfaced in that basement, perhaps a murder or a violent incident during one of those parties that had to be hushed up.

Those monthly parties, Owens learned, had an informal name. They called them Razzle Dazzle Nights.

"No one would know that," he told me, "unless they went through those darn Monrovia papers."

This is perhaps as close to proof as one could possibly hope for: a random name that some psychic had pulled out of thin air during some séance turned out to have a very specific connection to the hotel's history. Maybe this does tell us something about the Aztec, but what? It will never lead to a clear, complete narrative of events, as anyone who might have been able to tell us about what happened during those Razzle Dazzle nights is dead now.

Ghost stories like this will never have a perfect Hollywood resolution. Another LA ghost hunter, Michele Yu, once referred to this as "paranormal archaeology," which is as good an analogy as any: you get fragments that suggest histories, that hint at a purpose, but have nothing definitive to offer, which ultimately stare dumbly back at you.

Unlike those in search of some holy grail of definitive, objective evidence of supernatural life, Lisa Strouss seems interested in the paranormal more as a means of self-reflection. Though an avid believer, she told me that she herself had never seen a ghost. "I would like to have my own ghost story," she said, almost mournfully. "I really want to believe, but I keep discrediting my own stories. I'm my own worst skeptic." Besides, as she'll tell you, even if you have proof, what—really—does that get you? It's not just a question of finding proof of the paranormal, because "even when you get the evidence," she offered, "you're still at the same place you were before the evidence. You can prove all you want. It's like the god question: you come back to the same point."

This existential problem of proof is the thing that all ghost hunters have to wrestle with, something each person seems to face in a different way. "Say we take [proof] to a scientific board," Garcia surmised, "which is really what it's going to come down to. They're not going to say, 'Yeah, that's a voice from the dead.'" He's given this enough thought to know it'll never come down to a single sighting, a single EVP, a single video. "You gotta have so much, an overabundance of each event, and then you have a whole bunch of those events, and *then* you might have something." He stops for a second, perhaps taking in the quixotic nature of the quest he's set before himself, the enormity and the impossibility of a quest that's taken up the last seven years of his life, most of it in solitary pursuit. "It's going to take a lot more than what we're doing now, and a collective thought of everyone on the same page . . . and that's not going to happen."

If there are thirteen ways of looking at a blackbird, there are as many ways of looking at a ghost. For Bobby Garcia, it's a means of understanding science. For people like Richard Carradine and Craig Owens, ghost hunting is a way of unearthing history, of figuring out the past. For Lisa Strouss, who's left the LA ghost-hunting community, it's a means of understanding something about herself. But none of these kinds of discussions took place the night of the GHOULA event in Venice, and I couldn't help but feel that I was years late to a party long over—like showing up at Haight Ashbury after the '60s or CBGB's after the '70s. There was a brief moment in time, it seems, when a remarkable—remarkably weird and remarkably thoughtful—collection of passionate oddballs came together and found one another. Almost as soon as it had begun, the scene was co-opted, standardized, and commodified, and the thoughtful ones all scattered to the winds.

I was about to leave the Townhouse when, as promised, the bartender got off shift and offered to take us downstairs to the former speakeasy. We all trudged down to the event space, which, unsurprisingly, looked like an LA venue on an off night: stage at one end, bar along one wall, a smattering of velvet curtains and leather booths—including the one supposedly still inhabited by the former owner. As I watched these milquetoast ghost hunters mill about the room, furtively taking EVP recordings on their phones, asking one another if they saw anything, felt anything, I could've been in any bar in Los Angeles—heck, it *was* any bar in Los Angeles.

And then an old man rose up out of the crowd—a guy in his eighties at least, shock of white hair, baggy in his skin, someone who wasn't a ghost hunter but who'd heard about the GHOULA event, heard about Richard Carradine's fascination with LA history, and had come out for a drink, some son of a former mayor or councilman from decades ago, from some other time. He stood on the lowest step of the basement stairs, floating just above the rest of us, and he started to speak about old Venice, about the trolley line that used to run from Venice to Santa Monica, about the time when Orson Welles filmed *Touch of Evil* across the street, strange memories and stories of local corruption and gossip. He didn't really have any point, and he meandered, getting confused, trailing off, repeating himself, but none of this mattered. There—among the ghost hunters scurrying around, amid enthusiasm both naïve and cynical—there, for the briefest of moments, this ghost-made-flesh appeared above us, speaking of the forgotten and the fragmentary stories that make up a city, stories told barely above a whisper in basements such as this.

III

CIVIC-MINDED
SPIRITS

prisons and asylums, graveyards and
cemeteries, a park

Frank Wattron wasn't sure what to do. He'd been elected to the position of Navajo County sheriff three years earlier, in 1896, and in that time he had become known throughout the county and its county seat, Holbrook, as fair and tough-minded. With his black handlebar mustache and the sawed-off shotgun he kept under his black trench coat, Wattron looked ever the part of an Arizona lawman. Newspapers described him as "a generous, whole-souled man whom no one can charge with any dishonesty," though his capacity for boundless charity was matched by his mercurial temper and his reputation for being a "gruff, hard-boiled joker." He had a mild opium addiction, to which some attributed his mood swings, but he'd been liked well enough to get reelected. As the Holbrook *Argus* put it, "Hundreds of persons who read this article can no doubt recollect instances in which they have received personal favors from Mr. Wattron."

Now he had to figure out what do to about George Smiley. Smiley had been working for the Atchison, Topeka & Santa Fe Railway in 1899 as a trackwalker when he confronted a previous foreman over a missing paycheck. An argument broke out between the two men that quickly escalated, and before it was over Smiley had shot his former foreman in the back. Smiley was caught, convicted of murder, and sentenced to death, and his execution was set for December 8, 1899.

Wattron had no problem with seeing this murderer off to his reward: the case was clear-cut, the conviction straightforward, the punishment just. But it was Wattron's first execution, and he was obligated by Arizona statute to notify the public prior to the execution to ensure that witnesses would be present. Without any sense of how such notifications were supposed to look, Wattron composed an invitation that reflected his dark sense of humor:

> You are hereby cordially invited to attend the hanging of one George Smiley, murderer. His soul will be swung into eternity on December 8, 1899, at 3 o'clock p.m., sharp.
>
> Latest improved methods in the art of scientific strangulation will be employed and everything possible will be done to make the surroundings cheerful and the execution a success.
>
> F. J. Wattron, Sheriff of Navajo County.

Smiley's was the first major trial held in the brand-new county courthouse. Simple, elegant, defined by the bell tower rising up from its peaked roof and by its generous arched entryway, the courthouse was built to signify order and law in a lawless land, its tower looming over the small frontier town as though a beacon or some searching eye. And it was here that Smiley was to meet his end.

Wattron's tongue-in-cheek announcement of Smiley's impending execution soon hit the newswires and spread across the country. His gallows humor was met with a mixture of chagrin and outrage, bringing notoriety to the tiny county. Ultimately President William McKinley got word of it and, since Arizona Territory was under federal control, issued word to its governor to address the situation. Governor Nathan Oakes Murphy mandated a thirty-day stay of execution to give Wattron time to reissue the notification with a more funereal tone.

Wattron hated nothing as much as sham and hypocrisy, and no doubt saw this unwanted federal intrusion as more of the same. Perturbed, he issued a second execution announcement, this one in the style of a Victorian mourning card.

Framed in a black border, it read:

Revised Statutes of Arizona, Penal Code, Title X,
Section 1849, Page 807, makes it obligatory on sheriff
to issue invitations to executions,
form (unfortunately) not prescribed.

Holbrook, Arizona

Jan. 7, 1900.

With feelings of profound sorrow and regret, I hereby invite you to attend and witness the private, decent and humane execution of a human being; name, George Smiley, crime, murder.

The said George Smiley will be executed on Jan. 8, 1900, at 2 o'clock p.m.

You are expected to deport yourself in a respectful manner, and any "flippant" or "unseemly" language or conduct on your part will not be allowed. Conduct, on anyone's part, bordering on ribaldry and tending to mar the solemnity of the occasion will not be tolerated.

F. J. Wattron, Sheriff of Navajo County.

I would suggest that a committee, consisting of Governor Murphy, Editors Dunbar, Randolph and Hull, wait on our next legislature and have a form of invitation to executions embodied in our laws.

This time, to prevent any further interference, Wattron sent the invitation out a day before the execution. And on January 8, 1900, George Smiley, age thirty-seven, was hanged from the scaffolding of the courthouse—not only the first person executed on the courthouse grounds but the only legally executed criminal in the history of Navajo County.

The *Argus* noted in its January 13 edition that Smiley had converted to Catholicism shortly before his execution and received baptism and confession before going to his death. "Smiley exhibited great coolness and composure until the last," the paper reported. "He ascended the scaffold unassisted; he spoke clearly and without a tremor in his voice and showed not the slightest sign of nervousness." With his final words Smiley thanked Wattron and his deputies for their kindness.*

Such a report implies a sense of finality and closure and that Smiley went to his death calm and at peace. But according to Marita R. Keams, who worked in the courthouse building after it was converted into a museum in 1981, Smiley has since grown restive. Teenagers using a Ouija board one Halloween, she reports, claimed to have contacted a ghost who told them his name was George. Keams says she and other employees have felt and heard Smiley, that he has turned on the faucets in the men's restroom, and that she's felt him playing with her hair when no one is around. The prevailing feeling among those who work in the building is that Smiley haunts the place of his execution, awaiting a second reprieve from the president that has yet to come.

Whether you believe that Smiley haunts the courthouse may have

---

*Wattron's own death was considerably less serene: five years after the execution he overdosed on laudanum, and when friends came to aid him, he reportedly told them, "I have a ticket punched straight through to Hell with no stopovers" (*Crooked Trail to Holbrook*, 218).

something to do with your attitude toward capital punishment. Culturally, after all, attitudes on the subject vary widely and fluctuate over time, and it's likely not a coincidence that the stories of Smiley's restless soul have gained ground as the mode of his original punishment has lost popularity. The story recorded by the *Argus* suggests that Smiley's death sentence was instrumental in his reform: only when faced with his imminent execution did this wayward murderer find his way, facing death with peace and dignity. The ghost stories, on the other hand, suggest that Smiley's ghost haunts the courthouse grounds, still hoping for a reprieve.

Navajo County's Superior Court is now housed in a larger complex that includes not only an enlarged county jail but also the board of supervisors and other essential government services. Its architecture suggests a changing face of government: low-slung and economical, lacking ornament or ostentation, it projects frugality, a reluctance to spend taxpayer money. Arizona is no longer a Wild West frontier, so the power of government need not be telegraphed to the citizenry anymore. The new building is boring, but that is its point.

More so than houses, civic structures—not just courthouses but prisons, asylums, and other government buildings—are purpose-built. They are rarely constructed for convenience's sake; they are built to send a message. They may incorporate Greek or Roman colonnades and rotundas to suggest that their lineage stretches back millennia, as though to grant further legitimacy. They may—as is common with libraries of a certain era—have the names of famous philosophers, statesmen, artists, and writers carved into the exterior stone. When they are built simply or modestly, that is part of their message, too.

A common feature of many of these buildings is the idea of permanence: they're meant to last forever. And yet many of the ideas and philosophies that drive these constructions change over the course of time. Demographics shift, political affiliations change, new administrations are voted in, aesthetics evolve—but the buildings often are left behind, bearing traces of whatever impetus drove their construction.

How a public building—or, as we'll see, a cemetery or even a park—can come to be haunted has a lot to do with the evolution of our cultural ideas, which change faster than our landscape can keep up with, rendering these places obsolete, archaic, and anachronistic.

Unlike businesses or private residences, these civic-minded places have less control over their haunted reputations and less power to keep out the spirits and the spirit seekers. Partly this is out of necessity: places like the West Virginia State Penitentiary in Moundsville don't receive enough public funding to cover operating expenses and need the revenue from dark tourism to avoid the wrecking ball. Ghost stories have become an important tool for preservationists, as a means to keep alive buildings that have civic and cultural value, buildings that might otherwise get plowed under. But as inherently public places, they belong to the public imagination. You cannot keep a paranormal researcher out of a public park, after all. Hauntings keep alive neglected spaces and make them relevant to their communities once again.

CHAPTER NINE

MELANCHOLY CONTEMPLATION

Moundsville, WV

In the wilds of Greenbrier County, West Virginia, along Route 60, stands a particularly odd national landmark sign. Erected in 1979, in sixty-four words it tells the strange tale of the Greenbrier Ghost.

INTERRED IN NEARBY CEMETERY IS ZONA HEASTER SHUE. HER DEATH IN 1897 WAS PRESUMED NATURAL UNTIL HER SPIRIT APPEARED TO HER MOTHER TO DESCRIBE HOW SHE WAS KILLED BY HER HUSBAND EDWARD. AUTOPSY ON THE EXHUMED BODY VERIFIED THE APPARITION'S ACCOUNT. EDWARD, FOUND GUILTY OF MURDER, WAS SENTENCED TO THE STATE PRISON. ONLY KNOWN CASE IN WHICH TESTIMONY FROM GHOST HELPED CONVICT A MURDERER.

The husband's name was Erasmus Stribbling Trout Shue, not Edward, though he was known by most as Trout. When he arrived at the West Virginia State Penitentiary at Moundsville in 1897 as inmate number 3255, it was not his first time. A competent blacksmith, he'd been convicted of horse thievery and had spent twenty months in prison for it. His first marriage had been in 1885, and he'd divorced four years later under clouded circumstances (some would later claim that his wife had feared that he would kill her). In 1894 he married again, a woman named Lucy A. Tritt, who died less than a year into their marriage in February of the following year. Little is known about her death: the newspaper recorded only that she "died very suddenly at her home" and apparently never followed up on the cause of death. When Shue met Zona Heaster, she had several suitors, but she chose this newly arrived blacksmith, and in October 1896 they were married.

Once again it took less than a year before Shue's marriage ended in death. On the morning of January 22, 1897, he had been out running errands and had sent a young boy, Anderson Jones, to stop by his house and see if his wife needed anything. Jones found Zona's body on the floor, "stretched out perfectly straight with feet together, one hand lying by the side and the other lying across the body." Her head, according to news reports, "was slightly inclined to one side."

By the time the coroner, George Knapp, arrived, Shue had laid out his wife's body and was cradling her head and sobbing uncontrollably. Knapp, attempting to determine the cause of death, noticed some "slight discolorations on the right side of the neck and right cheek," but when he went to investigate further, Shue "protested so vigorously" that Knapp gave up and left the house, having made only a cursory investigation. He later reported that the woman had died from "an everlasting faint."

Zona Heaster Shue was taken to her mother's house and laid out for viewing, but during the wake her husband's behavior, according to eyewitness accounts, became increasingly erratic. He claimed to have dressed her body himself and seemed agitated whenever anyone came too close to it. He had placed a pillow at one side of her head so she should could "rest easier," he said. Even in such a state, people noticed an odd looseness to her head whenever the corpse was moved. She was buried the next day, Monday, January 25.

The ghost came shortly thereafter.

Shue's mother-in-law, Mary Jane Heaster, had always disapproved of the marriage. The news of her only daughter's death left her inconsolable, but in the days afterward she would claim that she began receiving regular visits from Zona's ghost. As she later would testify under oath, "It was no dream—she came back and told me that he was mad that she didn't have no meat cooked for supper." The ghost told Heaster that Shue had killed her, driven to rage by such petty things as a lack of meat. The ghost then told her that if she "could look down back of Aunt Martha Jones', in the meadow, in a rocky place; that I could look in a cellar behind some loose plank and see" some traces of blood where he had done it. Heaster did exactly as she was told and, sure enough, saw blood exactly where it had been indicated. Then, most significant, was this revelation: "She cames [sic] four times, and four nights; but the second night she told me that her neck was squeezed off at the first joint."

After several nights of this, Heaster could stand it no more and went to the county prosecutor, John Preston, telling him she believed that Zona's death was no accident and that Zona's ghost would haunt her until justice was done. Nearly a month after Zona's death, her body was disinterred and an inquest was convened. The body had kept well through the West Virginia winter; little decomposition had taken place. Though Mary Jane Heaster had claimed that the ghost had told her that her neck had been broken, the autopsy started with a search for signs of poison. Only after that came back negative did they investigate her neck, determining that Zona Heaster Shue had indeed had her neck broken and that without other bruises on her body that might indicate a fall or other accident, it was a strong likelihood that she had been murdered.

Shue was tried and convicted of his wife's murder that summer but, unusual in the case of murder, was not given the death penalty. Instead, he was sentenced to life imprisonment at the West Virginia Penitentiary in Moundsville. He never left there, dying behind bars on March 13, 1900.

✤

In the decades following Shue's death, the penitentiary gradually developed a reputation for its poor treatment of inmates—so much so that in

1981 a prisoner named Robert Crain sued the state, claiming cruel and unusual punishment and initiating a lengthy legal battle. In a 1986 opinion the West Virginia Supreme Court found a list of deplorable conditions so voluminous that they had difficulty accurately summarizing them. Back-flowing toilets leaking sewage onto the floor were common, as were bird droppings from the pigeons roosting in the eaves. The lack of temperature control meant freezing in winter and scorching heat in summer. "Because of lack of ventilation and cleanliness and sewage spills," the justices reported, "much of the living facility is permeated with a stench. Fire and safety hazards abound and are compounded by numerous health hazards in the food service area. Food is contaminated with hair, insects, and other foreign substances." The state's failure to remedy these problems in the ensuing years led finally to the facility's closure almost ten years later, in 1995.

The prison's ghosts moved in around the same time as the inmates were cleared out. One former inmate, William "Red" Snyder, who was murdered in his cell in 1992, has been heard calling out to tour guides and has occasionally shown up on EVP recordings. Shadowy figures have been seen in the hallways, and near the North Gate roams the indignant ghost of Arvil Adkins. Adkins had been one of three men condemned to death in 1938 for a botched kidnapping that had led to their victim's death. Adkins's hanging did not go smoothly; the trap door beneath him was sprung prematurely, and he plummeted twenty feet onto the concrete below. Still alive, the bloodied and injured Adkins was carried back upstairs on a stretcher to be hanged properly.

After 1995, the state turned the operation of the penitentiary over to the Moundsville Economic Development Council but provided no additional funds for its upkeep or restoration. So the council turned to the haunted reputation of the prison to keep it open to the public, running a staged haunted attraction each fall, the Dungeon of Horrors, and regular ghost-hunting sessions throughout the year.

The Dungeon of Horrors tour, according to one employee I spoke to who worked there for a season, didn't have to rely on ginned-up shocks. Even without any canned effects, strange sounds could be heard: dripping water from an unknown source and unidentified clanging sounds cutting through the eerie silence. As part of the tour, guides would recount real stories of murder, torture, and abuse that had taken place in the prison. Its reputation was such that a haunted tour could rely heavily on well-established facts.

Attractions like these have become enormously popular. Sociologist Margee Kerr explains that they are "frightening yet intriguing—creating a kind of attraction/repulsion dynamic." Though they're places we hope never to find ourselves confined in, we nonetheless are attracted to them because of what they stand for. In Kerr's words, "In the public act of confining the criminal, or the 'abnormal' other, societies reaffirm their shared values, the differences between 'us' and 'them' become visible, and the dividing lines are fortified." If you are terrified by the thought of one day finding yourself behind bars in a place like Moundsville, Kerr suggests you're also relieved by the recognition, at the tour's end, that you are not one of the "bad guys," and once past the gift shop you're allowed to go free back into civilization. The good attractions, she notes, push your boundaries while leaving you safe and inspired; the less reputable ones, on the other hand, "leave you there or drop you."

But perhaps we *should* be left slightly disturbed by a place like Moundsville. The employee I spoke to recalled how, after a month at that prison, the place began to work on him. There was little after-hours bonding among the staff; no sharing of beers or stories after a job well done. "No one wanted to stick around," he said.

Prison architecture evolved, after all, to elicit extremely specific emotional and physical reactions. While the idea of solitary confinement and cellular prisons grew out of the monastic tradition, in a punitive context isolation rarely produces rehabilitation. Repeated studies have, in fact, shown the opposite: that solitary confinement acts as a barrier to mental and physical health, creating increasing psychological instability and antisocial behavior among those subjected to it.

When prisons like Moundsville were being planned and built, little of this was known. Prior to the nineteenth century, prisons were temporary spaces. You were imprisoned while you were awaiting trial, and in some cases, after you'd been sentenced and were waiting for the sentence to be carried out. The punishments themselves were almost uniformly physical: beatings or death. The notion that imprisonment itself could be a punishment, that one could be made to pay for crimes by the loss of time, is a relatively recent phenomenon.

So at the time Moundsville was built, treatments like solitary confinement seemed novel, even humane. The commissioners appointed with the design and construction of Philadelphia's Eastern State Penitentiary wrote, "Its good design is to produce, by means of sufferings principally acting on the mind and accompanied with moral and religious instruction, a disposition to virtuous conduct, the only sure preventive of crime." Alone with only one's thoughts and a Bible, one could focus on penance and self-correction, unencumbered by the distractions of one's surroundings and any further temptation to sin once more.

But this wouldn't work with all criminals, of course, hence the other factor of Eastern State's design: its imposing façade, its castlelike exterior, which exudes a gothic dread to all passing by. This malevolent exterior was intentional, meant "to impress so great a dread and terror, as to deter the offender from the commission of crime in the state where the system of solitary confinement exists."

Moundsville, like Eastern State, was designed explicitly to spread this sense of gloom and melancholy, a means of further inspiring penance upon those trapped in its walls or those on the outside who might contemplate a life of crime. An 1826 encyclopedia noted, "The style of architecture of a prison, is a matter of no slight importance. It offers an effectual method of exciting the imagination to a most desirable point of abhorrence." Continuing, it recommended that "the exterior of a prison should, therefore, be formed in the heavy and sombre style, which most forcibly impresses the spectator with gloom and terror. Massive cornices, the absence of windows or other ornaments, small low doors, and the whole structure comparatively low, seem to include nearly all the points necessary to produce the desired effect."

The architects who designed institutions like Eastern State and Moundsville, then, attempted to inspire the same sense of foreboding that London's Newgate Prison had long been famous for, inciting in their inmates (in the words of one commentator) a sense of awe and "melancholy contemplation." Eastern State, though far more expensive than other prisons of the day, continually succeeded in creating this impression, at least among the law-abiding. "The design and execution impart a grave, severe, and awful character to the external aspect of this building," George Washington Smith noted in 1830. "The effect which it produces on the imagination of every passing spectator, is particularly impressive, solemn, and instructive."

Even today the prison feels deeply unsettling, and walking through its halls leaves you with a pervasive sense of unease. It feels both claustrophobic and endless, forlorn and merciless. The cool stone sucks out all the available heat in the room; no doubt the place gets unbearable in summer, but even when I visited in late April, it felt unnaturally chilled, as though the whole building were a cold spot. The walls ricochet sound in unexpected ways, making for strange echoes. Moundsville *works* on you, even as a tourist.

The prison also speaks to you, giving the history of its former occupants through the paintings and words that decorate the walls. Somewhat anomalously, the wardens at Moundsville began allowing prisoners to paint murals on the walls, starting in the 1960s until the prison's closure in 1995. The insides of Moundsville are covered with cryptic imagery, traces of the lives lived inside these walls—everything from the Teenage Mutant Ninja Turtles to lyrics by Guns N' Roses and Hank Williams. For the most part there is a mixture of fantasy and nature imagery (mountain waterfalls, medieval knights, dinosaurs), gang signs, Confederate flags, skulls and demons, along with cartoon characters. The prison failed to keep records of the artists, and aside from what's passed down in oral history, the purpose and meaning of the images have become ambiguous. Once a series of faceless cells and corridors, Moundsville today, through these murals, preserves strange, elliptical stories of the people who were once imprisoned here.

Many buildings—most notably the houses we live in, but, really, any building in which we spend a great deal of time—establish a kind of feedback loop with their inhabitants. Through the placement of furniture and decoration, patterns of wear and habit, even the unpacking of luggage in a hotel room, we arrange and order the spaces we move through to suit our needs. But this doesn't happen in a prison. The effect here is entirely one-way; the prison molds the inmate and gives the inmate no quarter to be himself or herself, to step out of line, to change the circumstances of the prison to suit personal needs. The caged-in hallways, the towering rows of identical cells, the naked toilets in plain sight—everything is de-signed to remind you that no human could live here, despite the reality that thousands do.

Eastern State Penitentiary gets more press than Moundsville—it's big-ger, more famous, and more likely to show up in online roundups as the "most haunted" prison. But it's also right in the middle of Philadelphia, hemmed in by restaurants and cafés and upscale salons and nice houses, and despite the gothic ambiance of its façade, it is integrated into the city. Moundsville is itself remote, and the prison rises out of the ground as an anomaly, forlorn and distant.

And then there's the mound across the street.

❧

Nearly seventy feet tall and nine hundred feet in circumference, consist-ing of some fifty-five thousand cubic yards of dirt, the Grave Creek Mound is the largest extant burial mound in the country. It was con-structed some two thousand years ago by the Adena, a culture that had mostly died out by the year 200. The Adena remain a mystery to anthropologists, and the very existence of the startling-looking mound has belied attempts to definitively explain its purpose or its creators.

Joseph Tomlinson discovered it in 1770. After a day on his land, south of Wheeling, he climbed a small knoll less than a quarter mile from his cabin, only to realize that he was standing not on a hill but on an enormous mound of excavated dirt that had been more or less hiding in plain sight. Gradually, it began to draw curiosity seekers, and theories abounded as to what might be inside the massive mound, with people speculating that it held the keys to ancient civilizations long gone. By 1838, the Tomlinsons had raised enough money to fund an excavation of the site.

The mound, as it happened, contained not mysteries to vast civilizations but only the remains of two individuals. A museum of sorts was created in the middle of the mound, where a visitor could pay a quarter to see the mound's contents. Upon entering the mound, one found a central room supported by a brick column. "Around the base of this column there is a circular shelf provided with wire cases," recorded one visitor in 1842, "in which the bones, head ornaments, and other objects of interest, found in the vaults are arranged. The place was dark, or but dimly lighted with a few tallow candles, which cast around a sepulchral glare on the wired skeleton and other bones spread around." But without a railroad or other easy access to Moundsville, the mound couldn't attract widespread excitement.

As a tourist attraction the Grave Creek Mound had failed by 1846, but over the years other attempts were made to wring some value from this inexplicable earthwork: a saloon was built on top of it at one point, and during the Civil War artillery cannons were stationed there. In 1874 a former warden of the penitentiary bought it; he first installed a dance platform on it but was hoping to use it to support a water tank to supply the prison and the town. This plan, too, failed, and the state finally purchased the site in 1909.

The mound was in serious disrepair by then. The state used prison labor to refill the holes in the mound and repair other damage. A cultural center was added, but while it does an admirable job of reconstructing early Adena culture, there's so much that simply isn't known. The mound stands as a monument to the gaps in our history, the things in the past that we can no longer access.

Numerous blogs have connected the haunted prison with the Grave Creek Mound via a variety of bizarre speculations involving aliens, buried giants, and more. The two structures are a study in contrasts: one ephemeral, composed of dirt, perpetually threatening to return to the land; the other cut from solid rock, utterly impregnable, not likely to ever come down except by the most strenuous effort. The mound has stubbornly resisted attempts by the local white population to monetize it, whereas the prison has been relatively successful in turning its legacy into much-needed funds that keep it alive. And while the Grave Creek Mound remains unknowable, the prison lends itself remarkably well to a narrative of crime and punishment, of good and evil.

∞∿◑ ◐∿∾

No matter your crime, once you were in Moundsville, your life was pretty much forfeit. The place was underfunded and understaffed, and there was no room for pity. The world of the penitentiary is one of lawlessness, of anarchy, which is in part why it's so frightening. By one estimate, at any given time in Moundsville's operating history, inmates outnumbered guards by at least 20 to 1. Designed to hold 650 inmates but often holding in excess of 2,000, it was staffed with fewer than 50 guards on shift at any given time during the day.

This chronic lack of guards and resources led, as one might expect, to a level of violence among the inmates that approached pure anarchy. In November 1992, a leader of the Aryan Brotherhood, "Red" Snyder, was stabbed repeatedly by his neighbor Rusty Lassiter. The two had been good friends, but a price on Snyder's head by a rival proved too enticing for Lassiter.

This betrayal perhaps accounts for why Snyder's restless ghost continues to haunt his cell, calling out to the former guards who now give tours of the prison. But his murder is only one of many instances of horrific brutality that have transpired behind the prison's walls. Its history is filled with savage violence by inmates—prominently involving rival gangs making examples of each other. Moundsville is perhaps most notorious for the underground recreation room—the Sugar Shack, as it was known—which was unsupervised and played host to countless beatings, rapes, and murders.

The desire for a quick and ready dispatch of justice underlies so many of our ghost tales. Part of our belief in ghosts, you could say, comes from our belief in perfect and unambiguous justice. As opposed to tales of, say, a poltergeist, a spirit that is mischievous without direction, or a demon or other actively malevolent spirit, ghost stories often revolve around crime and punishment. The story of Zona Heaster Shue's murder is a perfect example: a murderer nearly gets away with a crime, but the ghost returns to see justice done. The mother avenges the daughter, an inverted *Hamlet*, where the ghost will not rest until its relatives stand up for it. Indeed, the story of the Greenbrier Ghost is so perfectly literary that it almost seems like something out of a book.

But did a ghost actually help convict Trout Shue?

In the early 1980s author Katie Letcher Lyle, having heard the story of the Greenbrier Ghost from one of Trout Shue's descendants, set out to discover what was fact and what was fiction. She interviewed living descendants, scoured news stories and trial records, and while she found that the main elements of the story are by and large true, there are odd discrepancies between how Zona's story is usually told and the actual history.

For one, while Zona's mother did testify to having seen a ghost during Shue's murder trial, she did so at the behest of the defense, not the prosecution. John Preston, the prosecuting attorney, apparently thought the ghost story too fantastic to be of any actual help and did not call Mary

Jane Heaster as a witness for fear of sabotaging his case. It was the defense who summoned her to the stand, hoping to discredit the whole proceedings by implying it had been initiated by a hysterical mother.

Aside from her testimony in court, there is no other record of the ghost visiting Heaster until after the conviction, and the supposedly telling detail—that the ghost had told her mother about the broken veterbrae—doesn't explain why the autopsy (if done at the ghost's urging) would have started by searching for signs of poisoning.

Lyle came up with her own theory as to what really happened: In the January 28, 1897, edition of the *Greenbrier Independent*, news of Zona Heaster Shue's death was covered on page three, but on page one was a curious story out of Australia. "One of the most famous murder cases in Australia," it read, "was discovered by the ghost of the murdered man sitting on the rail of a dam (Australian for horse pond) into which his body had been thrown. Numberless people saw it, and the crime was duly brought home." The item continues:

> Years after, a dying man making his confession said that he invented the ghost. He witnessed the crime, but was threatened with death if he divulged it as he wished to, and the only way he saw out of the impasse was to affect to see the ghost where the body would be found. As soon as he started the story, such is the power of nervousness that numerous other people began to see it, until its fame reached such dimensions that a search was made and the body found, and the murderers brought to justice.

Mary Jane Heaster was no idiot, nor was she hysterical. She had strong suspicions that Shue had killed her daughter and that the local officials, whatever their own beliefs might have been, weren't doing anything about it. The Australian ghost story inspired her, according to Lyle, to concoct her own vision of justice, which she then used as leverage to spur the authorities back into action.

Lyle admits that, as Mary Jane Heaster is long dead and left no confession, this hypothesis is circumstantial. And yet so, too, was Shue's conviction. Though the autopsy proved that Zona was murdered, during the trial the prosecution provided no physical evidence that Trout was the culprit. He was convicted based entirely on his suspicious actions after her death.

The case of Trout Shue is unsettling, I think, not because of its supernatural element but because of the obviously roughshod manner in which justice was carried out. Shue might very well have been guilty; the people of Greenbrier certainly thought so. If so, why couldn't they convict him through more substantial means? What is more troublesome about Zona Heaster's story: that a possibly innocent man was convicted of her death based on nothing but circumstantial evidence? Or that a guilty man could not have been convicted through the accepted legal framework on which we usually rely?

The ghost story does away with this unsettling quandary. In the years since the verdict and Shue's death, the Greenbrier Ghost has come to stand for a kind of certainty, the same certainty we seek in the thick walls of an old prison. Offering a vision of pure justice, the unavenged ghost wipes away all the legal ambiguities of the case with a brush of a spectral hand, leaving only the pure truth.

CHAPTER TEN

THE STAIN

Danvers, MA, and Athens, OH

Towering above the local landscape on a hill in northeastern Massachusetts are the remains of the Danvers State Hospital, its imposing clock tower still looming over the traffic on nearby I-95. Here, it is said, John Hathorne—one of the head judges of the Salem witch trials, known for his harsh interrogations, his presumption of the guilt of the accused—built his home. In the curious way that America sometimes piles one tragedy upon another, as if to quarantine the evil, the land that had been Hathorne's became the site of the Danvers State Hospital, a place built with the best of all possible intentions that would, in time, be known as the worst of all possible worlds.

The hospital was made famous by H. P. Lovecraft, who used it as a model for his fictional Arkham Sanitarium. The real-life hospital was built in 1874 and has long had a host of legends attached to it. Even after the hospital was closed in 1992, its legacy as a haunted asylum remains.

If you call to mind a haunted mental asylum, you are undoubtedly thinking of Danvers: an ornate but sinister Victorian façade, long wings, and, in the center of the building, a glowering clock tower. This is no accident; Danvers is one of many asylums based on a similar model, a design by architect Thomas Kirkbride that was first implemented in 1848, at the

New Jersey State Lunatic Asylum in Trenton. By the end of the nineteenth century, Kirkbrides dotted the country, from Salem, Massachusetts, to Salem, Oregon—home of the Oregon State Insane Asylum (where Ken Kesey's novel *One Flew Over the Cuckoo's Nest* was set). But within the past few decades, most of these buildings have been abandoned, demolished, or repurposed—few still operate as mental health institutions.

Danvers began shuttering its facilities in the late 1960s and shut down entirely in 1992. In 2006, after a lengthy process, a developer bought the property and set about renovating what was left of the asylum into luxury condos; the hospital's massive wings were demolished, but the central administration building with its clock tower was preserved. Inside it smells of new carpet and fresh paint. If it feels eerie now, it's perhaps not because of its provenance as a haunted asylum but because of its utter generic feeling: once you step inside its doors, you could be in any modest hotel chain in the country.

∽◇◇∼

Unlike Moundsville and Eastern State, which were meant to exude a melancholy terror, their architecture part of the punishment, Danvers and its many sisters were designed to be welcoming, to reassure both patients and their families that they were in good, safe hands.

For centuries the mad belonged to the same group of society as the blind, the poor, the sick, and the elderly; all who could not work or otherwise easily contribute to society were more or less treated equally, regardless of the specificity of their situations. Prior to the rise of asylums, the mad were often sequestered in off-limits parts of their house. (Most famously, of course, in *Jane Eyre*, when Jane confronts the "madwoman in the attic," Bertha.) But gradually, in the seventeenth and eighteenth centuries, the first madhouses began offering a place where wealthy families could sequester relatives. The madhouse, in this light, was simply the attic, or the basement, of the house, made external and moved elsewhere.

Early madhouses were often revealed to be nightmares of abuse and neglect. Reports of incontinent patients hosed down with icy water, naked women chained haphazardly to the walls, fleas and rats rampant, and other horrors gradually prompted a desire for something more sanitary and humane. In England, Bethlehem Royal Hospital—more often known as Bedlam—became so associated with chaos, horror, and depravity that its name has entered the dictionary as a catchall for chaos and lunacy.

In 1843 Dorothea Dix emerged as a powerful voice calling for social reform. In a memorandum sent to the legislators of her home state of Massachusetts, she railed against "the present state of insane persons confined within this Commonwealth, in cages, closets, stalls, pens! Chained, naked, beaten with rods, and lashed into obedience!" She found instances of inmates padlocked in cellars, left in the dark to wail in torment for years without aid or treatment. Something had to give.

The "moral treatment," as it came to be known, became the solution: rather than chained and forgotten, patients would be unshackled and allowed to move about the asylum at will. Instead of being tortured and imprisoned, patients would work and play. Through labor and sports, hobbies and other recreations, the moral treatment promised rehabilitation and freedom from insanity. The moral model was held out as a means of actually curing patients, rather than simply bundling them out of sight. "All experience," Dix claimed, "showed that insanity reasonably treated is as curable as a cold or a fever."

The Kirkbride asylum came to be the architectural style most thoroughly associated in the United States with the moral treatment. Rather than terrifying, the new asylum would be inviting, surrounded by lawns and gardens that patients could tend themselves. The defining features of the Kirkbride asylum include the central administration building, stately and elegant, with a central tower and elongated wings, forming a shallow V that extends back farther and farther. Part of the beauty of this architectural model was that wings could always be added farther out indefinitely. As a result, they were often massive, growing to hundreds of thousands of square feet.

There was another reason for the ostentation in the Kirkbride design: while insanity, in its various forms, has accompanied humankind forever, the discipline of psychiatry was still nascent, and the idea of "treating" mental patients was not yet fully accepted. Kirkbride believed that, unlike other diseases, mental illness could not be treated at home, and required an institutional setting, but at the same time treated their asylums as home: doctors referred to themselves as "fathers," the asylum as "the house," the patients as "the family." The asylum provided a large and visible monument to psychiatry. Built with sturdy stone, designed with grace and care, it made real the role of the psychiatrist; like a badge or a uniform, the building itself established authority and legitimized the discipline. People could see and point to it as a place of healing; it allowed people to see insanity as a disease that could be cured, and a psychiatrist as the doctor to cure it. It also became a clearinghouse for all the various maladies that could now be grouped under the notion of mental health. The asylum, in its own way, created both the doctor and the patient.

Dozens of Kirkbride asylums were built throughout the country during the second half of the nineteenth century. They became a way for middle- and upper-class families to transfer care of sick relatives to private facilities where professionals could assume the burden of care. They were inseparable from the burgeoning industrialization of the day; academic Benjamin Reiss refers to the asylum as a "laboratory for the purification of culture and the production of useful citizens."

The Kirkbride asylum was meant to be the antidote to the kinds of horrific treatments at places like Bedlam. Why are we so afraid of them today?

❧❦❧

Kirkbride asylums are, by design, huge. Danvers was originally 70,000 square feet, but this is modest compared with some of her sisters. The

Trans-Allegheny Lunatic Asylum of West Virginia was 242,000 square feet; the Northern Michigan Asylum in Traverse City was, when completed, more than 380,000 square feet; Greystone in New Jersey and the Ridges in Athens, Ohio, were both more than 660,000 square feet.

Originally the asylums' size and amenities were subsidized by the affluent families who wanted the best for their relatives. But in the wake of the Civil War, veterans began to crowd the only federal Kirkbride asylum in Washington, D.C. (the Government Hospital for the Insane, since renamed St. Elizabeths Hospital), and it became clear that insanity was not simply a problem for those with money.

By the second half of the nineteenth century, psychiatric care fell more and more under state control. Private Kirkbride asylums were turned over to the states, and many states built their own in imitation of the same model. For the first time size and cost began to be an issue.

Public officials balked at lavishing taxpayer resources on so few inmates. One opponent, Hervey B. Wilbur, tallied up the cost of various asylums alongside their relative capacities: Danvers, built at a cost of $1.6 million, was designed to house only 450 patients; the Ridges, built for $950,000 for just 600 beds; Worcester State Hospital in Massachusetts, built for $1.25 million for only 450 beds; Greystone, built at a cost of $2.5 million for just 800 beds; and so on. Wilbur ultimately estimated that the Kirkbride asylums were costing around $2,600 per bed—and that excluded the site's land value and its furniture, to say nothing of its staff and upkeep.

The solution seemed to be to take these great buildings and cram into them as many humans as possible. Buildings that were meant to be expansive and give patients a great amount of freedom were now stuffed with bodies, creating a downward spiral of deplorable conditions, understaffing, overtaxed resources, and inhumane treatment.

Whatever the Kirkbride model promised by way of rehabilitation rates was effectively destroyed by this civic disengagement. The asylums became host to the worst kind of neglect and abuse that had typified their precursors—precisely what they had been designed to address.

By the end of the nineteenth century, the Kirkbride plan was being abandoned in favor of another form of architecture: the so-called cottage plan, which focused on campuses of smaller, freestanding buildings instead of giant, imposing façades. The Kirkbrides seemed anachronistic, reflective of an earlier age in which tax money was wasted on frivolous architectural details and massive floorplans.

In a short time the Kirkbride ideal went from being seen as progressive to being a symbol of neglect. And so the clock tower of the administration building became menacing and the loving touches meant to look like home became grotesque parodies.

⁓⁓ல ல⁓⁓

Through it all the stately façade of the Kirkbride asylums remained stately, even if now the boastful architecture projected not sanity and sanitary conditions but a living nightmare. Stories of deaths inside the walls, bodies forgotten, "treatment" that resembled sadistic torture, gradually gave way to stories of ghosts, poisoned land, and haunted buildings.

The ghost stories surrounding the haunting of Kirkbride asylums, like the Danvers Hospital, often originate in a very real, very troubled past. Danvers quickly became notorious for its overcrowding, with almost four times as many patients as the hospital was designed to house. Patients sometimes died out of sight of the staff and their bodies decomposed for days before they were noticed. A report from 1939 noted that more than 10 percent of the asylum's population had died within its walls. Add to the hospital's grisly reputation the ignoble distinction of being the place where the prefrontal lobotomy was refined and widely implemented. It's precisely this accumulation of horrors behind its walls that has led to the prevalence of spirits at Danvers and made it a mecca for paranormal enthusiasts. Thrill seekers trying to get access to the hospital even after it closed its doors led to heightened security on the property; more than 120 would-be ghost hunters have been arrested for trespassing since 2000.

Among those who claim to have seen things there is Jeralyn

Levasseur, who grew up on the grounds (her father, Gerald Richards, was a hospital administrator). Levasseur recalls apparitions angrily scowling at her and her sister when she was a child, and once in high school her bed-covers were yanked off in the middle of the night without warning. Levasseur explained her experiences as a function of the changing nature of psychiatric health: "If you think back to the beginnings of medical science and the things done to people," she told a local newspaper in 2003, "not because they thought they were doing bad, but because they were trying to do right, you have to wonder, did people think they were being tortured?"

The history of the asylum, as with the hospital, is the history of practices that once seemed necessary and now strike us as bizarre and troubling. Dr. Henry Cotton, who from 1907 to 1930 was the superintendent at the Trenton State Hospital (the former New Jersey State Lunatic Asylum, first of the Kirkbrides), performed savage surgeries on his patients for decades, extracting everything from teeth to stomachs in the belief that infections were contributing to his patients' psychological instability.

Haunted by such legacies, the ruins of the Kirkbride asylums—and their attendant lore—reveal how uncomfortable we've become with antiquated methods of "healing the sick." Whatever the intentions behind them, lobotomies, straitjackets, and aggressive shock therapy now strike us as barbaric and unnecessary and hover in the back of our collective consciousness. As a culture we still struggle with unresolvable questions that were once wrongly answered in places like these: Who is crazy? Are we crazy? And what can we do to assure ourselves that we aren't?

The stories of ghosts in the asylums are mostly driven by this anxiety, and for the most part they are the standard, vague stories without much substantiation. But if there is a particularly haunting symbol of the fall of the Kirkbrides—one that is verifiably real—it can be found in Athens, Ohio, in what's left of the Ridges.

The Ridges first opened in 1868 as the Athens Lunatic Asylum—a monstrous campus stretching more than eight hundred feet long. Rather than the single central tower of Danvers, the Ridges is marked by the dual towers of the main administration building, giving its profile vague echoes of Notre Dame.

The plan included not just decorative lakes and fields meant to soothe wandering intellects but also gardens, orchards, and eventually a dairy barn, all tended by the inmates, in an effort to make the facility entirely self-sufficient. For a time it even played host to an alligator, which lived in its fountain during the summer months.

The asylum was built to house just over five hundred patients, but the population quickly grew to double that; like other Kirkbrides, the site soon faced overcrowding. By the 1970s it was underfunded and ill managed, with inmates poorly accounted for and large portions of the complex boarded up or otherwise not in use. In such a setting emerged a ghost story so compelling it ended up in the *Journal of Forensic Sciences*—that of the ghost of Margaret Schilling.

A patient of the Ridges' Continued Care Unit, Schilling, then fifty-three years old, had general freedom of movement and no serious behavioral problems—she was a model patient, her behavior unremarkable in every way. But on December 1, 1978, she failed to show up for dinner, having disappeared without any sign. Within a few hours an extensive search was launched, with staff crisscrossing the wards in search of her. They didn't find her that night—a worrying sign, given the brutally cold winter that had set in.

It wasn't until January 11, 1979, more than a month later, that workers found Schilling's body in the attic of an abandoned wing. There was no sign of foul play. Schilling appeared to have taken off her clothes and folded them neatly before lying down to die on the cold floor. No one could say how long she'd been dead, but despite the cold winter, the room had been warm enough to allow for significant decay.

She left behind no clues as to how she'd ended up there or what had led to her death, but she did leave behind a gruesome mystery: when workers removed her decomposing corpse from the concrete floor, they found a stain in the shape of Schilling's body: a ghostly outline in chalky white, ringed by a fainter, darker outline. And despite how hard workers tried to clean the floor, the stain would not come off.

The stain of Margaret Schilling still remains. Over the years it's been the source of numerous ghost tales and rumors about the hospital, but Schilling's manifestation is not paranormal. A forensic team that investigated the stain in 2007 determined that the image was likely a result of a process called adipocere: the breakdown during decomposition of the body's fat into soap. The investigators found a waxy residue on the floor that had significantly altered the chemistry of the concrete itself, leaving it lighter than the surrounding area. While usually adipocere requires moist, enclosed conditions (say, those of a coffin buried in the right kind of soil), the forensic team's best guess was that Schilling's corpse had undergone some similar process despite the less-than-ideal conditions of the attic.

This strikes me as far more terrifying than an actual ghost. That this woman, placed in the asylum's care, was left to rot on this floor, her body imprinting itself on the cold, unforgiving concrete, seems more disturbing than any tale of an apparition or unidentified noise. Herself unable to tell her tale, Margaret Schilling nonetheless managed to leave an indictment of her caretakers, a savage rebuke of the years of psychiatry that has left a deep stain on our history.

⁓ ◦ ⁓

This regime of horrors wasn't always evident. Family members and officials who came to tour these asylums often failed to see anything amiss. One of the benefits of the Kirkbride layout, with its gently flanking wings moving farther and farther away from the main administration building, was that it allowed the facility to segregate patients based on the severity of their condition. Traditionally the more difficult patients—the violent, the noisy, the untreatable—were housed in the wings farthest out, while the more sedate and promising patients were kept closer to the main building.

Visiting relatives, shown the main building and the adjacent wings, left convinced that their relatives were in a stately, dignified place, not a madhouse. This was important, after all, so long as these institutions were private and depended on paying customers in the form of satisfied families. What went on behind closed doors would always remain a mystery.

Stories began to emerge of horrors inside via the reports of those who'd escaped. Some of the more sensational of these came from a man named Ebenezer Haskell. Haskell was involuntarily committed to the Pennsylvania Hospital for the Insane in 1866 and escaped twice, the second time breaking his leg in the process. After a jury deemed him sane, Haskell wrote a book about his incarceration and trial in which he cited a number of horrific examples of patient mistreatment, including what he claimed was called the "Spread Eagle Cure," a treatment that bore eerie similarities to the torture young Armstead Mason Newman endured in Lumpkin's Jail:

> A disorderly patient is stripped naked and thrown on his back, four men take hold of the limbs and stretch them out at right angles, then the doctor or some one of the attendants stands up on a chair or table and pours a number of buckets full of cold water on his face until life is nearly extinct, then the patient is removed to his dungeon cured of all diseases; the shock is so great it frequently produces *death*.

It's hard to say for sure how accurate Haskell's report was, particularly given his obvious ax to grind. But the lack of any clear information of what was going on, mixed with rumors and horror stories, only added to the picture the public began to form about the state of psychiatric care in general and at the asylum in particular.

The asylum in the nineteenth century embodies a tension between the visible and invisible—that is its most disturbing aspect. There is the highly visible and pronounced architecture, which projects one story, and there are the mostly invisible rooms on the edges, in the wings farthest out, hidden from public view.

Poe tapped into this tension in his short story "The System of Doctor Tarr and Professor Fether." A visitor to an unidentified asylum in France ("a fantastic château, much dilapidated, and indeed scarcely tenantable through age and neglect," one whose façade inspires the narrator with "absolute dread") is shown a model of humane treatment, though gradually it becomes apparent that something is off. Only in the climax of the story is it revealed that the patients have overtaken the asylum; they've taken to impersonating the doctors, while the doctors themselves, along with the staff, have been locked up as patients. In the story's final pages the doctors escape and riot; having been tarred and feathered, they unleash a terrifying fury on their captors, "fighting, stamping, scratching, and howling," having been rendered less than human by their captivity. It's a scene that speaks to the fine line between sanity and insanity. Once the doctors escape, they are as dangerous and as frightening as we've suspected the patients to be. Which is to say, once you're inside the walls of the asylum, objective sanity is all but impossible.

Asylums became haunted by what happened inside their walls and also by the walls themselves: an architecture that was purposely boastful but which spoke of a previous generation with different ideals, economic motives, and attitudes toward the sick. The moment when we were most optimistic about our ability to cure the mind is when we built our most ostentatious palaces to psychiatry. There is a danger, then, in telegraphing too prominently one's utopian ideals via architecture.

We design buildings not only for their utilitarian values but to project specific ideals and reflect our shared values. But these ideals and values are prone to change faster than the buildings. Shifting political fortunes, vacillating periods of excess and austerity, evolving attitudes about how the government should best serve its population—these all tend to move much faster than the time it takes for a building to outlive its usefulness.

❧

"These are America's castles," Robert Kirkbride told me, speaking of the hospitals built on the plan of his ancestor Thomas Kirkbride. An architect and architectural historian himself, Robert was involved with the effort to save one building in particular: Greystone Park Psychiatric Hospital, in Morristown, New Jersey. Less than a year after it was closed, in 2008, a scheme to demolish the massive building and replace it with town houses was put forward by the city, only to be defeated by concerned citizens who argued that the hospital deserved saving: even as a gargantuan gothic ruin, Greystone was an important part of New Jersey's history as well as a significant architectural landmark.

Cities have struggled to deal with these albatrosses—massive, unloved, associated with ghosts and an age gone by—as they've been decommissioned and treatment has moved elsewhere. Not only do they haunt our dreams; they haunt our local governments, who must figure out what to do with them. Many are on highly prized land that has developers salivating; even those that aren't are massive buildings that require resources to keep them from falling into disrepair. They are filled with asbestos and lead paint—toxic materials that are another kind of civic ghost, a remnant of a former idea now discarded.

Danvers's Kirkbride is a typical compromise, in which the most striking feature—the administration building's façade—was preserved, while the surrounding structures were demolished. Others have been made into malls, universities, and other structures. The Northern Michigan Asylum, in Traverse City, was reopened in 2005 as the Village, a complex of shops, restaurants, and residences. The Hudson River Psychiatric Hospital, in Poughkeepsie, New York, after sustaining damage from a lightning strike and two subsequent fires, is likewise being reborn as a mixed-use commercial site. Also in New York, the Buffalo State Asylum for the Insane is in the process of being transformed into a hotel and conference center.

Other buildings have not fared as well. The city of Morristown solicited redevelopment bids for Greystone, but despite receiving six serious proposals from developers, it finally opted to spend up to $50 million to tear down the structure. Greystone, like a ghost, did not go quietly. Built with solid concrete, it cost the state more than $30 million to knock it down.

Robert Kirkbride himself is haunted by a different aspect of these asylums: the very materials in their construction. The Northern Michigan Asylum, he points out, is a massive structure built entirely with a form of Michigan pine that has now vanished. Which is to say, these buildings carry another kind of history, another kind of legacy: the raw materials of our changing landscape, an archaeology of our past.

The problem of the haunted Kirkbride asylums—behemoth structures that reflect a failed utopian plan, that have lingered long after they fell from vogue—is representative of many civic structures that we've come to see as haunted. Victims of changing fortunes, they've accrued stories of death, despair, and haunting in part because of their misuse or because the government and the people who built them were attempting to make a statement that no longer resonates in the same way. If the Kirkbride asylums are haunted, they are haunted, you could say, by the difference between how history is conceived and how it plays out.

CHAPTER ELEVEN

AWAITING THE DEVIL'S COMING

Charleston, SC, and Douglas County, KS

The churchyard of the Unitarian Church in Charleston, South Carolina, is great with ghosts. Overgrown and rapturously baroque, the graveyard is evocative of the kind of Southern gothic that seems ripe for spirits and phantoms of all manner. A sign meets you at the entrance, proclaiming that the paths are uneven and the grave markers may be unstable. Grass pokes through the disintegrating brick walkways, tombstones tilt amid the foliage, moss-laden trees drape over paths. Individual plots are contained by elegant, lacy metalwork, and inside these quadrangles stately obelisks and humble crosses call out, asking you to keep the memory of the dead alive. The weeds and other flora are eager to reclaim the markers of the dead. In the years since a man named Ephraim Seabrook Mikell died, in 1836, the roots of a giant neighboring tree have begun to consume his tombstone, granite and wood fusing together. The legend across the tombstone now reads ACRED TO HIS MEMORY, the "S" now buried inside the tree itself.

"The Souls of the Dead appear frequently" in cemeteries, Joseph Addison wrote in 1711, attributing the thought to Plato, "and hover about the Places where their Bodies are buried, as still hankering after their old brutal Pleasures, and desiring again to enter the Body that gave them an

187

Opportunity of fulfilling them." Here in this churchyard is the Ravenel family plot, where one might look—in vain—for the marker of Annabel Ravenel. According to sources, Annabel haunts this cemetery, hankering after an old pleasure, waiting for her beloved soldier to return.

Her father, Dr. Edmund Ravenel, divided his time between Charleston and nearby Sullivan's Island and was famous as a conchologist (several species of mollusk are named for him, including Ravenel's scallop) when in 1824 he was appointed the first chair in chemistry and pharmacology of the brand-new South Carolina Medical College. In time he would be appointed its dean.

In 1827 Ravenel befriended a young soldier by the name of Edgar A. Perry, who was stationed at Fort Moultrie, on the tip of Sullivan's Island. Ravenel apparently functioned as something of a father figure to the young Perry, whose own parents had disinherited him. Eventually Perry met Ravenel's fourteen-year-old daughter, Annabel, and the two fell madly in love.

When Ravenel discovered his daughter was in love with Perry, he closed his house on Sullivan's Island and returned to Charleston. If he'd hoped that that was the end, it wasn't; Perry followed Annabel to Charleston, where they would meet in secret under the weeping willows of the Unitarian Church Cemetery. When these trysts were discovered, Ravenel locked his daughter in her room. Within a few months she had died of yellow fever.

In order to keep Perry from haunting Annabel's grave, as it were, Ravenel disguised her tombstone. Perry soon was mustered out of service and returned to his life. But Annabel still waits for him at their secret meeting place.

Annabel Ravenel's story seems somewhat archetypal of the ghost stories of the old South: a delicate Southern belle, ruled by her passions but trapped within a strict patriarchal system. With a love unrequited, a cruel father, and a tragic outcome, the tale has all the elements of a gothic romance; it is also a universal fairy tale inflected with the genteel manners and diseased miasmas of South Carolina.

The story is particularly endearing to the citizens of Charleston, though, because of the revelation, in 1885, that Edgar A. Perry was not this soldier's real name. "Perry" was a pseudonym of the man who'd go on to (mostly posthumous) fame as the author of "The Raven" and the "Tell-Tale Heart." Annabel's beloved was none other than Edgar Allan Poe.

Poe biographer Arthur Hobson Quinn believes it probable that Poe knew Ravenel while stationed at Sullivan's Island, and there is some likelihood that the conchologist was the basis for the character William Legrand in Poe's "The Gold Bug"—a man "well educated, with unusual powers of mind, but infected with misanthropy, and subject to perverse moods of alternate enthusiasm and melancholy. . . . His chief amusements were gunning and fishing, or sauntering along the beach and through the myrtles, in quest of shells or entomological specimens." Annabel Ravenel, many now believe, would later serve as the basis for Poe's famous poem "Annabel Lee," with Sullivan's Island as the "kingdom by the sea":

> It was many and many a year ago,
> In a kingdom by the sea,
> That a maiden there lived whom you may know
> By the name of Annabel Lee;
> And this maiden she lived with no other thought
> Than to love and be loved by me.

Having fallen in love with his beautiful maiden, the narrator of Poe's poem laments:

> So that her highborn kinsmen came
> And bore her away from me,
> To shut her up in a sepulchre
> In this kingdom by the sea.

All of which, it would seem, tracks with the details of the love affair of Annabel Ravenel and Edgar A. Perry. Theirs is a beautiful story, full of gothic longing, a wasting beauty (so typical of Poe's writing), an elegy for the dead, all spun around an overgrown, haunted cemetery. We should not be dissuaded by the fact that Edmund Ravenel had no daughter named Annabel. "*I* was a child and *she* was a child," Poe's narrator waxes, but if this is truly about a daughter of Edmund Ravenel, then they were children of different magnitudes, for when Poe was stationed at Sullivan's Island, Ravenel's eldest daughter, Mary Louisa, would have been a mere eighteen months old.

❧

The Unitarian Church no longer accepts new burials; the last remaining plots have been filled. Most burials in Charleston happen in much larger places, like Magnolia Cemetery and the more modern Live Oak Memorial Gardens. Magnolia Cemetery was dedicated in 1850, laid out on what was then the outskirts of the city. Unlike the Unitarian Church's cemetery, Magnolia is sprawling, open, and airy, dotted with pleasant lakes and generous views. Dubbed the "City of the Silent," it quickly became a prime tourist attraction for the city. "If you would see Charleston's greatest attraction drive to Magnolia Cemetery," *Appleton's Hand-Book of American Travel* advised in 1866. "This is indeed a lovely retreat; a scene of tangled woods and silvery waters, looking out upon the broad surface of the Cooper River, whose waters find their way into its pretty lake-lets, over which the majestic live-oaks hang their Druid mosses."

Large, rolling cemeteries like Magnolia, with their contemplative waters and acres of green, came about as a solution to a very pressing modern problem. Since the early Middle Ages, towns in Christian Europe (and later in North America) were laid out around a central church, and adjacent to that church would be the town's graveyard. It was necessary to be buried in consecrated ground so that one could await the Second Coming, and so graveyards were as centrally located as the churches they bordered.

This layout, with a churchyard at the center of town, worked fine in small towns, but with the rise of cities, it became untenable. For one thing, there were simply too many bodies to cram into a small plot of consecrated ground. As churches ran out of space, they would re-trench their graveyards and remove the bones to charnel houses or, in some cases, simply pile new corpses on top of the old. Churchgoers complained of the overwhelming foul odor of decaying bodies, with one critic suggesting the real reason behind burning incense during services was to mask the smell of decomposition. And while germ theory wouldn't be fully understood until the late nineteenth century, by the 1700s people already understood that dead bodies could breed disease. In 1744 a story circulated of a funeral procession in Montpellier, France: when workers opened a vault to inter a newly deceased body, a cloud of poisonous gas spewed forth, knocking the priest unconscious and killing three mourners.

The solution, city planners understood, was to move the bodies away from the church and outside of town—far, far outside of town. In 1804 Paris opened Père-Lachaise, a lush necropolis of 118 acres on the outskirts of the city. Green, rolling hills with widely spaced, stately monuments replaced the crammed, gloomy rows of decrepit tombstones, and mourners and picnickers alike were invited to spend their afternoons in Elysian idyll and quiet contemplation.

The so-called garden cemetery concept caught on quickly, and large cities everywhere began exchanging their cramped churchyards for pastoral campuses far removed from the urban metropolis. In the United States the first of these was Mount Auburn, outside Boston, opened in 1831, followed by New York's Green-Wood, in the faraway suburb of Brooklyn, in 1838. The most comprehensive plan was adopted by San Francisco when, in 1900, the city moved all its remaining remains to the tiny suburb of Colma. Fully 73 percent of Colma's land today is occupied by one of its seventeen cemeteries. "Colma," reads the town's motto, "where it's great to be alive!"

Keeping the living from encroaching on such places has proved difficult over time. Chicago's main cemetery, City Cemetery, was laid out in 1842, situated well beyond the city's northern limits, north of North Avenue and east of Clark Street. Subsequent cholera outbreaks strained its capacity, though, and the site itself was far from ideal for the long-term storage of bodies. Because of its low elevation, the cemetery was regularly flooded, and the waters had the undesirable effect of occasionally forcing coffins to the surface.

By 1858 the city was pressing up against the boundaries of the cemetery, and physician John H. Rauch spearheaded a movement to relocate the dead. Rauch, in line with prevailing medical understanding, argued that "the emanations of the dead are injurious to health and destructive to life"; he wanted to move the dead out of their swampy resting places and away from the city's population to a drier, forested location where trees could absorb the noxious gases of decomposition.

The city acted fast. In November Chicago's aldermen acquiesced to Rauch's pleas, agreeing to investigate the possibility of moving the cemetery to new grounds, and within months they had chartered a new corporation, the Rosehill Cemetery Company, to open up a new burial ground on the North Side. Rosehill Cemetery was inaugurated on July 28, 1859, and was followed that November by the founding of the rural Catholic cemetery Calvary, and finally Graceland, in 1860.

As with Rosehill, Graceland was built and operated by a private company chartered by the city. The cemetery's founder, lawyer, and land speculator Thomas Bryan, was intimately aware of the shortcomings of the old City Cemetery. When he had searched for a plot for his infant son, who'd died in 1855, he'd found City Cemetery "neglected" and in an "actually repulsive condition," which had induced him to search for land "for a rural burying ground, more remote from and more worthy of the city." Contrasted to the low-lying, marshy terrain of City Cemetery, Graceland would be on high ground, wooded with old-growth trees. It would be a place of rolling acres, graves ornate and stately, clean fresh air—an idyllic final resting spot. Landscaped with native trees and flowers, it would in time be described as the "most perfect expression" of the "modern, park-like cemetery."

The plan to build these cemeteries well outside city limits was never truly successful, since inevitably cities spread. Brooklyn is of course now incorporated into New York City, and the real estate surrounding Green-Wood is among the most expensive in the nation; one doesn't have to wonder how many salivating contractors would plow those bodies under in a heartbeat if given the chance to build high-rises. Likewise, Colma, California, is today surrounded on all sides by high-priced suburbs. Grace-land was a victim of its own success; it was so popular as a destination for day trips that it heightened the value of the surrounding real estate: orig-inally known as the township Lake View, the community adjacent to Graceland grew quickly after the cemetery was founded, first becoming its own city and then, in 1889, merging with Chicago itself.

∽◌◌◌∾

The shift wasn't just about urban space; it also had ramifications both religious and linguistic. For much of English history, a place where dead bodies were buried was known exclusively as a churchyard; this was true even if the land itself was not adjacent to a church (such as the mass burial pits dug in London during the Black Death). The word "cemetery," which comes from the Greek *koimētērion* and originally meant simply a dormitory or a place to sleep, had been adopted first by early Christians, who saw sleep as temporary and used the Latin *coemeterium* to refer to the tombs of martyrs, who were simply sleeping and would soon arise once more. By the fifteenth century "cemetery" had entered the English lexicon as an acceptable synonym for "churchyard," and it is not until the 1750s that "cemetery" had its own distinct definition: "a place where the dead are reposited," according to Samuel Johnson's 1755 dictionary. "Church-yard" still meant consecrated ground, but "cemetery" did not; any place that received remains could be a cemetery.

If "graveyard" and "cemetery" had once been more or less synonymous terms, now they represented two very distinct concepts: one tiny, central, and consecrated; the other expansive, distant, and civic in function. By moving the dead out of the grounds of the church, the garden cemetery could also become a place of national significance. At the dedication of Mount Auburn Cemetery, Supreme Court Justice Joseph Story spoke of transforming it into a "more efficient instrument to elevate Ambition, to stimulate Genius, and to dignify Learning." The grave, he argued, has "a voice of eloquence, nay, of super human eloquence," one that, among other things, "awakens a new enthusiasm for virtue," "calls up the images of the illustrious dead," and "demands of us, as men, as patriots, as Christians, as immortals, that the powers given by God should be devoted to his service, and the minds created by his love, should return to him with larger capacities for virtuous enjoyment, and with more spiritual and intellectual brightness." The eloquent voice of the dead, then, could and should be marshaled to enrich the living, to urge us to a higher calling and civic virtues.

Many small towns, of course, continue to use their churchyards. When I was in college in Oregon in the 1990s, I regularly drove past the Old Scotch Church, just off Highway 27 on unincorporated land near Hillsboro. The church itself is a historic monument, with a striking eight-sided steeple, and its churchyard contains the graves of several early Oregon settlers. It also contains fresh graves, including one for a young child, whose unique and singularly disquieting headstone was visible from the road as you drove by: a two-foot-tall Nerf basketball hoop.

Most of these smaller graveyards have stopped taking new occupants, and some cities, like San Francisco, have paved over their old churchyards for new real estate projects. (Only two cemeteries remain within San Francisco's city limits: one at the Mission Dolores Church, the other at the Presidio.) Others have simply fallen into disrepair. Without an influx of new bodies, these places gradually lost their mourners as well, which is to say that there are fewer and fewer people with a vested interest in maintaining them, and so many churchyards in America have become overgrown and melancholy.

And with the weeds come the ghosts.

ᴄᴏᴏ⌐ᴏᴏ

Churchyards make for good hauntings, not only because they are places of the dead but because they are anachronistic. As garden cemeteries became the norm, with their emphasis on spiritual uplift, old churchyards, almost out of necessity, came to be seen as their opposite: gloomy and forlorn, dire and dreary. While guidebooks were urging tourists to visit Mount Auburn, Magnolia Cemetery, and Arlington, folklorists were recording stories of supernatural disturbances at old graveyards. Ghosts emerge from places of neglect, and churchyards are the homes of the neglected dead.

The graveyard of St. Paul's Chapel, in lower Manhattan, is home to one such strange ghost: the Shakespearean actor George Frederick Cooke, who was buried there in 1812—most of him, at least. Cooke had been a tremendous success on the American stage when he came over from England in 1810, but he died just two short years later from alcoholism. He had a modest plot at St. Paul's until a fellow actor, Edmund Kean, paid to have his remains reinterred beneath a grander monument. The process was not without incident; Kean removed one of Cooke's toes as a keepsake ("it was a little black relic," recalled one observer, "and might have passed for a tobacco-stopper"). Additionally, Cooke's skull was stolen; no one knows who took it, but the doctor John W. Francis later had it in his possession and years later loaned it out for a performance of *Hamlet*, the deceased Shakespearean appearing in the role of Yorick. Cooke's skull now resides in the Scott Library of Thomas Jefferson University, but his headless ghost still haunts the churchyard of St. Paul's Chapel, looking for what's been stolen.

St. Paul's churchyard, at least, is still in good shape, well tended and surrounded by the bustling metropolis of New York City. Far from the madding crowds you'll find the Stull Cemetery, in Douglas County, Kansas, all the more legendary for its remoteness. Getting there isn't easy: after you leave the freeway near Lawrence, you take a series of back roads that even Google Maps doesn't fully understand. It takes perseverance, more than a little backtracking, and faith. You feel yourself leaving civilization behind as the gas stations and supermarkets fall away and you're drawn farther out into the untrammeled wilds of the country, dead lands not yet explored, or places that have deliberately been left and allowed to go to seed.

Stull is no longer a town; it's unincorporated land, and there are only a few buildings near the graveyard, including a church across the road and a shuttered bait-and-tackle shop. The graveyard itself rises up from the road, occupying the side of Emmanuel Hill and bordered by a chain-link fence. The tombstones these days are mostly in good condition, evenly spaced, with plenty of green grass and small clumps of brush between them. The Evangelical church across the street is new; the one originally attached to Stull's graveyard no longer stands.

The first haunting stories came from an item in the University of Kansas's student newspaper, the *University Daily Kansan*, in November 1974, which reported that the graveyard and its ruined church had been "haunted by legends of diabolical, supernatural happenings" for well over a century. One student recalled how, driving toward the cemetery, she'd seen a house glowing bright red, as if on fire, but as she got closer it returned to normal. An assistant instructor was quoted as saying that he'd heard people who'd gone ghost hunting at Stull would later have three- or four-hour memory lapses they could not explain. A student told the *Daily Kansan* that he and two friends had journeyed to Stull one night. "All of a sudden I heard a noise behind me and felt someone grab my arm," he said. "I'll never forget how cold the fingers felt." Assuming that it was one of his friends, he turned, only to find them both some twenty-five yards away.

Through the 1970s and '80s the *Daily Kansan* continued to report various stories from students—usually anonymous or identified only by their first names—of second- and thirdhand stories about Stull. Two men who'd been wandering in the cemetery felt a strong gust of wind, and when they returned to where they'd left their car in the road, they discovered it had mysteriously been moved to the other side of the highway and was facing the opposite direction. One woman claimed that as she and her friends drove up to the church, they saw before them a giant burning cross. A sophomore told the paper she'd been nine times to the cemetery and on one trip she'd left two of her friends in the abandoned church; she returned to find them lying "in awkward positions on the floor," a wooden cross lying beside them, and when she approached, one began to convulse about on the floor.

Eventually legends coalesced around a specific narrative of a deformed child who'd lived only a few days beyond birth and was buried at the cemetery in 1850. The child's deformity was attributed to a union between Satan and the child's mother, a witch. The ruins of Stull's former church supposedly contained a set of limestone steps that descended into the bowels of Hell; twice a year Satan himself would climb the steps to pay respects to his dead child. Some creative soul at some point suggested that a grave marked "Wittich" had something to do with this consort of the devil, or that the town was not named after its first postmaster, Sylvester Stull, but was in fact a corruption of the word "skull." A pine tree in the cemetery was identified as a preferred gallows for Kansas's witch population, as well as a few errant suicides. Both the Cure's Robert Smith and Pope John Paul II are said to have avoided Kansas because of Stull (the Cure's longtime keyboard player, Roger O'Donnell, denies this; the Vatican did not respond to requests for comments).

The Stull churchyard became the unhappy host to kids from the university, who would show up twice a year—on the spring equinox and at Halloween—in increasingly large numbers, drunk and rowdy and awaiting the devil's coming. In 1978, 150 people were reported to have shown up; by 1999 there were closer to 500. As the devil was a perpetual no-show, in his absence students hid behind trees or set off fireworks to scare their friends, tipped over tombstones or stole them for their dorm rooms, and generally made merry in the land of the dead. In 1985 *University Daily Kansan* reporter Michelle Worrall concluded that, based on the remains of six-packs scattered about the graveyard, "whatever lurks in the church satisfies its thirst with beer—not blood."

The legends of Stull appear to have been fabricated from whole cloth by the staff of the *University Daily Kansan*. Written by and for college students, articles by the paper amped up the folklore surrounding the cemetery further each year, relying on hearsay and rumor. Having unleashed this unholy monster, the paper in subsequent years tried to keep the beast at bay, as its reporting shifted not to ghosts but to the inevitable trespassing fines awaiting any student who came seeking Satan. "The real evil," the paper proclaimed in 1990, "has not been Satan but the vandalism that occurs on the church's grounds."

Increasingly attention turned to the graveyard's ruined church. A few local preservationists tried to save it and restore it to some semblance of its former state, even as it became a safety hazard. In the absence of any movement in either direction, the church was left untended and foreboding. This is what happens when you leave something vaguely gothic looking, something associated with death, to be reclaimed by nature—it gets claimed by thrill seekers, too.

The college kids were harder to exorcise than ghosts would have been, but the community has worked hard to drive them off. Preserving the graveyard was particularly important because, desolate as it may seem, the Stull Cemetery was and is still in use, and families do come to visit their loved ones. A chain-link fence went up to keep people out, and the Douglas County Sheriff's Department began patrolling the site. "When I used to patrol out there," Lieutenant Steve Lewis told the *University Daily Kansan* in 2013, "I would stop people and they would tell me that they were just trying to see something scary, and I told them they were looking at the scariest thing they were going to see all night, and I charged them with a misdemeanor."

The ruined church was finally torn down in 2002, after one of its few remaining walls fell in a storm, leaving an even more dangerous hazard. John Solbach, one of the local citizens who'd worked to save it, lamented its loss to local news site Lawrence.com: "A lot of history fell with that building. Those who wanted to see it preserved were heartsick that it was destroyed."

The demolition of the old church and the removal of the supposed hanging tree have (alongside efforts from law enforcement) helped to cut down on trespassers. A woman who declined to give her name to the paper decried the glut of drunk kids for abusing the cemetery where her ancestors were buried: "One man wrote and said a relative of mine was a werewolf, and that really made me mad." Solbach himself reported that he knew a man whose son was buried in the cemetery. "Some people came out there to have Halloween fun and they tipped over his son's tombstone. He found that out and he broke down and just cried like a baby."

These residents see nothing titillating, or eerie, or good-natured about the legends surrounding Stull's graveyard. "This story about it being haunted just tears the guts out of people," Solbach said. You could almost say that the people of Stull had been presented with something of a devil's bargain: the destruction of the church might have been the price that had to be paid to save the rest of the graveyard.

❧

Whereas some places—historic houses, hotels, prisons, and asylums—have found that there's good money to be had in ghost tours and catering to paranormal enthusiasts, cemeteries have had less success, and less interest, in going down that road. Unlike forlorn churchyards, modern cemeteries don't attract—and certainly don't encourage—the same kind of folklore and ghost stories. As still-functioning businesses, cemeteries like Graceland in Chicago and Forest Lawn in Los Angeles have little interest in being overrun by thrill seekers or conveying the image to potential clients that their loved ones' tombstones might be vandalized.

But that's not to say that ghosts haven't also found their way to the nation's modern cemeteries. Though they're not nearly as numerous as the stories that surround the older churchyards, such as Stull or Charleston's Unitarian graveyard, you can find them if you go looking. Find yourself in Chicago's Graceland and you may hear the crying of a young girl named Inez Clarke, who's buried on the cemetery's grounds.

Inez was only six years old when, in 1880, she was fatally struck by lightning. Her grave is marked by a beautiful stone statue of a young girl. Legs crossed, she sits atop a stone tree branch, her summer hat askew, an umbrella dangling in front of her legs. The entire statue, which reads only "Inez," is itself encased in glass atop the monument for John and Mary Clarke, and for years legends have maintained that Inez's ghost is still scared of lightning; during thunderstorms, people claim, her statue disappears entirely, returning only after the threat has passed.

Inez Clarke was actually Inez Briggs, who died on August 1, 1880, not of lightning but of diphtheria. Her mother had recently remarried, changing her name to Clarke, when her daughter died, and later she denied the existence of the children from the earlier marriage. Compounding the confusion, in Graceland's burial records "Inez Briggs" was mistakenly entered as "Amos Briggs." The story of the lightning strike was perhaps conjured from clues from the statue—the hat and umbrella—though most agree that the statue was made not for Inez but as a sample of the carver's work to drum up business.

The slight confusion surrounding the child's identity and the lack of a readily available explanation of the statue's meaning have contributed to the legend that has swirled up around her, and surely ghosts will follow wherever there is bad record keeping. Is the ghost of Inez Clarke an outlier in a cemetery mostly devoid of phantoms or a harbinger of more spirits to come? Just as we moved away from churchyard burials to cemeteries almost two hundred years ago, we are now, slowly, moving away from the garden cemeteries. Cremation is on the rise, as is green burial and other alternative forms. The era of the lavish, expensive funeral in the rolling hills of the garden cemetery may gradually be coming to an end. If our children or grandchildren have less and less cause to visit these places, they, too, may begin to suffer from neglect.

And if that happens, expect more ghosts to come keep Inez Clarke company.

CHAPTER TWELVE

OUR ILLUSTRIOUS DEAD

Shiloh, TN

I n Cold Harbor, Virginia, the battle commences again promptly at 1 a.m.—soldiers materialize from the earthworks amid the fields, engaging once more in a battle that seems to play on an endless loop. An hour to the south, at Fredericksburg, scene of one of the Civil War's bloodiest battles, ghost sentries stand guard, march in formation, and tend to their wounds. Ghosts of all manner roam the battlefield at Gettysburg: Shouted commands have been heard at Reynolds Woods, shadows roam Little Round Top, and a ragged Texas infantryman known as "the hippie" has appeared to some at Devil's Den. At Manassas, where the first and second battles of Bull Run were fought, a charred smell hangs in the air, which writer Mark Nesbitt has surmised may be a remnant of Sullivan Ballou, the Union major who was killed at the First Battle of Bull Run and whose body was desecrated and burned by Confederate soldiers after the battle.

At Shiloh a visitor reported seeing a young Confederate soldier sleeping against a wall. "He was lying down on the moss with his knees up," she later recalled. "He had one arm lying on his cheek, and one arm at his side with his hat over his face. I said, 'Is he sleeping it off from last night? Is he OK? He appears to be OK.' We stood there watching the kid. It was sort of a strange thing to find in the woods. And then he wasn't there. He just dissolved in the air."

Many tourists at Shiloh have seen the nameless Union drummer boy. The story, as it's often passed down, is that as a Union offensive began to turn bad, the commanding officer called out a retreat, but the drummer boy instead gave the call once again to attack. Furious, the commanding officer asked him why, and the boy replied that he only knew one signal: attack. But by then, due to the boy's error, the Union forces had rallied and had taken the hill they'd been fighting for. The commanding officer later sought out the young boy to thank him, only to find he'd fallen in the fighting.

∾◦◦∾

Civil War cemeteries loom large in the American consciousness. After all, the most famous piece of American oration, the Gettysburg Address, was delivered at the dedication of one such cemetery. Lincoln's speech, brief and iconic, makes a simple and elegant point: it is beyond the power of any great speaker—including the president—to consecrate this, since only the bodies of the dead soldiers can do this, and it is they on whom the foundation of the United States rests. At the heart of Lincoln's speech is this solemn belief that the greatness of the country lies in its ghosts, to whom we are constantly indebted.

The creation of the Civil War battlefield cemeteries began in 1867, with the wounds of the war still fresh. The conflict was so savage in its destruction of human life that many men were simply unaccounted for; by the end the lists of casualties included only a third of the total number of men estimated to be missing or killed. By early 1866 journalists, politicians, and humanitarians began clamoring for a system of national cemeteries to honor the fallen. James Fowler Russling, in *Harper's New Monthly Magazine*, asked:

> Shall we permit their honored graves, holding the best ashes
> of the land and proudest of the century, to be left liable to

desecration by hostile hands, or to be obliterated quickly by time and nature, as among other nations and in other ages? Or rather shall we not at once gather their remains tenderly together into great national cemeteries, few in number but centrally located; beautify and adorn these in a moderate but just way, and solemnly commit them to posterity as a part of the precious price our generation paid for the Union, to be the republic's legacy and the nation's inheritance for evermore?

Spurred by these calls to action, the North began to gather its dead, to build monuments not just to individual sufferers but also to the country as a whole. What started at Gettysburg and at a former POW camp at Andersonville was quickly incorporated into a national program, one that ultimately led to seventy-four national cemeteries holding a collective 303,536 dead, at a cost of $4 million—what historian Drew Gilpin Faust has called "arguably the most elaborate federal program undertaken in nearly a century of American nationhood."

Throughout, the goal, explicit and implicit, was not just to provide proper burial for those who'd died in war and been left on the battlefield but also to build on a narrative of the United States in the wake of the war that had almost destroyed it. A nation that had won a battle fought partly over states' rights could not now allow its obligation to the dead to fall to the states; the cemeteries of the Civil War must be overseen by the federal government while uniting the states under this larger sovereignty.

The creation of the Civil War battlefield cemeteries also coincided neatly with the transition from churchyards to garden cemeteries. Coming at the end of that major evolution, in which burial grounds shifted from a religious setting to a civic institution, the battlefield cemeteries became a symbol of how Americans strove to make meaning from dead bodies. These men would never rest in family plots and the cemeteries of their hometowns. Instead, their bodies would consecrate the fields of battle, imbuing these lands with an extra symbolic weight. Thomas W. Laqueur notes that "the body, by the fact of its physical location, infuses its meaning into the land where it rests and decomposes"—what mattered was that these men be buried where they fell. The battlefield cemeteries and the preservation of the battlefields themselves were means of creating a more perfect union, of commemorating a loss that couldn't be fully reckoned with.

The ghosts that have more or less always existed on these fields—ghosts without name or identification, often even without allegiance to the North or the South—would seem to further help unite us. Rooted to these resonant places, they keep alive acts of heroism, relive moments of courage, and remind us of their sacrifice.

∽∾⚬∾∾

But this wasn't always the case. While the federal government was burying the Union dead, the economically destroyed South saw its own dead lying fallow and untended. The work of burying Confederate soldiers fell to civilians and became a grassroots movement that gave a purpose of sorts to defeated Southern culture. Southern whites undertook ad hoc attempts to bury their dead, often raising money through the community to cover burial costs and tombstones. This work was largely the provenance of women—grieving mothers and widows who would honor fallen Confederates one last time. Mourning the Southern dead became a way to subtly repudiate the Union and reject the war's outcome. At a consecration in Savannah, Georgia, of the Confederate dead who'd fallen at Gettysburg, Father Abram Ryan, the so-called poet laureate of the Confederacy, recited an elegy for the dead who'd fallen in a cause "though lost, still just."

The reincorporation of the Confederate dead into the fold took time. In 1900 Congress appropriated funds for a dedicated Confederate section within Arlington Cemetery, and in 1906 the federal government established the Commission for Marking Graves of Confederate Dead, which incorporated earlier ad hoc Confederate cemeteries into the national park system. Finally, the dead of the Confederacy had a permanent home alongside the dead of the Union. The sleeping Southern boy at Shiloh now could haunt alongside the famous Union drummer, the two boys united in the afterlife.

But this left close to four decades in which the Confederate dead had no home to haunt, and in those years, particularly in the immediate wake of the Civil War, it would appear that they roamed free.

∽◌◌∾

"Sometimes we would meet one or two people and they'd ride right on by," a former slave would later say about the years following the Civil War, "and nobody would speak or say nothing, but just keep straight forward; just the foremost ones that would see them would say, 'Shiloh,' and then they'd all hang their heads, or turn their heads, and nobody would say anything." Stories circulated of an incident in Attakapas Parish, Louisiana: A freedman was awakened one night by a night traveler, who asked for some water. The man filled a bucket with water and gave it to the stranger, who proceeded to drink the entire bucket, then demanded another. After he had drunk the bucket dry a second time and then a third, he thanked the man, telling him how thirsty he'd been, that he had traveled more than a thousand miles in the last twenty-four hours, and that that was the best drink of water he'd had since he'd been killed at Shiloh.

The ghosts rose from Shiloh, from Vicksburg, from Cold Harbor and Antietam. In southeastern Tennessee, travelers noticed a strange, foreboding sentinel keeping watch in front of a dilapidated house on a hill. Occasionally someone asked him who he was; and the reply, in low, sepulchral tones, returned: "A spirit from the other world. I was killed at Chickamauga." Ghosts stood guard over dilapidated plantations and, like the man in Attakapas, they rode through the night, demanding water to quench an unquenchable thirst, hanging their heads low, speaking in guttural voices, telling all who asked of their deaths on the field of battle.

One former slave would remember, decades later, ghosts who approached him one night and told him "they had come from Manassas Gap to see that the poor widows are not imposed upon. They also said that the rebels were not going to let the taxes be paid. From the two things you would infer that they were rebels killed at Manassas. They said they were risen from the dead, and that they were rebels, too." A man in South Carolina was awakened one night by a hammering at his door and voices demanding he come outside. Shadowy figures came forth, wanting to know how he'd voted in recent elections—whether for the radical Republicans or for the Democrats—and when he told them he'd voted Republican, one ghost stuck the barrel of a pistol under his chin and dragged him into the woods. There they demanded that he remove his shirt. "What do you all want to whip me for," he pleaded; "what have I done?" The figures replied, "Off with your shirt; if you don't you shall go dead. We come from Manassas graveyard; and by Christ we want to get back to our graveyard and cover up before day, by Christ." These ghosts then whipped him ten to fifteen times, by his recollection, before releasing him, telling him, "You must promise to vote the democratic ticket, or you go dead before we leave you."

What began in Pulaski, Tennessee, as a series of pranks—born when a few bored Confederate veterans formed a club whose only mandate was that its members "have fun, make mischief, and play pranks on the public"—grew quickly into the nation's first major terrorist organization, focused chiefly on harassing recently freed slaves and the Northerners who'd come to empower them. The six founders took their name from a gibberish distortion of the Greek for "circle," *kuklos*, adding the word "Klan" at the end to emphasis their Scottish heritage: the Ku Klux Klan, a name instantly mysterious, terrifying, what one founder described as the sound of "bones rattling together."

In its first incarnation the Klan led a regime of terror throughout the South, harassing, beating, torturing, and killing hundreds and thousands in their quest to maintain white supremacy. With an economy built on the exploitation of free labor, the South in the years following the Civil War was left not only with a ravaged and defeated landscape but with its most fundamental economic structure invalidated by the Emancipation Proclamation and the Thirteenth Amendment. The sharecropping system, and eventually Jim Crow laws, would become proxies for slavery in the sense that, for all Southern whites' racism toward the black community, these freed slaves were still vital to the economy and could not be allowed to migrate to the North. Just as slave owners had prevented blacks from escaping prior to the Civil War, it now became equally imperative to discourage this movement among liberated slaves, a job taken up by the Klan.

It was an enforcement that relied heavily on the presence of ghosts. The man who woke in the middle of the night to find a ghost from Shiloh demanding water was later identified only as a "radical negro," as were most of the victims of the Klan. Members would arrive at the home of a black family in the dead of night, dressed in sheets or other makeshift costumes (the formal robes associated with the Klan would come much later), claiming to be the ghosts of Confederate soldiers killed at various battles. Often stories of these visits would involve some sort of simple stage magic trickery: a skeletal hand would be inserted in a robe so that when a Klansman offered to shake someone's hand, they would get instead a disembodied hand. Another common ruse involved rigging an oilskin bag beneath the robe with a hose going to the mouth so the Klansman could appear to drink voluminous amounts of water.

Whether or not these stage tricks were actually employed or just folktales told by the Klan is a matter of much debate. Even if the stories were real, it's doubtful that such rudimentary jokes were believable. As Wyn Craig Wade notes in his history of the Klan, despite the stereotype of black people being more susceptible to superstition than whites, "the Klan legends of terrified 'darkies' scurrying from ghosts of the Confederate dead probably say more about the aggrandizement of the white ego than about black gullibility." Put another way, it's probable that a freedman awakened in the middle of the night by a (likely) drunk Confederate veteran pretending to be a ghost had plenty to be frightened of that was not supernatural. Wade notes that "it has been suggested that blacks might have played into the Klansmen's hands, hoping that their feigned fright would avert a more violent form of intimidation. It then becomes a question of who was controlling whom."

How often these implausible-sounding pranks were actually employed, and what psychological effect they had on their victims, might never be fully known. But the spectral aspect of the Klan was one of its defining features in its early years. Central goals were to keep liberated slaves in the South to prop up the economy and to keep out white "carpetbaggers" who'd come to provide education and resources to newly liberated slaves. As Gladys-Marie Fry notes in her book *Night Riders in Black Folk History*, "The concept of returning Confederate dead was meant to suggest that the slave regime had not ended, though the South was subdued, and that former controls were still being perpetrated." If anything, the goal was to prove that these ghosts were even more powerful, having returned from the grave and been elevated to a new supernatural status. Southern whites tried—usually unsuccessfully—to convince freedmen and -women that moving north was futile, since spirits of the Confederate dead could follow them anywhere, no longer limited by their physical bodies. In Edward H. Dixon's fantastical novel *The Terrible Mysteries of the Ku-Klux-Klan*, a Klan leader proudly proclaims, "The Klux is the living dead, and it is the strength of weakness. Bound hand and foot with cords that gall and eat into running sores the dead flesh, the living Klux riseth and walketh abroad in the black night."

The use of ghosts as a means of social control predated the Klan. Slave owners employed so-called patterollers, usually poor whites, who would patrol the countryside at night; such patrols would regularly use spook stories, among other tactics, to help keep enslaved people from escaping. "The fraudulent ghost," Fry writes, "was the first in a gradually developed system of night-riding creatures, the fear of which was fostered by whites for the purpose of slave control." A man in a white sheet on horseback riding ominously through a forest could help substantiate rumors that the forest was haunted and that those who valued their lives best avoid it. By spreading ghost stories, Southern whites hoped to limit the unauthorized movement of black people. If cemeteries, crossroads, and forests came to be known particularly as haunted, it's because they presented the easiest means of escape and had to be patrolled.

Now it's common to think of such places as the provenance of spirits. We have stories for such places: a tragic death, forlorn lovers, a devil waiting to make a deal—stories that reflect a rich tradition of American folklore. But all this might have come much later, and these places might have first earned their haunted reputation through much more deviant methods. In the ghost-haunted legacies of many of these public spaces lies a hidden history of patrolling and limiting access. These should be places more or less open to all—meeting points, thoroughfares, public property, the sacred resting places of the dead. But in many parts of the country where access to these places have long been restricted, the spirits of the dead have been marshaled as one more weapon to be used by an invisible army.

CHAPTER THIRTEEN

THE WIND THROUGH CATHEDRAL PARK

Portland, OR

In the video there is first the image of kids, their flashlights to their chins, then giggling in the darkness. One is named Isaiah, another Vinnie, the third Jamison—beyond that there's not much more information about them. They could be in their early twenties, but they continue to giggle like schoolchildren. The camera drops, there's fumbling. They could be drunk, high. They're clearly enjoying themselves, barely keeping it together.

They are beneath the St. Johns Bridge in Portland, Oregon. Portland's bridges are so spectacular that one of the city's many nicknames is "Bridge City," but St. Johns is perhaps its most beautiful. A dual suspension bridge patinaed in copper green, it rises above the Willamette River like a smaller, more refined Golden Gate Bridge. On the west side it crosses over NW St. Helens Road before meeting NW Bridge Avenue; on the east side of the river the bridge towers above a gentle slope, descending gracefully into Portland's St. Johns district.

The land under the bridge on the east side is now called Cathedral Park, named for the sweeping gothic arches that form the supports for the bridge above it. It captures a great deal of the city's scenic beauty: the gently flowing river, the hints of industrialization dwarfed by the mountains and the evergreens all around. It is, though, surprisingly noisy: the cars rushing by a hundred feet above your head and the wind coursing through the gothic arches all around you combine to create a sense of voices and howlings that accompany you throughout the park. On the bridge's supports signs blare out warnings: DANGER: FALLING OBJECTS, PARK AT YOUR OWN RISK.

The kids who have made this YouTube video are there for the ghost of Thelma Taylor. In 1949 Taylor, then fifteen years old, was abducted from under the bridge. At the time there was no park, just dirt, junk, and bushes spilling out in all directions. Taylor was hitching a ride to a summer job when she was picked up by Morris Leland, a twenty-two-year-old drifter.

A week after Taylor's disappearance, police pulled Leland over for stealing a car and took him down to the police station, where, without prompting, he asked to talk to a homicide detective. He proceeded to make a full confession, describing in detail how he'd murdered Taylor, covered her body in driftwood, and wiped his prints off her lunch pail before leaving the scene. He offered to take the police to the place where he'd left her remains. Until that moment he was just a petty criminal who'd stolen a few cars. The murder of Thelma Taylor was something else entirely, and it was weighing on him when he blurted out his confession to the detective. He was tried in 1951, quickly found guilty, and sentenced to death. After several unsuccessful appeals, Leland went to Oregon's gas chamber in 1953.

The stories told about Taylor are predictably gruesome: she was raped and tortured for seven days, they say, before she was finally killed. "Oh yeah," one diner owner told the local news in a 2013 special about the murdered girl, "I've been down there at night and heard her scream, 'Help me, help me—somebody help me!'" This is why people come to find Taylor: they want the chills that go with a brush with death, the intoxication that comes with being close to mortality. Writer Andy Weeks, in his guide *Haunted Oregon*, advises that you "visit the area and see if you can hear the unearthly screams of now-deceased Thelma. They won't be pretty sounds if you hear them, but ones that will make your skin crawl." What better way to spend a chilly evening than trying to scare yourself into feeling alive?

The screams you may hear at Cathedral Park, screams that twine themselves with the wind as it whips up from the water and through the arches of the St Johns Bridge, come, so they say, from the bridge itself, from the massive stone pylons anchoring the span looming above you. When Thelma Taylor was murdered, the theory goes, the bridge itself "recorded" the event and now plays back the horror it once witnessed.

As the guidebook *Ghosthunting Oregon* claims, paranormal researchers say Cathedral Park is an area "primed for a haunting": the water from the river and the limestone blocks used to build St. Johns Bridge are associated with a phenomenon called residual haunting. Also sometimes called the stone tape theory, the belief is that certain inanimate objects are primed to record imprints of certain action that they then play back later. As *Ghosthunting Oregon* puts it, "Inanimate materials, such as stone, can absorb energy from the living, much as a tape recorder absorbs the voice of the living, especially during episodes of high tension, anxiety, and fear. Once this energy is stored, it can also be released, resulting in the display, or replay, of the recorded events."

The residual haunting theory was first popularized by an anthropologist named T. C. Lethbridge, whose career began to decline as he became more and more obsessed with ghosts and spirits. His 1961 book *Ghost and Ghoul* offered no room for skeptics ("The question is not whether people see ghosts or not. There is ample evidence that they do so") and turned instead to a mechanism that could explain spirits, a mechanism that relied less on the afterlife and more on the psychic abilities of the living. Rather than see spirits as distinct entities, capable of agency and will after death, he argued that we the living act as spiritual television projectors, capable of sending ideas mentally that are then picked up by others and interpreted as ghosts. The majority of ghosts, Lethbridge concluded, "are no more than mental pictures produced by living people," and in the burgeoning technology of television he found a perfect metaphor. Ghosts, he concluded, "appear to be no more and no less than television pictures. The television picture is a man-made ghost."

Lethbridge wasn't the first to propose such an idea. Sir Oliver Lodge, in his 1908 book *Man and the Universe*, speaks of how a haunted house has "photographed" a past tragedy. But Lethbridge's ideas caught fire in England, perhaps because of the strong association with television, and in 1972 BBC Two broadcast a made-for-TV film, *The Stone Tape*, inspired by Lethbridge's idea of television ghosts. A team of scientists who've relocated to new headquarters in a Victorian mansion with a reputation of being haunted discover that the ghosts they're seeing are a sort of playback loop of an earlier tragedy. The stone tape's playback abilities depend greatly on the individual acting as the receiver—haunting here, in its simplest form, is a psychic interplay between place and person, between a past tragedy and a present witness's ability to attune herself to that tragedy.

In this version of haunting, ghosts are not able to harm or otherwise disturb the living, even though the images called forth may be traumatic or terrifying. With many of the ghost hunters I've talked to, from California to Louisiana, residual haunting is put forth as the most popular explanation for hauntings, even if its mechanism is as implausible as the Spiritualist version of ghosts. It holds out the promise that no matter how creepy the environment, the ghost hunter won't be harmed, and yet still manages to give people the thrill they want to feel that much more alive.

The kind of ghost that haunts Cathedral Park, local ghost researcher Jefferson Davis told me, is an important question. "Is it a remnant spirit, is it a self-aware spirit, or is it something else?" Davis was born in the Pacific Northwest, and he has been fascinated with ghosts from an early age. He describes himself as a "comfortable skeptic": "I believe in the possibility," he said, but he hasn't seen or heard anything that he believes beyond a shadow of a doubt to be confirmation of the paranormal. "I'm just waiting for something to happen."

Davis's background is in anthropology, so he's trained to see ghost stories as expressions of larger cultural trends and indicative of communal beliefs. If the traditional ghost story formula involves a restless ghost, a task left undone, an injustice not yet addressed, the residual haunting formula doesn't require this—Thelma Taylor's killer, after all, was brought to justice, and so her spirit need not call out to the living to aid her.

The Cathedral Park ghost instead seems to exist as a cautionary tale. Local historian Jim Speirs, who grew up in North Portland, didn't remember much about the murder when he first began writing about Thelma Taylor for the *St. Johns Review* in 2009. "What I do recall is a vague, scary story that circulated around Roosevelt when I attended school there in the 60's," he later wrote. "That tale was of a ghost that haunted the bowels of the St. Johns Bridge . . . and that the place was to be avoided." This, of course, was easy enough to do, since at the time there was no park; "the area," Speirs remembered, "was acres of tangled wild blackberries, stunted trees, abandoned cars, piles of garbage, menacing underbrush, and passing hobo derelicts."

Taylor's story is important for someone like Davis precisely because it's a true story that nonetheless has all the hallmarks of a fictitious urban legend. "A lot of hauntings are not symbolic, a lot of hauntings really happened, and that's what makes it interesting," Davis told me, speaking specifically to how a story like this blurs drama and melodrama, making the archetypal aspects of Thelma's story so closely intertwined with facts that it becomes hard to separate the two.

⤜⟳⟲⤛

Erik Meharry isn't sure exactly when he became interested in Thelma Taylor. He'd grown up just outside Portland, and like most kids in the area, he knew the story as just something to scare kids from hitchhiking, nothing specific. Now he works as an investigator for the public defender's office, but at the time he began delving into the life of Thelma Taylor, he was working at a mortuary. ("I got in the funeral business by accident," he told me; "they needed someone to pick up the bodies.") On-call for twenty-four hours at a time, he was living in the funeral home, and at some point—though he says it was unrelated to his job—he became deeply interested in Taylor's life. He doesn't remember exactly what it was that caught his attention. "Mostly," he said, "I just felt *bad* for her."

He started researching—collecting news clippings and trial records, stuff that went beyond the urban legends and ghost stories. For all the belief that Taylor haunts Cathedral Park, Meharry learned that she was killed eight blocks away from the bridge. She wasn't raped, and though it was a week before Leland was caught and confessed, the murder itself happened the morning after the kidnapping; there was no prolonged imprisonment.

In 2012 Meharry put up a Facebook page about Taylor, mainly to keep her memory alive but also to sort out the truth from the lore. On September 25, 2012, about eight months after he'd launched the page, he received a message from a woman named Paulette Jarrett. It was brief and to the point: "Thelma Taylor is my sister—who are you?"

⁓⊙⌒⌒

In an oft-quoted passage from his book *Lies Across America*, James W. Loewen writes of a distinction between the dead made by Kiswahili speakers in east and central Africa:

> According to John Mbiti, Kiswahili speakers divide the deceased into two categories: sasha and zamani. The recently departed whose time on earth overlapped with people still here are the sasha, the living-dead. They are not wholly dead, for

they still live in the memories of the living, who can call them to mind, create their likeness in art, and bring them to life in anecdote. When the last person to know an ancestor dies, that ancestor leaves the sasha for the zamani, the dead. As generalized ancestors, the zamani are not forgotten but revered. . . . But they are not living-dead. There is a difference.

Loewen uses this distinction to critique the historical problems in many of the monuments and markers that dot the country. While history is most accurately documented while it is in living memory—the sasha—civic monuments are often products of zamani, and they are, for Loewen, ideologically loaded: "Not primarily motivated by loss or grief, zamani monuments and markers usually go up to serve the political exigencies of the time of their erection." Memorials honoring Confederate war heroes, or the victims of 9/11—hashed out and argued over, long delayed and deployed by politicians for any number of personal ends—typify the kind of zamani monument that has little connection to the actual dead or loss that a sasha monument, like a temporary roadside memorial or a simple gravestone, might honor.

While Loewen is primarily concerned with public monuments, his distinction gives us another lens for understanding ghost stories and how those stories evolve over time. As I've gathered ghost stories over the past decade, I've seen historical specificity reduced to the same clichés and melodrama over and over again. Ghost stories become, in this light, a kind of fetishization of the past, detached from the actual history—a kind of frozen moment in which all of the past mirrors itself. The French philosopher Jean Baudrillard once wrote, "It is not the passion (whether of objects or subjects) for substances that speaks in fetishism, it is the *passion for the code*," and in the melodramatic ghosts we find a passion not for individual stories or histories so much as for a certain set of clichés repeated over and over again. This is the effect of zamani memory: without first-person accounts, without personal memories, the stories become monuments that must serve larger purposes.

~~∽∽◦∽∽~~

Case in point: Cathedral Park itself. One obviously false aspect of the story of Thelma Taylor is where she died: not in the park but some eight blocks away. And yet, despite being easily disproven, the incorrect location has become an integral part of the legend. Why in particular does this fallacy persevere?

The bridge was opened in 1931. But despite such fanfare, the park itself was not built until the 1970s and not dedicated until May 1980. The decision to turn this land into a park was an attempt to capitalize on the dead space under the bridge's long span and to eradicate the kind of forces that might otherwise gather in such dead spaces.

Parks like Cathedral Park are part of a general movement in urban planning under the rubric of what's called adaptive reuse: otherwise-dead zones in the city that have been repurposed. Perhaps the most famous and successful example is the High Line in New York City, an elevated railway trestle that's been converted into a linear park. The idea here is to convert eyesores into habitable spaces.

Adaptive reuse projects have of course also included former Kirkbride asylums, and as with those asylums, it should come as little surprise that many projects bear haunted legacies. A local tour company offers a haunted tour of the High Line, with stories of ghosts like a mysterious figure who lived below the tracks, a "West Side Cowboy" who fell to his death, and various children who died and now haunt the park. Another adaptive reuse project in New York, lower Manhattan's Battery Park, is also haunted, this one by vice president Aaron Burr and his daughter, Theodosia. These buildings and parks attract ghosts because they *are* ghosts: once abandoned, they've been reconstituted, given a new life after death. It shouldn't be surprising that stories of the past cling to them, manifesting themselves in ghost stories and unexplained occurrences.

Cathedral Park, a place that feels new and refurbished but can't entirely cover up the scar of what it was before, was always destined to be haunted. It can't escape the monstrous bridge looming above it, the incongruity of the bustle of traffic and the park environs. It can't escape the wind that tears through it at all hours, the wail and moan that rushes through it. Even had Thelma Taylor never come here at all, one way or another Cathedral Park would've found its ghost.

❧

Kevin Brockmeier's 2006 *The Brief History of the Dead* literalizes the difference between sasha and zamani; it takes place in the city of the sasha dead. In the novel it's the place where those newly deceased go while someone alive still remembers them, a place they leave only once there is no one left alive to keep them in living memory. Thelma Taylor belongs here, in a very different city of the dead than where most ghosts roam. Victorian ladies, Confederate soldiers, silent film starlets—they may have descendants, but they aren't kept alive in living memory. Thelma Taylor's story is unlike many I've come across, simply because there are still so many who remember her.

After Jim Speirs first wrote about Taylor in the *St. Johns Review*, he received several e-mails from people who remembered her in life. Having awakened memories decades old, he collected various e-mails he'd received in a blog post; one woman remembered Taylor from grade school and attending her funeral; "even though Morris had been caught," she wrote, "we were still scared stiff." The murder changed the landscape, turning the world from a place of wonder to one of deep suspicion. While North Portland high schoolers once went to the bridge for expansive views of the Willamette as it flowed into the city, they stopped going near the bridge altogether after the murder. "My friend Thelma is still down there, and I don't care how good the music becomes, or how pretty the park is, I will NEVER step on that land again!" George Parrish remembered Taylor as well: "She was skinny and underdeveloped, but that's just the odd age she was when I knew her. We were classmates . . . but I don't remember much about her, and doubt if I'd remember her at all if she hadn't been killed."

Another man e-mailed Speirs about the killer himself. "It's been a long time," Bill Grubb told Speirs, "but we knew Leland was weird, he didn't have any friends that I can recall, and he was always doing something stupid. . . . He always had a knife, and that made us weary [sic] of him . . . he was always playing with a knife."

Paulette Jarrett was only three years old when her sister was murdered, but she still has two clear memories: one of Thelma sitting outside with her friends, and another of finding her in the living room chewing gum and asking for a piece. "So she pulls it out of her mouth and hands it to me," she told me. "Well, I had a screaming fit, I did not want something out of her mouth—I wanted my own piece! And of course Mom comes around the corner, asking what the heck's going on, and Thelma said, 'Well, she asked for gum, so I gave it to her and she refused it.'" As a memory on its own, it's not much, but it's a snippet of a life, of a person who could be more than just the story of her death. Jarrett still has a cache of photos of her sister—dressed in their father's uniform, posing for a school portrait, living the life of a perfectly normal teenager. Jarrett, who spent the rest of her childhood sheltered because her mother wouldn't allow her to go anywhere by herself, told me that mostly she wonders how Thelma would have turned out if she'd lived. "I just wish I'd known her a little better."

❧

The ghost stories that swarm around Thelma Taylor suggest what happens when an actual life maps too closely on an urban legend. Taylor's disappearance and murder became a warning about hitchhiking or loitering in desolate places. The details were never terribly important—the important thing was to scare people into listening. It was an easy conversion from a life to a lesson, from sasha to zamani, from the messy world of a human being's thoughts, desires, and memories to a cautionary tale.

When I asked Davis about whether it was ethical to give tours or tell stories about Taylor's death, he seemed somewhat conflicted by the genuine moral conundrums involved. "None of us wants to set out to ruin the day—or the month or the year—of someone else's life, like the family member of someone who's been killed." Like many ghost hunters I've interviewed, Davis genuinely believes that his work is not exploitive, that he does his best to get out the true story, to report terrible events without sensationalizing them, without trying to make a buck off of someone else's trauma. At the same time, though, he told me, he maintains his right to tell these stories, since no matter what you do, "People will get offended and misunderstand."

Only when I mentioned the video I'd seen, of the kids in the park trying to contact Taylor's ghost, did Davis push back sharply. "The people smiling and laughing," he said, "they're having a quasi-religious experience: they're trying to contact the other side. You can't gauge from a video what's going on in someone else's mind."

"Have fun with it," said Meharry. "Why not? If you want to go have fun, as long as you're not hurting anyone else, knock yourself out." He admitted that Taylor and the bridge is a good story: an archetypal ghost story about a young girl's tragedy. But then he paused and looked off. "But I've spent so much time on Thelma Taylor, and I know her family, so I'm kinda on guard and a little bit defensive.

"Do it with other ghost stories," he said finally, "but leave this one alone."

Myself, I tend to think of ghost stories as a natural way of preserving—or at least attempting to preserve—a history that might otherwise go unnoticed and forgotten. The story of Cathedral Park, like too many ghost stories, blurs the fact in favor of gory inventions and puts a premium on the thrill of the ghost hunt, the brush with death, rather than on the actual life that was lost in 1949.

At the same time that it's a personal story for this family, it's also a civic story, a story about a community, and the ghost of Cathedral Park isn't merely a cheap stunt, a sensationalized grab for cash. As a cautionary tale, it's a legend that encourages teenagers to turn down rides from strangers, and even if we just leave it here, the ghost story of Thelma Taylor isn't a bad thing. If the casual reiteration of that story—handed down from generation to generation, unmoored from specificity and unnaturally gruesome—helps to prevent another death like hers, it's worth it . . . even if there are those who'd wish it would wait at least until she leaves the city of Sasha and enters the land of Zamani.

❧

As I was researching for this book, I was startled to find myself reading about a longtime friend's fiancé. I'd never known him in life, because a few months before their marriage, he'd walked out onto the fourth-floor balcony of his college dorm and then shot himself, falling to the ground below.

More than fifteen years later his life has become a ghost story, his death an explanation for unexplained chills and creepy sensations that students feel in the dorm. As a legend it's so vague that it's hardly worth mentioning, except that behind the banality is a very real story and a man who left behind people who loved him.

I never expected to be this close to an urban legend. I'd certainly never expected that a friend's tragedy would become a ghost story in so few years. What was once a person's unbearable loss is now someone else's "strange noises and voices," a reminder of how quickly a personal tragedy can be molded, in the hands of strangers, into folklore, taking on a life of its own. Maybe the purpose of a story like this, the reason it gets told and retold, is to shine a light on the very real problem of college depression, to let those suffering know that they're not alone, to encourage them to find support.

More likely, it's just something to pass the time.

IV

USELESS MEMORY

cities and towns

I n the fall of 2004 I attended a conference in Binghamton, New York, almost two hundred miles from Manhattan along the Pennsylvania border. My flight arrived late at night, and I caught a cab to my hotel—a hotel that, when I had booked it, had been called the Ramada Limited, but by the time I arrived had been sold (Ramada no longer finding much of value in Binghamton) to a private operator. It was late but I was on West Coast time and still very much alert, and as we drove to the hotel the chatty cabdriver unfurled an endlessly depressing history of Binghamton.

Driving down Front Street toward my hotel, the cabdriver let me know, "This street used to be in the Guinness Book of Records for the most bars on a single street." A dubious claim (and one that several other towns also boast) but still impossible not to hear the pathos in his voice as he listed them as we drove: "That used to be a bar"—he gestured to an empty lot— "and that used to be a bar"—now a Laundromat—"and there, and there, and there, too. All gone now." He continued this the length of the empty, lifeless street. And then he told me about the curse.

No white person from Binghamton, he said, is ever able to leave. Even if you move away, sooner or later you'll be drawn back in. It's the curse on the city, he said, laid on it by the Native Americans who once lived here—revenge for the violence inflicted on them centuries ago, a revenge that is only now coming to fruition.

Binghamton is built on land once occupied by the Onondaga and Oneida people, who, along with the Mohawk, Cayuga, Seneca, and Tuscarora, once made up the Iroquois Confederacy. Most of these tribes sided with the British during the Revolutionary War, and in 1779 Major General John Sullivan led a contingent of American troops through the heart of New York in a scorched-earth campaign, laying waste to at least forty Iroquois villages throughout the state, including the Onondaga and Oneida land that is now Binghamton.

The curse, supposedly, is in the water itself, which saps the drinker of any desire to leave town. Binghamton doesn't have anything close to the reputation of other haunted cities, but mentions of the curse surface occasionally, often in the form of a joke: a lame excuse offered for those townies without the motivation to leave, a dumb anecdote to entertain friends. But the night I heard of it from the cabdriver who bore me into the town's heart, there was no mistaking the sadness in his words, the ache in his voice, as he tried to make sense of his town and what had happened to it.

Binghamton might have lost its bars and its jobs, but what it does have is carousel horses. The benevolent owner of the massive Endicott Johnson shoe factory had given back to the town generously, from building cinemas for his workers to donating six antique carousels for free public use in local parks; stand-alone horses also dot the downtown streets. Once meant to look jolly and inviting, they've taken on a different pallor amid the vacant storefronts. With their mouths open and their ears flared back, the horses could be screaming, or running from a fire—or trying to escape Binghamton itself.

Which is not to say that Binghamton doesn't have dreams of recovering. An investment in Binghamton University, part of the State University of New York system, has helped revitalize the local economy, and the population has stabilized. But the city sustained massive damage during floods in recent years and in 2009 was the site of a mass shooting, when a man named Jiverly Wong killed thirteen people and wounded four before turning his gun on himself. Wong, a Vietnamese immigrant who'd lived in the United States since the early '80s and had become a naturalized citizen, had been taking English classes at the American Civic Association, and on April 3, 2009, he returned to his former classroom and began killing his classmates, along with a substitute teacher. In a letter he'd mailed to a local news station shortly before the killings, Wong hinted that his deepening psychosis was at least in part due to low job prospects.

So Binghamton has experienced its share of hardships and tragedies, and a curse—stretching back as it does to the earliest confrontations between whites and Iroquois—encompasses all of them. Binghamton's troubles were due not to outsourcing or demographic shifts but to an age-old conflict, an act of revenge for violence committed more than two hundred years ago.

And what's more, the specific aspect of the haunting is unusual: rather than whites being driven from the land they wrongfully seized, they're not able to leave. The city in decline is a trap, a dead-end street. The curse on Binghamton renders the city a spectral penal colony, one whose borders are nebulous but still mystically enforced.

How does an entire city come to see itself as haunted? At what point does a city cease to simply have a few haunted buildings and instead begin to define itself as a haunted city?

※

Most cities commemorate their pasts, often with statues, plaques, renamed streets, or even parades. But cities that are haunted don't just try to keep the past alive; they seem to straddle past and present, as though two versions of the same city are overlaid on top of each other. To paraphrase Hamlet, hounded by the ghost of his father: time in these places is "out of joint." The past seethes in the streets, always on people's lips, always at the edge of one's vision. In such places the past may be dead but it isn't past.

Disjointed history can be a great way to raise money through tourism, as places like Salem, New Orleans, and Savannah have found, but only if that history can be packaged in a way that doesn't offend anyone. Savannah, for example, is famous for its ghosts and its glamorous, dark past, and many tour operators there do a brisk business in ghost tours—but, as former tour guide Elena Gormley later wrote of her experience, the ghost stories she recited would turn the city's turbulent past into a pleasant night's outing. "A few stories came across as fairly light," she wrote, "but most repackaged the rape, abuse, and lynching of vulnerable women into family friendly entertainment."

There are, for example, the stories surrounding the beautiful Sorrel-Weed House, an elegant Greek Revival mansion built in 1841 for Francis Sorrel, a prosperous plantation owner. Though married, Sorrel was secretly having an affair with one of his slaves, a Haitian woman named Molly. In 1860 his wife, Matilda, discovered the affair and threw herself out a third-story window, smashing her head on the paving stones below. Shortly thereafter, Molly was found hanging from a noose in the carriage house, another supposed suicide.

Not unlike the story of Chloe at the Myrtles Plantation, the tour script presents a well-worn version of the Jezebel narrative: a sexually aggressive black woman destabilizing a white man's marriage. Gormley offers another, far more plausible version of events: Francis's wife "may have committed suicide after she discovered her husband had raped his slave, and in the story, Molly's suffering didn't end there. At the tale's conclusion, a group of men, who some locals allege may have been Francis and his sons, lynched her."

As part of the tour script, Gormley would play an EVP recording provided for her that supposedly documented the paranormal screams of Molly from beyond the grave. "Help! Get out! Oh my God!" a disembodied voice on the tape would cry out, and whenever she would ask the guests what they'd heard, Gormley notes, the "white tourists always made smart comments. Once, on a charter tour for auto parts managers, a man yelled, 'Sounds like my regional manager!' His buddies all laughed."

Savannah, like a number of historic cities (New Orleans and Washington, D.C., among them), requires that anyone who gives a tour (ghost or otherwise) pass a test of the city's history. ("Where did Savannah's major Revolutionary War battle take place?" "At which cemetery can graves of the victims of the 1820 yellow fever outbreak be found?" "In which square is the Greene Monument located?") A way to ensure a base level of quality and lack of misinformation, it's notoriously difficult—the college professor who wrote it estimates that it would take three months of full-time studying to master.

But the real goal of the test seems to cement certain narratives of the city over others. Gormley believes that the test is ideologically slanted toward minimizing controversial or problematic aspects of the city's history in favor of things that portray it in a neutral or positive light. "The city's very obsessed with its brand," she told me. This may explain why several groups filed suit against the city, alleging that the test infringed on their right to free speech. "By limiting the universe of speakers to those who have memorized and regurgitated the City's official version of Savannah history," attorneys for the plaintiffs argued, "the City plainly hopes to ensure that tour guides draw upon that official narrative in their speech to tourists." In the fall of 2015 the city backed down, dropping the testing requirement and moving instead to restrict the available hours in which tour groups were allowed in primarily residential areas.

Of the Sorrel-Weed House the testing manual mentions only that it is a "distinguished" building built in 1841 on the southwest corner of Harris and Bull streets. There is no mention of Francis Sorrel's relationship with his slave Molly, nor of her death or the death of Sorrel's wife, Matilda. As Tiya Miles discovered when she began researching the house, the story probably is fictionalized. Miles hypothesizes that the Molly legend was concocted by brothers Stephen and Philip Bader sometime after they purchased the house in 1996 and began renovations (Stephen Bader, however, contends that he has documents attesting to the veracity of the story). Not only could they capitalize on Savannah's reputation, established by John Berendt's 1994 book *Midnight in the Garden of Good and Evil*, as a creepy, haunted city; they could also get away with a half-renovated house, she adds, playing up its ruined, gloomy state of disrepair as part of its haunted aura. And so, for all the city's emphasis on its daunting test of factually correct history, licensed tour companies still do a brisk business on fabricated stories and distortions.

❧

Binghamton isn't trading on its curse to sell tickets to walking tours (not yet, at least). For every city basing a tourist industry on its famous hauntings, there are a dozen other cities that have come to be known as haunted in a different way, one devoid of the charm and cheer of a Salem or Savannah. These cities are haunted by what they once were, what they might have been; towns haunted by some series of past failures or tragedies that encompass more than one or two buildings and swept up the whole city.

For better or worse, the language of hauntings and ghosts is a convenient metaphor for a whole host of problems not connected to the supernatural, and the recourse to such vocabulary becomes a means to process or make sense of experiences that can otherwise seem overwhelming and mystifying.

A city obsessed by its ghosts seems to be weighed down by a conflicted view of the past. Something close to melancholy: a weight it can't quite let go of, a lingering sadness. And though we don't often think of the United States in these terms, this melancholy is as much a part of our history as our triumphs.

CHAPTER FOURTEEN

THE WET GRAVE

New Orleans, LA

Walk through the streets of New Orleans, and you're beset on all sides by ghosts. In the French Quarter it's best early in the evening, when the day-trippers have gone home and what's left of the tourists have quarantined themselves on Bourbon Street or in tucked-away white-napkin restaurants. You can slip past these places into the gloom of old New Orleans, in and out of the pools of light from the streetlamps, in and out of the past.

Perhaps, if you are lucky, it'll be raining—the cool, clarifying rain that drives out the humidity and the tourists—and you'll be free to walk the cobblestones alone. Through the soft hum of the rain pelting the streets, you might hear a murmur of a song, something maybe coming from a nearby bar or perhaps somewhere more distant. Not something you'd hear at a bar. What folklorist Jeanne deLavigne described as "a song which rises like slow smoke from the heavy ashes of experience, fanned by the winds of perplexity."

New Orleans, Lafcadio Hearn once wrote, is a place that "actually resembles no other city on the face of the earth, yet it recalls vague memories of a hundred cities." You are at once in the arcades of nineteenth-century Paris or a Spanish port city and yet still in the bowels of a swamp.

The dampness only adds to the mystery, creating halos of mist around the lights, adding a heaviness to the air that you can't shake; it's a dampness that Hearn called "spectral, mysterious, inexplicable."

Soon the nightly ghost tours will be out, traipsing the quarter in clumps of fifteen to twenty people, gathering at corners to hear stories that stretch credulity but that have been honed through years of telling, polished to a high sheen for maximum intensity.

On the 700 block of Royal Street, a naked woman will appear on the roof of one building under the moonlight. Before and after the Civil War, white men sometimes kept octoroon mistresses—women who passed as white but who had an exotic charm about them. Because of the notorious one-drop rule (the notion that a single drop of black blood makes an individual black), such women could be discarded at will by wealthy men shuttling back to their wives or on to the next mistress. In this particular house, though, things turned out differently.

The wealthy Frenchman who lived here kept a mistress, whose name is sometimes given as Julie. He never saw her as anything more than a plaything, but she fell in love with him nonetheless. After repeatedly denying her entreaties to marry her, he devised a cruel prank and told her that if she lasted an entire night on the roof fully naked, he would marry her. Whether or not he thought that would be the end of it, he underestimated her resolve, and she ascended to the roof and disrobed, preparing to spend the night there to prove her love. At some point before dawn, she caught a chill, and she died shortly thereafter. She can still be seen, they say, when the moonlight is right. Not unlike the story of Chloe at the Myrtles Plantation, Julie is a stock character: the tragic mulatto who wants to join white society but is rebuffed by her white lover, with fatal consequences—a reminder that many of New Orleans's ghost stories are more concerned with affirming stereotypes than with offering proof of the paranormal.

Which is not to say that the city doesn't try hard to convince you it's haunted. As deLavigne wrote in the introductory note to her *Ghost Stories of Old New Orleans,* "There is not a corner of the city that does not harbor some unearthly visitor in one guise or another. They hug close as feathers on a bird." New Orleans is very haunted. New Orleans ghost hunter David Laville told me that the three-hundred-yard radius around Jackson Square is the most haunted place in the country. Asked why, he gives four reasons. First, because the city's so old. Second, its long history of tragedies: not just fires and floods but disastrous outbreaks of cholera and yellow fever, among other epidemics. Third, its history of violence: crime, of course, but the city is also known for public executions in the main square and a preponderance of duels to settle disputes. Fourth, all this activity has, for centuries, been packed into the tiny area of the French Quarter. He offers, finally, a fifth reason: "It's just a city that everybody loves, so, naturally, the people who lived and died here—they don't want to leave."

New Orleans's inordinate obsession with death stems in part from the constant dance it's had with the geology of the area; the city may be old, but the ground on which it stands is new. In a place with such a high water table, it's hard to bury corpses six feet under, so New Orleans is unique among American cities for its necropolises filled with elaborate—and aboveground—mausoleums. These cities of death parallel the city of the living: in places like St. Louis Cemetery #1, just across Basin Street from the French Quarter, family crypts have the stately grandeur of the fine villas they neighbor, though some have begun to majestically decay into ruins. Those who can't afford a grand crypt are entombed along the wall, in vaults sometimes referred to as "bake ovens."

New Orleans is particularly cruel to the corpse, whose bacteria thrive in the humid, temperate environment. A body in the Northeast or Midwest will keep longer, if it's winter; a body in the Southwest will dry out; but in the Pelican State the environment is perfect for the work of decay. In New Orleans you cannot avoid the fact of death and decomposition. The living and the dead have always occupied close quarters here, which helps explain why the city, over the years, has become death-haunted.

There are, of course, ghosts in St. Louis #2, as there are in all of New Orleans's graveyards and cemeteries. But you need not leave the French Quarter on a night like this to find ghosts. From Royal Street wend your way to the Hotel Provincial, on Chartres Street, which guides will tell you operated as a hospital during the Civil War. Countless men died within its walls, some from wounds received in battle but many from the barbaric methods of healing employed on them. Guests on the fifth floor claim to see a doctor, still in his bloodied apron, walking the halls. Forget for a moment that the building was operating during the war as a hair salon, according to journalist Paul Oswell. Allow yourself instead to be captivated by the city's spells, its love of the tall tale and legend, and let yourself be carried on past the Hotel Provincial to the corner of Governor Nicholls and Royal.

On the southeastern corner stands a particularly majestic building, the highlight of any ghost tour in the French Quarter, a place of legend: the Lalaurie Mansion.

∼⌒◦⌒∼

The Lalaurie Mansion is larger than many of the houses in the French Quarter, its façade stretching down both streets. It's been a part of New Orleans's tourist industry for more than a century; by the 1890s the mansion was already being advertised as a haunted house. An Italian immigrant who bought it in 1893, Fortunato Greco, complained that its "reputation for spooks" had rendered it unsalable. In order to make a profit off his white elephant, he hung signs announcing that it was not haunted and charged people ten cents if they wanted to come in and see for themselves. Within a few years he'd made enough on ghost tours that he opened a thematic bar on the ground floor, the Haunted Exchange. In the early twentieth century the building was cut up into tenement slums and occupied by immigrant Italian and Sicilian families; the tradition continued, children charging five cents for tours of the haunted house while they dragged chains across the attic floor and ran past windows dressed in sheets. In an 1895 guide to New Orleans, Henry C. Castellanos wrote that while "no spirits wander through its wide halls," there was indeed a curse on the house "that follows every one who has ever attempted to make it a permanent habitation . . . every venture has proved a ruinous failure." That curse may help explain why actor Nicolas Cage, who bought the house in 2006, lost it to foreclosure only three years later.

The house was built in 1831 by Delphine and Louis Lalaurie. Louis was her third husband. Delphine's first marriage had been to Ramon López y Ángulo de la Candelaria, when she was fourteen and he was a thirty-five-year-old widower. López y Ángulo died in a shipwreck five years later, while Delphine was pregnant with their child. The day she turned twenty (March 7, 1805), she married again, to another widower more than twice her age. Her second husband, Jean Paul Blanque, died in 1815, leaving her a widow once more. Having inherited considerable real estate holdings upon her mother's death, she was already wealthy when she met Louis Lalaurie, a doctor, with whom she had a child out of wedlock before marrying him in 1828. The marriage, according to friends, was not a happy one. As the young doctor was still establishing his medical practice, their lavish lifestyle was funded by his wife's considerable real estate holdings and other assets. By 1832 their marriage had grown so intolerable that she petitioned a judge to allow the couple to reside separately.

It was during her third marriage that Delphine's reputation for beating slaves emerged. Several times in the late 1820s and early 1830s she was accused of what a neighbor termed "barbarous treatment of her slaves contrary to law": willfully mistreating them, incarcerating them, and depriving them of necessities.* Despite these allegations Lalaurie repeatedly

---

*While it's true that there were laws against the mistreatment of slaves, it would be a stretch to draw from this that New Orleans was a place where enslaved blacks had it good. According to Article 38 of the city's Code Noir, a slave absent without leave for one month would "have his ears cut off and [be] branded on one shoulder with the fleur-de-lys; if he is guilty of a second offense . . . , he shall be hamstrung and also branded with the fleur-de-lys on the other shoulder, and a third time, he will be put to death."

escaped prosecution, since testimony by slaves against whites was inadmissible. Court records don't preserve the specifics of her alleged crimes, but what is clear is that an unusually high number of her slaves died while they were owned by her. Later apologists tried to justify this by asserting that Delphine Lalaurie's mother was killed at the hands of slaves, either in the Saint-Domingue slave rebellion or by family slaves—but neither of these stories bears any ring of truth.

The Lalaurie legend truly begins on the morning of Thursday, April 10, 1834, with a fire. It broke out first in the kitchen, on the first floor of the outbuilding. A crowd quickly gathered, both firefighters and dozens of concerned onlookers, as the flames quickly started to spread to the slave quarters above the kitchen.

A local judge asked Delphine's husband for permission to have the slaves moved to a place of safety and was met with a harsh rebuke. "There are those who would be better employed," Louis spat at him, "if they would attend to their own affairs instead of officiously intermeddling with the concerns of other people." Neighbors already believed that the slave quarters were operated by the Lalauries as something of a prison, and the judge, thankfully, ignored the doctor's insult and had the doors to the slave quarters broken down. Rescuers found a horrible sight: "several wretched negroes," reported the *Louisiana Courier*, "their bodies covered with scars and loaded with chains." The *New Orleans Bee* gave a similar account, of "seven slaves, more or less horribly mutilated . . . suspended by the neck with their limbs stretched and torn from one extremity to the other. . . . They had been confined . . . for several months in the situation from which they had thus been providentially rescued, and had merely been kept in existence to prolong their sufferings and to make them taste all that the most refined cruelty could inflict." An elderly woman claimed to the mayor that she had been the one who'd set the house on fire, "with the intention of terminating the sufferings of herself and her companions, or perishing in the flames."

It was too much for the people of New Orleans to take. Even in a city that was built on slave labor, whose slave markets—the largest in the country—were a symbol of the vile predation on black bodies by speculators and planters, the cruelty found at the Lalaurie Mansion and the desperate act of an old woman struck a deep chord. The *Bee* reported that after Delphine's slaves were removed from the house and taken to the jail for their safety, "at least two thousand persons visited the jail to be convinced . . . of the sufferings experienced by these unhappy ones. Several have also seen the instruments which were used by these villains: pincers that were applied to their victims to make them suffer all manner of tortures, iron collars with sharpened points, and a number of other instruments for punishment impossible to describe." The newspapers did their part to whip the citizens into a frenzy; the *Louisiana Advertiser* editorialized its hope that "justice will be done and the guilty be brought to punishment."

It was too late for justice: the Lalauries had already fled. They left their home the afternoon of the fire, first making their way to New York City, then crossing the Atlantic on their way to France. By the time the mob arrived at the mansion, Delphine and her husband were already gone, so a crowd "composed of all classes and colors" broke in and destroyed everything in sight. According to the *Bee*, the riot "continued unabated for the whole of the evening" and into the next morning. By the time the sheriff dispersed the mob, nearly the entire edifice of the building had been pulled down, and all that was left of the house was its walls.

Delphine Lalaurie died in Paris, in exile, in 1849. Her remains were eventually repatriated to New Orleans. Despite the outrage of the people of New Orleans regarding the treatment of the Lalauries' slaves, the newspapers of the period are entirely silent on what happened to them after they were rescued.

Judging by contemporary news reports, it's clear that the Lalauries' treatment of their slaves was absolutely horrific, without excuse. They displayed an utter savagery and indifference toward their fellow men and women, which they hid behind a veneer of civilized society. But what is also undeniably clear is that in the decades since that 1834 fire, the accounts of the Lalaurie Mansion have been consistently amplified and exaggerated as storytellers and historians have continued to pile atrocity on top of atrocity, blurring the historical record in a way that does no small amount of insult to the actual victims of Delphine and her husband.

As the house has become known as haunted, Delphine Lalaurie has come to be seen as a figure of monstrous duality: both her elegance and her sadism have been exaggerated for effect. Herbert Asbury (author of *Gangs of New York*) wrote of her that "this bewitching and engaging creature, who entertained the great of New Orleans at her sumptuous table and fascinated her guests by the brilliance of her wit, in reality had the heart of a sadistic demon and was unquestionably mad." Jeanne deLavigne, in her inimitable style, writes:

> Madame Lalaurie, under her soft and beautiful exterior, possessed a demon's soul. Laughing and lovely to her friends and family, she would suddenly fly into rages which none but her slaves ever saw. On these occasions (which were by no means rare), her sadistic appetite seemed never appeased until she had inflicted on one or more of her black servitors some hideous form of torture. As her word was law in that house, and as she had the power to punish in ways far more excruciating than mere death, she could command and receive assistance in her diabolical drama.

In deLavigne's telling, the first responders to that fateful fire found naked men chained to the wall, "their eyes gouged out, their fingernails pulled off by the roots"; others "had their joints skinned and festering, great holes in their buttocks where the flesh had been sliced away, their ears hanging by shreds, their tongues drawn out and sewed to their chins, severed hands stitched to bellies," and on and on. Women whose orifices were crammed with ash and chicken offal, or smeared with honey to attract masses of ants. "There were holes in skulls, where a rough stick had been inserted to stir the brains."

This is how Lalaurie's reputation has solidified over the years: as a figure of barbaric cruelty par excellence, a Creole Marquise de Sade. Despite some attempts at rehabilitation by the white community, and by Lalaurie's own descendants, in the first half of the twentieth century, this is the image of her that endures. This is how she is portrayed by Kathy Bates in *American Horror Story*: not just cruel but a sadist beyond compare, one who reduces black bodies into objects.

It's not clear why subsequent accounts of the Lalaurie Mansion have exaggerated this story to such a great degree. The imprisonment and barbaric conditions of those enslaved apparently became, at some point, insufficient to raise the pity and sympathy of visitors. Why were the actual crimes not enough?

⌒⌒⊙⌒⌒

Writing of New Orleans's history, the scholar Joseph Roach notes that here "memory operates as both quotation and invention, an improvisation on borrowed themes, with claims on the future as well as the past." Ghosts are part of the city's tourism now, like jazz and voodoo, brothels and booze. If places like Richmond, Virginia, have built a tourist industry by effacing certain aspects of their past, New Orleans has thrived by trumpeting these same aspects, though in the process there are bound to be inventions alongside the quotations, elaborations accompanying the documentation.

The city has always used its black culture as a commodity, taking living culture from the fringes and repackaging it for tourists in the French Quarter. Jazz, pioneered by poor blacks living in brothels, is now an upscale entertainment. The dynamic religious practices of the city, which combine Catholicism, evangelical Protestantism, and voodoo, are flattened out and reduced solely to the exoticism of voodoo, which is further misrepresented. And while Disneyland has borrowed the culture and aesthetics of the French Quarter for its "New Orleans Square," the opposite could also be said: New Orleans has borrowed heavily from Disneyland's tactics and aesthetics, in creating a French Quarter that exudes a mysterious allure while promising safety for tourists.

For those of us who don't live there, the image of New Orleans that comes to mind is that of a bifurcated city. In the French Quarter one finds music, laughter, excess, and fun while beyond its invisible walls lie the specter of poverty and crime. As welcoming as Louisiana's tourist board assures the city is, tour operators and guidebooks also warn about straying too far from the quarter. A recent Fodor's guide to New Orleans, for example, recommends a visit to St. Louis Cemetery #3 for its beautiful sepulchral architecture and its ghost stories but also cautions, "This is a higher crime area, so take a group tour to see it." For all the violence described on a typical New Orleans ghost tour, this violence is contrasted against ominous warnings of a different kind of violent experience. And by telling tales of two cities, New Orleans's tourist industry only further heightens the economic disparity of the city.

Scholar Anna Hartnell refers to the French Quarter as a "site of translation," in which the living, breathing aspects of the city—complicated, ambiguous, sometimes dangerous, but also palpably alive—are translated into a safe commodity to experience in easily digestible packages. Anthropologist Helen A. Regis more bluntly calls this "spatial apartheid." The ghost stories are part of this mythmaking, of packaging the city for consumption, not unlike the branding of Salem. They tread on the city's violent past while sectioning off that violence into a distant, romanticized past, a past that no longer has any connection to the city's actual politics, racial relations, or history.

❧❧❧

The Lalaurie Mansion offers a particularly stark example of this. For years it was left as a ruin. When Harriet Martineau, the English sociologist who abhorred slavery and used her travelogues to urge its abolition, visited New Orleans in 1836, she stumbled upon what was left of the house. "The house stands, and is meant to stand, in its ruined state," she later wrote. "It was the strange sight of its gaping windows and empty walls, in the midst of a busy street, which excited my wonder, and was the cause of my being told the story, the first time." Asking around, Martineau gathered eyewitness accounts and other local lore, filling in the gaps of the story of the house, but she was "requested on the spot not to publish it as exhibiting a fair specimen of slave-holding in New Orleans"; Lalaurie's crimes could be held up only as an exception, not the rule. This, Martineau was willing to concede, but she quickly added that "it is a revelation of what, may happen in a slave-holding country, and can happen nowhere else. Even on the mildest supposition that the case admits of,—that Madame Lalaurie was insane, there remains the fact that the insanity could have taken such a direction, and perpetrated such deeds nowhere but in a slave country."

But even left as a ruin, Lalaurie Mansion wasn't considered haunted. It wouldn't acquire that reputation until the publication of a short piece by George Washington Cable, "The 'Haunted House' in Royal Street," which appeared in 1889. In Cable's telling, the house exudes an uneasy aura:

> The house is very still. As you stand a moment in the middle of the drawing-room looking at each other you hear the walls and floors saying those soft nothings to one another that they so often say when left to themselves. While you are looking straight at one of the large doors that lead into the hall its lock gives a whispered click and the door slowly swings open. No cat, no draft, you and ——— exchange a silent smile and rather like the mystery; but do you know? That is an old trick of those doors, and has made many an emotional girl smile less instead of more; although I doubt not any carpenter could explain it.

Cable and his two research assistants unearthed contemporary news-paper accounts and interviewed those present at the riot and their descendants. While he recounts the grotesque stories of the Lalauries, he's far more concerned with a different troubling event that happened within the house's walls. Because for Cable, who was an ardent champion of the rights of the black community in the postwar South, the mistreatment and torture of Delphine's slaves is only the first—and not the most pressing—horror that occurred on that corner of Royale Street.

By 1872 the house had been rebuilt and was operating as a public high school for girls. The Lower Girls' High School, as it was called, had been integrated and had some twenty black students attending. In 1874 a group of young white boys took it upon themselves to purge the school system of black students. They forcibly removed three black women from one school and a few days later the teenagers arrived at the Lower Girls' High School, where they intimidated the black students there and finally drove them out. Neither the school superintendent nor the police intervened, and the local paper, the *Daily Picayune*, congratulated these "young regulators" on their "admirable firmness and propriety."

Whatever the severity of Delphine and Louis Lalaurie's crimes, the mansion's reputation as "haunted" didn't begin until after this second tragedy, as though the first outrage wasn't enough to prove by itself that something sinister inhabited the house's walls. Cable saw Delphine Lalaurie's outrages as part of an endemic, systematic brutality that also included these "young regulators"—the true evil haunting the mansion's walls.

Abolitionists like Harriet Martineau seized on the story of Lalaurie because they saw it as exemplary of a horrific system. If they embellished a little bit, it was only as a means of highlighting what they saw as the intrinsic barbarism of slavery. In the years since slavery ended, as Delphine Lalaurie's crimes have been so exaggerated as to defy all rational conception, she's been transformed from a brutal slave owner to something outright demonic, a sadist without a soul, an emblem of pure evil. Rather than becoming emblematic of slavery, then, she's become its opposite: an outlier, an exception. Apologists can thus seize on the story of the Lalaurie Mansion for completely apposite ends: here is a sole example of cruel barbarism that was completely at odds with the "civilized" institution of slavery, with its fair treatment of slaves.* New Orleans exists on this kind of mythmaking, on turning tragedy into story, on making legends as a means of building and rebuilding.

⤜⤏⦵⦵⤌⤛

From the Lalaurie Mansion, head toward Canal Street. If it's still raining, you hear that same strange music when you reach Jackson Square, a humming you can barely make out, a singing without a voice. By now you know it's not coming from any bar or any band in the plaza. It's always close but just out of earshot, and it disappears when the rain stops.

They will tell you it's the voice of Père Dagobert, a Capuchin monk who came to New Orleans in 1722, known for a voice like "liquid honey," a benevolent presence throughout New Orleans in the mid-eighteenth century. In 1745 he was appointed priest of the St. Louis Cathedral, the central church in the French Quarter. Universally beloved, Père Dagobert was a pillar of the community, a man people came to for all manner of problems.

Not much historical data has been preserved of Père Dagobert, but he participated in a strange drama in the annals of New Orleans history. When France announced that it was turning Louisiana over to the Spanish crown in 1768, local Creoles rose up in bloodless rebellion, driving out the newly arrived governor. Spain responded by sending Alexander O'Reilly as his replacement: O'Reilly was an Irish officer who abandoned the English army in favor of Catholic Spain and rose through the ranks of the Spanish army. When he arrived in New Orleans in August

---

*In deLavigne's account of Lalaurie's torture, there's a foul irony in her mention that some slaves were found with their "ears hanging by shreds," considering that cutting off ears was a legal, sanctioned punishment for escaping slaves, which deLavigne repackages as a torture beyond the pale.

1769, he immediately set out to put down the rebellion. Offering friendship, he invited the leaders of the rebellion over for dinner, where he had them arrested. Of the ten men accused of being ringleaders, O'Reilly had five of them—Nicolas Chauvin de Lafrénière, Jean Baptiste Noyan, Pierre Caresse, Pierre Marquis, and Joseph Milhet—executed by firing squad in the Place d'Armes (now Jackson Square), on October 25, 1769. Afterward he commanded that their bodies be left where they fell as a deterrent to any other would-be conspirators.

The slain men's families went to Père Dagobert, believing that, as a priest, he would be allowed to remove the bodies and give them proper burial. The priest had never before run afoul of the law and appeared reticent to violate O'Reilly's orders. In deLavigne's telling, Père Dagobert replied to the women who'd come to him, "Wait here until night. I have a great deal to do. Spain is on us like a wolfpack. Do not venture out, for any reason whatsoever. Tell your prayer beads, and sleep a little if you can." And so, the story goes, they waited for night, to see if Père Dagobert could redeem the fallen bodies of their loved ones.

That night a rain started as the Spanish troops stood guard. And then Père Dagobert emerged, somehow attended by an entire funeral procession of mourners, and without being noticed, they retrieved the bodies of those men, carrying them through the city through the night, singing "Kyrie eleison, kyrie eleison"—"Lord, have mercy"—as they made their way to St. Louis Cemetery, under the oblivious eyes of the Spanish guards. No one knew how Père Dagobert could lead so many people, carrying those five bodies, those long blocks to the graveyard, singing all the while, and never be stopped, but many New Orleanians will tell you that on nights when it rains, you can still hear his voice singing softly, "Kyrie eleison, kyrie eleison . . ."

But by now you're past the square, and the colonial intrigues of centuries ago have likewise faded. Across Canal Street a new kind of ghost begins to appear. A local tour guide told me that several National Guard troops were driving down this street one night in the aftermath of 2005's

Hurricane Katrina when the driver saw in his headlights a group of disheveled pedestrians, who seemed to appear from out of nowhere. Going far too fast to avoid them, he braced for impact, but they disappeared as quickly as they'd appeared.

Other responders who came to New Orleans in the wake of Katrina found ghosts as well. If you keep walking far enough down St. Charles Street, you'll reach the Sophie B. Wright Charter School, on Napoleon Avenue. During Katrina, the California National Guard was stationed here, and several Guardsmen reported strange goings-on. Sergeant Robin Hairston told a local television station, "I was in my sleeping bag and I opened my eyes and in the doorway was a little girl. It wasn't my imagination." Ghost sightings at Sophie B. Wright were confirmed by another member of the Guard: Specialist Rosales Leanor. "I was using the restroom and I just saw a little shadow," Leanor reported, "kind of looming in front of me." A third soldier claimed that when she opened a cleaning supply closet, she saw a little girl laughing.

This is unsurprising. After Katrina, bodies were left unburied for days, and some were never buried at all, washed away into Lake Pontchartrain and the Mississippi River. The disaster, the ineptitude of the response, and the breakdown of civil services created an entirely new relationship between the dead and the living. As Michael Osterholm, a doctor on the scene, later told the *Washington Post*, "One of the many lessons to emerge from Hurricane Katrina is that Americans are not accustomed to seeing unattended bodies on the streets of a major city." As with soldiers in combat, those who survived Katrina have faced a variety of emotional fallout as they attempt to process what happened. As one resident said on the ten-year anniversary of the storm's landfall, "Even cities feel trauma. It's not just people."

For a city that has long translated its tragic past into tourist entertainment, the response to the devastation wrought by Hurricane Katrina has moved along lines both predictable and unexpected. Within months of the event, disaster tourism had already sprung up. Visitors came to New

Orleans now not just for gumbo and beignets but to photograph the ravaged Lower Ninth Ward and get a firsthand glimpse of what the disaster
had wrought. Before long, tour companies had organized this fascination
with poverty and destruction into bus tours that narrate and contextualize
the storm. Too often, critics have suggested, these tours write out of history New Orleans's poor black citizens, focusing instead on ecological
issues and depopulated ruins. But this is what New Orleans has always
done: take culture from its populations at the margins, smooth off the
rough edges, and sell it to tourists around the globe. As with jazz, voodoo,
and ghosts, so, too, with Katrina.

Given the city's history of selling trauma, will those killed in the wake
of Katrina find themselves in the illustrious company of New Orleans's
famous ghosts? Ghost stories, for good or ill, are how cities make sense of
themselves: how they narrate the tragedies of their past, weave cautionary
tales for the future. More than ten years later, the water has receded and
some of the scars have healed, if unevenly. Yet even as the city continues
to rebuild, some spirits remain.

Meanwhile, you've arrived at the corner of Jackson Avenue and Magazine Street, where the high-end burger joint Charcoal's stands, home to
the ghost of Vera Smith.

✒♦♦✒

A squat, two-story brick rectangle, Charcoal's is, as one reviewer dubbed
it, a "mammoth temple of burger worship." Inside are reclaimed-wood
bars, low-wattage vintage lightbulbs dangling from the ceiling, and jars of
pickled vegetables lining the wall. And, of course, burgers. "As Gourmet
as a Burger Gets" is Charcoal's tagline, and this seems fairly accurate: you
can get your choice of not only beef, chicken, and veggie burgers but also
antelope, elk, buffalo, venison, shrimp, and salmon. In short, anything you
could possibly want in a burger.

The restaurant's opening did not go well: a brand-new meat grinder
failed, water lines inexplicably broke, and other strange mishaps troubled

the place. Charcoal's struggled to get a foothold in the community, and business was slow. The idea that the place was haunted started as a joke among employees, a way to explain the problems, but about a year after it opened, the restaurant's owners, Craig Walker, Jr., and Blaine Prestenbach, announced that the problems were in fact due to the ghost of Vera Smith, who'd died on that corner eight years before, at the height of the storm.

No one knows for sure what happened to Vera Smith. The sixty-five-year-old went out on August 29, the night after Katrina made landfall. According to her common-law husband, C. N. "Max" Keene, she went out to find cigarettes and beer; the next morning her body was found at the intersection of Jackson and Magazine. Most likely she was hit by a drunk driver who fled the scene, but what is beyond doubt is that by then Katrina had begun its decimation of the city, and as the crisis escalated and emergency response focused exclusively on the living, Smith's body was left unattended and abandoned. Keene, himself also elderly and not in great health, laid a sheet over Vera's body, unsure of what else to do in those days of nightmare and chaos.

"I saw a bloodied corpse weeping body fluids onto the street," resident John R. Lee later told reporters. Aghast at finding Vera's body in such a horrific state, seemingly ignored even as it started to rot in the heat and humidity, Lee went to the police, begging them to take care of the body. The cops refused, claiming that their priority was the living, and when Lee asked if he could move the body himself, they told him this was illegal. The only thing the cops were prepared to do, they told Lee, was to let Vera Smith's body rot on the street until they got around to dealing with it.

Lee refused to accept this answer, and finally, after enough badgering, the police allowed him to bury her, so long as he didn't move the body. So he set about building a makeshift grave for her, right there on the corner of Jackson and Magazine.

A few other neighbors joined in to help and managed to cover her body with a white tarp, which they then weighted down with bricks.

Another neighbor, artist Maggie McEleney, painted on top of the tarp a cross and a few stark words: HERE LIES VERA. GOD HELP US.

Vera's body was ultimately recovered and cremated; her remains were sent to relatives in Texas, where she was given, finally, a proper burial. She has not been forgotten in New Orleans, though. The neighbors who knew Smith later made a more lasting memorial for her at the site of her death: built by the local artist Simon Hardeveld, the memorial was a simple iron cross at the center of which was a clock face wound in barbed wire. Above the clock were the words VERA, DIED AUG 29, '05.

It might have been then that the stories of Vera's ghost began to appear. At one point the property owner, who'd been having difficulty finding someone to take the lot off his hands, became convinced that Hardeveld's memorial was some kind of voodoo charm preventing him from selling the lot and took a sledgehammer to the memorial, almost completely destroying it.

Vera's spirit would not depart so easily. In a city filled with tragedies, Vera Smith's death became emblematic of the horror of Katrina, what a local shopkeeper referred to as "symbol of the quiet suffering people endured." In part because her death remains a mystery—the official autopsy noted her injuries were not consistent with being hit by a car, and left the cause of her death as undetermined. In part because she was loved.

Many assumed, given the situation and the fact that she'd struggled sometimes with alcohol, that she had been homeless, a drifter, a no one. But she had two daughters in Texas and a network of friends and loved ones in the community. Known for her costume jewelry, her brightly colored wigs, and her elaborate dresses, she lived with two small dogs and her common-law husband. "She was not a sad woman. She had a very good life. In the neighborhood, everyone knew her and loved her," Hardeveld said.

A woman like Vera deserved much more—more assistance during the storm, more dignity in death. The work of Lee and the other neighbors who gathered to help became a defiant gesture in the face of the storm and the ineptitude, poverty, and failures of the city. Even in the depths of such anguish and despair, this much could be done.

When Abraham Lincoln addressed the dead at Gettysburg, he made plain that it was the bodies of the fallen that consecrated the burial ground, not words. So, too, with New Orleans, whose ground was consecrated by the bodies of men and women like Vera Smith. The corner of Jackson and Magazine is a *haunt*, a place we must always come back to. To be haunted by Vera is to return to this place, to remember.

Because of stories like Vera's, the ghost of Père Dagobert has become increasingly important to New Orleans, leading this phantasmal funeral procession through the night rains, singing, "Kyrie eleison, kyrie eleison"— Lord, have mercy, God help us—promising to bury the bodies that have been left to rot, offering rites for all those that have been abandoned. His legacy is a reminder that, no matter what else happens, we must care for our dead.

As for Charcoal's: after a year the owners commissioned Hardeveld— the artist who'd built the original memorial for Vera—to create a second memorial honoring her, this one attached to the restaurant, in hopes that it would quiet her spirit. One neighbor told me there were those who felt that the ghost story was likely fictitious and that Charcoal's used Vera's death as a marketing ploy to raise interest and business. But this is what New Orleans has always done, and this may just be the next stage of mythmaking for a city that manages to remain the same even as it's constantly reborn. When co-owner Walker told reporters, "Our message to Vera is our heart and soul is in this restaurant. We want you to support us," it may not matter whether or not he was speaking to a paranormal entity or simply through Vera to the people who remembered her and wanted her honored.

One way or another, regardless of motives, regardless of what you believe, Vera has returned to her corner. On the side of the building facing Jackson Avenue is a small fountain adorned with a cross and flanked by two wings: one that reads VERA, DIED AUG 29 '05, and the other, a sly play on words, that reads QUI VERA SERA—"Who is Vera, will be."

CHAPTER FIFTEEN

AMONG THE RUINS

Detroit, MI

T he ghost of Daniel Scotten didn't wait long to materialize. Prior to his death, in 1899, Scotten had been a titan of Detroit's business community, beloved by everyone who knew him. He'd started the Hiawatha Tobacco Company and turned it into a massive enterprise, complete with a monstrous factory on Fort Street. Woodcuts of the building show a stately rectangular building with arched windows along its first floor and a giant American flag flying from the roof. In an age when factory owners could be less than humane toward their workers, Scotten built a reputation as a philanthropist, funneling his wealth back into the city, even leaving stacks of firewood out for workers or anyone else who needed them to get through the long Michigan winter.

Shortly after Scotten died, his factory was closed and put up for sale. Once a beacon of Detroit's manufacturing success, it now sat dark and empty, an imposing tombstone to Scotten's legacy, a leering monolith with an uncertain future at the dawn of the twentieth century. Two of his former workers were walking past it when they were confronted by what they later described as "the figure of a man, white and terrible," which sent them both screaming in fright. Despite their terror, they recognized the ghost as their former boss, who bellowed at them, "Ever more must I walk until the smoke comes out of the chimneys of the old plant."

By June of the following year, ownership of the factory had transferred to Scotten's nephew Owen Scotten, who reopened the plant. The smoke of industry began once again spewing from its chimneys, and the ghost disappeared. It has not been seen since, not even after the company relocated to Buffalo, New York, in 1969, or after the Detroit factory was demolished in 1971—where it once stood, on the corner of Fort Street and Campau (since renamed Scotten Street), there's now a parking lot.

One wonders if we'll see the ghost of James Ward Packard on the city's east side, roaming the grounds of the massive, forty-acre Packard Automotive Plant. The plant, one of the most modern factories when it opened in 1903, operated until 1958, when the Packard brand died, but continued to be inhabited by various other businesses until the 1990s. Since then it has stood vacant, looming, ghostly—a sprawling ruin, a symbol of devastation stretching twelve city blocks.

A number of investors have tried to purchase the property and revitalize it, but despite vague plans for the future, it remains a wreckage a half mile long, a playground for vandals and disaster tourists. And if the ghost of Packard is here, no one's yet seen him.

Goethe wrote in 1827,

> America, you have it better
> Than our old continent,
> You have no ruined castles
> And no ancient basalt.
> Your inner life remains untroubled
> By useless memory
> And futile strife.

That was then. Now, almost two hundred years later, we've started to catch up to old Europe. We have plenty of ruined castles now, plenty of wasted strife to call our own.

Detroit has its abandoned hotels and office buildings, towering over the skyline but emptied out within. The once-beautiful theaters of a golden age, neo-Renaissance temples that have been left to decay and deteriorate. In these formerly grand palaces, failing plaster now drips from gouged ceilings and the sweeping balconies and cornices lord it over trash and dust. One such place, the Michigan Theatre, was converted into a parking garage; its vaulted ceilings are still visible above the cars and trucks.

These buildings have become the playgrounds of urban explorers, who've taken to breaking in where necessary to see the insides of abandoned hulks and fallen beauties. Before it was boarded up, the Roosevelt Warehouse at the corner of Fourteenth and Marantette was a popular destination. In use as a book depository for the Detroit public schools when it was heavily damaged by fire in 1987, it was subsequently abandoned, the school district leaving behind a surplus of usable supplies, including hundreds of books. In the slow decay of the building, trees have sprouted from the wreckage and books and other supplies left behind, offering a particularly stark image of Detroit's abandonment and, to some extent, its rebirth—or at least its reclamation by nature.

Detroit's downtown is anchored by the mammoth Renaissance Center. It was designed by John Portman, the same architect who designed LA's Westin Bonaventure, and the two properties are markedly similar, except that the seven-tower Renaissance Center is larger and its central core—a Marriott—is much taller. Inside, though, is the same style of confusing atrium, the same sense of a Piranesi prison come to life. But unlike the Bonaventure, the Renaissance Center isn't haunted. Why would it be? There are so, so many other haunted buildings in Detroit.

Ghosts fester in places untended to, where the usual patterns of behavior aren't or can't be enforced. Where once-regular places become strange, where it's no longer clear what a building's function was. Where the shadows multiply and nothing restricts your mind from projecting your thoughts and dreams and nightmares onto the walls and corridors. New Orleans gets its haunted reputation in no small part from carefully scripted stories that have been cultivated over decades, a way of packaging the city's history for tourists. Detroit's haunting feels more organic, sprung from the wreckage like a ghost from the well at the bottom of some forlorn dungeon.

⌇⌇⌇

"In the ruin history has physically merged into the setting," the German philosopher Walter Benjamin once commented. The ruin does not give history eternal life, he added; rather, it transforms the past into a thing that offers only "irresistible decay." As moss and foliage reclaim the remains of an old statue or aqueduct, the normally sharp line between the works of humanity and nature blur. A young Gustave Flaubert wrote of the "deep and ample joy" that filled him upon seeing ruins and their "embrace of nature, coming swiftly to bury the work of man the moment his hand is no longer there to defend it." A few decades earlier, the Reverend William Gilpin wrote similarly that "a ruin is a sacred thing. Rooted for ages in the soil; assimilated to it; and become, as it were, a part of it; we consider it as a work of nature, rather than of art." Sacred and enigmatic, for centuries ruins have been seen as appropriate places for philosophical reflection; it's not a coincidence that two of the best-known Romantic poems, Wordsworth's "Lines Composed a Few Miles Above Tintern Abbey" and Shelley's "Ozymandias," are both meditations on ruin.

In the same way that a ghost story told on a dark night might quicken one's pulse, ruins have a strange attraction, an exhilaration that accompanies the melancholy contemplation. Faced with the pitiless passage of time, the reality of one's own insignificance, we are awakened to our own death without actually facing a life-threatening experience. The eighteenth-century French writer and encyclopedist Denis Diderot spoke for many of us when he wrote:

> The ideas that ruins awaken in me are grand. Everything vanishes, everything dies, everything passes, only time endures. How old it is this world! I walk between two eternities. Everywhere I cast my eyes, the objects which surround me announce an end and make me yield to that end which awaits me. What is my ephemeral existence in comparison with that of the rock which is effaced, this valley which is forged, with this forest that trembles, with these masses suspended above my head which rumbles. I see the marble tombs crumble into dust; and I do not want to die!

Detroit is filled with ruins like no other city. And certainly they are beautiful. The buildings that remain are primarily from a single period: the early decades of the twentieth century, when the rise of the automobile catapulted Detroit to the forefront of American consciousness. We may think of the city as a petrified ruin, but for the first century of its history, it focused on new construction instead of preservation. Very little of its architecture from the nineteenth century still stands; much of it was demolished to make way for the great Art Deco and Beaux-Arts landmarks of the early twentieth century, when the city was in its heyday.

So many people fetishize Detroit's ruins in particular, because loving other ruins is often off-limits. "Is it unseemly now or ever to talk about the beauty of the World Trade Center ruins?" Sarah Boxer asked in the *New York Times* in 2002, and while the cultural consensus seems to be yes, Detroit is fair game, or so it would seem. Detroit has become our nation's favorite morality tale: a series of ineffectual mayors, bad public policy, and servitude to unions have all allowed a popular conception that Detroit "deserves" its fate. Just as we once visited circus sideshows, gawking at the

Bearded Lady and the Dog-Faced Boy—freaks whose display not only titillated but reminded customers that they were themselves normal—those of us who don't live in the Motor City peer at its haunted architecture to remind ourselves that our lives are normal. An architectural freak show, these ruins are both cautionary tale and stone and copper mementos mori, reminders that we, too, will all one day age and die. The haunted theaters of Detroit entice outsiders because they suggest decadence, extravagant wasting. The Michigan Theatre that is now a parking garage—what can that mean except a perverse excess, as though Beaux-Art landmarks are so plentiful here that you can throw them away.

In 2009 Detroit-based writer and photographer James D. Griffioen complained to *Vice Magazine* about the prevalence of a certain kind of image of Detroit: one of blight and destruction and little else. Professional photographers from around the world had been contacting him, asking for tours of the city, but he soon sensed a pattern. "At first you're really flattered by it, like 'Whoa, these professional guys are interested in what I have to say and show them.' But you get worn down trying to show them all the different sides of the city, then watching them go back and write the same story as everyone else. The photographers are the worst. Basically the only thing they're interested in shooting is ruin porn." The term Griffioen coined, "ruin porn," caught on and has since become ubiquitous, a phrase describing a certain kind of approach to urban decay, one that for better or worse has become associated with Detroit. In these images the ruins of places like the Roosevelt Warehouse and the Packard Plant are captured in their eerie beauty.

In the past few years the subgenre of ruin porn has exploded; coffee-table books that depict Detroit's abandoned spaces in lush, stunning photography have become a reliable industry. In works like Andrew Moore's *Detroit Disassembled*, Yves Marchand and Romain Meffre's *The Ruins of Detroit*, and the architectural history *Lost Detroit: Stories Behind the Motor City's Majestic Ruins*, by Dan Austin and Sean Doerr, Detroit is captured in its faded glory and displayed, like an anatomized corpse on a dissecting table, for the rest of us to gaze upon with awe and delighted terror.

⁓⊙⊙⁓

A mile and a half from the train station is Detroit's Masonic Temple, the largest such building in the country. A sixteen-story gothic behemoth with more than one thousand rooms, it was built by George D. Mason to display the pride of a city that had only recently begun to emerge as the manufacturing hub of an entire nation. As Detroit, and the Masonic lodge, have fallen on hard times in the past few decades, ghost stories have emerged about the lodge, including a popular one about Mason himself. As it's told on one Web site:

> Mr. Mason went slightly overboard when financing the construction of the building, and eventually went bankrupt, whereupon his wife left him. Overwhelmingly depressed about his financial and personal circumstances, Mason jumped to his death from the roof of the temple. Security guards claim to see his ghost to this day, ascending the steps to the roof. The temple, abundant with cold spots, inexplicable shadows, and slamming doors, is known to intimidate visitors with the eerie feeling of being watched.

A popular story, yes, but among the most patently false and easily disproved ghost stories out there. Mason was eighty-eight at the time of his death, from natural causes (as any quick Google search will tell you), which took place more than twenty years after the Masonic Temple was finished. And yet the story has cachet in part because it reflects a narrative that many have about Detroit: one of ostentatious overreach, folly, and death from financial ruin. So even though it's obviously false, it still gets told and retold.

If the legend of Mason's ghost reflects the downfall of the city, other ghosts stand guard trying to ward off further ruin. Such is the strange ghost of Colonel Philetus Norris, who appears at the haunted Two-Way Inn, several miles north of downtown. Even had he not returned as a ghost, his life would have been spectacular enough. Born in 1821 Norris served in the Union Army during the Civil War, rising to the rank of colonel and working as a spy in Confederate territory. After the war he served in the Ohio legislature before moving to Detroit, building the home for himself that is now the Two-Way Inn. He stayed in Detroit until he was hired to become the superintendent of Yellowstone National Park. In his later years he did ethnographic research for the Smithsonian Institution, dying in Kentucky and returning to Detroit only to be buried.

In photographs Norris looks every bit the Wild West mountain man, sporting a full, bushy beard and dressed entirely in buckskin. It's this figure that has been seen repeatedly in the Two-Way Inn: the frontiersman image easily recognizable in the postindustrial landscape, an unlikely candidate for protector of the Motor City.

In most retellings of the story of Norris's ghost, he's credited with protecting the inn from arson, which has long been endemic in Detroit. As with Daniel Scotten, you could say Norris's ghost is looking out for the city, acting as a steward against its decline, militating against its abandonment. It is rare for the supernatural to adopt such a civic responsibility, but here in Detroit it is perhaps essential.

Ghost stories like this reveal an evolving attitude toward buildings after their collapse. The remnants left behind after a ruinous rapture, they've become burdens a city must bear and a constant reminder of a past now faded. The ghost stories of Detroit that focus on its old buildings are of a different caliber from those that center on the gothic high-rises of Manhattan or Chicago, where land is precious and useless buildings don't stick around. The reputation of the Merchant's House in Manhattan comes in no small part from the contrast with the surrounding buildings: an anachronistic anomaly in a bustling, forward-looking metropolis. In Detroit the ghosts stand guard, preserving the past against the decay of the future. They command the living to reclaim the former pride of these factories and mansions, or, like Mason, they lament their own folly and hubris.

And then there is the curious figure of the Nain Rouge, the mysterious Red Dwarf that's haunted Detroit for more than three hundred years. If Daniel Scotten and Philetus Norris are the supernatural defenders of Detroit, the Nain Rouge is the city's assailant. If George Mason laments the end of the city's glory days, the Nain Rouge celebrates it.

∽◦∾

Stories of the Nain Rouge begin with the founding of the city. In 1701 Antoine Laumet de La Mothe Cadillac (the French explorer who would found Detroit) had been in attendance at a lavish ball in Quebec when a strange fortune-teller appeared. The author of the 1883 collection *Legends of Le Détroit*, Marie Caroline Watson Hamlin (about whom not much else is known), who tells the story that follows, described her as "a woman of unusual height, a dark, swarthy complexion, restless, glittering eyes, strangely fashioned garments yet in harmony with her face." On her shoulder was perched a small black cat, which would lick her ear occasionally during her sessions, leading some to assume that the devil was whispering instructions through the body of the feline.

Finally she came to Cadillac, who bade her to tell him his fortune as well. "Sieur," she told him, "yours is a strange destiny. A dangerous journey you will soon undertake; you will found a great city which one day will have more inhabitants than New France now possesses; many children will nestle around your fireside." But as with Macbeth's fortune, there was another side to Cadillac's future: "Dark clouds are arising and I see dimly your star," the fortune-teller went on. "The policy you intend pursuing in selling liquor to the savages, contrary to the advice of the Jesuits will cause you much trouble, and be the cause of your ruin. In years to come your colony will be the scene of strife and bloodshed, the Indians will be treacherous, the hated English will struggle for its possession, but under a new flag it will reach a height of prosperity which you never in your wildest dreams pictured."

Confused, Cadillac pressed her for more information, and she ended her tale with this warning: "Your future and theirs lie in your own hands, beware of undue ambition; it will mar all your plans. Appease the Nain Rouge. Beware of offending him. Should you be thus unfortunate not a vestige of your inheritance will be given to your heirs. Your name will be scarcely known in the city you founded."

That same year Cadillac founded the settlement that would in time grow to be Detroit, and as it flourished quickly, he became arrogant and proud, disregarding the soothsayer's warnings. One night when he and his wife were out walking, on the path in front of them jumped "the uncouth figure of a dwarf, very red in the face, with a bright, glistening eye; instead of burning it froze, instead of possessing depth [it] emitted a cold gleam like the reflection from a polished surface, bewildering and dazzling all who came within its focus. A grinning mouth displaying sharp, pointed teeth, completed this strange face." Unwisely, Cadillac struck the dwarf with his cane, shouting, "Get out of my way, you red imp!" The Nain Rouge responded with a fiendish, mocking laugh, then disappeared.

True to the fortune-teller's predictions, Cadillac's own fortunes soon fell precipitously, and in the years since, the Nain Rouge has become not simply a personal antagonist but a villain for the city as a whole. He is seen shortly before every major disaster that's befallen Detroit. Just as Binghamton has its curse, Detroit has its Red Dwarf.

In another collection of folktales, Charles M. Skinner writes that the Nain Rouge was "seen scampering along the shore on the night before the attack on Bloody Run, when the brook that afterward bore this name turned red with the blood of soldiers. People saw it in the smoky streets when the city was burned in 1805, and on the morning of Hull's surrender it was found grinning in the fog."

Little record of the dwarf, a harbinger of tragic romanticism and falls from grace, can be found in the years of the city's great boom. Only starting in the 1960s did the Nain Rouge supposedly return, making an appearance again shortly before the devastating race riots of 1967. In the decades since, he's shown up again before major ice storms and other calamities.

～◇◇◇～

Meanwhile, another class of ghosts has emerged here. Among the most iconic images of contemporary Detroit is Yves Marchand and Romain Meffre's image of Michigan Central Station: their photograph takes the building head-on, cropping it so closely that there's nothing else in the frame: no sky, no land, no other buildings. The building is imposing, and the impression it gives can be quite chilling. But what's not captured in the image is what was happening behind them as they took the photograph. Across the street from Michigan Central Station is a row of shops and restaurants, including a barbershop and a real estate firm, a fancy espresso place, a barbecue joint, and a vodka bar.

The simple fact, after all, is that while ruin porn focuses on abandoned buildings, devoid of any humanity, Detroit is not empty. As historian Thomas J. Sugrue notes, "Detroit might be depopulated, but it's not a blank slate. Over 700,000 people, more than four-fifths of them Black, call the city home. For them, Detroit's ruins are not romantic: they are a taunting reminder of how the city has lost capital and jobs, and how many lives have been ruined in the process." The images of emptied buildings have to efface blue-collar workers who are almost always just out of frame. They have their own stories, of course, these lives that exist just beyond the camera's eye—and they haunt the aesthetic of ruin porn with their refusal to vanish.

Our ruins are not centuries-old testaments to the civilizations long gone; they are not the mysterious ciphers of Stonehenge or ancient Egypt. They have been birthed in modern memory, documented for all to see. And ruin porn photographs offer no way to understand the decline we're witnessing; they're anti-history, even as they embody the past and its decline. A ghost story's reduction of a complex moment or the history of a building into a series of clichés is reproduced in beautifully staged photos that fetishize the past without truly representing it. Ruin porn is the visual analog of the ghost story.

Meanwhile, Detroit is still teeming with people. It's one of the top twenty largest cities in America—more populous than Seattle, Denver, Boston, or Washington, D.C. It's down from its historic highs of two million people, to be sure, and its massive size means a lower population density, but it's by no means empty. On the contrary, on an early spring weekend, Detroit's downtown struck me as a good deal more lively than Chicago's Loop or downtown Los Angeles would have been at the same time. To see Detroit as a ruin—and as nothing but a ruin—is to see it emptied out of people. It is to erase some 713,000 residents from view. It is to transform them, against their will, into ghosts.

⁓⊙⌒⌒

Sometimes, though, the ghosts fight back. Since 2010, on the first Sunday of spring each year a parade is held for the Nain Rouge, where he confronts the city and is symbolically driven out of town. Half Mardi Gras parade, half Burning Man (though nowhere near as large or elaborate or well attended), the Marche du Nain Rouge is a strange, if entertaining, way to spend a Sunday morning in March. Fire jugglers accompany a float made to look like a giant cockroach, on top of which stands the Nain Rouge himself—or at least an actor portraying him, in full black leather and an appropriately demonic red mask. From his perch he mocks the crowd to the strains of Black Sabbath's "War Pigs," shouting, "You think you can defeat me! You'll never be able to defeat me!"; "You thought you got rid of me but I'm back!"; "You won't succeed, Detroit! I'll make you fail!"

Parade goers wave signs blaming the Red Dwarf for their troubles (NAIN BROKE MY TIRE, read one) or in support of the antagonist (DON'T DREAD THE RED!; SUPPORT THE SHORT!; STOP NAIN SHAMING!), while he claims credit for petty annoyances: "I fed your dog chocolates!" or "I cc'ed the wrong e-mail to everyone you know!" But even here there can be a harder edge beneath the veneer. "I put all the toxins in the air and the lead in the soil," he taunts. "I raised the parking ticket to $45." He seems to ally himself with the Republicans in control of the state government ("I support right to work"; "I gerrymandered Michigan!") as well as the new influx of white hipsters ("I think gentrification is excellent urban planning"; "I'm working on the new hipster political correctness"). The crowd on hand is overwhelmingly white, and young; participating in a public shaming of themselves, these gentrifiers perhaps hope to absolve themselves of some guilt. A carnivalesque scapegoat, the Nain Rouge can function as a release valve for pent-up annoyances and anxieties, which is the most you can hope for from any ghost.

It's hard to know for sure what lies in store for a city like Detroit, one that has so much promise and potential and so many dedicated citizens but that still has so many obstacles standing in its way. It's hard to know how much longer the Nain Rouge will return to pester the citizens and frustrate their dreams. From the rooftop of the massive Masonic Temple, the ghost of the building's architect, George Mason, looks down on the city, watching. Once, years before, he was allowed to rest in peace, but then he was resurrected, not unlike the Nain Rouge, and remade into a symbol of the city's tragic fortunes.

Perhaps, in the years to come, he may be able to rest in peace once more.

CHAPTER SIXTEEN

HILLSDALE, USA

The road to Hill House leads through Hillsdale. In Shirley Jackson's *The Haunting of Hill House*, Eleanor Vance is given detailed instructions on getting to the eponymous mansion and is advised explicitly not to ask about the mansion once she gets to the small town closest to her haunted destination. "I am making these directions so detailed," Dr. Montague writes to her in a letter, "because it is inadvisable to stop in Hillsdale to ask your way. The people there are rude to strangers and openly hostile to anyone inquiring about Hill House." And it's true: the people of Hillsdale feel an immediate distrust of this mousy Eleanor Vance who's preparing to spend several months at the haunted mansion.

In Jackson's novel Hill House's creator, Hugh Crain, materializes almost from nowhere, without a backstory and certainly not as a citizen of Hillsdale—his decision for choosing Hillsdale remains a mystery. Though Crain builds Hill House for his wife and family, his wife dies minutes before first laying eyes on it, as the carriage taking her to her new home overturns in the driveway. Bringing up his two children alone in the murky mansion, Crain eventually marries twice more, though both subsequent wives also come to untimely ends: the second from a fall, the third from consumption. It's not clear why things go so horribly wrong, only that Crain's house unleashes some unspeakable evil, or is itself that evil—an evil that lingers long after he himself is dead. Stuck with a darkness on the edge of town, the people of Hillsdale must contend with this new architectural evil perpetually on their periphery.

Why do the poor townspeople hate the haunted mansion? Well, because they're poor. They can't afford to move away, to uproot their families, even after some rich eccentric has uncorked some terrible spirit just outside town. "People *leave* this town," a Hillsdale resident tells Eleanor, "they don't *come* here." The archetypal haunted house story is fundamentally about class: new money who doesn't understand the land or the people or the history blunders into the landscape, attempting to buy his way into a community, blithely oblivious to the locals. A legend goes unheeded, a terrible secret is unearthed, sacred land is disturbed, and so forth. The townspeople grow resentful because, by the force of economics, they are imprisoned by the rich and their folly.

Shirley Jackson never specifies exactly where Hillsdale is, or even in which state it can be found. Take "Route 39 to Ashton," Dr. Montague's letter instructs Eleanor, "and then turn left onto Route 5 going west"—that's about it. For a long time I'd assumed it was in New England; Jackson was living in Vermont when she wrote the novel, and that's where director Robert Wise sets *The Haunting*, his adaptation of the novel: in "the most remote part of New England." But while there are about a dozen Ashtons throughout the country, none are in New England. There is, however, an Ashton, Illinois, right near the intersection of State Route 5 and State Route 38.

So Hill House might actually be in the Land of Lincoln. If you look closely, though, every state has its Hillsdale: a town beset by a local haunting, a paranormal real estate problem, a conflict between the haves and have-nots that plays out in supernatural terms.

~~~◦◦◦~~~

As Salem has taught us, nothing brings out ghosts like property disputes. Events played out similarly sinister in Nyack, New York, a few decades ago. Helen Ackley had advertised her house as haunted for more than a decade before she put it up for sale in 1989; for years she had opened it up for local walking tours of haunted Nyack, and it had once been featured in *Reader's Digest*. But it was only *after* Jeffrey Stambovsky bought the house that he became aware of the rumors and the house's reputation. Stambovsky, who'd lived in New York City and wasn't up to speed on local lore, argued that the presence of ghosts lowered the value of the house, and he sued Ackley for failing to inform him of its haunted past.

West Virginia's Greenbrier Ghost would not be the last instance of the supernatural entering into American case law, and *Stambovsky v. Ackley* worked its way slowly through the courts. After a lower court dismissed Stambovsky's claim under the principle of caveat emptor (as the buyer of the home, it was his responsibility to do his due diligence), he appealed, and in a New York state appellate opinion, Justice Israel Rubin finally agreed with him.

Rubin's decision began by more or less sidestepping the question of whether or not the house was actually haunted: "Whether the source of the spectral apparitions seen by defendant seller are parapsychic or psychogenic," Rubin wrote, was irrelevant, since Ackley had repeatedly advertised her house as having ghosts: "defendant is estopped to deny their existence and, as a matter of law, the house is haunted."

Rubin recognized Stambovsky's predicament: though it was reasonable to expect the buyer to check for termites, water damage, and other possible faults, it struck him as unreasonable to expect a buyer to check for paranormal problems. "From the perspective of a person in the position of plaintiff herein, a very practical problem arises with respect to the discovery of a paranormal phenomenon: 'Who you gonna call?'" Rubin wrote, clearly having fun with his decision. Imagining prospective buyers having to hire not just a structural engineer and a pest-control consultant but also a ghost hunter, the court concluded that "the notion that a haunting is a condition which can and should be ascertained upon reasonable inspection of the premises is a hobgoblin which should be exorcised from the body of legal precedent and laid quietly to rest." Narrowly tailoring his decision, Rubin did reject Stambovsky's claim that Ackley had acted fraudulently, arguing that any attempt to recover actual damages from Ackley hadn't "a ghost of a chance." But, "moved by the spirit of equity," Rubin ordered the contract voided, awarding Stambovsky his original down payment.

Almost twenty years later the Pennsylvania Supreme Court would take on many of the same issues, though they would reach a significantly different outcome. In 2008 Janet Milliken sued the previous owners of her home in Thornton. The home had been the scene of a gruesome murder-suicide; it was subsequently bought cheaply at auction by Kathleen and Joseph Jacono, who renovated it and then resold it to Milliken. Milliken, who'd moved from California with her two young children after her husband's death, had no idea of the house's gruesome past and soon found her family beset with a number of ghostly encounters. After finally learning the true history of her house, she brought suit against the Jaconos, claiming that they'd purposefully withheld information that materially affected the value of the house.

Milliken v. Jacono went all the way to the Pennsylvania Supreme Court, and as part of her case Milliken brought in Randall Bell, a California appraiser whose specialty was consulting on properties that were "psychologically stigmatized." He'd first come to fame assisting with the sale of the condo where Nicole Brown Simpson and Ronald Goldman had been murdered. He'd also consulted on the house where Sharon Tate and four others were murdered by the Manson family, JonBenet Ramsey's former house, and the Rancho Santa Fe mansion where thirty-nine members of the Heaven's Gate cult committed suicide, as well as other places that bore the stain of a violent, sensationalized past. Bell himself doesn't believe in ghosts, but he recognizes that the perception of ghosts or a history involving violence can affect a home's resale value. "A haunted house is a perception," he's said. "If a property is perceived as haunted, it's haunted. If you don't think it's haunted, it isn't." Bell, along with Milliken's lawyers, argued that whether or not ghosts were really haunting the house was irrelevant; what mattered was that the house's history was affecting its price, and that the Jaconos had been obligated to disclose this during the sale.

Ultimately the court sided with the Jaconos, not Milliken. "One cannot quantify the psychological impact of different genres of murder, or suicide," it wrote in its opinion. Psychological stigma, no matter its subjective effect on some, presented the court with such a slippery slope of possibilities that there was no way for them to contemplate it as a material defect: "Does a bloodless death by poisoning or overdose create a less significant 'defect' than a bloody one from a stabbing or shooting? How would one treat other violent crimes such as rape, assault, home invasion, or child abuse? What if the killings were elsewhere, but the sadistic serial killer lived there? What if satanic rituals were performed in the house?" Unlike the New York court, the Pennsylvania justices put the onus entirely on the buyer: caveat emptor—buyer beware.

If *Milliken v. Jacono* was expected to settle, definitively, the question of whether ghosts can affect property values, it most assuredly has not, and the belief that a building's reputation as haunted can have a legitimate impact on its value has resurfaced over the years in sometimes unexpected ways. In Brooklyn the former Caledonian Hospital, overlooking the south side of Prospect Park, was transformed in 2014 into a luxury rental property, and almost immediately the ghosts moved in. Stories of strange smells, unexplained sounds, and other haunted phenomena began to emerge, and three doormen quit over the course of six months. One doorman who'd quit reportedly told a neighbor that 123 on the Park, as the building's now known, is "a messed-up place to work because it's haunted." The managing director of the property group that manages the building confirmed to local papers that there was high staff turnover and that there have been issues in renting units.

But these unexplained spirits may have a more predictable origin. Writing for *Gothamist*, Lauren Evans wondered whether the ghosts were themselves "understandably perturbed by the gentrification of their longtime home" and had "organized to retaliate." When she poked around the property trying to verify the haunting, she was told by employees that the ghost rumors had been started by neighbors, who were concerned that the high-priced apartments would drive up their own rents. Meanwhile, prospective renters at 123 on the Park have themselves apparently tried to use the ghosts as a bargaining chip, asking for reduced rents since their apartments already have occupants. In landscapes such as New York City, where real estate and issues of gentrification are already fraught, it doesn't much matter if the ghosts are real or not; what matters is the financial leverage they may provide.

I'd felt this myself firsthand when my wife and I were searching for our first home, in 2008, when the country's real estate market was in free fall. In many of the strange houses we looked at, I felt the hints of lives left behind by the foreclosure crisis, and the odd, haunting feeling such traces could engender. But nowhere did I feel it as strongly as in the one house we came to call the Happy Murder Castle.

Standing midway up the side of a hill off Alvarado Boulevard in Los Angeles's Echo Park neighborhood, even from a distance it stood out against the other homes. Driving up to it, we could see the faux flagstone that had been painted on some, but not all, of its walls. It was just up the street from an elementary school and might have once doubled as an unlicensed day care; perhaps the castle look had seemed inviting to children at one point. The citrus trees on the property were untended and filled with ripe and rotting fruit, and from those trees rose the back bedroom, complete with plywood crenellations to complete the medieval tower aesthetic. Meanwhile, the front of the house still bore the evidence of its former life as a 1920s bungalow. This was an architectural version of *The Fly*: two incompatible species gratuitously grafted together, resulting in an utter monstrosity.

As we walked in, we found another couple on their way out. They smiled grimly and said merely, "Hope you brought your mask," on their way past us. The owners, we learned, had left the taps dripping, so that pools of black mold festered beneath the sinks, but that was only the beginning. The house had once been half its current size, and the additions boggled the mind: the only door to the backyard was through a bathroom, and off the kitchen was something too wide to be a hallway, too small to be a room. This "room," in turn, led to that back bedroom tower, which amazingly had a ceiling painted with a marginal trompe l'oeil: scarf-draped cherubs blowing trumpets amid wispy clouds. It was hard to imagine how anyone could have made a home here, but we walked through it anyway, drinking in its distorted weirdness, its history measured out in garish juxtapositions. We were about to leave when our real estate agent noted something we'd overlooked: scrawled in pencil on the living room wall were the words A MURDERER LIVED HERE.

The feeling I got from the house stayed with me for weeks, even after we'd ended our search. (We didn't put in an offer on the house, unsurprisingly.) The Happy Murder Castle was disquieting, uncanny, possessed of an uneasy sense I've rarely felt in any structure; I'll admit there are times I'm tempted to call it haunted. We tell ourselves ghost stories perhaps because we truly believe in the paranormal—or perhaps because we just need a word, a term, a story for that vague feeling that would be too silly to admit in other terms.

After our trip to the Happy Murder Castle, I Googled the address, along with "murderer," "killer," "child molester," every combination I could think of. I came up with nothing. Unlike in Pennsylvania, in California a real estate agent has to notify you if a death has occurred in a house within the past three years, but that wouldn't include a murderer who lived there and did his or her killing elsewhere or a murderer who was never caught. It's possible, I suppose, that a murderer really did live there. But the truth is likely far more obvious, more quotidian, more biting. These were homeowners who bought at an inflated price before the market crashed and now found themselves underwater; they finally lost their home like so many thousands of others. Those penciled words were, like the black mold, likely an attempt to make their home as unappealing as they could, an albatross around the neck of the bank that had taken it from them. Forced out, the home's previous owners' memories linger in that house—bitter and spiteful spirits, mingling with a sense of melancholy and regret.

~~~

Wherever they are now, who can say. But this, too, you could say, is part of the American story, as we have always been people who move on, leaving behind wreckage and fragments in our wake. We will continue, despite our best intentions, to make haunted houses and cities, for we are endlessly mobile, leaving a pockmarked landscape of abandoned places in our wake. Like hermit crabs, Americans tend to abandon one home for the next, leaving behind a former dwelling to be either repurposed by its next occupant or left as detritus.

"We left the valley with reluctant feet, looking backward at every turn in the steep grade, much as our first parents must have lingered on the confines of Eden," a correspondent for the *Cincinnati Enquirer* wrote in 1875, signing her dispatch with only the name "Abigail." A travelogue through eastern California out of the Sierra Nevadas, Abigail's short article offers an early perspective on the changing nature of the country in the wake of the early mining booms. "We ate our first lunch under a great Sequoia tree, named 'Illinois,' and sped down into the Valley of the Stanislaus, and up to Sonora, through the deserted mining towns, like the ghosts of their departed prosperity. The country is ruined now for all agricultural purposes for ages, every inch of soil having been washed away, only the unsightly piles and ridges of stone and washed gravel left. The gold was dearly purchased at such a price."

Abigail's article, according to the Oxford English Dictionary, is the earliest use of the word "ghost" to denote an abandoned town. "Ghost town" would find increasing favor in the lexicon, particularly starting in the 1920s, as the last vestiges of the boomtown West dried up. In his 1931 popular history of mining in California and Nevada, *Here They Dug the*

Gold, George F. Willison wrote, "Today all lie ghost towns smelling of the long slow processes of ruin and decay," cementing the term as an idiom that has since become ubiquitous. As more and more of these towns dried up, confronting us with a strange new landscape, a term was needed, and the language of ghosts presented itself.

Many ghost towns, naturally, also claim to be haunted. The ruined town of Garnet, Montana, is one, named for the rich vein of gold, the Garnet lode, that birthed it. Its population peaked at a thousand residents in 1895, but within ten years it had dwindled to less than two hundred. A fire destroyed the business district in 1912, and the last resident died in 1947. Given over to the elements, the remaining buildings gradually fell to ruin until preservationists, along with the Bureau of Land Management, stabilized the remains and opened the town to visitors. When the tourists are gone, though, the ghosts appear—so says resident ghost historian Ellen Baumler. Officially employed as the interpretive historian for the Montana Historical Society, Baumler writes books on Montana's haunted past on the side, and she cites Garnet as among many ghost towns that now have spirits. "Sometimes, in the deep winter quiet, a piano tinkles in Kelley's Saloon and the spirits dance to ghostly music," she writes in her *Montana Chillers*. "Men's voices echo in the empty rooms. But the moment a living, human hand touches the building, the noises stop."

Ghost towns feel haunted because, even if they will never again host living society, they remain filled with hints of those who once lived there. Our imaginations cannot help but project onto these ruins the ghosts of the people who've left indelible traces, and these spirits can spring to life with just a shift in the wind, a creaking board, or a distant animal call. Far more comforting, after all, to believe that someone—even if not someone living—is still making use of these shacks, saloons, and general stores.

Americans aren't the only people to leave behind ghost towns, but we are particularly adept at it, as our peripatetic nature drives us from claim to claim, stake to stake, leaving behind not much but rubble and clapboard houses. The ghost town has become a defining feature of the West and its mythology, and as the country's manufacturing economy fell on hard times, it became the defining feature of an emptied-out rust belt. In the early years of a new century, we're poised to see more and more ghost towns emerge. As places like Manhattan and San Francisco become uninhabitable to all but the richest 0.01 percent, driving out even their own service workers, internal migration will continue and new places will become abandoned. A 2014 article in the *New York Times* suggested that as global warming increases, Americans will empty out the Southwest in favor of places like Maine, Oregon, and Alaska. Spurred by a global warming dust bowl, we'll move north, and in time Phoenix, Sacramento, and Los Angeles may come to be as ghost-haunted as Detroit seems now.

We live among the undead, in cities of ghosts. The buildings that used to have meaning and purpose—not only houses but banks and government buildings—have been emptied of what they once meant, and yet they remain, haunting us. Those of us who can, leave, moving on to new cities that we hope are not yet beset by the dead. Those of us who can't, like the residents of Hillsdale, Illinois, remain behind, haunted by forces larger than ourselves, imprisoned by the folly of the rich who have unleashed some unspeakable dread from which we cannot escape.

GHOSTS OF A NEW MACHINE

Allendale, CA

W hen Jessamyn West and her sister, Kate, moved into their father's home in Westport, Massachusetts, after his death in 2011, they didn't expect to find it haunted. Their father, Tom West, had been a hardware developer and program manager who'd achieved a certain measure of fame when his work was documented in Tracy Kidder's Pulitzer Prize–winning *The Soul of a New Machine*. Kidder's 1981 book followed West and his team as they developed a new computer for Data General: the Eclipse MV/8000. As a result of Kidder's book, riding as it did the early wave of the 1980s computer revolution, Tom West came to be seen as something of a symbol for the burgeoning tech economy, a standard-bearer of a brave new future.

And yet he left behind ghosts. When Jessamyn, who works as a community technology librarian, and Kate, an administrative officer in the Massachusetts State Police, moved into what they came to call the Museum of Dad, lights would turn themselves on and off without reason or human input—as though their father's spirit was still there with them, moving through the house, making his appointed rounds. A motion sensor set up in the driveway would go off randomly, even when no one was near the house, signaling the imminent return of something only it could see. Jessamyn told me, "I often thought the house was lonely without my dad in it."

There was, of course, an easy explanation for this, even if not an easy solution. Tom West, always on the cutting edge of technology, had wired the house with an X10 automated lighting system and a series of other automated systems, all of which were set up to follow his rhythms without having to have him lift a finger. In many rooms outlets and light switches had been replaced by nodes embedded in the walls that were driven by a configuration file on his laptop.

West's house was an early incarnation of what's now called the Internet of Things: a future in which not just phones and computers are connected to the Internet but light switches and refrigerators and security alarms and laundry machines—all connected via Wi-Fi and Bluetooth, automating our homes in myriad ways. The Internet of Things was still at a relatively primitive stage when West wired his house in 2010, and so mostly he only was able to automate the lighting and plumbing, but this was more than enough to create strange and unsettling effects after his death.

Jessamyn and Kate noticed at one point that their electricity bills had spiked. After some sleuthing they found an irrigation pump that had come on mysteriously—a pump that, as far as Jessamyn could determine, hadn't worked for several years. In the basement a Shop Vac would turn on by itself mysteriously at random hours. The toilet water became inexplicably hot at one point, breeding bacteria in the toilets that left the bathrooms with foul odors.

These are the kinds of freak occurrences that lead people to think a place is haunted, but in the case of West's house, it was more obviously a complicated electronic protocol that was gradually falling apart, without a clear blueprint that would allow either daughter to understand the problem. Jessamyn found herself trapped in the garage one day when she realized that the only way to open the door was through a remote that had gone missing; ultimately she had to dismantle the door manually. The toilet problem, the women learned, was the result of a water pump in the basement whose existence—let alone purpose—was unknown to them until it failed.

Even knowing that the lights in West's house weren't being controlled by spirits, they still posed problems. Some of the lights were timed in ways that made sense, such as coming on at five in the evening; others followed Tom's more idiosyncratic routines—routines that were never spelled out in a will or passed on to his heirs. The lights abruptly turning off at ten at night were meant to urge West to go to bed, a feature that was infuriating to anyone not on a similar schedule. To compound the confusion, the hard drive on the laptop that held the data crashed, making it difficult (though by no means impossible) to reprogram the house. Jessamyn and Kate debugged the most egregious programs and hired electricians to work through the rest. What remains, they've since learned to live with—the back porch still doesn't have a light switch.

When West worked for the microcomputer manufacturer Data General, he was known for a saying he'd written on a whiteboard in his office: *not everything worth doing is worth doing well*. When Tracy Kidder asked him for a translation, he offered, "If you can do a quick-and-dirty job and it works, do it." Now, after his death, his daughters are living with the strange ramifications of this philosophy as it relates to West's own house, where an idiosyncratic and sometimes jury-rigged home infrastructure is now gradually falling apart.

A house that more or less operates under its own control, automated and animated and no longer requiring input from its living inhabitants—in such a strange new dwelling lies one glimpse of the future of hauntings. The house was set up for Tom West himself—his rhythms and habits, his patterns and haunts. With him gone, the house continues in many ways to respect those patterns of being, asserting them on its new occupants as though they, too, are obliged to adopt their father's modes of being. And should the house be sold, Jessamyn admitted, the next occupants will have to reckon, one way or another, with these same protocols, since there's no way to rid the house entirely of them, short of gutting its electrical and plumbing systems altogether. Which is to say, the house is cursed—benignly cursed, but cursed all the same. The spirit of Tom West is going to inhabit it for a long time to come.

❧

Ray Bradbury had already imagined the Internet of Things in a 1950 short story that's turned out to be one of the more prescient stories of all time: "There Will Come Soft Rains." Set in the year 2026, the story follows a day in the (artificial) life of a fully automated house in the possibly fictional town of Allendale, California, a house that goes about its domestic duties—washing dishes, cleaning rooms, reciting poetry for entertainment—all the while unaware that its inhabitants, the McClellan family, are all dead, atomized in a nuclear explosion. It's a rare science fiction story that, aside from the nuclear holocaust part, has so far accurately predicted the future—an automated home so fully integrated that it can essentially function without us. If we're not there yet, this is certainly the dream of futurists, designers, and advertisers, and 2026 seems a pretty reasonable date.

Often characterized as science fiction, Bradbury's story is also a ghost story: a story of a haunted house. Sentient, the house acts of its own accord, an inanimate place animated, its poltergeists moving about. "Bridge tables sprouted from patio walls. Playing cards fluttered onto pads in a shower of pips. Martinis manifested on an oaken bench with egg-salad sandwiches. Music played. But the tables were silent and the cards untouched. At four o'clock the tables folded like great butterflies back through the paneled walls." Bradbury gives us the kind of house one expects from Disneyland's Haunted Mansion, where unseen ghosts flit about, frolicking and enjoying themselves as though still living. The story's title comes from a Sara Teasdale poem, which describes how nature will be unaffected by humanity's destruction, how the frogs and birds and trees will remain oblivious to humanity's final wars, apathetic and unmoved by the end of us—which Bradbury in turn extends to our technological marvels, continuing, undead and ghosted, after our own dear departures.

But in Bradbury's futuristic ghost story, who is haunting whom? The house, after all, is mostly self-sufficient, and the real ghosts are its missing occupants. The only remaining traces of the McClellan family are the ghostly traces on the walls outside:

> The entire west face of the house was black, save for five places. Here the silhouette in paint of a man mowing a lawn. Here, as in a photograph, a woman bent to pick flowers. Still farther over, their images burned on wood in one titanic instant, a small boy, hands flung into the air; higher up, the image of a thrown ball, and opposite him a girl, hands raised to catch a ball which never came down. The five spots of paint—the man, the woman, the children, the ball—remained. The rest was a thin charcoaled layer.

No longer living inhabitants, the McClellan family haunt their own house. Their lives, their hobbies and relations and jobs and desires and loves, are evident everywhere in the house, but they themselves are not. The true protagonist is the house itself, and it is the house's own life-and-death struggle that we witness, its former inhabitants now merely the specters that haunt its walls. In this way, too, Bradbury might have been onto something: With the coming of the Internet of Things, automated houses may mean not that the houses themselves are haunted but that we ourselves become the ghosts, mere guests obligated to the thing that once represented security.

❧❧❧

Which isn't to say there aren't scientists working to disabuse us once and for all of our belief in spirits, proving them to be nothing more than phantasms of the mind that can be easily controlled and replicated in the laboratory. In 2014 researchers from the École Polytechnique Fédérale de Lausanne, in Switzerland, figured out a way to manufacture ghosts, thus suggesting that they're really all in our minds. A participant in their experiment would control a robot directly behind her or him, causing the robot to touch the participant's back when commanded. But sometimes the robot would delay its actions by a half second, sometimes not. The confusion caused by the expectation of a reaction and the slight delay interrupted participants' sense of their own sensorimotor input enough that they thought their own actions were that of another person—creating the "feeling of presence" in the subjects: a ghost behind them who wasn't really there.

"Our brain possesses several representations of our body in space," researcher Giulio Rognini explained. "Under normal conditions, it is able to assemble a unified self-perception of the self from these representations. But when the system malfunctions because of disease—or, in this case, a robot—this can sometimes create a second representation of one's own body, which is no longer perceived as 'me' but as someone else, a 'presence.'" For skeptics, studies like these can be powerful ammunition to convince those who've "felt something" that what they're really feeling are just manifestations of their own minds.

Even if science can help explain to us how our brains concoct ghosts, it won't explain their importance in our lives, and it will do little to dispel our belief of them. For even though communication technologies have made mammoth strides since the days when the telegraph inspired Spiritualists, the same technological static and gremlins are still with us. YouTube videos, with their often low resolution, shuttering frame rates, and other technical glitches, seem to some to evidence the paranormal. The conspiracy-minded and those looking for proof of spirits scour online videos for such static to interpret. A video of a young Japanese girl titled "Look at Her Face, Scary," in which her face dissolves slightly as she delivers a classroom presentation, has more than sixteen million views.

On the contrary, as technology changes our world at a speed so fast we can barely keep pace, it may be the case that our world will become increasingly haunted. Take the well-known phenomenon of the "Uncanny Valley" as one example: as computer-generated images and robots become more and more lifelike, they will paradoxically become more, not less, creepy. The closer they are to human, the more tiny faults—dead eyes, jerky movements—become magnified and unsettling. Japanese roboticist Masahiro Mori has been credited with first theorizing the problem, known as far back as 1970, but the idea didn't really gain traction until after 2000, when digital animation advanced sufficiently to make it a reality. And though designers and animators have made progress since first diagnosing the problem, what the Uncanny Valley reveals is that technological innovation often creates ghosts as fast as it dispels them.

Part of the reason that ghosts stay with us is that they remain a compelling mechanism to explain so much that is unknown in our lives. They enter and reenter our lexicon to explain the unexplainable, to represent the unrepresentable, to give a word to that which we don't understand. If scientists truly believe they are capable of dispelling the ghosts from our lives, then we'll have to replace them with some viable cultural conversation that offers an equally meaningful way of understanding death and the past.

And then there is social media, which has also created its share of ghosts. For several months in 2009, Facebook urged me to "reconnect" with a friend I hadn't spoken to in a while—but what Facebook was asking was impossible, since she had died earlier that year. To see her profile show up occasionally on my Facebook feed was never not jarring, particularly since Facebook's algorithms could not tell (and seemed to have no interest in learning) that she was dead. Because your online life lives on after you (unless you leave specific instructions on deactivating it) and because these sites depend on constant engagement, those who've left us have become cyber revenants.

This return of the dead happens more often than we think, and often with disturbing resonances. Images of Rehtaeh Parsons, a seventeen-year-old Canadian girl who committed suicide after a campaign of cyberbullying, began appearing after her death online as part of ads that beckoned: "Meet Canadian girls for friendship, dating or relationships. Sign up now!" The algorithm that crawled the Web, grabbed these images, and repurposed them for advertising had no idea—was never programmed to have an idea—about Parsons's life, her backstory, her death, or how her image's sudden reappearance could be so traumatic for those suddenly faced with it. This is how ghosts will continue to haunt us in the coming years: the unintended return of the dead via sites and algorithms that aren't yet programmed to let the dead rest.

Social media sites like Facebook, Twitter, and Instagram have in many ways replaced (or at least complemented) the cafés, parks, and bars where we gather; it's little wonder, then, that they've also become populated with ghosts. Physical places become haunted because of creaky doors, odd construction, and other quirks of architecture that get transformed in our minds into the paranormal. Online it's still a question of architecture: coding and algorithms with unintended consequences, like an uncanny hallway, which open up unexpected nightmares. And, as with physical architecture, it's unlikely that we'll ever dispel these ghosts in the machine entirely; coding, after all, is a human endeavor, and like architecture, it's prone to a thousand variables that can never be fully controlled.

Our belief (or lack thereof) in ghosts ultimately reflects the way we face death. Those of us who fear mortality can often find comfort in a belief in life after death, and those whom we fail to mourn properly may return to haunt us. If we can't find a way to design our cyber temples of the future in such a way as to accommodate the departed, we can expect their return in ways as surprising as they are unsettling.

⚭

Ghost stories are about how we face, or fail to face, the past—how we process information, how we narrate our past, and how we make sense of the gaps in that history. During my conversation with Eric Meharry about the ghost of Thelma Taylor, he mentioned that we may see fewer ghosts like Taylor's in the future, simply because we're so inundated with information, particularly about gruesome killings and other tragedies that tend to be fodder for ghost stories. "Lack of information is part of the recipe," Meharry told me, and today's ubiquitous news coverage—an endless online stream of updates, gossip, and posts by citizen journalists—is making that air of mystery more scarce. "Information," he said, "is killing ghost stories."

When I asked him if this was a good thing or not, he replied, "I don't know. The romantic idea of a lonely person haunting a place is slowly disappearing . . . the idea is becoming a ghost, I guess."

Then again, the glut of facts and the preponderance of evidence create as many gaps as they fill, leading to a swirling cacophony of information. There will never be a complete record, particularly when it comes to scenes of great emotional complexity. We can, for example, expect ghosts to continue to follow national tragedies—ghosts such as the mysterious woman who appeared in the Fresh Kills, New York, landfill in the days following September 11, 2001. Dressed in a World War II Red Cross outfit, holding a tray of sandwiches, the spectral aid worker appeared to a number of individuals, who claimed to be able to see her only from a distance and who said she vanished as they approached.

Besides, even if we could dispel them once and for all, we need them too badly. The language of ghosts is a means of coping with the unfamiliar, and if they sometimes require that we overlook the truth, that may be a price we're willing to pay. In some ways we don't want to know too much about the true story, since whatever happens, we can't break the spell— because the ghost is too important.

ACKNOWLEDGMENTS

This book could not have been written without help. Thanks to everyone who shared with me a ghost story or who directed me to a haunted house, hotel, prison, park, cemetery, or other haunted place. I'm also grateful to everyone who accompanied me on various ghost tours and ghost-hunting adventures, particularly: Elise Blackwell, Emily Mandel, Elizabeth Harper, Chelsey Johnson, Eric Bebernitz, Alex Dickey, Karl Erickson, and Gretchen Larsen. Thanks to all of the ghost hunters, historians, and tour guides who spoke with me for this project. In particular, thanks to Robert Kirkbride, Michele Yu, Kim Cooper, Richard Schave, Ben Miller, Margaret McGovern, Erik Meharry, and Jessamyn West, whose ideas gave me much-needed perspective throughout the process of writing this book.

Special thanks to Paulette Jarrett for sharing her stories with me.

Suzanne Fischer helped me work out the structure and format of this book through our early conversations, and I'm grateful for her feedback and her friendship. This book also benefited immensely from talks with Michelle Legro, Franz Potter, Kara Thompson, and Evan Kindley. Special thanks to Liberty Hardy for her unwavering support of this project and her all-around excellence. Thanks to Brenna Murray for research assistance.

Some of the first ideas of this book were worked out at lectures I presented at Machine Project in Los Angeles, Acme Studio in Brooklyn,

Odd Salon in San Francisco, and Death Salon Philadelphia at the Müt-ter Museum. Thanks to these venues and their staffs, particularly Mark Allen, Annetta Black, and Rachel James. Thanks to Dan Piepenbring at the *Paris Review* and Jane Friedman at the *Virginia Quarterly Review* for publishing early essays that would go on to become parts of this book. Thanks also to Fred Ramey and everyone at Unbridled Books.

I've also been fortunate to have surrounded myself with several differ-ent communities of writers, artists, and scholars who've helped nurture this project from its very beginning. At the Morbid Anatomy Museum, thanks to Tracy Hurley Martin, Joanna Ebenstein, Tonya Hurley, Laeti-tia Barbier, and Cristina Preda, without all of whom this book might not have happened. Thanks also to Caitlin Doughty, Megan Rosenbloom, Sarah Troop, and everyone at the Order of the Good Death for their constant support and inspiration. And thanks especially to the fabulous people at Betalevel: Jason Brown, Heather Parlato, Sean Deyoe, Amar Ravva, Dave Eng, Ariana Kelly, and Amina Cain.

A writer could not ask for a better agent than Anna Sproul-Latimer, whose enthusiasm for this project, along with her constant insight and expertise, made it happen. I am overwhelmed with gratitude for the sup-port I've received from her and everyone else at the Ross Yoon Agency. At Viking, my editor, Melanie Tortoroli, shaped and refined this manu-script and made it far better than I could have on my own. Thanks also to everyone else at Viking who's worked so hard on this book.

Thanks to my parents for taking me to the Winchester Mystery House so many times when I was a child and for supporting my youthful Stephen King obsession. Above all, thanks to Nicole, for having come so far with me through all the strangeness and for making the journey so much fun.

NOTES

AUTHOR'S NOTE

xiii   **"All argument is against it; but all belief is for it":** James Boswell, *The Life of Samuel Johnson, LL.D.* (London: Wordsworth Classics of World Literature, 1999), 635.

INTRODUCTION: ANATOMY OF A HAUNTING (NEW YORK, NY)

2   **Samuel Lenox Tredwell, Gertrude's brother:** Stories of the ghosts at the Merchant's House Museum have been collected in Andrew Bellov, *Some Say They Never Left: Tales of the Strange and Inexplicable at the Merchant's House Museum* (New York: Merchant's House Museum, 2007).

3   **"in the form of an old man":** Pliny the Younger, *The Letters of Caius Plinius Caecilius Secundus,* trans. William Melmoth, ed. Rev. F. C. T. Bosanquet (London: George Bell and Sons, 1905), 250.

3   **"made a sign with his hand":** Ibid., 251.

3   **45 percent of Americans:** Lee Speigel, "Spooky Number of Americans Believe in Ghosts," *Huffington Post,* February 8, 2013.

4   **The house was bought by Seabury Tredwell:** The best history of the Merchant's House Museum is Mary L. Knapp, *An Old Merchant's House: Life at Home in New York City, 1835–65* (New York: Girandole Books, 2012).

6   **known as a "memory palace":** On memory palaces, see Frances A. Yates, *The Art of Memory* (London: Routledge, 2001).

7   **"a representation of the unrepresentable":** Thomas W. Laqueur, *The Work of the Dead: A Cultural History of Mortal Remains* (Princeton, NJ: Princeton University Press, 2015), 69.

8 **changed shape through the decades:** See Judith Richardson, *Possessions: The History and Uses of Haunting in the Hudson Valley* (Cambridge: Harvard University Press, 2003), 103–9.

8 **a 2002 book containing the Leeds legend:** See Dennis William Hauck, *Haunted Places: The National Directory* (New York: Penguin, 2002), 297.

9 **"the return of the repressed":** Sigmund Freud, *Introductory Lessons on Psycho-Analysis,* trans. James Strachey (New York: W. W. Norton, 1989), 29.

10 **"allow access to dissonant knowledge":** Quoted in Tiya Miles, *Tales from the Haunted South: Dark Tourism and Memories of Slavery from the Civil War Era* (Chapel Hill: University of North Carolina Press, 2015), 10.

I: THE UNHOMELY

16 **"This house, which seemed somehow":** Shirley Jackson, *The Haunting of Hill House,* in *Novels and Stories* (New York: Library of America, 2010), 265.

17 **"the present writer must plead guilty":** Sigmund Freud, *The Uncanny,* trans. David McLintock (London: Penguin, 2003), 124.

18 **"shelters daydreaming"** and **"allows one to dream":** Gaston Bachelard, *The Poetics of Space,* trans. Maria Jolas (Boston: Beacon Press, 1994), 68.

18–19 **"Every corner in a house":** Ibid., 136.

19 **"The places in which we have *experienced*":** Ibid., 6.

19 **"When we concentrate on a material object":** Vladimir Nabokov, *Transparent Things* (New York: Vintage International, 1989), 1.

CHAPTER ONE: THE SECRET STAIRCASE (SALEM, MA)

21 **"Houses of any antiquity in New England":** Nathaniel Hawthorne, *Mosses from an Old Manse* (New York: Modern Library, 2003), 14.

22 **"Oh, there are subjects enough":** Quoted in James R. Mellow, *Nathaniel Hawthorne in His Times* (Baltimore: Johns Hopkins University Press, 1998), 175.

23 **it's "a rusty wooden house":** Nathaniel Hawthorne, *The House of the Seven Gables,* in *Collected Novels* (New York: Library of America, 1983), 355.

23 **"a great many times":** Ibid., 424.

24 **"form a patina, a part of the thing itself":** Lorinda R R. Goodwin, "Salem's House of the Seven Gables as Historic Site," in Dane Anthony Morrison and Nancy Lusignan Schultz, *Salem: Place, Myth, and Memory* (Boston: Northeastern University Press, 2015), 300.

24 **"what appears to be a teenage girl":** Ghost sightings at the House of the Seven Gables have been collected at www.graveaddiction.com/sevengab.html.

26 **"convince mankind—or, indeed":** Hawthorne, *House of the Seven Gables,* 352.

26 **"when no man shall build":** Ibid., 510.

27 **"pinching and pricking" her "dreadfully":** There are numerous accounts of the Salem witch crisis of 1692; the two I found to be most helpful are Mary Beth Norton, *In the Devil's Snare: The Salem Witchcraft Crisis of 1692* (New York: Vintage

Books, 2003), and Bernard Rosenthal, *Salem Story: Reading the Witch Trials of 1692* (Cambridge: Cambridge University Press, 1993).

28   **"by his warrant hath caused"**: Quoted in Rosenthal, *Salem Story*, 195.

28   **"with a ghastly look"**: Hawthorne, *House of the Seven Gables*, 358. See also Rosenthal, *Salem Story*, 87.

29   **"you are a lyer"**: Quoted in Rosenthal, *Salem Story*, 87.

29   **According to the nineteenth-century historian Thomas Hutchinson:** Thomas Hutchinson, *The History of Massachusetts from the First Settlement Thereof in 1628, Until the Year 1750* (Boston: 1795), 2:56.

30   **"My first visit to the House"**: Caroline O. Emmerton, *The Chronicles of Three Old Houses* (Salem, MA: House of Seven Gables Settlement Association, 1985), 29.

30   **"To console me my friends"**: Ibid., 34.

31   **"pine tree sixpence and a book"**: Ibid., 29.

31   **"Of what use for smuggling"**: Ibid., 18.

31   **"Can there be any doubt"**: Ibid., 15–16.

32   **"Thinking it over," Emmerton writes:** Ibid., 39.

32   **"For it seems to me"**: Ibid., 38.

33   **any legal or financial obligation to the victims' descendants:** The 1957 bill named only Ann Pudeator and "certain other persons"; it wasn't until 2001 that the last five women were cleared by name. "Massachusetts Clears 5 from Salem Witch Trials," *New York Times*, November 2, 2001.

33   **The town seems caught between past and present:** See Frances Hill, "Salem as Witch City," in Morrison and Schultz, *Salem: Place, Myth, and Memory*, 283–98.

34   **"the crimes for which they had been arrested":** J. K. Rowling, "History of Magic in North America," Piece Two, "Seventeenth Century and Beyond," www.pottermore.com.

CHAPTER TWO: SHIFTING GROUND (ST. FRANCISVILLE, LA)

37   **"unable to defeat Satan":** Norton, *In the Devil's Snare*, 226.

37   **"The pavements of the Main-street":** Nathaniel Hawthorne, "Main Street," in *Tales and Sketches* (New York: Library of America, 1982), 1028.

39   **either mostly or wholly fictitious:** See Miles, *Tales from the Haunted South*, chapter 2.

40   **she soon found herself beset by paranormal events of all kinds:** Frances Kermeen, *The Myrtles Plantation: The True Story of America's Most Haunted House* (New York: Grand Central Publishing, 2005). Despite the book's subtitle, the copyright page lists Kermeen's book as a work of fiction.

42   **When the Lutzes bought their dream home:** Jay Anson, *The Amityville Horror* (New York: Pocket Star Books, 2005).

42   **"as an enclosure for the sick":** Ibid., 122.

42   **"the Shinnecock did not use this tract":** Ibid.

42 **Johnson-Meyers channeled the spirit:** William Grimes, "Hans Holzer, Ghost Hunter, Dies at 89," *New York Times,* April 29, 2009.

43 **provided the couple with salient details:** See Ric Osuna, *The Night the DeFeos Died: Reinvestigating the Amityville Murders* (Bloomington, IN: Xlibris, 2002).

43 **a massive legal battle against the Maliseet:** Renée L. Bergland, *The National Uncanny: Indian Ghosts and American Subjects* (Hanover, NH: University Press of New England, 2000), 162–9.

44 **"Honey, do we *own* this?":** Stephen King, *Pet Sematary* (New York: Pocket Books, 1983), 26.

44 **"Now the Micmacs, the state of Maine":** Ibid., 244.

44 **"Who does own it":** Ibid., 260.

44 **"the Indians chose that spot":** Kermeen, *Myrtles Plantation,* 2.

45 **At the end of the last ice age:** See Richard Campanella, *Bienville's Dilemma: A Historical Geography of New Orleans* (Lafayette, LA: Center for Louisiana Studies, 2008), 77.

46 **"past small sandy islands":** Quoted in Campanella, *Bienville's Dilemma,* 78.

46 **In 1968 a guard:** Michael F. P. Doming, "The Tale of the Tunica Treasure," *Harvard Crimson,* October 13, 1983.

47 **"I found the thing":** "Court Denies Claim to Items Found on Indian Burial Site," *New York Times,* December 31, 1986.

CHAPTER THREE: THE ENDLESS HOUSE (SAN JOSE, CA)

50 **The basic facts of how the house got started:** The definitive biography of Sarah Winchester is Mary Jo Ignoffo, *Captive of the Labyrinth* (Columbia: University of Missouri Press, 2010).

50 **"expected that someday Hill House":** Jackson, *Haunting of Hill House,* 315.

51 **"There's the psychological aspect of the place":** Steven Henry Madoff, "Guns and Ghosts: The Winchester Witch Project," *New York Times,* February 27, 2005.

51 **"At one séance":** Quoted in the press release "Rose Red: The Stephen King Mini-Series on ABC Inspired by a Real-Life Ghost Story," www.winchestermystery house.com, January 27, 2002.

55 **In 1857 he had bought:** For a history of the Winchester Repeating Arms Company, see R. L. Wilson, *Winchester: An American Legend* (New York: Chartwell Books, 2004).

57 **San Francisco's population grew:** Susan Craddock, *City of Plagues: Disease, Poverty, and Deviance in San Francisco* (Minneapolis: University of Minnesota Press, 2000), 30.

57 **"Nor is sickness that scourge of humanity":** Quoted in Susan Craddock, *City of Plagues,* 25.

57 **by 1900 one-fourth of all migrants to California:** Ibid., 23.

58 **its great Electric Light Tower:** See Linda S. Larson, *San Jose's Monument to Progress: The Electric Light Tower* (San Jose, CA: San Jose Historical Museum Association, 1989).

58   "For the first time the citizens": Quoted in ibid., 9.

58   "California was a hot-bed": Quoted in Kevin Starr, *Americans and the California Dream: 1850–1915* (New York: Oxford University Press, 1973), 110.

59   "I am constantly having to make an upheaval": Sarah Winchester to Jennie Bennett, June 11, 1898, Bennett Family Papers, Connecticut Historical Society.

59   "If I did not get so easily tired out": Ibid.

59   "I hope some day": Sarah Winchester to Jennie Bennett, May 14, 1898.

60   "they did not want to encourage young girls": Sara Holmes Boutelle, *Julia Morgan, Architect* (New York: Abbeville Press, 1988), 30.

61   "I began to understand that everything": Charles Dickens, *Great Expectations* (London: Penguin, 1996), 60.

64   By 1895 unemployment: See Samuel Rezneck, "Unemployment, Unrest, and Relief in the United States During the Depression of 1893–97," *Journal of Political Economy* 61, no. 4: 324.

64   "dark, mysterious, crafty, wicked": Quoted in David A. Zimmerman, *Panic!: Markets, Crises, and Crowds in American Fiction* (Chapel Hill: University of North Carolina Press, 2006), 65.

64   "It is probably safe to say": H. P. Robinson, "The Humiliating Report of the Strike Commission," *Forum* 18 (September 1894–February 1895): 523; quoted in Rezneck, "Unemployment, Unrest, and Relief in the United States during the Depression of 1893–97," 335.

64–65 "result of rural rumors": "Only Gossip: No Truth in the Story of the Winchester Palace," *San Jose Evening News*, October 11, 1897.

66   "appraised as of no value": Ignoffo, *Captive of the Labyrinth*, 206.

67   "The whole thing is beautifully inlaid": *Oregon Daily Journal*, November 3, 1924.

67   "as sane and clear headed a woman": Quoted in Ignoffo, *Captive of the Labyrinth*, 165.

CHAPTER FOUR: THE RATHOLE REVELATION (GEORGETOWN, NY, AND BULL VALLEY, IL)

69   "found that if he put his chisel": "Brown's Free Hall—Inspiration and Will," *Banner of Light*, January 18, 1879.

70   they had been communicating with the spirit of a dead man: There are many good histories of the Fox sisters; among them is Frank Podmore, *Modern Spiritualism: A History and a Criticism* (London: Methuen and Company, 1902), especially volume 2.

70   "I then asked if Mr. ———": Quoted in ibid., 181.

71   in Philadelphia there were another: Podmore, I:183.

71   "his wonderful persistence has well-nigh conquered": "Brown's Free Hall—Inspiration and Will," *Banner of Light*, January 18, 1879. Italics in original.

72   one more "paroxysm of humbug": John Dix, *Transatlantic Tracings* (London: W. Tweedie, Strand, 1853), 244.

72 Emerson called it the "rathole revelation": Quoted in Daniel Conway Moncure, *Emerson at Home and Abroad* (London: Trübner & Co., 1883), 189.

72 "have mistaken flatulence for inspiration": Ralph Waldo Emerson, *The Journals and Miscellaneous Notebooks of Ralph Waldo Emerson, 1854–1861,* ed. Susan Sutton Smith and Harrison Hayford (Cambridge, MA: Belknap Press, 1978), 254.

72 "I hate this shallow Americanism": Ralph Waldo Emerson, "Success," in *The Complete Works of Ralph Waldo Emerson,* ed. Edward Waldo Emerson (New York: AMS Press, 1904), vol. 7, 290.

73 "It is the secret of the world": Ralph Waldo Emerson, "Nominalist and Realist," in *Essays and Lectures* (New York: Library of America, 1983), 584.

73 our attitudes toward death were changing: On the changing social role of the dead body, see Ruth Richardson, *Death, Dissection and the Destitute* (London: Phoenix Press, 1988).

74 In short order Spiritualism became dominated by women: An excellent history of Spiritualism that traces its feminist roots is Ann Braude, *Radical Spirits: Spiritualism and Women's Rights in Nineteenth-Century America* (Bloomington: Indiana University Press, 2001).

74 "the only religious sect in the world": Quoted in ibid., 2.

74 "have always assumed that woman": Quoted in ibid., 3.

76 "This fellow had been taught": Quoted in Ignoffo, *Captive of the Labyrinth,* 209.

77 most economical shape for a stall is a wedge: J. C. Loudon, *An Encyclopaedia of Cottage, Farm, and Villa Architecture and Furniture* (London: Longman, Brown, Green, and Longmans, 1846), 375–76.

78 In 1995 the village clerk: Christine Winter, "Bull Valley Home Haunted Only by Reputation," *Chicago Tribune,* September 27, 1995.

78 "There's never been anything to those stories": Ibid.

78 "It's just something creepy that kids like to say about the place": Ibid.

79 "walking toward a group of pine trees": Carri Williams, "The Demon Walking Near the Stickney Mansion," www.trueghosttales.com/paranormal/the-demon-walking-near-the-stickney-mansion, April 13, 2011.

79 "put fear aside, and you may well encounter the divine there": MotherEarthPrayers, "Spirit House Society," YouTube video, February 28, 2011.

80 according to one study: Kathleen Weldon, "Paradise Polled: Americans and the Afterlife," *Huffington Post,* June 17, 2015.

CHAPTER FIVE: THE FAMILY THAT WOULD NOT LIVE
(ST. LOUIS, MO)

82 The Lemp family story: A history of the Lemp family and their brewing empire can be found in Rebecca F. Pittman, *The History and Haunting of the Lemp Mansion* (Loveland, CO: Wonderland Productions, 2015).

82 His marriage to Lillian fell apart: See Pittman, *The History and Haunting of the Lemp Mansion,* 237–39.

83   **Tradition holds that Charles:** Ibid., 347–53.

85   **Media and medium were two sides of the same coin:** See Jeffrey Sconce, *Haunted Media: Electronic Presence from Telegraphy to Television* (Durham, NC: Duke University Press, 2000).

86   **"Here is night brothers, here the birds burn":** Quoted in ibid., 88.

86   **"Secret reports . . . it is bad here":** Quoted in ibid., 91.

86   **"to empirically provable reality with a factual background":** Konstantin Raudive, *Breakthrough: An Amazing Experiment in Electronic Communication with the Dead* (New York: Lancer Books, 1971), 2.

90   **"I will take it with me now":** See Pittman, *History and Haunting of the Lemp Mansion*, 229–30.

90   **according to historian Davidson Mullgardt:** See Jeannette Cooperman, "The Last Lemp," *St. Louis Magazine,* May 15, 2015.

91   **"Our desire and passion is to let the wonderful people":** Quoted in Cooperman, "The Last Lemp."

91   **just one more example of someone trying to capitalize:** See ibid.

II: AFTER HOURS

95   **If the guidebooks are to be believed:** Legends of the hauntings at the Stanley Hotel can be found in, among other places, Sherri Granato, *Haunted America and Other Paranormal Travels* (Bloomington, IN: LifeRich, 2015).

96   **"heat, light, and cook meals exclusively with electricity":** A short but reliable history of the Stanley is in Phyllis Perry, *It Happened in Rocky Mountain National Park* (Guilford, CT: Morris Book Publishing, 2008), 38–41.

96   **"We found ourselves the only guests":** Quoted in Gary A. Warner, "Guests and Ghosts: Relax at the Colorado Hotel That Inspired *The Shining,*" *Victor Valley Daily Press,* December 14, 2002.

97   **"I don't know why this person":** Quoted in Gregory Lee Sullivan, "Visiting the Oldest Bookstore in America—And Its Resident Ghost," *Guardian,* February 25, 2016.

97   **A former employee delightfully named Putt-Putt:** Dan Koeppel, "Ghost Sightings Aren't Spooking Sales at Toys 'R' Us," *Chicago Tribune,* June 23, 1991.

98   **"He's a classic case":** Sylvia Browne, *Visits from the Afterlife: The Truth About Haunting Spirits and Reunions with Lost Loved Ones* (New York: New American Library, 2004), 75.

99   **As if to prove the point:** Stories of other Toys "R" Us stores that are reputedly haunted have been collected at http://ghosts.org/haunted-toys-r-us-sunnyvale-ca.

99   **independent analyses of her work:** Sylvia Browne's record has been analyzed in Joseph Gomes, "Prophet Motive," *Brill's Content,* November 27, 2000.

99   **"go to the light of God":** Browne, *Visits from the Afterlife,* 76.

CHAPTER SIX: A DEVILISH PLACE (RICHMOND, VA)

103 **There are ghosts everywhere:** For the best collections of the various hauntings in Shockoe Bottom, see Pamela Kinney, *Haunted Richmond* (Atglen, PA: Schiffer Publishing, 2007), and Scott Bergman and Sandi Bergman, *Haunted Richmond: The Shadows of Shockoe* (Charleston, SC: Haunted America, 2007).

104 **Virginia was home to the earliest settlements in North America:** Interview with the author, April 26, 2015.

105 **"delightfully situated on eight hills":** Charles Dickens, *American Notes,* quoted in Jack Trammell, *The Richmond Slave Trade: The Economic Backbone of the Old Dominion* (Charleston, SC: History Press, 2012), 74–5.

106 **"The exposure of ordinary goods":** Frederick Law Olmsted, *A Journey in the Seaboard Slave States, with Remarks About Their Economy,* quoted in Trammell, *Richmond Slave Trade,* 77–8.

106 **"were taken from the cars":** Solomon Northup, *Twelve Years a Slave* (New York: Penguin Books, 2012), 33.

107 **"a large yellow man, quite stout":** Ibid., 35.

107 **"In this building Lumpkin was accustomed":** James B. Simmons, "Lumpkin's Slave Jail," in Charles H. Corey, *A History of the Richmond Theological Seminary: Reminiscences of Thirty Years' Work among the Colored People of the South* (Richmond, VA: J. W. Randolph Company, 1895), 76.

108 **"On the floor of that room":** Quoted in Ned Sublette and Constance Sublette, *The American Slave Coast: A History of the Slave-Breeding Industry* (Chicago: Lawrence Hill Books), 586.

108 **"the epicenter of some of the most profound":** Bergman and Bergman, *Haunted Richmond,* 11.

108 **"The area surrounding the Shockoe Valley":** Ibid.

108 **"We have been able to find very little":** Ibid., 18.

109 **"If a premature exit from this world":** Ibid., 11.

109 **There the president is heard:** Accounts of Thomas Jefferson's ghost can be found in Charles A. Stanfield, *Haunted Presidents: Ghosts in the Lives of the Chief Executives* (Mechanicsburg, PA: Stackpole Books, 2010).

110 **"we have the wolf by the ears":** Quoted in Philip J. Schwarz, *Slave Laws in Virginia* (Athens: University of Georgia Press, 2010), 36.

110 **"not a fear of ghosts":** Miles, *Tales from the Haunted South,* 40.

110 **The only way to keep alive the white world:** As historian Philip J. Schwarz notes, Jefferson "believed that conformity to the law of slavery constituted a civic duty, protected him from some of the dangers inherent in slavery, preserved his liberty to hold humans in bondage, and even, secondarily, gave some personal security to the enslaved." He saw himself, in other words, as having a moral obligation to preserve the order of things, even if the order was itself immoral. And yet, Schwarz adds, it wasn't just his "deep attachment to the mores of his society" that

led him to defend slavery: "his 'conspicuous consumption,' and his chronic debt problem held him captive to bondage." Schwarz, *Slave Laws in Virginia*, 35.

111 **"It is better to buy none in families":** Quoted in Edward E. Baptist, *The Half Has Never Been Told: Slavery and the Making of American Capitalism* (New York: Basic Books, 2014), 102.

111 **This was not unintentional:** Ibid., 188.

111 **also of their memory in death:** See Vincent Brown, *The Reaper's Garden: Death and Power in the World of Atlantic Slavery* (Cambridge: Harvard University Press, 2008).

111 **"the new zombie body of slavery":** Baptist, *The Half Has Never Been Told*, 147.

112 **"Not a house in the country":** Toni Morrison, *Beloved* (New York: Plume, 1988), 5.

113 **"John May come back":** Jane Arrington, *Born in Slavery: Slave Narratives from the Federal Writers' Project, 1936–1938, North Carolina Narratives*, Vol. 11 (Federal Writers' Project, United States Work Projects Administration; Manuscript Division, Library of Congress, digital ID: mesn 111/048044), 46.

113 **"One night we was driving":** George Bollinger, *Born in Slavery: Slave Narratives from the Federal Writers' Project, 1936–1938, Missouri Narratives*, Vol. 10 (Federal Writers' Project, United States Work Projects Administration; Manuscript Division, Library of Congress, digital ID: mesn 100/041036), 36.

113 **A woman named Florida Clayton:** Florida Clayton, quoted in *Born in Slavery: Slave Narratives from the Federal Writers' Project, 1936–1938, Florida Narratives*, Vol. 3 (Federal Writers' Project, United States Work Projects Administration; Manuscript Division, Library of Congress, digital ID: mesn 030/065062), 62–63.

114 **"place where there is a high fence":** Thomas Lewis, *Born in Slavery: Slave Narratives from the Federal Writers' Project, 1936–1938, Indiana Narratives*, Vol. 5 (Federal Writers' Project, United States Work Projects Administration; Manuscript Division, Library of Congress, digital ID: mesn 050/127123), 126–27.

114 **"When the nights were still":** "Slave and Negro Lore," *Born in Slavery: Slave Narratives from the Federal Writers' Project, 1936–1938, Missouri Narratives*, Vol. 10 (Federal Writers' Project, United States Work Projects Administration; Manuscript Division, Library of Congress, digital ID: mesn 100/208203), 204.

114 **"How come I knows dey rides me?":** "Foots Get Tired from Choppin' Cotton," *Born in Slavery: Slave Narratives from the Federal Writers' Project, 1936–1938, Alabama Narratives*, Vol. 1 (Federal Writers' Project, United States Work Projects Administration; Manuscript Division, Library of Congress, digital ID: mesn 010/435429), 430–31.

114 **One woman in Tennessee:** Recounted in Baptist, *The Half Has Never Been Told*, 148.

114–15 **A man identified only as Uncle Louis:** "Psychology of a Runaway Slave," *Born in Slavery: Slave Narratives from the Federal Writers' Project, 1936–1938, Alabama*

Narratives, Vol. 1 (Federal Writers' Project, United States Work Projects Administration; Manuscript Division, Library of Congress, digital ID: mesn 010/269263), 265–66.

115 **"The legacy of Wall Street":** Trammell, *Richmond Slave Trade,* 116.

116 **an archaeological team largely funded:** See Abigail Tucker, "Digging Up the Past at a Richmond Jail: The Excavation of a Notorious Jail Recalls Richmond's Leading Role in the Slave Trade," *Smithsonian Magazine,* March 2009.

117 **"I started weeping and couldn't stop":** Ibid.

117 **"It doesn't escape me for one moment":** Caitlin Dewey, "Transcript: Lupita Nyong'o's Emotional Oscars Acceptance Speech," *Washington Post,* March 2, 2014.

CHAPTER SEVEN: BABY (RENO, NV)

119 **that of Bella Rawhide and Timber Kate:** Bella and Kate's story is recounted in a number of places, including James Reynolds, *Ghosts in American Houses* (New York: Paperback Library, 1955), and Ken Summers, *Queer Hauntings: True Tales of Gay and Lesbian Ghosts* (Maple Shade, NJ: Heritage Press, 2009).

123 **"a seedy biker bar":** Alexa Albert, *Brothel: The Mustang Ranch and Its Women* (New York: Ballantine, 2001), 12.

125 **In 2013 investigators from the reality show:** "Mustang Ranch," *Ghost Adventures,* Travel Channel, October 18, 2013.

126 **"Baby apparently likes water":** Interview with the author, December 2, 2014.

128 **"This is the epitome of caregiving":** Interview with the author, December 1, 2014.

CHAPTER EIGHT: PASSING THROUGH (LOS ANGELES, CA)

132 **"There are many stories about ghostly presence":** Quoted in Dennis Romero, "Laura Finley's Death at Old Biltmore Hotel in Downtown L.A. Perplexes Investigators: A Commenter Suggests the Place Is Haunted," *LA Weekly,* October 27, 2010.

133 **"not a superstitious man":** Wilkie Collins, *Miss or Mrs?, The Haunted Hotel, The Guilty River* (Oxford: Oxford University Press, 1993), 172.

133 **"How many times":** Interview with the author, August 3, 2012.

134 **"We're two different people":** Interview with the author, August 12, 2012.

136 **"I think he's a corrupt cop":** Interview with the author, August 2, 2012.

137 **unusual repetition, or "involuntary repetition":** Freud, *The Uncanny,* 145.

137 **"The uncanny is home defamiliarized":** Wayne Koestenbaum, *Hotel Theory* (New York: Soft Skull Press, 2007), 116.

138 **"an old hotel that had once been exclusive":** Raymond Chandler, "Nevada Gas," in *Collected Stories* (New York: Alfred A. Knopf, 2002), 238.

139 **Amateur sleuths became obsessed with the video:** Josh Dean's "American Horror Story: The Cecil Hotel" (on the Web site *Matter,* October 27, 2015)

recounts the history of the Internet's fascination with Lam's death, as well as the subsequent police investigation.

140   **"ghost ship floating adrift"**: Quoted in Lynnea Chapman King, *The Coen Brothers Encyclopedia* (Lanham, MD: Rowan and Littlefield, 2014), 7.

142   **"It does not wish to be a part of the city"**: Frederic Jameson, *Postmodernism: Or, The Cultural Logic of Late Capitalism* (Durham, NC: Duke University Press, 2003), 42.

142   **"You are likely to move around"**: Charles Willard Moore, *A City Observed, Los Angeles: A Guide to Its Architecture and Landscapes* (New York: Random House, 1984), 16.

146   **"We want proof"**: LA Ghost Patrol, "LAGP on Fox News 11 at Suicide Bridge," YouTube video, March 10, 2012.

147   **"paranormal archaeology"**: Interview with the author, August 3, 2012.

III: CIVIC-MINDED SPIRITS

153   **"a generous, whole-souled man"**: Lloyd C. Henning, quoted in Leland J. Hanchett, *The Crooked Trail to Holbrook: An Arizona Cattle Trail* (Phoenix, AZ: Arrowhead Press, 1993), 217.

153   **"Hundreds of persons"**: Ibid., 215.

154   **that reflected his dark sense of humor:** Both funeral announcements can be found in, among other places, ibid., 216–17.

156   **"Smiley exhibited great coolness"**: Holbrook *Argus*, January 13, 1900, quoted in Linda Kor, "New Marker Recognizes Smiley's Place in Navajo County History," *Arizona Journal*, July 24, 2015.

156   **But according to Marita R. Keems:** See Antonio R. Garcez, *Arizona Ghost Stories* (Moriarty, NM: Red Rabbit Press, 2012).

CHAPTER NINE: MELANCHOLY CONTEMPLATION
(MOUNDSVILLE, WV)

159   **The husband's name was Erasmus Stribbling Trout Shue:** Shue's biography is recounted in Katie Letcher Lyle, *The Man Who Wanted Seven Wives: The Greenbrier Ghost and the Famous Murder Mystery of 1897* (Charleston, SC: Quarrier Press, 1999).

160   **"stretched out perfectly straight"**: Quoted in ibid., 9.

160   **"slight discoloration on the right side"**: Ibid.

161   **"It was no dream"**: Ibid., 118.

162   **"Because of lack of ventilation"**: *Crain v. Bordenkircher*, 342 S.E.2d 422, Supreme Court of Appeals of West Virginia, 1986.

162   **Adkins had been one of three men:** Stan Bumgardner and Christine Kreiser, "'Thy Brother's Blood': Capital Punishment in West Virginia," *West Virginia Historical Society Quarterly*, http://www.wvculture.org/history/wvhs/wvhs941.html.

162   **according to one employee I spoke to:** Benjamin Miller, interview with the author, November 1, 2015.

163   **"frightening yet intriguing"**: Margee Kerr, *Scream: Chilling Adventures in the Science of Fear* (New York: Public Affairs, 2015), 54–5.

163 **"leave you there or drop you"**: Ibid., 64.

164 **"Its good design"**: "Report of the Commissioners Appointed to Superintend the Erection of the Eastern Penitentiary, Near Philadelphia, on the Penal Code," in Samuel Hazard, ed., *The Register of Pennsylvania, Devoted to the Preservation of Facts and Documents, and Every Other Kind of Useful Information Respecting the State of Pennsylvania* (Philadelphia: W. F. Geddes, 1828), vol. 1, 264.

164 **"to impress so great a dread"**: Ibid.

164 **"The style of architecture of a prison"**: Quoted in Elmer Barnes, *The Evolution of Penology in Pennsylvania: A Study in American Social History* (Indianapolis, IN: Bobbs-Merrill, 1927), 143.

165 **a sense of awe and "melancholy contemplation"**: Charles C. Western, *Remarks Upon Prison Discipline* (London: James Ridgway, 1821), 22.

165 **"The design and execution impart"**: John Wilkes, *Encyclopaedia Londinensis* (London: G. Jones, 1826), vol. 21, 421–2.

167 **Joseph Tomlinson discovered it in 1770:** For a history of the Grave Creek Mound from its rediscovery to the present, see Delf Norona, *Moundsville's Mammoth Mound* (Moundsville: West Virginia Archeological Society, 1954).

167 **"Around the base of this column"**: Quoted in ibid., 34.

170 **"One of the most famous murder cases in Australia"**: Quoted in Lyle, *Man Who Wanted Seven Wives*, 159.

CHAPTER TEN: THE STAIN (DANVERS, MA, AND ATHENS, OH)

175 **"the present state of insane persons"**: Quoted in Andrew Scull, *Madness in Civilization: A Cultural History of Insanity, from the Bible to Freud, from the Madhouse to Modern Medicine* (Princeton, NJ: Princeton University Press, 2015), 192.

175 **"All experience"**: Quoted in ibid., 207.

176 **"laboratory for the purification of culture"**: Benjamin Reiss, *Theaters of Madness: Insane Asylums and Nineteenth-Century American Culture* (Chicago: University of Chicago Press, 2008), 79.

177 **One opponent, Hervey B. Wilbur:** See Carla Yanni, *The Architecture of Madness: Insane Asylums in the United States* (Minneapolis: University of Minnesota Press, 2007), 165.

178 **A report from 1939:** "The Commonwealth of Massachusetts Annual Report of the Trustees of the Danvers State Hospital for the Year Ending November 30, 1939, 11. Found online at http://abandonedasylum.com/yahoo_site_admin1/assets/docs/danvers1939.14582704.pdf.

179 **"If you think back to the beginnings"**: Quoted in Michael Puffer, "The Lore, and Lure, of Danvers State Hospital," *Danvers Herald*, October 29, 2003.

179 **Dr. Henry Cotton, who from 1907 to 1930:** See Andrew Scull, *Madhouse: A Tale of Megalomania and Modern Medicine* (New Haven: Yale University Press, 2005).

180 **In such a setting emerged a ghost story:** Carolyn M. Zimmermann, Ünige A. Laskay, and Glen P. Jackson, "Analysis of Suspected Trace Human Remains from

an Indoor Concrete Surface," *Journal of Forensic Sciences* 53, no. 6 (November 2008): 1437–42.

182 **"A disorderly patient is stripped naked":** *The Trial of Ebenezer Haskell, in Lunacy, and His Acquittal Before Judge Brewster, in November, 1868, Together with a Brief Sketch of the Mode of Treatment of Lunatics in Different Asylums in This Country and in England* (Philadelphia, 1869), 43.

183 **"a fantastic château, much dilapidated":** Edgar Allan Poe, "The System of Doctor Tarr and Professor Fether," in *Poetry and Tales* (New York: Library of America, 1984), 699–716.

184 **"These are America's castles":** Interview with the author, July 5, 2015.

185 **cost the state more than $30 million:** William Westhoven, "Greystone Fading into Black," *Daily Record,* October 10, 2015.

CHAPTER ELEVEN: AWAITING THE DEVIL'S COMING
(CHARLESTON, SC, AND DOUGLAS COUNTY, KS)

187 **"The Souls of the Dead appear frequently":** Joseph Addison, *The Spectator,* No. 90, June 13, 1711.

188 **Her father, Dr. Edmund Ravenel:** Ravenel's life and career is discussed in Lester D. Stephens, *Science, Race, and Religion in the American South: John Bachman and the Charleston Circle of Naturalists, 1815–1895* (Chapel Hill: University of North Carolina Press, 2000).

189 **Poe knew Ravenel while stationed at Sullivan's Island:** See Arthur Hobson Quinn, *Edgar Allan Poe: A Critical Biography* (Baltimore, MD: Johns Hopkins University Press, 1998), 130.

189 **"well-educated, with unusual powers":** Poe, "The Gold Bug," in *Poetry and Tales,* 561.

190 **We should not be dissuaded:** Some have suggested that Annabel may not have been Edmund Ravenel's daughter but perhaps a niece or other relative. But the exhaustive Ravenel genealogical records reveal no such plausible candidate; there are very few Annabels, Annabelles, Annas or Annes, and all either died in childhood or were born after Poe himself died.

190 **"If you would see Charleston's greatest attraction":** Edward Hepple Hall, *Appleton's Hand-Book of American Travel* (New York: D. Appleton & Co., 1866), 353.

191 **graveyards were as centrally located:** On the history and evolution of the graveyard, see Colin Dickey, "Necropolis," *Lapham's Quarterly* 3, no. 4 (Fall 2010).

191 **In 1744 a story circulated:** See John McManners, *Death and the Enlightenment: Changing Attitudes to Death Among Christians and Unbelievers in Eighteenth-Century France* (Oxford: Oxford University Press, 1985), 313.

191 **Fully 73 percent of Colma's land:** Carol Pogash, "Colma, Calif., Is a Town of 2.2 Square Miles, Most of It Six Feet Deep," *New York Times,* December 9, 2006.

192   **"the emanations of the dead":** Quoted in Christopher Vernon, *Graceland Cemetery: A Design History* (Amherst: University of Massachusetts Press, 2011), 26.

192   **and finally Graceland:** On the history of Graceland, see ibid.

192   **"neglected" and in an "actually repulsive condition":** Quoted in ibid., 28.

193   **described as the "most perfect expression":** Wilhelm Miller, quoted in ibid., 177.

193   **For much of English history:** A concise history of the etymology of "graveyard" and "cemetery" can be found in Laqueur, *Work of the Dead*, 118–21.

194   **"more efficient instrument to elevate Ambition":** Joseph Story, *An Address Delivered on the Dedication of the Cemetery at Mount Auburn, September 24, 1831* (Boston: Joseph T. and Edwin Buckingham, 1831), 14.

195   **"it was a little black relic":** Dutton Cook, *On the Stage: Studies of Theatrical History and the Actor's Art* (London: Sampson Low, Marston, Searl, and Rivington, 1883), vol. 1, 224.

195   **Additionally, Cooke's skull was stolen:** Ibid., 224–5.

196   **"haunted by legends of diabolical, supernatural happenings":** Jain Penner, "Legend of Devil Haunts Tiny Town," *University Daily Kansan,* November 5, 1974.

196   **"All of a sudden I heard a noise":** Ibid.

197   **"in awkward positions on the floor":** Tom Ramstack, "Devil Bypasses Cemetery," *University Daily Kansan,* March 22, 1978.

198   **"whatever lurks in the church":** Michelle Worrall, "Ghostly Tales Haunt Town's Graveyard," *University Daily Kansan,* April 16, 1985.

198   **"The real evil," the paper proclaimed:** Elicia Hill, "Vandalism at Stull's Mythical 'Gate to Hell' Frustrates Residents," *University Daily Kansan,* November 1, 1990.

198   **"When I used to patrol out there":** Tom Dehart, "Rumors, Urban Legends Surround Stull Cemetery," *University Daily Kansan,* October 31, 2013.

199   **"A lot of history fell":** Richard Gintowt, "Hell Hath No Fury," www.lawrence.com, October 26, 2004.

199   **"One man wrote and said a relative of mine":** Ibid.

199   **"This story about it being haunted":** Ibid.

200   **Inez was only six years old:** On the ghost of Inez Clarke, see Tom Ogden, *Haunted Cemeteries: Creepy Crypts, Spine-Tingling Spirits, and Midnight Mayhem* (Guilford, CT: Globe Pequot Press, 2010), 21; and Jeff Morris and Vince Shields, *Chicago Haunted Handbook: 99 Ghostly Places You Can Visit in and Around the Windy City* (Covington, KY: Clerisy Press, 2013), 21–2.

200   **a sample of the carver's work to drum up business:** An exhaustive search into the history of the statue can be found in John J. Binder and William G. Willard, "The Mysterious Statue of Inez 'Clarke,'" *Chicago Genealogist* 44, no. 1, 3–7.

CHAPTER TWELVE: OUR ILLUSTRIOUS DEAD (SHILOH, TN)

203 **In Cold Harbor, Virginia:** There are many books about ghosts of Civil War battlefields, including Beth Brown, *Haunted Battlefields: Virginia's Civil War Ghosts* (Atglen, PA: Schiffer Publishing, 2008); Mark Nesbitt, *Civil War Ghost Trails: Stories from America's Most Haunted Battlefields* (Mechanicsburg, PA: Stackpole Publishing, 2012); and Daniel Cohen, *Civil War Ghosts* (New York: Scholastic, 1999).

203 **"He was lying down on the moss":** Alan Brown, *Tales from the Haunted South* (Jackson: University Press of Mississippi, 2004), 239.

204 **The creation of the Civil War battlefield cemeteries:** On the creation of the Civil War battlefield monuments, see Drew Gilpin Faust, *This Republic of Suffering: Death and the American Civil War* (New York: Vintage Books, 2008), chapter 7.

204 **"Shall we permit their honored graves":** James F. Russling, "National Cemeteries," *Harper's New Monthly Magazine* (August 1866), 311–12.

205 **"arguably the most elaborate federal program":** Faust, *This Republic of Suffering*, 219.

206 **"the body, by the fact of its physical location":** Laqueur, *Work of the Dead*, 54.

206 **"though lost, still just":** Quoted in Faust, *This Republic of Suffering*, 245.

207 **"Sometimes we would meet one or two people":** Quoted in Gladys-Marie Fry, *Night Riders in Black Folk History* (Chapel Hill: University of North Carolina Press, 1975), 137.

207 **Stories circulated of an incident:** Wyn Craig Wade, *The Fiery Cross: The Ku Klux Klan in America* (New York: Oxford University Press, 1987), 36.

207 **"A spirit from the other world":** Walter Lynnwood Fleming, *Documentary History of Reconstruction: Political, Military, Social, Religious, Educational & Industrial, 1865 to the Present Time* (Cleveland: Arthur H. Clark, 1907), vol. 2, 361.

208 **"they had come from Manassas Gap":** Quoted in Fry, *Night Riders*, 137.

208 **"What do you all want to whip me for":** Quoted in Fleming, *Documentary History of Reconstruction*, 371–3.

208 **"bones rattling together":** Wade, *Fiery Cross*, 33.

209 **simple stage magic trickery:** Ibid., 35–36.

209 **"the Klan legends of terrified 'darkies'":** Ibid., 36–7.

210 **"it has been suggested that blacks":** Ibid.

210 **"The concept of returning Confederate dead":** Fry, *Night Riders*, 136.

210 **"The Klux is the living dead":** Edward H. Dixon, *The Terrible Mysteries of the Ku-Klux-Klan* (New York: n.p., 1868), 43.

210 **"The fraudulent ghost," Fry writes:** Fry, *Night Riders*, 73.

CHAPTER THIRTEEN: THE WIND THROUGH CATHEDRAL PARK (PORTLAND, OR)

213 **In the video there is first the image:** GuerrillaFilms1, "Amateur Ghost Hunting in Cathedral Park," YouTube video, November 3, 2010.

214 **"Oh yeah," one diner owner told the local news:** Tim Becker, "Thelma Taylor: Phantom in Cathedral Park?" www.koin.com, October 29, 2015.

214 **"visit the area and see":** Andy Weeks, *Haunted Oregon: Ghosts and Strange Phenomena of the Beaver State* (Mechanicsburg, PA: Stackpole Books, 2014), 20.

215 **"Inanimate materials, such as stone":** Donna Stewart, *Ghosthunting Oregon* (Cincinnati: Clerisy Press, 2014), 22.

215 **"The question is not whether people see ghosts":** T. C. Lethbridge, *Ghost and Ghoul* (London: Routledge and Kegan Paul, 1961), 36.

215–16 **"are no more than mental pictures":** Ibid., 151.

216 **a haunted house has "photographed" a past tragedy:** Oliver Lodge, *Man and the Universe: A Study in the Influence of the Advance in Scientific Knowledge upon Our Understanding of Christianity* (London: Methuen and Co., 1908), 194.

216 **"Is it a remnant spirit":** Interview with the author, March 9, 2015.

217 **"a vague, scary story that circulated":** Jim Speirs, "Speaking of Ghosts," deathinspadesandmore.blogspot.com, July 9, 2010.

218 **"I just felt *bad* for her":** Interview with the author, March 2, 2015.

218 **"According to John Mbiti":** James W. Loewen, *Lies Across America: What Our Historic Sites Get Wrong* (New York: Touchstone, 2000), 24.

219 **"Not primarily motivated by loss or grief":** Ibid.

219 **"It is not the passion":** Jean Baudrillard, *For a Critique of a Political Economy of the Sign*, trans. Charles Levin (St. Louis: Telos Press, 1981), 92.

221 **in the city of the sasha dead:** Kevin Brockmeier, *The Brief History of the Dead* (New York: Vintage, 2006).

221 **Having awakened memories decades old:** See Speirs, "Speaking of Ghosts," deathinspadesandmore.blogspot.com, July 9, 2010.

222 **"So she pulls it out of her mouth":** Interview with the author, January 10, 2016.

IV: USELESS MEMORY

228 **a dumb anecdote to entertain friends:** A user named "niki-mullins" commented on the Virtual Tourist Web site, "Also some say the water was cursed by Indians. And that if you drink it, that you'll be stuck here no matter how hard you try to leave. As far as for me I didn't grow up here, THANK GOD, but the curse seems to be holding up no matter what." Another user on the same page, "matt 999tye," concurs: "Honestly, I am not superstitious or anything, but this curse may be true. All my drive and passion for leaving Binghamton has vanished. Binghamton is not a recommended tourist area." See https://www.virtualtourist.com/travel/ North_America/United_States_of_America/New_York_State/Binghamton-837475/ Warnings_or_Dangers-Binghamton-TG-C-1.html.

230 **"A few stories came across as fairly light":** Elena Gormley, "Ghost Tours Turn Women's Abuse into Family Friendly Entertainment," Broadly.vice.com, October 10, 2015.

230 **"may have committed suicide":** Ibid.

231 **"white tourists always made smart comments":** Ibid.

231   **"The city's very obsessed with its brand":** Interview with the author, November 5, 2015.

231   **"By limiting the universe of speakers":** "Savannah Tour Guides Say City Uses Testing to Control Speech," Associated Press, August 15, 2015.

231   **the story is probably fictionalized:** See Miles, *Tales from the Haunted South*, chapter 1.

232   **Stephen Bader, however, contends:** Jamie Caskey, "Stephen Bader Responds (TAPS at Sorrel-Weed)," http://hauntedsavannah.blogspot.com/2005/11/stephen-bader-responds-taps-at-sorrel.html, November 15, 2005.

CHAPTER FOURTEEN: THE WET GRAVE (NEW ORLEANS, LA)

233   **"a song which rises like slow smoke":** Jeanne deLavigne, *Ghost Stories of Old New Orleans* (Baton Rouge: Louisiana State University Press, 2013), 3.

233   **"actually resembles no other city":** Lafcadio Hearn, *American Writings* (New York: Library of America, 2009), 670.

234   **"spectral, mysterious, inexplicable":** Ibid., 680.

234   **The wealthy Frenchman who lived here:** This story is told, among other places, in deLavigne's *Ghost Stories of Old New Orleans*, under the title "The Golden Brown Woman."

235   **"It's just a city that everybody loves":** Interview with the author, February 4, 2015.

236   **the building was operating:** Paul Oswell, *New Orleans Historic Hotels* (Charleston, SC: The History Press, 2014), 136.

236   **already being advertised as a haunted house:** The best history of the Lalaurie Mansion and its notorious owner is Carolyn Morrow Long, *Madame Lalaurie: Mistress of the Haunted House* (Gainesville: University Press of Florida, 2012).

237   **"no spirits wander through its wide halls":** Henry C. Castellanos, *New Orleans as It Was: Episodes of Louisiana Life* (Baton Rouge: Louisiana State University Press, 1978), 62.

237   **"barbarous treatment of her slaves contrary to law":** Quoted in Long, *Madame Lalaurie*, 79.

238   **"There are those who would be better employed":** Quoted in ibid., 90.

238   **"several wretched negroes":** Ibid.

238   **"seven slaves, more or less horribly mutilated":** Ibid.

238   **"with the intention of terminating the sufferings":** Ibid.

239   **"at least two thousand persons visited":** Ibid., 91.

239   **"justice will be done and the guilty be brought to punishment":** Ibid.

240   **"this bewitching and engaging creature":** Herbert Asbury, *The French Quarter: An Informal History of New Orleans* (New York: Alfred A. Knopf, 2003), 248.

240   **"Madame Lalaurie, under her soft and beautiful exterior":** deLavigne, *Ghost Stories of Old New Orleans*, 257.

241   **"memory operates as both quotation and invention":** Joseph Roach, *Cities of the Dead: Circum-Atlantic Performance* (New York: Columbia University Press, 1996), 33.

242   "This is a higher crime area": Quoted in Anna Hartnell, "Katrina Tourism and a Tale of Two Cities: Visualizing Race and Class in New Orleans," *American Quarterly* 61, no. 3: 725.

242   "site of translation": Ibid., 723.

242   "spatial apartheid": Quoted in ibid., 732.

243   "The house stands, and is meant to stand": Harriet Martineau, *Retrospect of Western Travel* (London: Saunders and Otley, 1838), vol. 1, 263.

243   "The house is very still": George Washington Cable, "The 'Haunted House' in Royal Street," in *Strange True Tales of Louisiana* (New York: Charles Scribner's Sons, 1889), 195.

244   "admirable firmness and propriety": Quoted in Long, *Madame Lalaurie*, 158.

246   "Wait here until night": deLavigne, *Ghost Stories of Old New Orleans*, 13.

247   "I was in my sleeping bag": Janet Yee, "Guardsmen Sense Ghostly Presence in New Orleans," KPIX, CBS5, San Francisco, September 23, 2005.

247   "One of the many lessons": Ceci Connolly, "A Grisly but Essential Issue," *Washington Post*, June 9, 2006.

247   "Even cities feel trauma": Andrew Buncombe, "Hurricane Katrina 10th Anniversary: New Orleans Is Haunted by the Death of Vera Smith," *The Independent*, August 24, 2015.

248   "mammoth temple of burger worship": Sarah Baird, "Review: Charcoal's Gourmet Burger Bar," *Gambit*, October 13, 2014.

249   "I saw a bloodied corpse weeping body fluids": Chris Rose, "Vera Smith's Makeshift Garden District Grave Endures as a Most Unlikely—and Poignant—Katrina Memorial," *Times-Picayune*, October 25, 2009.

250   "symbol of the quiet suffering people endured": "Vera Smith's Death After Hurricane Katrina Still Haunts New Orleans Neighborhood," Associated Press, August 19, 2015.

250   "She was not a sad woman": "New Orleans Restaurant Reportedly Haunted by Hurricane Katrina Victim," www.aol.com, August 24, 2015.

251   "Our message to Vera": Kenny Lopez, "Hurricane Katrina Victim Haunting New Orleans Burger Joint?," wgno.com, December 10, 2013.

CHAPTER FIFTEEN: AMONG THE RUINS (DETROIT, MI)

253   "the figure of a man, white and terrible": See Amy Elliott Bragg, *Hidden History of Detroit* (Charleston, SC: History Press, 2011), 120.

254   "America, you have it better": Johann Wolfgang von Goethe, "Den Vereinigten Staaten," in *Goethes Werke: I. Abtheilung, 5 Band* (Tokyo: Sansyusya, 1975), 137.

256   "In the ruin history has physically merged": Walter Benjamin, *The Origin of German Tragic Drama*, trans. John Osborne (London: Verso, 2009), 178.

256   "deep and ample joy": Gustave Flaubert, *The Letters of Gustave Flaubert, 1830–1857*, ed. and trans. Francis Steegmuller (Cambridge, MA: Belknap Press, 1980), 71.

256 **"a ruin is a sacred thing":** William Gilpin, *Observations, Relative Chiefly to Pictur-esque Beauty, Made in the Year 1772, on Several Parts of England, Particularly the Mountains and Lakes of Cumberland and Westmoreland,* 3rd ed. (London: T. Caddell and W. Davies, 1808), vol. 2, 183.

257 **"The ideas that ruins awaken in me":** Denis Diderot, quoted in Michael S. Roth with Claire Lyons and Charles Merewether, *Irresistible Decay: Ruins Reclaimed* (Los Angeles: Getty Research Institute for the History of Art and the Humanities, 1997), 59.

257 **"Is it unseemly now or ever":** Sarah Boxer, "Even in a Moonscape of Tragedy, Beauty Is in the Eye," *New York Times,* May 23, 2002.

258 **"At first you're really flattered":** Quoted in Dora Apel, *Beautiful Terrible Ruins: Detroit and the Anxiety of Decline* (New Brunswick, NJ: Rutgers University Press, 2015), 20.

259 **"Mr. Mason went slightly overboard":** Claire Moore, "Top Ten Most Haunted Places in Michigan," www.awesomemitten.com/ten-haunted-places-in-michigan, October 20, 2012.

261 **"a woman of unusual height":** Marie Caroline Watson Hamlin, *Legends of Le Détroit* (Detroit: Thorndike Nourse, 1884), 25–30.

262 **"seen scampering along the shore":** Charles M. Skinner, *Myths and Legends of Our Own Land* (Auckland, NZ: Floating Press, 2013), 460.

263 **"Detroit might be depopulated":** Thomas J., Sugrue, "Notown: Good News: A Few Hipsters Are Rediscovering Detroit. Bad News: Everything Else," *Democracy: a Journal of Ideas,* Spring 2013, no. 28.

CHAPTER SIXTEEN: HILLSDALE, USA

267 **"I am making these directions so detailed":** Jackson, *Haunting of Hill House,* 252.

268 **"People *leave* this town":** Ibid., 259.

268 **Take "Route 39 to Ashton":** Ibid., 252.

268 **"the most remote part of New England":** *The Haunting,* directed by Robert Wise, 1963.

269 **"Whether the source of the spectral apparitions":** *Stambovsky v. Ackley,* 169 A.D.2d 254, Appellate Division of the Supreme Court of New York, First Department, 1991.

270 **In 2008 Janet Milliken:** On the history of the house in Thornton, Pennsylvania, see Will Hunt and Matt Wolfe, "The Ghosts of Pickering Trail," *Atavist Magazine,* read.atavist.com/the-ghosts-of-pickering-trail.

270 **"If a property is perceived as haunted":** Quoted in ibid.

271 **"One cannot quantify the psychological impact":** *Milliken v. Jacono,* J-87-2013, Supreme Court of Pennsylvania, 2014.

271 **"a messed-up place to work because it's haunted":** Frank Rosario, Chris Perez, and Jennifer Gould Kell, "Ghosts Scare Staff Away from Luxury Rental Building," *New York Post,* May 18, 2015.

271 **"understandably perturbed by the gentrification"**: Lauren Evans, "Anti-Gentrification Ghosts Haunt Luxury Flatbush Development," *Gothamist*, May 19, 2015.

274 **"We left the valley with reluctant feet"**: Abigail, "Pacific Coast Letter," *Cincinnati Enquirer*, July 2, 1875.

275 **"Today all lie ghost towns"**: George F. Willison, *Here They Dug for the Gold* (New York: Brentano's, 1931), 71.

275 **"Sometimes, in the deep winter quiet"**: Ellen Baumler, *Montana Chillers: 13 True Tales of Ghosts and Hauntings* (Helena, MT: Farcountry Press, 2009), 61.

276 **A 2014 article in the *New York Times***: Jennifer A. Kingson, "Portland Will Still Be Cool, but Anchorage May Be the Place to Be," *New York Times*, September 22, 2014.

EPILOGUE: GHOSTS OF A NEW MACHINE (ALLENDALE, CA)

278 **"I often thought the house was lonely"**: Interview with the author, January 3, 2016.

279 **"If you can do a quick-and-dirty job"**: Tracy Kidder, *The Soul of a New Machine* (New York: Back Bay Books, 1981), 119.

280 **"Bridge tables sprouted from patio walls"**: Ray Bradbury, "There Will Come Soft Rains," in *The Martian Chronicles* (New York: Simon & Schuster, 2012), 224.

281 **"The entire west face of the house"**: Ibid., 222.

282 **"Our brain possesses several representations"**: Sheila M. Eldred, "Do Ghosts Live in Our Brains?" *Discovery News*, November 6, 2014.

282 **A video of a young Japanese girl**: See Matthew Battles, "Distributed Ghosts in the Machine," *The Atlantic*, March 28, 2011.

283 **Images of Rehtaeh Parsons**: Katherine Jacobsen, "Facebook Mystery: How Did Rehteah Parsons Image End Up on Dating Ad?" *Christian Science Monitor*, September 18, 2013.

285 **"Lack of information is part of the recipe"**: Interview with the author, March 2, 2015.

285 **the mysterious woman who appeared**: Patricia Pearson, "The 9/11 Survivors Who Were Guided to Safety by Spirits," *Daily Mail*, May 19, 2014.

INDEX

San Jose, Calif., 49, 57–58, 64
  Winchester Mystery House in, 49–53,
    57–67, 69, 76, 78, 83, 97, 125
San Jose Daily Herald, 58
San Jose Daily News, 58, 62
San Jose Evening News, 64–65
Santa Clara Valley, 49, 50, 58, 65–66
sasha and zamani categories, 218–22, 224
Satan, devil, 76, 77, 197–98
Savannah, Ga., 230
  Sorrel-Weed House in, 230–32
Schelling, Friedrich, 17
Schilling, Margaret, 180–81
Sconce, Jeffrey, 86n
Scott, Frank, 136, 146–47
Scott, Margaret, 33
Scotten, Daniel, 253–54, 260, 261
Scotten, Owen, 254
Senner, Madis, 79
September 11 terrorist attacks, 257, 285
Shakers, 77
Shakespeare, William, 5n, 71
  Hamlet, 195, 229
Shelley, Percy Bysshe, 256
Shiloh, Tenn., 203–4, 207, 209
Shining, The (King), 43, 51, 96
Shockoe Bottom, 103–9, 111, 115–17
Short, Elizabeth, 131, 137
Shue, Erasmus Stribbling Trout, 159–61,
    169–71
Shue, Zona Heaster (Greenbrier Ghost),
    159–61, 169–71, 269
Simmons, James B., 107, 108
Simpson, Nicole Brown, 270
Skinner, Charles M., 8, 262
slaves, slavery, 8, 9, 105, 110–15, 209, 210,
    242–45
  Chloe, 39–40, 48, 110, 230, 234
  collected stories of, 112–14
  Jefferson and, 109–10
  Lalaurie and, 237–41, 243–45
  Molly, 230–31
  in New Orleans, 237n, 238–39, 243
  paterollers and, 210–11
  in Richmond, 104–8, 111, 115–17
  Three-Fifths Compromise and, 112
Slave Trail Commission, 117
Smiley, George, 153–57

Smith, George Washington, 165
Smith, Horace, 55
Smith, Robert, 197
Smith, Vera, 248–51
Snyder, William "Red," 162, 168–69
Sochotsky, Cheryl, 91
social media, 283, 284
Solbach, John, 199
Sophie B. Wright Charter School, 247
Sorrel, Francis, 230, 231
Sorrel, Matilda, 230, 231
Sorrel-Weed House, 230–32
Soul of a New Machine, The (Kidder), 277
Speirs, Jim, 217, 221–22
Spiritualism, 70–80, 86–87, 216
  first appearance of word, 72
  telegraph and, 85, 282
  Transcendentalism and, 72–74
  women and, 74–75, 80
Spiritual Telegraph, 85
Sprague, Antoinette (Nettie), 57, 58
Sprague, Homer, 54, 57, 58
Stacy-Judd, Robert, 135
Staffleback, Ma, 122
Stambovsky, Jeffrey, 269–70
Stanley, Freelan O., 95–96
Stanley Hotel, 95–96, 97, 101
Stanton, Elizabeth Cady, 74
Stay on Main (Cecil Hotel), 137–41
Stickney, George, 76–77, 79
Stickney, Sylvia Beckley, 76–77, 79
Stickney House, 76–79, 83
Stirling, Mary Catherine, 38
Stirling, Ruffin, 38
Stone, Bill, 113
Stone Tape, The, 216
stone tape theory, 215–17
Story, Joseph, 194
Stoughton, William, 28
Strouss, Lisa, 133–34, 137, 144–48
Stull, Sylvester, 197
Stull Cemetery, 196–200
suffragists, 74–75
Sugrue, Thomas J., 263
suicide, 58
Sullivan, John, 228
Sunset Boulevard, 140
Sutherlands, The (Harris), 8

THE WORLD
ACCORDING TO
JOAN
DIDION

THE WORLD
ACCORDING TO
JOAN
DIDION

EVELYN McDONNELL

HarperOne
An Imprint of HarperCollins*Publishers*

FIRST EDITION

Designed by Elina Cohen
Illustrations by Anne Muntges
Photograph on p. x courtesy of Julia Armstrong-Totten.
Photograph on p. 48 by Robert Weidner.
Photograph on p. 151 by John Bryson/Getty Images.
Photograph on p. 236 by Chris Felver/Getty Images.
Paper art on p. vi courtesy of Shutterstock/ArtKio.

Library of Congress Cataloging-in-Publication Data is available upon request.

ISBN 978-0-06-328907-9

23 24 25 26 27 LBC 5 4 3 2 1

To the J & J of my world,
John and Judy.
I love you, Dad.

And to Sarah Lazin, my agent for three decades and counting.
Without her, this book would not be in your hands.

Remember what it was to be me. . . .

—Joan Didion, "On Keeping a Notebook"

CONTENTS

Joan Didion circa 1943.

Gold

Most of us have a Joan Didion origin story: the article, or book, or photograph, or quote that first made us want to know more about this quiet oracle. Maybe you saw a Julian Wasser photograph of an unsmiling woman in a full-length long-sleeved dress with her back against her Corvette Stingray and her splayed right hand clutching a cigarette, and you said to yourself, "She's a writer?! I want to be a writer." Maybe you were a disaffected youth following a beatnik dream on the road to San Francisco in 1979 when your mom sent you the 1968 collection *Slouching Towards Bethlehem* and advised you to read the titular article, in which Didion exposes the

Haight-Ashbury hippie trip.* Maybe you just read the famous first line from her book *The White Album*—"We tell ourselves stories in order to live"—nodded, and sharpened your pencil.

That quote is one of the most famous of Didion's many literary jewels, and the most subject to interpretation. On one hand, it's an invitation: By writing in the first-person plural—"We"—she includes and empowers the reader. We are all storytellers, she says, and we all have the existential human right—as basic as food, water, and shelter—to tell our stories. Didion's embrace of her readers coupled with her openness about herself is an act of radical generosity. She told her story to encourage us to tell ours.

But the essay, like so much of Didion's writing, is also an indictment of narrative's ability to limit and distort reality—and Joan includes herself in this indictment. She empowers us and she warns us: Stories can be lies. "We live entirely, especially if we are writers, by the imposition of a narrative line upon disparate images, 'ideas' with which we have learned to freeze the shifting phantasmagoria which is our actual experience," she says in *The White Album*. Narrative was her expertise and her enemy.

We live in an age of reckonings over who gets to tell stories and how and why. Didion faced this abyss as a young woman beginning her career and her family, and her transparency about this dissolution was her, and our, saving grace. "I've had to struggle all my life against my own apprehensions, my own false ideas, my own distorted perceptions," she said in a commencement ad-

---

* This is writer David L. Ulin's origin story, and he didn't stop at that essay: He kept reading until he became the editor of the Library of America anthologies of Joan Didion's writing.

dress at the University of California, Riverside, in 1975. "I've had to work very hard, make myself unhappy, give up ideas that made me comfortable, trying to apprehend social reality. I've spent my entire adult life, it seems to me, in a state of profound culture shock. I wish I were unique in this, but I'm not."

Didion expressed many of her foundational concepts first in speeches like these, mostly at universities, to younger audiences. This is part of what has made her legacy so transformative for multiple generations. She was literally speaking to us, passing on what she had learned. "It takes an act of will to live in the world, which is what I'm talking about today," she said at Riverside. "By living in the world, I mean really trying to see it, look at it, trying to make connections. And that's not easy, it takes work. You have to keep stripping yourself down, examining everything you see, getting rid of whatever is blinding you."

Then she offered this advice: "Throw yourself into the convulsion of the world."

Beginning in the 1960s with her journalism and first novel, Joan Didion reshaped the geography of American literature by redirecting readers' attention away from the East and toward the way the sun set over the Pacific Ocean. There were other great California writers before, during, and after her, of course, but there was something about the way this woman documented the real lives of the West that was new, riveting, and transformational. She wrote about the world she knew—the rivers, the freeways, the mountains, the movie stars, the ocean, the orchids—and she wrote about it with such an eye for detail and an ear for music, and with such a mix of appreciation and skepticism, that she put us in her places. In her eighty-seven years, Joan Didion wrote five novels, hundreds of articles (many of which were collected in books), several movies, and a play. She was a much-photographed literary celebrity and a fashion icon. Her death on December 23, 2021, launched a tsunami of tributes from other writers, but also from actors, musicians, filmmakers, artists, politicians, and her legion of fans. Even those who criticize her acknowledge her craft and legacy.

Didion's writing was often extremely personal; she confessed her madness, her grief, her guilt, her love, her failures. And yet there is something of the cipher about her. She was extremely reticent in person and kept much of her life private. Her writings were windows into her world, but she kept the doors locked. When she died, it felt like she took the keys with her. After Joan Didion passed, I threw myself into the convulsion of her world. It was a place I thought I knew, but I had so much to learn.

Mine is one of the more common Didion origin stories: In college, I read "Some Dreamers of the Golden Dream," Joan Didion's 1966 article about a murder in San Bernadino. I was taking one of the two journalism courses my school offered, and our textbook was the anthology *The New Journalism*, edited by Tom Wolfe. I was not generally interested in crime stories, but "Dreamers" was no ordinary whodunit. Didion's subject was not homicide; her subject was the Inland Empire (the rather grandiose name for the exurban area east of Los Angeles). The mystery Didion was trying to solve was not whether Lucille Miller killed her husband, setting their VW bug on fire with Gordon "Cork" Miller inside (that was evident, her story made clear). The question that puzzled the writer was much bigger than that of one marriage gone wrong.

Where had the dream gone wrong?

The golden dream. The California dream. The American dream. The dream, and its bad turn, was the theme of much of Joan Didion's work. She may have been the golden girl of the Golden State who lived the literary golden dream, but she saw the darkness and danger of the mines. "This is a story about love and death in the golden land, and begins with the country," reads the first sentence of "Some Dreamers." It's not a conventional news lede, but it is one of the more famous openings in American letters. It could be the first sentence of this book.

Didion's dream was etched in dread, outlined in black shadows—a chiaroscuro study. "The center was not holding," the queen of California noir warned about the changing times in her 1967 article on Haight-Ashbury, "Slouching Towards Bethlehem." She was paraphrasing the Irish poet William Butler Yeats, writing about World War I; the conflict in Vietnam loomed over Didion's landscape. In the third act of her life, her center did indeed let go—her husband of four decades, the writer John Gregory Dunne, and their thirty-nine-year-old daughter, Quintana Roo Dunne, died during a torturous twenty-month stretch, leaving Joan alone in New York City, a single woman, age seventy. No longer the dreamer in the golden land, but a stranger in a strange land.

"The idea of the golden dream infuses all her work," says Steffie Nelson. She was so compelled by Didion's influence on the literary scene she found when she moved from New York out West that she edited an anthology about it, *Slouching Towards Los Angeles: Living and Writing by Joan Didion's Light.* "She sees this potential—she also calls it the shimmer—but the golden dream, in particular, applies to California. She was enraptured by this idea of the potential of California, whether that was being a pioneer crossing the prairie to get to the West, or an aspiring starlet trying to become a Hollywood star."

Didion knew quite a bit about pioneers and starlets. She was born in California, as were four generations of her family before her. These deep roots were intrinsic to her identity. As early as eighth grade, she celebrated them in writing: "They who came to California were not the self-satisfied, happy and content people, but the adventurous, the restless, and the daring. They were different even from those who settled in other Western states. They didn't come West for homes and security, but for adventure and money," she wrote, voicing early skepticism of imperial ambitions. The words come from a speech for her graduation from Arden School, which was then, in 1948, on the agrarian eastern edge of Sacramento but is now a public education institution firmly planted in a grid that includes Taco Bell, Kaiser Permanente, and Big 5 Sporting Goods.

There is a common misperception that Didion was an Angeleno. She did live in various parts of Los Angeles for twenty-four years, and she did document that city with a keen simpatico like no other writer had done before. But the story begins with the country. She was born and raised in Sacramento, the capital city that sits atop California's agrarian Central Valley, in the middle of the state. It was here, in a land made verdant and volatile by the convergence of two rivers, between the snow-capped range of the Sierra Nevada—where many would-be settlers met their death in the journey to the West—and the coastal range that became the home of vineyards and universities, that Didion's ancestors settled.

The Matthew Kilgore Cemetery lies on the eastern outskirts of Sacramento, on what was once the Kilgore Ranch but is now a typical suburban sprawl called Rancho Cordova. On a steamy June morning in 2022, I'm sitting beneath an oak tree with Jeanne Didion Huggins and John Didion, two of the seven children of Robert "Bob" Eldridge Didion, the brother of Joan's father, Frank "Sonny" Reese Didion. The canopy provides some protection from the notorious Central Valley heat, which tops one hundred degrees by midday. The cousins of "Joanie," as they still call her, are telling me the history of their Kilgore ancestors, whose graves lie fifty feet from where we sit. The tiniest little acorns occasionally fall onto the picnic table as they show me the bound book that includes the diary of one ancestor's passage through the Sierra Nevada to the golden land.

"A lot of people who came to California wrote diaries because it was such an undertaking," Huggins says. "They knew they were participating in a historical adventure. I don't know if anybody in my generation could ever have done anything like this." In the slanting handwriting of the nineteenth-century diary, I see the forbear of Joan's notebooks, one of which I had perused two days earlier in the Joan Didion collection at the University of California, Berkeley.

Sacramento is the oldest incorporated city in California, dating back to 1850, the same year California became a state. Before a

Swiss con man named John Augustus Sutter convinced the Mexican government in 1839 to give him 48,000 acres of land at the junction of the Sacramento and American Rivers, the area was populated by the Maidu, Patwin Wintun, and Miwok, people who understood the improvisation necessary to live in an area of ecological whimsy and who based their diet on the smallest provenance: acorns. The indigenous tribes did not try to cultivate or control the land, because they obeyed the laws of the water and knew that nature had its own method of providing nutrition: tender protein encased in a hard shell wearing a jaunty little cap.

Settlers had other ideas. Sutter built a typical, square, European fort here in 1840. There was no war taking place, except of course for the invasion of native land. Sutter's Fort is now a state park in the heart of Sacramento. Schoolchildren visit regularly, baking cookies in the old stone ovens, walking the grounds where indigenous people were once enslaved. Didion must have come here on those field trips, her connection to the city's settlement a source of childhood pride, as made evident by her ardent Arden speech. Sutter was a wily capitalist who hitched his wagon to whomever was in charge: first the Mexican government, then the United States of America. Sutter's Fort was perfectly positioned west of the mountain passes through which more and more wagon trains were coming. The fort was a gateway, providing shelter and sustenance to the growing number of colonizers, including some of Didion's ancestors.

Then the trickle became traffic. In 1848 James Marshall, a carpenter building a mill for Sutter on the southern fork of the American River, saw a glint in the water. He scratched the yellow rock.

It was soft. After that, the Maidu, Patwin Wintun, and Miwok didn't stand a chance.

The Golden State is not so named just because of the way the light falls on the Pacific Coast, or for its fields of yellow poppies, or after the color the grass on the hills gets bleached in the endless summer sun. Gold, the precious metal, is the state mineral. "Eureka," the Greek word for "I found it" that Marshall reportedly shouted when he identified those nuggets, has been on California's seal since it was created in 1849. In the four years after Marshall's discovery, the state's settler population grew from 14,000 to 250,000, even as the indigenous inhabitants were displaced and destroyed. Settlers came for the gold and they stayed for the weather, for the light, for the flowers.

The golden dream was a dream of gold.

As an adult, Joan Didion came to understand this origin story very well. In fact, expansionism, so-called manifest destiny, became a central theme of her writing. "The American empire was one of her great subjects," writer David Rieff, son of an acclaimed writer, Susan Sontag, himself, told me. "She understood it. In some ways Joan was always an insider. The American establishment was material to her."

Her subject was the Inland Empire.

Her subject was the American empire.

In 1948, one century after Marshall's Eureka moment, at a school just a quick jog from where her great-great-grandfather Matthew Kilgore settled, Didion was enthralled by her "pioneer" heritage. She acknowledged its roots in the ore-rich Sierra Nevada region known as "the Mother Lode," where "they mined gold by day and danced by night," as she wrote in her Arden speech. But at thirteen, she was more interested in the lesson about hard work than in considering stolen goods and land. "It would be easy for us to sit back and enjoy the results of the past. But we can't do this. We can't stop and become satisfied and content. We must live up to our heritage, go on to better and greater things for California."

We know about Joan's Arden graduation speech because she excerpts it in *Where I Was From*, her 2003 book in which she rigorously examines her own embrace of the Golden State narrative. In which she goes on to better and greater things by ripping up the myth of heritage.

One of the things I admire most about Joan Didion is her ability to refuse satisfaction. To listen. To change. *Where I Was From*, not *Where I Am From*. She chose every word with machinelike precision.

Joan Didion was born December 5, 1934, at Mercy Hospital in Sacramento. It was the middle of the Depression. She was the first child of Frank and Eduene; her brother James (a.k.a. Jim or Jimmy) joined her five years later. She spent her early years in modest houses in the centrally located neighborhoods of Curtis Park and Poverty Ridge (a name given in Sacramento's early days, before it became a neighborhood of comfortable two-story homes). Oaks, willows, eucalyptus, pines, and sycamores line the wide streets, which are mostly laid out in a grid. With the exception of a few years during World War II, when her father was stationed around the States doing accounting for the army, Joan grew up here in what is known as the City of Trees.

"I was born in Sacramento, and lived in California most of my life. I learned to swim in the Sacramento and the American, before the dams. I learned to drive on the levees up and down-river from Sacramento," she wrote in *Where I Was From*. She attended public schools, studied at the public library downtown. She left in 1953 to go to the University of California, Berkeley, for four years, then moved to New York, where she worked for magazines for eight years. She returned to California and lived as a writer in LA for twenty-four years, then moved back to New York, where she spent the last thirty-three years of her life. Although she never lived in Sacramento after college, she came back frequently to visit her parents for holidays and birthdays, until very late in Frank's and Eduene's lives, when they moved to Carmel with Jim.

The 2017 film *Lady Bird*, directed by Greta Gerwig, is about a creative, troubled young woman, played by Saoirse Ronan, who is desperate to get out of Sacramento and secretly applies to colleges back East. The film opens with a quote from Didion: "Anybody who talks about California hedonism has never spent a Christmas in Sacramento."

The adult Didion came home also to write, in the big house in Fair Oaks that her parents moved to in her teens. Back then it was on the city's eastern edge; now it's a posh suburban neigh-borhood, between Arden School and Kilgore Cemetery. Still, when I drove down the street one day, a gaggle of wild turkeys loitered a few doors down. This is a region where it's not unusual to see wildlife on the lawn. The day I visited Robert Weidner, Joan's college boyfriend, at his home north of San Francisco, a doe and two fawns stood at the end of the driveway as I got ready to leave. One fawn stared at us, curious, then finally bounded away to join its family.

On a beautiful afternoon the summer after her death, I drove up the Pacific Coast Highway to Trancas, the Malibu neighborhood that Joan Didion called home from 1971 to 1978, when she was in her late thirties and early forties. Place was not just a setting in her writing; it was a character. She wrote vividly about locations and their influences on people and events. Her own life can be divided into eras based on locales—time and space in tandem. Of all her locations—Sacramento, Berkeley, Manhattan, Portuguese Bend, Franklin Avenue, Brentwood Park, Manhattan again— Trancas is the one that most draws my imagination, my desire. She, her husband, and their young daughter lived in a house on a cliff between the Pacific Coast Highway and the ocean here. It was a storybook Southern California existence: the ocean, celebrities, a sports car, and a small community of creative friends, including a handsome handyman named Harrison Ford. (Let's pause here for a second to reflect on the experience of having the future Han Solo fixing things around your groovy Malibu pad.) Didion was a famous novelist and journalist; network news programs came to interview her with the ocean rolling in the background. The large living room had red terra-cotta tile floors, white walls, a redwood ceiling, and a wall of glass facing the sea. She said that the glare of the sun was so bright that they gradually moved all their chairs to dark corners.

"They just had a scene and everyone was there," says Katrina vanden Heuvel, publisher of *The Nation*. Vanden Heuvel's mother, the writer Jean Stein, rented a house in Trancas in 1973—the year of the Watergate hearings. Joan and Jean would visit each other, as they did for the rest of their lives. "There was open air, and they would eat overlooking the water."

Malibu is at once a haven of multimillion-dollar beachfront designer mansions owned by movie and music stars and moguls, and a paradise for surfers splitting their time between their vans and the waves. Stretches of the rocky coast are famously unreachable by regular folks, despite federal law and multiple lawsuits guaranteeing public access to all coastal land. The Michigan-born architect John Lautner built some of his most to-die-for houses here, concrete abodes with boulders in the living rooms. But there are also several spots where plebeians like me can dip our toes into the salt water: the legendary surf break of Zuma Beach or small parks such as El Sol and El Matador. At multiple stretches of the coast from here all the way up to Big Sur, you can pull your rig over and just park between the freeway and the Pacific, surfing from sunrise to sunset.

Songs of the 1970s romanticized this bucolic beach lifestyle: America's "Ventura Highway" (1972) ("Where the days are longer / The nights are stronger / Than moonshine"), Seals and Crofts's "Summer Breeze" (1972) ("Blowin' through the jasmine in my mind"), and Albert Hammond's "It Never Rains in Southern California" (1972) ("But girl, don't they warn ya, / It pours, man, it pours"). The most coveted plaything of young girls my age—Quintana's age—was Malibu Barbie: the tan, blond fashion doll with the groovy clothes and beach bus accessory.

I understand that this—beach, glamour, mountains, surf—is a California cliché: overdetermined, romanticized, privileged. And yet this topography figures prominently in my own childhood mythology; it's a place that has shaped who I am. One of my earliest memories is of riding this road with my brother, my parents, and Jackie, a single, sporty, adventurous woman I would later in life realize was Mom's lesbian friend, at the wheel. While Jackie drove the two-lane coastal freeway, Brett and I stuck our heads out the open windows like a pair of dogs, breathing in that summer breeze. I remember that ride as an experience of pure, free joy, a feeling too rare in our young lives then. When I was four, my family had moved from LA to a small town in Wisconsin. My memory of that coastal drive must be from an early return to the place of my birth, right around the time the Didion-Dunnes moved to Trancas. Malibu is my paradise lost, my golden dream. "Whenever I feel troubled, I think about the sea," Joan wrote to herself in a note while she was working on her 1970 novel about a woman driving around Southern California, *Play It As It Lays*.

Revisiting Malibu as an adult, decades older than my parents were back in those dog days, that happiness comes flooding back. I steer my car around the PCH curves, feeling the salt on my skin, the wind in my hair. Trancas is at the far northern edge of Malibu, more than twenty miles to Santa Monica, an hour at best in traffic. It's far enough that the Didion-Dunnes (as people called them) would stay at the Beverly Wilshire when they had business in LA. The vibe out here beneath the Santa Monica Mountains is more rural than urban; it must have felt familiar to the woman who grew up on rivers and levees. The local shopping plaza, a wooden complex where Joan bought groceries and shared news with neighbors, is called the Trancas Country Market, though the goods sold are for extremely well-heeled farmers. The story begins with the country.

I pull into El Pescador, a state beach less than a mile south of Didion's Trancas home. There are only a few cars in the parking lot. It's a short hike down to the beach. The water is aquamarine, the sand white, the sky azure. It's a relatively calm summer day and the ocean is warmer than where I live in San Pedro, though still bracing when I dive under a wave. It's hard to describe just how tranquil and beautiful the California coast can be: The sea and the sky are vast expanses of blue, free of obstructions, pollution, noise, negativity. There are just a dozen of us in this little cove that is bordered on either side by shy, exotic houses that try to avoid the public eye even as they court attention. If you love nature, like I do, like Joan—who said she always loved to live with a view of the ocean—it's idyllic.

And yet, Joan Didion would leave paradise for days, weeks, and then forever. She sought her jackpot in journalistic explorations of new places, people, and cultures. She was a small woman with a giant intellectual curiosity that led her to adventures and assertions far from Sacramento. She interviewed the Doors and Joan Baez, wrote screenplays for Barbra Streisand and Al Pacino. In 1960s America, she decried both the cops and the counterculture. She watched corpses being dissected in Miami. In war-destroyed El Salvador, the bodies didn't make it to a morgue: She saw them rotting on the streets, half eaten by animals, or dumped down a hillside. In Hawai'i, she watched a family bury their son killed in Vietnam in the former volcano crater known as the Punchbowl. She penetrated the surface rhetoric of court cases from Riverside, California, to New York City. She took on kings and kingmakers: Ronald Reagan, Bill Clinton, George W. Bush, Dick Cheney, Martha Stewart. When many commentators lapsed into a silence disguised as patriotism, Didion called out the way the Bush administration used 9/11 to advance its reactionary agenda of warmongering and censorship. At the same time, she praised the triumph of beauty over banality, whether in the artwork of Georgia O'Keeffe and Robert Mapplethorpe, the writing of Ernest Hemingway and Elizabeth Hardwick, or the orchids of Amado Vazquez, her Malibu friend.

Didion had a way of penetrating beneath the surface of events to a deeper, and often unstable, core. She did this not by asking lots of questions, but by standing back and observing. "She listened!" the photographer Julian Wasser, whose images of Joan adorn many a writer's dorm room and have provided his own professional mother lode, told me in 2022, a few months before his death. "She didn't talk; she observed." This ability to fade into the wallpaper and take in the scene was one of the keys to Didion's success. As she wrote in the intro to the first collection of her writing, *Slouching Towards Bethlehem*, "My only advantage as a reporter is that I am so physically small, so temperamentally unobtrusive, and so neurotically inarticulate that people tend to forget that my presence runs counter to their best interests."

The introvert's revenge.

It's important to note that Didion was one of only two women included in *The New Journalism* (the other was Barbara Gold-smith). Wolfe proclaimed in the introduction that the writers in his book were "dethroning the novel as the number one literary genre, starting the first new direction in American literature in half a century." But this was primarily a revolution for white men; meet the new journalism, same as the old journalism. It may have been a time of genre experimentation and immersive reporting, but the journalism of the 1960s could also be a sausage party. Covering crime, civil war, drugs, politicians, and rock stars, Didion broke ground for writers, for Californians, and for women.

Didion had a keen eye for the telling detail, an ear for the perfect quote. In 1967, she went to San Francisco to try to understand what was happening among the thousands of young people who were leaving their homes and flooding the Haight-Ashbury neighborhood. It was called the Summer of Love, but Didion approached the scene with an essential journalistic tool: skepticism.

Rather than merely interviewing officials and spokespeople (though she did plenty of that), Didion embedded herself in the hangouts and homes of young people trying to forge new lifestyles. This immersion in the real lives of subjects, rather than a reliance on static statements or interviews, did herald a new kind of journalism. "When I first went to San Francisco in that cold late spring of 1967 I did not even know what I wanted to find out, and so I just stayed around a while, and made a few friends," she wrote. For weeks she became a fly on the wall.

The resulting piece, "Slouching Towards Bethlehem," offers a bravura performance of the old writing adage: Show, don't tell. Joan sketches scene after scene of musicians, artists, cops, organizers, young people, and young people's children in places including an interrogation room, a space called the Warehouse, and a Janis Joplin with Big Brother and the Holding Company concert. Didion doesn't lecture, she describes, often in a stream of consciousness that seems to imitate an acid trip: "They are all pretty and two of them still have baby fat and one of them dances by herself with her eyes closed," she says of girls who hang around rock groups. She lets her subjects talk. "I've had this old lady for a couple of months now, maybe she makes something special for my dinner and I come in three days late and tell her I've been balling some other chick, well, maybe she shouts a little but then I say 'That's me, baby,' and she laughs and says 'That's you, Max.'"

"Slouching" is at once empathetic and terrifying: a view of the counterculture as not a revolution, but a dissolution. Joan threw herself into the convulsion of the world, looked at it plainly, and wrote it all down.

In the 2017 documentary *Joan Didion: The Center Will Not Hold*, Didion describes the Eureka moment when she interviewed Susan. The five-year-old was wearing white lipstick and was in "High Kindergarten," as the child herself put it. Susan was tripping on LSD.

This was the journalistic jackpot, the reveal that rewarded weeks of patient observation and exposed the grim bedrock beneath the flimsy rhetoric of peace and love.

And, "It was gold," Joan tells the filmmaker as she waves her long, skinny, age-spotted arms, a small grin lighting the famous face now carved with wrinkles. "You live for moments like that when you are doing a piece."

Notebook

Joan Didion began corresponding with the world at age five. The dusty house in the quiet Sacramento neighborhood contained her body, but her mind, restless, wandered to distant places. Her mother was busy with Joan's new baby brother and couldn't give her daughter the attention she had become accustomed to. So the former librarian handed her eldest a Big Five tablet "with the sensible suggestion that I stop whining and learn to amuse myself by writing down my thoughts," as Didion later recalled in "On Keeping a Notebook." And so Joan Didion wrote.

Her first entry in that first notebook was a short story in which the protagonist falls asleep freezing in the Arctic, only to wake up in the Sahara and die from the heat by noon. As Didion herself noted, this initial effort at fiction reveals "a certain pre-dilection for the extreme which has dogged me into adult life." The five-year-old Didion had yet to travel far from her home in Sacramento, where the temperature regularly topped 100 in the summer and where winter rains could make the Sacramento and American Rivers overflow. The tundra and the desert must have seemed like appealing, albeit dangerous, alternatives. Writing down her thoughts turned into not an amusement but a calling. Over the next eight decades, Didion would become one of the most acclaimed voices of her generation, known particularly for her skill at writing about place.

I picture the hand that held the pen: long, expressive fingers, fair skin, manicured nails. Didion wrote in a cursive whose letters didn't always connect. There are gaps inside words, where, for less than a moment, she lifted nib from page—and then returned to the flow. She wrote mostly in ink, sometimes pencil, her letters slanting to the right, with lovely loops in her *P*s, *Q*s, *D*s, *J*s, and *R*s: a distinctive penmanship that is easily legible in the many letters and thank-yous that she wrote, less so in her notebooks, notes to herself, and revisions to the typed pages of manuscripts.

Joan Didion wrote and wrote. Words got worked and re-worked. It's at once humbling to peruse early drafts of revered books—*Slouching Towards Bethlehem, The White Album, Miami, After Henry*—and reassuring to witness the process of imagina-tion, self-doubt, excision, and revision. Words did not burst in precise formation from Joan Didion's brain and land on the page pristine. She crossed whole passages out. Her rigor is apparent in the final product. It took time and labor to get there. Take notes. Type them up. Mark up the typed pages with red ink, or blue ink, even pencil. Type again. Repeat.

It is at once intimidating and inspiring to go through her papers.* HER papers. The notes she handwrote, the drafts she typed and retyped. On lined yellow legal sheets. On books of notecards. On ivory and blue and yellow typewriter paper. On the backs of business cards and envelopes and playlists from airplane entertainment systems. Outlining. Revising. Getting it right. A process at once so familiar, and yet so impressive. Her wide left typewriter margin and crinkly vellum paper. Pages with rectangular sections scissored out of them. Scraps of deleted typed notes stapled onto pages. Always thinking. Refining. The process behind the familiar finished product. How the sausage gets made.

A newspaper clipping about a massacre in the Virgin Islands. A handwritten Pablo Neruda poem about weariness, copied from a 1974 *Esquire*, according to Didion's note. A piece of tablet paper with two handwritten sentences: "I have always longed to live underwater" and "Whenever I feel troubled I think about the sea." A typed letter of notes from her beloved editor, Henry Robbins: "I do wish you'd go over the opening paragraphs on pp. 2–3 with an especially close eye." Notes from "JGD," John Gregory Dunne, her husband: "She should flick off the head of her cigarette rather than stub it out." The occasional brown stain on the edges of paper: Coffee? Coke? Bourbon?

---

* Manuscripts and notes for her books up to *After Henry* are housed at the Bancroft Library in Berkeley. Other materials were purchased after her death by the New York Public Library and will be available to the public in 2025.

Sentences evolved. *Play It As It Lays*, Didion's second novel, published in 1970, is about an actor, Maria, who is past the edge of a nervous breakdown. An early draft describes Maria's first movie role thus: "She played a girl surfer who stops surfing and improves her grades after being raped by the members of a motorcycle gang." That backstory gradually gets pared down in subsequent drafts to the published version: "A girl who was raped by the members of a motorcycle gang." Why? No notes indicate the reason the narration was condensed. What was the initial thinking, and how did it change? Was Joan punishing the girl for choosing surf over school? Or was she critiquing this kind of sexist Hollywood trope? Did she decide the critique worked best when made concise and thereby generalized? For Didion, words were earned, not spent.

Didion assiduously avoided the pat answer or obvious noun. To define the "shimmer" that, in her seminal 1976 essay "Why I Write," she said she saw around the pictures in her head, she zoomed in, not out. Don't go for the easy explanation. Break on through to the other side, as one of her more famous subjects, Jim Morrison, sang.

There is a torn piece of lined paper in the working notes for *Play It As It Lays*. On this scrap, the name "Maria" is underlined at the top. It is hard to read every word of the first two sentences— "When you are a little girl . . ." it begins—but the last sentence is clear: "It is very bad to be depressed on the west coast of America."

From the day her mother gave her that tablet Didion "felt compelled to write things down." Over the years, she would jot words on hotel stationery, on the margins of manuscripts, and yes, in notebooks. These were not diaries. "Keepers of private notebooks are a different breed altogether," she wrote in 1966. "The point of my keeping a notebook has never been, nor is it now, to have an accurate factual record of what I've been doing or thinking. That would be a different impulse entirely, an instinct for reality which I sometimes envy but do not possess." Instead, she put thoughts, quotes, images, fantasies on paper. She recorded what was in her mind, not her reality. *"Remember what it was to be me*: that is always the point."

Joan Didion was a writer's writer, a master of her craft. It's not surprising that her death on December 23, 2021, at the age of eighty-seven, unleashed an outpouring of obituaries, tributes, tweets, and memes, followed by the obligatory backlash. Within six months of her death, Didion was on the cover of three differ-ent magazines (*The Atlantic*, *Alta*, and *Document*). She had inspired generations of us to become close observers of the world, relent-less reporters, unsentimental critics, inventive novelists, and me-ticulous stylists. She wrote memoirs, screenplays, literature, and essays, and she helped invent literary journalism. She loved po-etry, quoting it frequently in her work—most famously the Yeats poem that gives *Slouching Towards Bethlehem* its title—but I only know of her having written one poem, for Dunne's book *Vegas*. She had her greatest success in her third act, with the 2005 National Book Award–winning bestselling memoir *The Year of Magical Thinking*, and was prolific until Parkinson's robbed her of move-ment and speech.

Writers revere Didion because her choice of language was at once original and precise. Even those who question her politics acknowledge her artistry. There is a reason for every word, and a word for every reason, and they are all inimitably, recognizably Didion. And then she connected those words with a musical flow that is as thrilling as it is controlled. "Grammar is a piano I play by ear, since I seem to have been out of school the year the rules were mentioned," she explained in "Why I Write." "All I know about grammar is its infinite power. To shift the structure of a sentence alters the meaning of that sentence, as definitely and inflexibly as the position of a camera alters the meaning of the object photographed."

The writerly love of Didion is not just idolatrous: It's aspirational. Even if we find her politics sometimes blindered by privilege, if she exuded cool while we blow hot, how could we not want to be Joan Didion? She became a world-traveling literary celebrity and an ageless style icon not because she sold out her impeccable craft, but because she was simply that good at what she did. Who knew that having a formidable intellect and a way with words could get you a Corvette Stingray and an oceanfront house? Well, we all knew after Didion did it.

Didion is also a writer's writer because she wrote frequently *about* writing. Over and over, in essays and interviews, she offered advice and encouragement. She told Jill Krementz that when she was almost done with a book, she slept in the same room with it: "Somehow the book doesn't leave you when you're asleep right next to it." She was also said to have kept her manuscripts in the freezer when she was stuck. By revealing her own creative process, she demystified the art of narrative for multiple generations—she passed the baton from Hemingway—"a man to whom words mattered," she wrote—to us. Her words help us understand our craft and our passion. She didn't just school us; she armed us. Making rhetorical devices transparent—exposing "political fictions," as she called them—was one of her prime objectives. Writing wasn't just a career choice; it was a mission—who she was, why she was, how she was: "A person whose most absorbed and passionate hours are spent arranging words on pieces of paper," she said in "Why I Write." "I write entirely to find out what I'm thinking, what I'm looking at, what I see and what it means. What I want and what I fear."

If you know instantly what she means by these words, you must be a writer.

When I don't write . . . "It is very bad to be depressed on the west coast of America."

Which isn't to say you have to be a writer to love Joan Didion. One of the fascinating things about La Didion, as the writer Richard Rodriguez calls her, is how, six decades after the start of her career, she continues to inspire fashion, film, songs, and memes. At age eighty-one she was the face of a Céline ad campaign. Her words provide the epitaph for Greta Gerwig's coming-of-age millennial movie *Lady Bird.* Dee Rees (*Mudbound, Bessie*) directed a film of Didion's novel *The Last Thing He Wanted* in 2020. Didion inspired two tracks on the 2022 album by singer and songwriter Andrew Bird, "Atomized" and "Lone Didion." "'Atomized' is attempting to update Yeats' 'The Second Coming' and Didion's 'Slouching Towards Bethlehem' as there is a fifty-year interval between the three," Bird said in an email interview. That year also, the bassist and artist Jill Emery painted a portrait of Joan alongside such subjects as the Pretenders, Bob Dylan, and the Stooges. Didion, after all, became an icon of 1960s culture in part by writing about, and hanging out with, rock stars.

Contextualizing Didion's ongoing resonance with multiple generations of dreamers and memers was one of the goals for this book. But I also wanted to dig beneath the hype, to the actual work that inspired it, and reconnect that work to the extraordinary life of the woman who created it. I did not intend to write an exhaustive biography. Tracy Daugherty did an excellent job of that with *The Last Love Song* in 2015, and until the rest of her papers are ready for public viewing, exhaustive is still in the offing. What I wanted to do instead was trace Didion's legacy in the wake of her death and map the narrative of her life by visiting the places she lived and wrote about. Along the way, I talked to many of the people who knew her best: family, friends, co-workers, fans. This is not Joan's complete story. It is more of a notebook, trying to remember what it was for her to be her, at different places and different times. I am fascinated by the ways in which she changed, from the Sacramento-bred Goldwater Republican to the Upper East Side liberal, from a proud daughter of pioneers to the first serious white writer to stand up for the falsely accused defendants in the Central Park rape case. Call it Joan's arc. In my travels through pages and places, I discovered a person who was so much more than the small woman in giant sunglasses, whose work went far beyond hippies and rock stars and Santa Ana winds, who beautifully but relentlessly laid bare the fictions that we tell ourselves, and each other, in order to live.

Like a notebook, this story proceeds in a fragmented style. As Joan's writing did, it embodies to some degree the atomization she prophesized. It is not a narrative log of events; it is more like an associative legend for a map, with each chapter named after an object that figured large in Didion's imaginary—gold, snake, hotel, orchid—and therefore, it leaps around and across space and time. Occasionally I insert myself into the narrative. Joan could be a very informed, impartial writer, but one of the keys to her appeal is the way she often personalized her work. For her first piece for *Life* magazine, she wrote not about the war in Vietnam as she had wanted (her editor wouldn't send her because "the guys" were already covering it); instead, she wrote that she was in the Royal Hawaiian Hotel in Honolulu, "in lieu of filing for divorce. I tell you this not as aimless revelation but because I want you to know, as you read me, precisely who I am and where I am and what is on my mind." This intensely private woman lived intensely publicly. That is one of the contradictions that makes her story so compelling, and relatable.

I never interviewed or even met Joan. She was more of a living legend to me, someone I read, taught, admired, emulated—from afar. But as I burrowed into her life and work, I realized how close our worlds came. She was born within one year of my mother; I was born within two years of her daughter. We are both native daughters of California. We lived in New York at the same time, though she was an Upper East Side celebrity and I was a Lower East Side punkette. We both wrote in order to live. We both thought about the sea whenever we felt troubled.

It is at once a joy and a burden to write about a writer with such immense talent. It's like making a film about Alfred Hitchcock or writing a song about Joni Mitchell. One of the ways Didion taught herself to write was by typing pages of Ernest Hemingway's writing. I did the same with her books. I thought that by following in her footsteps, I might be able to walk like Joan. I observed many of her tricks: Extremely long sentences whose strings of clauses are so artfully woven they flow like silk scarves. These soliloquies alternate with extremely short sentences: two, three, four words. Phrases—key ideas—get repeated, like refrains in a song. Signature clauses: "As it happens," "As it were," "Another picture," "Here." Titles that begin with the word "on" ("On Keeping a Notebook," "On Self-Respect"). Stories that are revealed incrementally, in growing, overlapping loops. First-person voice that is often stunningly, if archly, revelatory. A distanced observation that can be devastating in its summary dismissiveness.

You'll see those tricks here, some of them conscious gimmicks on my part, some of them so woven into the fabric of my writing I don't know they are stolen goods. While our maps sometimes aligned, I could never imitate Joan Didion's gait. It is as unique as her handwriting. As anyone's handwriting. I am infinitely grateful for where the journey through her life and work took me, and I hope this book will be a guide for you as well.

Snake

Joan Didion was a bit of a goth. Beginning with her first short story about death in the desert, she was drawn to dark subjects: cannibals, bikers, Jim Morrison, Dick Cheney. Her favorite house was the old governor's mansion in Sacramento, a towering compendium of gothic arches and Victorian cupolas. As a teen, and for years afterward, she would drive to the outskirts of Sacramento, park next to the Matthew Kilgore Cemetery, sit on the fender of her car, and read a book. In these three acres of white marble gravestones, her connections to the land ran deep. Her great-great-great-grandparents Matthew and Massa Kilgore and their children and grandchildren are buried in the cemetery's southeast corner. The Kilgores tried to build a ranch in this area east of Sutter's Fort, but the deluges defeated them, so they moved closer to the Sacramento River, where earthen levees were being built. The obelisk that marks the final resting places of the Ohio-born patriarch and matriarch remains. Its inscription marks the precise ages of Matthew (eighty-one years and two days) and Massa (seventy-seven years, four months, and twenty-nine days) on their deaths in 1882 and 1876.

Decades later their pensive descendent regularly drove to this still-quiet refuge to read in the company of dead souls. Then one day, as Joan pulled up to park, a rattlesnake slithered from behind a broken stone only to disappear in the grass. "I never again got out of the car," she wrote in *Where I Was From*.

Joan Didion had an obsession with snakes. They are almost comically prevalent in her writing—or rather, fear of their presence is everywhere. While researching this book, I used color-coded Post-its to mark recurring motifs in her texts. Red stands for snake. My Didion library has a crimson fringe.

Snakes make their first appearance in the third paragraph of her first book, set in Sacramento, *Run River*. Everett, the husband of the central character, Lily, has a .38 with which he once shot a snake, a foreshadowing of worse violence to come. In chapter 6, Lily recalls being afraid of possible snakes in an irrigation ditch and Everett picking her up and holding her to soothe her. In Didion's famous "love song" to John Wayne, "There had been ahuehuete trees in Durango; a waterfall, rattlesnakes." Snakes are so central to *Play It As It Lays* that the original cover features a coiled serpent; Quintana called it "the snake book." In her essay "Los Angeles Notebook," Didion's neighbor hears a rattlesnake. In *Blue Nights* the house cleaner yells "Vibora!" to rattle a nosy social worker. Joan recalls running over a black snake in "On Keeping a

Notebook." In "California Notes" she writes of "rattlers in the dry grass" and of the California novelist Gertrude Atherton "cutting snakes in two with an axe." (Here was a feminist role model Didion could embrace!) Writing for *Vogue* in 1961, she references the superstition that "self-respect is a kind of charm against snakes." In 1965, she is in Death Valley and she imagines she hears a rattlesnake, "but my husband says that it is a faucet, a paper rustling, the wind." Also that year, writing about her childhood in "Notes from a Native Daughter," she admits, "I was a nervous child, afraid of sinkholes and afraid of snakes, and perhaps that was the beginning of my error."

In the documentary *The Center Will Not Hold*, the director, her nephew Griffin Dunne, asks Didion about her reptilian obsession. "They were always on my mind," she says. "You had to avoid them."

Then she turns the tables on her questioner: "Do you have snakes?" she asks, grimacing.

"I just take a rake and kill them," Dunne attempts to reassure her.

"Killing a snake is the same as having a snake," she says, not mollified.

Snakes are an extremely common literary motif, of course, playing the main villain in the Book of Genesis itself. The propagandists who espoused the concept of manifest destiny decreed the American West an Eden "allotted by Providence for the free development of our yearly multiplying millions" (that is, white settlers), in the words of journalist John L. O'Sullivan. In her youth, Didion bought into pastoralism. In a 1962 review of Evelyn Waugh for the *National Review*, she wrote, "the banishment from

Eden is our one great tale," adding that "hardness of mind"—the moral clarity whose rarity she lamented—is "almost invariably held at arm's length, the way Eve should have held that snake."

The obviousness of the serpent metaphor may seem beneath the rhetorical talents of the queen of literary journalism. But for Didion, the fear was real, not merely symbolic. She grew up in a landscape where snakes were plentiful. California has almost fifty species, including seven types of venomous rattlers. Snakes were more than a literary device for Joan: They embodied a very real but also primal, even ancestral, fear.

Fellow Sacramentan Robert Weidner, Joan's boyfriend during her college years, recalls an experience she had with him early in their relationship, which may have inspired the scene by the ditch in *Run River.*

A highlight of social life in Sacramento is the river party: a gathering on the shores of the American and the Sacramento, on boats on the rivers, even in the rivers. Between her studies in high school and at the University of California, Berkeley, Didion attended junior college in Sacramento. There she met Maurice Read, who became a good friend; he introduced her to his friend Robert Weidner. Bob remembers them arriving at a river party—a beer bust, he calls it. "She wouldn't get out of the car," he recalls. "She was afraid of snakes. I assured her that, 'don't worry, I'll take care of you.' Then she got out of the car with me." (Read remembers this story differently; he recalls them bringing her beers as she sat in the car all night. Maybe that was a different river party.)

Unfortunately, rather than gallantly taking care of her, the man Didion later married was a herpetophobe too. "Everywhere I go, I am afraid of seeing snakes," John Gregory Dunne wrote in an article titled "I Hate Them" for the *Saturday Evening Post.* In fact, Joan's obsession with snakes seems minor compared to John's terror. Perhaps that fueled her continued interest in legless reptiles: How could they reduce the brilliant man she loved to a quivering wreck? How could his fear be so intense that it would keep him away from the nature that she grew up in—that it kept him out of Central Park, even?

It was Joan's grandfather—Eduene's father, Herman Jerrett, a miner and writer—who taught Joan the "code of the West" when it came to rattlesnakes: If you see one, kill it. If that meant getting out of the car and going into the brush after it, so be it. That was your duty to the next person who might come across this vermin and not have the luxury of a car or a shotgun or an axe.

Joan Didion relentlessly hunted snakes in human form, even as she spread the fruit of knowledge. You could say it was her prime objective: to expose corruption, lies, cruelty, hypocrisy, and the abuses of power.

Because she hosted Hollywood parties where authors, politicians, artists, and stars mingled, then carried on this tradition on New York's Upper East Side, and because she wrote about LA, and New York, and Miami so memorably, we tend to think of Joan Didion as an urbane, urban figure. But it is fundamental to her identity that she grew up in a natural environment. At one point she wanted to be an oceanographer, and in a world where STEM is encouraged for girls, maybe she would have been. A love of nature—particularly flowers, ocean, and sky—as well as a fear of nature—fires, floods, and snakes—animate her writing and are central to the core of who Joan Didion was. "Don't you think that sometimes people are formed by the landscape they grow up in?"

she said in a 1971 interview. "There's a picture of the valley there, that particular look of absolutely flat land and that sense of things growing, it formed everything I ever think of or ever do or am."

Donner Lake lies in the Sierra Nevada mountains at almost six thousand feet, one hundred miles from downtown Sacramento. It's shaped like a bean and lined with "cabins" whose retail prices start at $700,000. The fairly typical resort, recreational area, just twenty miles from the larger and more famous Lake Tahoe, offers fishing, hiking, paddleboards, boats. Except the alpine lake is named after one of the most infamous incidents in American history: In 1846 a group of would-be settlers known as the Donner-Reed party, or simply the Donner Party, attempted an alleged shortcut to the Central Valley and became stuck in a blizzard in what was then the Truckee Pass. Trapped for months, the men, women, and children turned to eating their horses, dogs, and finally, the bodies of the humans who had already died. This episode of cannibalism, of manifest destiny embodied as ouroboros—a snake eating its own tail—lives on in the geographical names of this tourist region.

Joan swam in Donner Lake as a youth and was obsessed with its macabre past. The connection wasn't mere gothic prurience: Her own ancestors almost came to the same fate. Nancy Hardin Cornwall, her great-great-great-grandmother on her mother's side, traveled with the Donner Party but wisely chose not to follow them through Truckee, taking the more accepted trail to Oregon. Didion's lineage taught her to follow convention; her fascination was with the road less traveled. She kept a photo of the

Sierras near Donner Lake in her study in Brentwood and in her parents' house, perhaps as a cautionary tale.

As her mother, Eduene, liked to remind the Didion side of Joan's family, her ancestors came West even before the Kilgores. Joan Didion was raised on the folklore of the Cornwalls, the Jerretts, the Kilgores, the Reeses; a piece of appliqué made by Nancy Cornwall hung in her Malibu home and her New York apartment. Even in *Where I Was From,* a book in which Didion has a self-reckoning with her own mythical roots, you can feel her stubborn pride in this frontier lineage, particularly its strong, no-nonsense matriarchs and the risks they took to find a new way of being. "These women in my family would seem to have been pragmatic and in their deepest instincts clinically radical, given to breaking clean with everyone and everything they knew," she wrote. For Didion, separating from her roots was itself a way of following her roots.

Being able to trace one's heritage back to the American Revolution, as Didion can, is no small distinction in a nation where most of us come from more recent immigrant stock. In California in particular, the final frontier, the place where "here, beneath the immense bleached sky, is where we run out of continent," as Didion wrote, only a small group of residents can connect their ancestry five generations back to the Golden Land itself. In my immediate friend group in LA, I am one of the few people I know who comes close, and the farthest I go back is three generations. I have a picture of the house my grandfather was born in: a two-story white wooden building surrounded by wilderness. It looks like it was in the middle of nowhere but in fact was a domicile in Downey, the eastern LA suburb that later housed the Apollo space program, the oldest continually operating McDonald's restaurant, and the 1970s sibling pop stars the Carpenters.

Of course, one of the reasons so few Californians can trace their lineage to previous centuries is because our ancestors destroyed and displaced the people who came before us. These descendants of Europeans that we once called pioneers but now describe as settler colonizers came from back east. They came from farms in Ohio and small towns in Arkansas. They were looking for a better life: land to plow, fresh starts, religious freedom, a place to raise a family, natives to convert and/or control. They were looking for gold.

Didion's maternal great-grandfather was a 49er—one of the hundreds of thousands of prospectors so named because of the peak year of the Gold Rush. His son was a miner, geologist, and author. Herman Daniel Jerrett taught his granddaughter Joan how to distinguish gold ore from serpentine (a green metal that is named after its snakeskin-like appearance), even though by that time "gold was no more worth mining than serpentine and the distinction academic, or possibly wishful," Didion recalled. Jerrett penned two books about El Dorado: His love of science and of writing rubbed off on his granddaughter. In *California's El Dorado Yesterday and Today*, you can hear the precursor to Joan's Californian pride—the urge to stake a claim for the state's importance in the history of the continent—and her personal, pragmatic prose: "I am no historian," her grandfather wrote. "Neither am I a journalist, but merely a native El Doradoan, who writes in the urgent hope of drawing attention of the public of America and tourist of foreign climes to a land of which so little is known, respecting its historical importance, fertility, scenic wonders, genial climate, and natural wealth."

This is classic boosterism, the Sunshine mythology that the late Mike Davis writes about in his seminal history of Los Angeles, *City of Quartz*—civic pride conveniently free of the mention of genocide. Interestingly, Davis categorizes Joan Didion's writing with Sunshine's opposite: LA Noir. In fact, the granddaughter did not fall that far from the tree: Like her grandfather, she loved her home state—even when she bemoaned it.

Herman's wife influenced Joan in different ways. Edna Magee Jerrett was accustomed to the finer things in life, "although she knows enough about mountains to shake out her boots for snakes every morning." She gifted her grandchild items such as an ounce of Elizabeth Arden On Dit in a crystal bottle and a hat with "gossamer Italian straw and French silk cornflowers and a heavy satin label that read 'Lilly Daché.'" These lessons in couture also stayed with Didion. Decades later, when Joan shared a bucket seat with a woman in a taxi on her way to the front line in El Salvador, she could identify the scent the passenger wore: Arpège.

On her father's side, Didion's paternal grandmother, Ethel Reese, was the great-granddaughter of Matthew Kilgore, the patriarch after whom the family cemetery is named. She bore two boys, Frank Reese and Robert Eldridge, then died when they were young, in the Spanish flu epidemic. Her husband, Joseph Frank Didion, Joan's grandfather, was a property assessor and school board member. His second wife, Genevieve, was a grand dame of the city, assisting in the founding of Sacramento State College, finding residences for homeless children, helping to raise money for statues and historic preservation, buying and restoring old houses, and serving on the Sacramento school board for thirty-two years after initially inheriting her husband's seat. A school in north Sacramento is named after Genevieve Didion. "For most of my childhood growing up, it was my grandmother who was famous," says Joan's cousin, Julia Armstrong-Totten. (Her mother, Mary, was one of three children of Joseph Frank and Genevieve.) "When people talked about the Didion family, it was my grandmother that people were talking about." Among her many civic accomplishments, Genevieve Didion organized the planting of a camellia grove by the state capitol. It may have been from this formidable matriarch that Joan inherited her love of flowers.

Armstrong-Totten remembers their grandmother as a formidable but caring woman. Her cousin recalled Genevieve less fondly, perhaps having absorbed her father's feelings about "the old hell on wheels," as he used to refer to his stepmother (according to Jeanne Didion). While Joan spins lyrical passages about her grandmothers Ethel Reese and Edna Jerrett in *Where I Was From*, she subtly mocks Genevieve Didion's historical whitewashing. She also has little positive to say about "the man to whom I sometimes referred as 'Grandfather Didion,' but never addressed directly, from the time I was a small child until the day he died in 1953, by any form more familiar than 'Mr. Didion.'" Joan's critique of this stern patriarch's "startling taciturnity" recalls the saying about the pot and the kettle.

Frank Reese Didion, known to his family as Sonny, was quiet like his father, and also like Joseph Frank, rail thin. There tended to be two types in the Didion clan: The skinny quiet ones and the stouter talkers. Opposites also attracted: Talkers married listeners, and vice versa. Frank and Eduene married January 1, 1934, on his twenty-sixth birthday; she was twenty-three. Less than one year later, their first child, Joan, was born. "There was this kind of really skinny frail gene, best way I can describe it. And Joan definitely had that," Armstrong-Totten says.

Joan's only sibling was born in 1939. Jim took after his heartier, more extroverted mother. That year the Didions moved to a two-story house on U Street in Sacramento, with cedar shingles and brick columns. Nothing fancy, but a nice home in a good neighborhood. Then on December 7, 1941, everything changed.

Decades later Joan wrote that she considered the Japanese attack on a US naval base when she had just turned seven years old the defining event of her generation. When she visited Pearl Harbor for the first time in 1966, she wept from the moment she saw the battleship the *Utah* in 50 feet of water until the tour boat had passed the turret of the *Arizona*.

World War II upended Didion's life, severing her from Sacramento and everything she knew. "Nothing [was] the same ever again," she wrote in "Letter from Paradise, 21° 19′ N., 157° 52′ W." Her father enlisted, and in 1942 and 1943, the Didions shuffled from Sacramento to Tacoma to Durham to Colorado Springs, as Frank did accounting for the army. The sufferings of itineracy were mild compared to what other families experienced during World War II, but "this was not . . . a sheltered childhood," Didion wrote with characteristic understatement in *Blue Nights*. Joan saw her mother cry for the first time in one of many downtown streets after finally emerging from a military housing office full of women and children, having failed again to find a room; "it seemed to be the end of some rope, one day too many on which there would be no place for us to stay." In North Carolina, the family rented a room in the house of a preacher and his family. One day Eduene saw Jim reach from his playpen

toward something and she froze: A copperhead lurked just beyond his reach.

When peace came, her family had to start all over again in
Sacramento. The Didions moved not back to Poverty Ridge but to
a Quonset hut in undeveloped acreage east of town. Rudimentary
wartime structures built out of curved, corrugated steel, Quonset
huts provided temporary housing to many families after World
War II. This was essentially a glorified camp, and yet the family had a nostalgia for these times. "I remember Eduene telling
me that was her favorite place of every home they ever lived in,"
Armstrong-Totten says. "It was probably a big adventure."

These were the years in which Joan went to Arden School,
which, as she said in 1975 at UC Riverside, "was in a district that
was just in the process of changing from rural to suburban. You
know, the kind of school in which some of us had sheep dogs—
dogs that ran sheep—and some of us had fancy Old English Sheep
Dogs." (I don't believe that her family owned any pets while she
was growing up, but as an adult, Didion had a Bouvier des Flan-
dres and a Wheaten terrier.) She wrote of a house surrounded by
dirt. She and Jimmy wanted a swimming pool; it can hit 120 degrees in Sacramento in the summer, and it's unclear if the hut had
a bathroom let alone air conditioning. Frank told them to start
digging. Her cousin John remembers visiting his relatives here
fondly. In old Sacramento, there was a class divide between Joan's
father, Frank, and his brother, Bob. When their mother died, the
young boys were separated: Frank went with their father and stepmother, Genevieve; Bob stayed with their aunt Pearl. "Joan was one
side of the family, we were the other side. We were snot-nosed kids,
they were exposed to other things," Bob's son John Didion says.

But in the country, the brothers were equal again. Together, their households could roar with laughter. The Didions were great jokers and storytellers, Jeanne says. Even though she tended to taciturnity, Joanie had that side of her as well. "She just had that great sense of humor, that her dad and my dad had, and she could be teasy, she could be kind of coquettish," her cousin says. "She could be very, very warm. I didn't see her ever when she wasn't warm."

And yet it was also out here, in this metal hut in these fields, that Joan must have learned to watch out for snakes.

These were boom times for America in general and California in particular, and in real estate, the heretofore dilettantish Frank Didion found his calling. Ethel Reese left her sons a trust that included prime property. Joan's father developed, sold, and reinvested this inheritance slowly and steadily, carefully buying ranches and empty lots, keeping an eye on them, turning them over. Jimmy watched and learned, eventually taking over the family business and ultimately becoming the president of Coldwell Banker Commercial and CEO of the real estate and investment firm CB Richard Ellis.

Joan picked up the family knack for real estate too: She would become known for her beautiful homes in Portuguese Bend, Malibu, and Brentwood Park. This was another interest she shared with Genevieve, whose civic duties included rehabbing old Sactown residences. It was Genevieve and Joseph Frank who, around 1949, purchased the building that is commonly known as the "Didion house." Joan's family moved into the stately four-story

Victorian building at the corner of Twenty-Second and T Streets, with its columns and porches. Here, in this house that she compared to a wedding cake, Didion received her infamous rejection letter from Stanford University, which she pinned to the wall.

In 1953, after Joseph Frank Didion died, Genevieve moved into the wedding cake and Joan moved with her family, to their own place, back on the eastern outskirts of town near Arden, where turkeys roamed. For decades, Joan would return to this Storybook country estate with its circular drive and pond, to her old pink bedroom with the photo of Donner Lake, and write. "She never wanted to talk about what she was working on," her cousin Jeanne Didion remembers.

The Didions were well known in Sacramento. Didion Hardware, founded in 1952, was a neighborhood institution run by Bob Didion, Joan's uncle. Joan's grandfather and step-grandmother played important roles in key community organizations. Among other civic engagements, Joseph Frank Didion was active in the Native Sons of the Golden West, a fraternal organization dedicated to celebrating the glory days of California, particularly the Gold Rush era. Genevieve was prominent in its female counterpart, the Native Daughters.

As with many American institutions, white supremacy was embedded in these organizations' bones. "Another activity we have been engaged in for over a quarter of a century is entitled 'Keep California for the White Race,'" boasts an annual report of the Native Sons published one year after Joan's birth. "This work is just as important today as it was twenty-five years ago, as there are organizations working in this and other States on the Pacific Coast to create a sentiment for Japan in order that she may have

a quota granted by Congress that will permit her nationals to enter the same as those of the Caucasian Race. The vigilance of the
members of our Order, as well as that of the American Legion and
the American Federation of Labor, has so far defeated every move
made in that direction and with the same vigilance in the future I
feel sure we will thwart any scheme started in the interest of these
Orientals whereby they may have the privilege of sending a quota
to this country."

Ironically, the camellias that Genevieve planted around the
California capitol are Asian imports.

Rake through the leaves of American history—military, labor,
fraternal, literary—and you'll find snakes.

To understand Joan Didion, and the arc of her life, you have to know
her roots in the country and this deep American conservatism—
where she was from. I don't know that Didion knew about this
exact passage that I found in Genevieve's papers at the Center for
Sacramento History, but she must have known about the racism
embedded in the Golden Sons and Daughters, which was typical rhetoric for organizations of its kind and time. Joan definitely
knew that her mother admired the John Birch Society, a far-right
organization founded in 1958 that was anticommunist, anti-
feminist, antifederalist, and pro–conspiracy theory. Eduene told
her daughter that "class" was not a word they used: "It's not the
way we think." Of course, not thinking about class is something
only someone for whom class has never been an impediment can
afford to do. The twelve-year-old Didion had read *Middletown*,
the famous 1927 study of small-town American culture, and was

beginning to question her elders about things like socioeconomic structures, as she later wrote in *Where I Was From*. But Joan never lost her distrust of big government, and of politicians, and like her parents, the young Didion voted for the arch conservative Barry Goldwater in 1964. In the 1960s, she wrote book reviews for the *National Review*, William F. Buckley Jr.'s journal for the Republican cultural elite—mostly because Buckley was one of the few editors who saw past her gender to her talent.

Some critics can't forgive Didion for these original sins. "She taught me that one could write about Sacramento, that, indeed, Sacramento was a literary landscape. In that sense, she gave me my life as a writer. No small gift!" says the writer Richard Rodriguez, who grew up in Sacramento as "a son of Mexican immigrants." "But I sensed early our difference and was put off by that difference, which loomed ever-larger than our similarities or points of comparison."

But the Sacramento to which Didion remained sentimentally attached, like many of us do to our hometowns, is not that of the camellia grove, which she in fact mocked. It is the people she went to public school with, whom she drank beer with at the river parties. In 1988, the year she moved back to New York and the year she spent covering presidential primaries and conventions for the *New York Review of Books*, she missed these Sacramentans still, maybe more than ever: "It had not been by accident that the people with whom I had preferred to spend time in high school had, on the whole, hung out in gas stations," she wrote in "Insider Baseball." "They had not run for student body office. They had not gone to Yale or Swarthmore or DePauw, nor had they even applied. They had gotten drafted, gone through basic at Fort Ord. . . . They paid their bills or did not pay their bills, made down payments on tract houses, led lives on that social and economic edge referred to, in Washington and among those whose preferred locus is Washington, as 'out there.'" Maybe because she had grown up feeling alienated in a government town, Didion always saw herself as "out there."

A close reading of Didion's work reveals that a prime agenda was to expose the moral bankruptcy of the myth of the golden land and the entire rhetoric of westward expansionism. Her subject was the American empire. It took her years to fully grasp and articulate this, in part because she resisted it, especially as long as her parents were alive. "I didn't want to figure out California because whatever I figured out would be different from the California my mother and father had told me about," she said in 2006. There are topics—the fate of the Miwok Indians, the exploitation of Mexican immigrants in the fields that her family owned, for instance—that she never did publicly address. But in incremental pieces—speeches, essays, notes—that were then gathered together in 2003, after her parents' deaths, as *Where I Was From*, she clearly and overtly reveals and removes her blinders on her own past. She laments her middle-school optimism and deconstructs the fallacies of her own first novel, *Run River*, and its perpetuation of frontier myths. She interrogates California narratives written by authors from Josiah Royce to Frank Norris to William Faulkner to Joan Didion. She documents exclusionary institutions from the Bohemian Club to the Spur Posse. Released from her loyalty to her mother—the woman who gave her the tools and instructions to start writing at age five, and to whom she was so deeply bound that she interred Eduene's remains in the same columbarium as

John Gregory Dunne, Quintana Roo, and finally, herself—Joan Didion lets it all go: "All of it . . . the dream of America, the entire enchantment under which I had lived my life." Like her foremothers, she breaks clean with everyone and everything she knew.

Herman Daniel Jerrett taught his progeny to kill rattlesnakes on sight. Except when Eduene Didion saw the copperhead by Jim's crib, she froze. Years later, when Joan Didion saw the rattler at Kilgore Cemetery, she never even got out of the car. The Didion women violated the code of the West.

There are other ways to handle phobias, ways to kill your fears not their subjects. As a child, Didion may have seemed scared, weak, nervous. But beneath that external frailty, she developed a core of iron. She eventually learned not to try to run from or annihilate her terrors. She faced them. She stared them down.

In 1970 Joan Didion and John Gregory Dunne spent a month driving around the American South. They cruised blue highways and stayed in small towns. They talked to hairdressers and writers and politicians, Black and white. "Sycamores and pit vipers," as she wrote in *South and West*, her book, published decades later, documenting this odyssey. She embarked on her trip below the Mason-Dixon Line with romantic notions about southern agrarian culture. She left enlightened and disturbed.

Between New Orleans and Biloxi, the Didion-Dunnes pulled over in the rain at a sign advertising a reptile farm. A tourist trap based on creatures that slither and squeeze was a strange choice of pit stop for two people with snake phobias. But in they went. Joan and John saw monkeys, boa constrictors in shipping boxes, and no proprietor or employee. They were standing inside the reptile house talking to another family when Joan realized the box on which she was leaning, which she had thought was empty, housed a copperhead. Back to the road through the rain they ran. "I slipped and fell in the mud and had an instant of irrational panic that there were snakes in the mud and all around me," she wrote.

In *The Year of Magical Thinking*, Didion says, "memories are what you no longer want to remember." Asked by an interviewer for *Sactown Magazine* if facing her memories through the book allowed her to move on, Didion answered: "The image I always have in my mind is a snake. A snake doesn't hurt you if you know it's there. It's not going to bite you if you keep it in your eyeline all of the time. So, in a way, this is keeping the snake in my eyeline." The teenager who was afraid to leave her car grew into the woman who lined up her sights on pundits, politicians, and police. She stared death in the face, turned tragedy into a national book award. Didion mastered the power of observation and the power of grammar. Who needs shotguns?

Joan Didion in San Francisco in 1956.

4

Typewriter

Joan Didion looks straight at the camera, with her fist curled in front of her mouth—as if to indicate it is through her hands that the taciturn thinker speaks. Appropriately, a manual typewriter takes up half the frame in this iconic black-and-white photo taken by Nancy Ellison in 1976.

When she was a teenager, Didion taught herself to type and to write by pecking out stories by Ernest Hemingway and Joseph Conrad on an Olivetti Lettera 22. Her goal: "To learn how the sentences worked," she told the *Paris Review*. Thus began her immersion in the physical act as well as the craft of writing. Call it a form of machine learning. "I'm only myself in front of my typewriter," Didion once told an editor at *Ms.* magazine.

At some point her father, in one of his random financial

schemes, bought a load of Royal 200 typewriters, one of which became Didion's accomplice. She took it with her everywhere. A typewriter is included in the carry-on items in the packing list she published in *The White Album*. Her idea was not to write on the plane, but while she waited in the airport, she would sit "and start typing the day's notes." This is one of many instructive lessons offered by Joan Didion. She must have hauled a typewriter with her in 1955, when, at age twenty, she took a train alone from Boston back to Sacramento, after a month spent in *Mademoiselle*'s guest editor program. She typed multiple letters to her *Mademoiselle* colleague and college friend Peggy LaViolette on hotel stationery along the way. "Never being one to throw myself wholeheartedly into Adventure, I carefully got a seat alone, barricaded myself in with wicker basket, typewriter, mangled copies of old magazines and thought I could sleep all night," she typed in one missive.

Many writers become so attached to a physical process that changing tools with the times is not easy; some never manage it. Neil Gaiman, the futurist, has said he prefers to write his novels in longhand. I still print out my writing and edit it on paper, a routine I was chuffed to hear Didion recommend to Hilton Als in an interview late in her life. Over the decades Didion graduated from notebook to manual typewriter to electric typewriter to computer, again demonstrating her openness to progress. Still, she did complain to author Maxine Hong Kingston about the transition to electric in a 1978 letter, saying that combined with moving and quitting smoking, the "reprogramming . . . had caused an inordinate amount of stress." She switched to a computer in 1987 and eventually came to love the editing capabilities of word processing programs. "It did for me what geometry was supposed to have done," she said.

Writers are prone to obsessive interest in other writers' processes. We write because we are readers, and we read, in part, to see how others write. Didion was a bookworm. When she wasn't sitting on the fender of her car, she was far from the snakes at the Sacramento library on a Friday night with her friend Maurice, or maybe her gal pal Nancy Kennedy (whose brother Anthony later became a Supreme Court justice and spoke at Joan's memorial). Photos and videos document her various homes stacked floor to ceiling with books. Among the items sold at auction by her estate in 2022 were Didion's collections of works by George Orwell, Elizabeth Hardwick, Joyce Carol Oates, and Norman Mailer.

Joan was an avid consumer of culture in general, with broad interests that did not divide art into high and low: She named one anthology after a Yeats poem, another after a Beatles album. Writer and friend Calvin Trillin called her Brentwood home "the West Coast literary consulate," but she and Dunne largely financed it with Hollywood hack work. She loved biker films, interviewed Jim Morrison for the *Saturday Evening Post* and Joan Baez for the *New York Times*, wrote an important essay about Georgia O'Keeffe, and was close friends with writer and artist Eve Babitz (*Slow Days, Fast Company*) and writer and screenwriter Nora Ephron (*When Harry Met Sally*).

There's a 1971 interview with Joan on YouTube, posted by the Center for Sacramento History. Some of the audio is missing, but the footage of Didion in her office in her Franklin Avenue house is, well, pure gold. She's wearing a brown flared miniskirt and a black V-neck shirt that fastens in the back. She has tucked her shoulder-length strawberry blond hair behind her ears, as she did, and freckles dot her cheeks. She's talking about growing up in rural environments; her Valley accent is strong. I'm not talking San Fernando Valley here; I'm talking the almost southern twang of the Central Valley, that Didion said she picked up from the many refugees from the Oklahoma dust bowl with whom she went to school. This is how Didion spoke: not with the English accent of Vanessa Redgrave, who portrayed her in the stage version of *The Year of Magical Thinking*, or the crisp patrician consonants of Barbara Caruso, who reads the audiobook of that text, but like a freckle-faced country girl. The camera pans across shelves full of books and books piled on the desk, lingering on volumes written by Didion and Dunne. Joan snips an article out of a newspaper in front of a cabinet of haphazardly placed manila folders, presumably full of other clippings. She's talking about worrying herself sick about a comma being out of place while admitting she doesn't have the same fastidious approach to her housekeeping. (This is the secret life of women writers: We can't be good mothers, wives, daughters, writers, cooks, *and* housekeepers.) She sits on a black leather couch with leopard-print pillows, smoking a cigarette and reading a paperback that's open on her lap.

"I like words and I'm very excited by seeing what can be done with words," she says. "*Play It As It Lays* is a very short novel. I worked on it for five years but when I finished it, I thought every word was exactly right. Now I can't even read it because words pop out at me, or sentences that I think ought to be changed."

Didion once told a participant in a writing seminar that to get through writer's block, you had to write one sentence, and then another, and then another.

To be a writer, you must write.

Writing was not actually her first ambition: She wanted to act. "I didn't realize then that it's the same impulse," she told the *Paris Review*. "It's make-believe. It's performance. The only difference being that a writer can do it all alone."

Didion similarly described the power of writing as a solitary act of imagination in the 1971 TV interview: "Writing provides me with a perfectly legitimate excuse for being alone and working out little fantasies."

I picture the teenage Joan Didion alone in her room in front of a typewriter. She rolls the paper in and out, trying to get the top perfectly aligned. She hits the keys that leave the letters indented in black ink on vellum paper. When the carriage that holds the paper has finished its journey across the machine, she slides it back and starts the next line. As she figures out the mechanics of the Olivetti, she simultaneously re-creates Ernest Hemingway's "perfect" sentences, as she called them. She learns the simplicity of his word choice, the strength of his utilitarian syntax. "There was just something magnetic to me in the arrangement of those sentences. Because they were so simple—or rather they appeared to be so simple, but they weren't," she told the *Paris Review*.

And Didion learns how to be a woman alone. Not a secretary, or a stenographer, or all the other supporting roles women were taught to play on typewriters, but a writer.

Lone Didion.

Bob Weidner was Joan Didion's boyfriend for five years, throughout her undergraduate education and for a year after she graduated.

He recalls the scene in the off-campus Berkeley apartment that he shared with their mutual friend Maurice Read while they were all undergraduates: "His girlfriend would be there, and I'd be there. And Maurice and I were probably studying and Libby [Read's girlfriend] was probably studying. And Joan might be typing something on a typewriter. But I never looked at what she was typing." (Maybe that's why the relationship didn't last longer than five years.)

Berkeley was not Joan's first choice.

Joan Didion wanted to go to Stanford University. It was considered the best school on the West Coast. All her friends applied and got in. She didn't.

She later wrote that she considered swallowing a bottle of pills as she stared at the rejection letter. (She may have given up acting, but she held on to drama queen tendencies.) She settled on tacking it to the wall of her bedroom.

Instead of attempting suicide, Joan Didion enrolled in Sacramento's community college for one semester and applied to the University of California, Berkeley. (She had been so certain she would get into Stanford, she hadn't applied elsewhere.) She spent the summer and the fall going to drive-in movies and attending river parties. In spring, she joined the student body at Berkeley.

"So it worked out all right, my single experience in that most conventional middle-class confrontation, the child vs. the Admissions Committee," she wrote sixteen years later in a column for the *Saturday Evening Post*. The essay offers a still timely admonishment to parents not to try to live their lives through their children: "Finding one's role at 17 is problem enough, without being handed somebody else's script."

Berkeley lies in the hills to the east of San Francisco Bay, about eighty miles southwest of Sacramento. When Joan went to college there, you could take the train or drive Highways 40 or 24. Interstates 80 and 5 have since replaced those routes. But there was and is another way to get to campus that will give you a feeling for what this area was like before the interstates and the suburbs and the semis. Take the river roads from Sacramento through the delta to the Berkeley Hills and drive through Joan Didion's past.

The Sacramento is a wide workhorse, the largest river in California. It runs down from the northern mountains to the Central Valley, where dams, aqueducts, and levees channel and divert its flow to provide hydroelectric power for the state, drinking water for faraway Los Angeles, and irrigation for farms, ranches, and vineyards. Didion was fascinated by the engineering intricacies that turned a largely arid state into one of the world's great agricultural providers. In 1977 she visited the Operations Control Center for the California State Water Project in her hometown and fell in love. "My own reverence for water has always taken the form of this constant meditation upon where the water is, of an obsessive interest not in the politics of water but in the waterworks themselves, in the movement of water through aqueducts and siphons and pumps and forebays and afterbays and weirs and drains, in plumbing on the grand scale," she wrote in *The White Album*.

The Sacramento also provides a site for recreation and relaxation. It's not uncommon to see sailboats amid the many skiffs and powerboats in its deep channel. The paddleboat the *Delta King* used to ferry travelers overnight from San Francisco Bay to Sactown, offering gambling and alcohol along the way. Now it's permanently docked and serves as a hotel adjacent to Old Town, the embarcadero that was redeveloped in the 1960s in an effort that,

Didion wrote, "derived from the same spirit of civic boosterism" that had led her grandmother to plant the Camellia Grove. Joan called the wooden sidewalks of this revamped Front Street "no more than a theme, a decorative effect" in *Where I Was From*—a stroll in their contrived frontier nostalgia cinched her ultimate disenchantment with her entire upbringing.

The boater in me couldn't resist the opportunity to stay on this repurposed vessel of California history. The nights I slept on the *Delta King*, I was awakened by the barking of three California sea lions who had swum up from the Pacific and were encamped on a deck on the opposite riverbank. Humpback whales have been known to make their way to John Sutter's old stomping grounds. It's an area where the sea meets the river, salt water mixes with fresh, farmers and fishermen shake hands.

Levees line both sides of the Sacramento, preventing it from flooding. The river roads run mostly on top of the earthen berms. Didion used to drive both north and south out of Sacramento on these thrilling, perilous streets. There are no shoulders next to the two-lane blacktops, just the tops of the stately oaks, syca- mores, and walnuts that grow below. It's a precipitous two-story drop, into farms on one side, the river on the other. Small wonder two characters die in a car crash out here in *Run River*, the end of their illicit love affair signaled by the headlights piercing the dark waters.

Sometimes the roads cross small canals that lead to bypasses that are part of the complicated flood-control plan, or they tra- verse the river itself. Sacramento is famous for these bridges, made predominantly of steel; Lady Bird and her mom drive across them in Greta Gerwig's movie. Many of the two-story farmhouses sit atop aboveground basements because of the history of flooding. Corn, pears, grapes, cherries, wheat, asparagus, rice, and more grow here. In *Run River*, Everett constantly worries about a break in a levee that could destroy the fields of hops. Now, the signs of vineyards and wineries beckon river road warriors. The combination of the narrow byways and wine tastings seems like a bad idea, like Old Town version 2.

Keep driving and you're soon in what they call the delta area, where the Sacramento and San Joaquin Rivers merge and mingle into the bay. The whole estuary has a Mississippi vibe, from the houseboats to the fishing shacks to the crawdads to the farmers in pickups. Drive some more, around Mount Diablo and through Contra Costa County, and you'll arrive at Berkeley via the hilltops, with the bay unrolling like a blue blanket below you to the Golden Gate—that Pacific Ocean horizon that Didion never tired of. "Late afternoon on the West Coast ends with the sky doing all its brilliant stuff," she said in 2006.

Berkeley is first and foremost a college town. "Cal," as the school is known, is the original of the University of California land-grant schools, established in 1868, and is still the esteemed public university system's star campus. Its bucolic, stately grounds slope down from the woodsy hills, where Didion used to see the glow of the nuclear Bevatron, a particle accelerator where the subatomic bits called antiprotons were discovered during Joan's junior year. A creek flows past the tower where the carillon bells chime every hour, past the Bancroft Library, down to the fancy bronze Sather Gate. Joan attended school here a decade before the free speech movement made Berkeley synonymous with Vietnam-era protests; during her years, 1953–56, the Beats were just beginning to make their presence known, particularly in nearby San Francisco, where the bookstore City Lights would become their mecca. Didion didn't think much of their "pseudo-avant garde," as she wrote to her friend Peggy.

Nor did she immediately find her groove at Berkeley. She joined Delta Delta Delta, an international sorority first founded at Boston University, but she moved out of the house after her first year. In the Tri-Delta photograph in the 1954 Cal yearbook, all forty-two of the white-skinned women sport pageboy haircuts, including Joan; she is one of a handful of the sisters who make a bold stylistic leap by wearing a shirt that is not white. Throughout her life, Didion would not be much of a joiner. She was dating Weidner, but for a while he was away in the Coast Guard, so she wrote him letters. "She didn't write a regular letter like most people wrote, you know; she had really interesting things to say," Weidner says. (The letters were all burned along with other Weidner documents in a fire years later.)

Joan was quiet, introverted. In Sacramento, her skill and intellect hadn't been taken seriously. That was about to change. "She told me that one of her high school teachers, an English teacher at McClatchy [high school], said she'd never make it as a writer. And that really gave her extra impetus to show that guy or that woman," Bob says.

At the typewriter, at Berkeley, writing essays and articles and short stories, she began to make herself heard. She wrote for the campus newspaper, the *Daily Cal*, editing special fashion issues with her friend Peggy. She also interviewed W. H. Auden when he came to campus. "At college, she interviewed bigshot authors and stuff like that. So she could overcome her shyness. And she would catch on to any little subtle thing that somebody might say and be able to expand on it," Weidner recalls.

It was particularly at the school's literary magazine, *Occident*, that Didion found a platform for her creative intellect. She worked her way up to the top of the masthead her final semester and published a short story in that spring 1956 issue. It's striking how many motifs and settings that would become classic Didion are evident in her first published fiction, "Sunset." The college senior foreshadows everything she is going to say in forty-seven years about where she was from. While she doesn't precisely name it, the location is clearly the Central Valley. There's an old cemetery that has Kilgores buried in it, a river, golden fields, and oak and willow trees (but no snakes!). The central character is a woman in her midtwenties in an unhappy marriage with a man her mother's age. Already, Didion's disillusionment with the golden dreams of her upbringing is the main theme: The land has been subdivided, her childhood house sold. "I always thought that some day I'd come back to the valley to live. But now I couldn't. Everything seems to be gone." Didion was just eighty miles from home, but she might as well have been eight thousand.

Didion found teachers at Berkeley who recognized her cunning and creativity and taught her to think in new ways about literature and writing. She studied new criticism under the revered professor and theorist Mark Schorer. For her final exam to complete her bachelor's degree, Didion wrote about the philosophical implications of Henry James's technique: "For James was ultimately interested in beauty, in the perception and organization of beauty, in art—and this seems to me the end toward which all his writing directed."

In "Sunset" and her final exam, Didion's voice and style are already honed. She has superb control of the flow of words, like she is swimming in the American River. She places transitional words at the front of her sentences like a musician marking a new verse, repeats words to emphasize a beat. And the subjects are pure Didion: truth and beauty in literature, life and death in the Central Valley. "Now she was committed to it, committed to this twilight visit to her father's grave, and so they drove on through the lines of oak and willow trees that one never really notices until the sun is almost down."

Professor Henry Nash Smith gave her final an A and commented, "I believe you have truly remarkable abilities as a critic."

By this time, Didion was already on her way, leaving not just the aspersions of Sacramento gatekeepers behind, but leaving the Golden State itself.

The discipline Didion learned sitting at the typewriter stayed with her for seven decades. "When I'm working on a book, I constantly retype my own sentences," she said in 2006. "Every day I go back to page one and just retype what I have. It gets me into a rhythm."

In 2004, nine months after her husband died suddenly, Joan Didion sat herself in front of her computer. She had lost her capacity for rational thought. She found her self at the keys. Three months later, she completed the book that would become her biggest seller and win her the awards that had been long overdue. "It was like sitting down at the typewriter and bleeding," she told *O, The Oprah Magazine.*

Building

Another picture: San Francisco's Nob Hill, 1956, in black and white. It could be the intersection of Mason and California, which, four years later, Joan Didion described in "San Francisco Job Hunt," her second ever article for a national magazine, *Mademoiselle*: "Standing on the corner, you look down the vertiginous length of California Street directly into the bay—almost as if into a well." Joan stands in front of a streetcar with a brick building behind it. The college senior looks stylish in a dark coat that she made herself and clutches a white hat firmly in both hands. Her hair is cut in a bob with short bangs, she's wearing dark lipstick, and she's in three-quarters profile, looking off into the distance: a West Coast Audrey Hepburn. The river girl has become the city woman.

Didion included the photograph, taken by Bob Weidner, in her application for the *Vogue* magazine Prix de Paris contest, which had as its top award a chance to spend time in the City of Light. The contest was a childhood dream: During one of the Didion family's stays in a strange city during World War II, Eduene saw it advertised and, projecting her own fantasies of a more worldly life, told her daughter some day she should enter. Joan didn't let the fantasy die.

The application was a bit of an exercise in inanity for the woman of "truly remarkable abilities." The prompts included: "Plan a weekend wardrobe that will fit in an overnight bag—a wardrobe that might be featured on two pages of *Vogue*. Specify activities planned for the weekend." (Perhaps this exercise prompted one of Didion's more famous pieces of writing: the packing list she included in *The White Album*.) Also, "Prepare an article on beauty for a college issue of *Vogue*. Describe an ideal and possible program of daily and weekly routines for a college girl—to take care of face, hands, figure, etc." Typical women's magazine fare. Didion could write this stuff in her sleep after editing those *Daily Californian* fashion issues. She later said she wrote about the San Francisco architect William Wilson Wurster, who headed Berkeley's architectural school at the time. This must have been to answer the prompt "Write a 300 word feature article on an outstanding person in the field of your major," though English, not architecture, was Joan's major. It was her roommate, Shirley Stephenson (later Friedman), who studied decorative arts and architecture. Perhaps Didion fudged the guidelines because like her, Wurster was from the Central Valley (Stockton) and a Berkeley alumni, and his "everyday modernism" style was similarly influenced by the flat lands and temperate climate of California. He is credited with creating the first ranch house, making high design affordable to the middle class. That she chose him as a subject shows her range as not just a literary student but a cultural critic—and her special affinity for design. Didion could turn a mundane assignment into an opportunity to make a statement.

Maybe because of her father's growing real estate business, Didion had a lifelong interest in buildings—in the way the human need for shelter can be elevated to an art form. She was interested in not just style, but engineering: She wrote about the Hoover Dam and the California water system with the awe of a western nerd. Her own enviable abodes evidenced the family knack for "location, location, location," her keen sense of design, and her privileged upbringing. She wrote essays about the American mall, the Getty Villa, the mansions of Newport, and the governor's residences in Sacramento (the old Victorian one and the one Ronald Reagan built, neither of which were then, in 1977, or are now occupied by governors, a conspicuous waste of taxpayers' dollars by a multigenerational legacy of bipartisan officials; Didion was also critiquing political showmanship). She called the old Governor's Mansion, which she stayed in once as a teen, "at that time my favorite house in the world, and probably still is." Her Mc-Clatchy High School classmate, the daughter of then governor

Earl Warren, hosted a party in this three-story Victorian bauble. "The bedrooms are big and private and high-ceilinged and they do not open on the swimming pool and one can imagine reading in one of them, or writing a book, or closing the door and crying until dinner," Didion wrote in 1977.

In 1929 the English writer Virginia Woolf wrote a seminal essay about the difficulties of being a woman writer. Having a space to read, to write, to close the door and cry, was so essential to this feminist call to action that Woolf called the canonical work "A Room of One's Own." And yet Didion's refusal to read Woolf sparked a feud between her and her friend Eve Babitz over the privileges—like spacious homes—that Joan took for granted.

In 1956, Joan Didion won the Vogue Prix de Paris with her Wurster essay and other writings. Only she didn't want the two prizes offered: a two-week trip to Paris or a grand in cash. She wanted a job in New York. During her junior year, Didion had won a different competition: to be one of twenty guest editors at *Mademoiselle* magazine in Manhattan. For one month in the summer of 1955, she lived at the famous Barbizon Hotel for women and walked the few blocks to the magazine's offices on Madison Avenue. Joan was hooked. Thus her request to swap in the job for her prize.

She got the position at *Vogue*.

Still, her boyfriend at the time says, Didion hesitated. (In this, she was in good company: In 1951 a Vassar student won the Prix by writing about people she wished she had known. Jacqueline Bouvier wound up turning the prize down for even better opportunities and in a few years became world famous as Jackie Kennedy.) Wanting was not the same as doing. New York was a long way from Sacramento, physically and mentally.

"She was reluctant to go to New York, very scared about it. She was kind of shy in those days," Weidner recalls. "I told her—and these are my exact words, I remember like it was earlier this morning—I said, Joan, if you don't go, you're going to spend the rest of your life wondering what your life would have been like if you had gone."

Joan went. Within a year, the move had changed her. "All anyone in this generation wants is security and group belonging," she wrote in a 1957 letter to her family, "and what will happen to the world if nobody is willing to risk that security to gain the big things?" Decades later, she told Hilton Als: "I was never a fan of people who don't leave home. . . . It just seems part of your duty in life." For eight years New York City became Didion's graduate school, her vocational training, her sexual awakening, her playground, her heartbreak, her home.

The thirty-story Graybar Building rises above Lexington Avenue between Forty-Third and Forty-Fourth Streets. It holds its own amid the midcentury modernist masterpieces of midtown Manhattan, rubbing shoulders with Grand Central Terminal and gazing across the avenue at the Chrysler Building—probably *my* favorite building in the world. (And I have the tattoo to prove it.) The Graybar's five-story entryway is framed by 20-foot concrete carvings of guardian figures in robes. Inside, the terrazzo floors gleam and a mere mailbox is a golden objet d'art deco, featuring a frieze of flowers, hourglasses, vases, and a winged helmet that invite the graceful deposit of your letters.

Vogue is published by the company Conde Nast, which in 1956 was headquartered in the Graybar. From a window here, Didion could see the lighted signs advertising *TIME* and *Life* above Rockefeller Plaza. (Later, she would become a columnist for *Life*.) After work, she would walk out of the Graybar, beneath the gaze of the chrome eagle gargoyles of the Chrysler Building, up Lexington, past all the store windows and restaurants, the taxis and trees, breathing in "the lambent air, all the sweet promises of money and summer," to her Upper East Side apartment. Joan Didion fell in love with New York, she wrote in "Goodbye to All That"; she fell hard for the sense "that something extraordinary would happen any minute, any day, any month."

"Goodbye to All That," written in 1967, is one of Didion's great articles. In swelling, lyric prose, she describes what it is like to be a young person, a young woman, on your own for the first time, passing through the doorway to adulthood, eking out a living, staying up and out all night, in the greatest city in the world. Its long expository paragraphs never seem long enough, so light is their rhythm, so delightful their humor: If she needed money, "I could write a syndicated column for teenagers under the name 'Debbi Lynn' or I could smuggle gold into India or I could become a $100 call girl." Here is Didion's signature eye, and ear, and nose for detail, for precise perfumes, in this case Fleur de Rocaille and L'Air du Temps. Here is her love of words: *tureens, chiffon, monastic.* Here are the sentences, sometimes a

Hemingwayesque two words ("Vermouth cassis."), sometimes a Jamesian sixty-eight, but always tracking, never losing their way from subject to predicate and back. And here is that subject, the relatable I, Joan Didion, portrait of the artist as a young woman.

Ironically, the article is her kiss-off to the Big Apple. The smells sour, the high becomes a hangover, the lover a torturer, the job a chore. But oh, the night before the morning after!

It's not an original story. That is part of its appeal; so many of us can relate to Joan's tale of the city. She follows in the footsteps of Sister Carrie, the titular character of Theodore Dreiser's great 1900 novel, who comes to New York from the farms of Wisconsin (hello!), via Chicago, to try her hand at Didion's first love, acting. Jacqueline Susann bowdlerized the story of the tragic thespian in 1966's trashy spectacular *Valley of the Dolls.* Sylvia Plath based her novel *The Bell Jar* on her own experience in *Mademoiselle*'s guest editor program just two years before Didion. But Manhattan's relentless pursuit of money disoriented and depressed the Massachusetts poet, feelings Didion would eventually experience as well. Fast forward to the 1990s and Candace Bushnell writing a magazine column not for teenagers, but about her erotic adventures; *Sex and the City* would become great TV and bad films. And then there's Lena Dunham.

New York City is a superlative place to be a young woman. The freedom of anonymity. The potential for fame. The dearth of gossipy neighbors. The people watching. The all-night diners. The shopping. The newsstands. The dancing. The sex. The music. The art. The light. "You pass a window, you walk to Central Park, you find yourself swimming in the color blue," Didion wrote in *Blue Nights*.

"Extraordinary things" did happen for Joan in New York.

New York City was and is the center of American publishing. As Joan put it in that 1960 *Mademoiselle* article, which was ostensibly about job prospects for women in San Francisco but wound up being an endorsement of her new home: "New York remains the single American city built upon a complex web of industries, including those few industries that offer women big jobs and big money: fashion, advertising, television, magazine publishing." All of the major book and magazine publishers and the most important newspapers—the *New York Times* and the *Wall Street Journal*—were and are there. The city also houses significant players in all the other media—television, radio, record companies, film, advertising—though Los Angeles beats NYC in the sphere of moving images. It is the most important American city for visual arts, fashion, and theater, not to mention finance. If you want to be a writer and have culture as your subject, it is an almost required rite of passage to do time in the Big Apple. I state this with reluctance, as someone who resisted the city's mercenary pull at first and broke from it after twelve years of obeisance, then found supportive and generative bases in Miami and LA. I know there are great American writers, particularly in California, who have never done their time in Gotham. But I also know I do not regret one second of those dozen years I lived beneath the lights of the Chrysler Building, even if I too eventually said goodbye to all that.

Joan Didion gained essential skills, made lifelong professional and personal relationships, learned how the publishing industry works, got great writing clips, and published her first book in the eight years she lived in New York. She started humbly, paying her dues—writing merchandising copy for *Vogue*. Initially, she was bored. "Work is dull and tedious," she wrote to her family in 1957. "I can hardly wait to quit." But the quick learner worked her way up the magazine ranks to film reviewer. The process of turning ideas into paragraphs on glossy paper every month—"The minutiae of proofs and layouts . . . working late on the nights the magazine went to press, sitting and reading *Variety* and waiting for the copy desk to call"—satisfied her creative intellect and her need for order.

Even the mundane tasks were fulfilling. Much of her early work at *Vogue* is unbylined: ad copy, photo captions, a society column. But it was in these anonymous, minimal spaces that Didion learned how to master Hemingwayesque brevity, to use every word necessary—and not a single word more. Didion had studied the tools of new criticism and how to write fiction under author Mark Schorer at Berkeley. At *Vogue*, she learned the tight, functional economy of public prose. Her editor, Allene Talmey, would assign her to write a story in three hundred words, then, when she was finished, tell her to pare it down to fifty. "We wrote long and published short and by doing that Joan learned to write," Talmey told the *New York Times*. Didion compared the experience to "training with the Rockettes," the famous Radio City Music Hall dancers. Like the Rockettes' high-heeled kicks, the words had to be precise and copious in meaning. "We were connoisseurs of synonyms. We were collectors of verbs," Didion wrote in 1978. "It was at *Vogue* that I learned a kind of ease with words, a way of regarding words not as mirrors of my own inadequacy but as tools, toys, weapons to be deployed strategically on a page."

Note the military analogy. Didion famously, in "Why I Write," called writing "a hostile act." "You're trying to make somebody see something the way you see it, trying to impose your idea, your picture," she explained in an interview. *Vogue* was boot camp. Drilled into its cadets was the importance of discipline, of making deadlines, of filling the page with words even when your head is filled with anxiety—and of being in the right place at the right time.

An early break arrived when another writer—"a real writer," as opposed to a staffer like Joan, as she later said—failed at these lessons, not delivering an assigned manuscript. The story had already been teased on the cover for the August 1961 issue: "Self-Respect—Its Source, Its Power." In this case, Didion had to turn the five words of the cover promo into a precise number of not just words but characters, as the story had already been laid out. She completed the training exercise in two one- to two-hour sittings after her daytime tasks were finished, in the empty *Vogue* offices at the Graybar. "In retrospect we know how to write when we begin; what we learn from doing it is what writing was for," she said in 2007, recounting the origins of "On Self-Respect" in her acceptance speech for a lifetime achievement award from the National Book Foundation.

That 1961 essay is in *Slouching Towards Bethlehem.* It was not Joan's first cover story for *Vogue* though: Her personal essay on jealousy was teased on the cover of the June 1961 issue. In these and her October 1961 piece "Take No for an Answer," we get early examples of one of the platforms she became most known for: the first-person essay.

In "Jealousy: Is It a Curable Illness?" Didion largely stays in third-person narration. The article offers a breezy tour through pop psychology and well-known historical and literary entities: Cleopatra, Madame Bovary, Descartes. Then she offers this resonant observation: "Because extraordinary beauty or intelligence or success in anyone, however deserving, presents a subtle threat to our self-esteem, we love best those possessed of some fatal flaw, some saving evidence of their own mortality." She doesn't drop the "I" bomb until the second page, and then it's to anonymously describe a friend: "*I* once knew a young woman, both beautiful and gifted, made incoherent by an affair between her estranged (by quite mutual agreement) husband." We don't get a window into the author herself until the fourth and last column, when she gives us this quintessential Didion biography: "When I was 18, I mourned because I could not at once be a Rose Bowl princess and a mediaeval scholar—I was naturally equipped to be neither; because I could not both write for *The New Republic* and spend my afternoon tea-dancing at the Palace Hotel in San Francisco. No one among my acquaintances in 1953 went tea-dancing at the Palace, but my mother had, in 1927. The jealous make exactly such demands upon themselves: there is simply no pleasing them." Here, at age twenty-six, are Didion's desire to be both bookish and the belle of the ball, her obsession with the golden past, and her envy of the example set by Eduene. She is both self-effacing and a scold—an excellent rhetorical combination.

Interestingly, for the morality lesson at the story's end, the writer eschews the obvious Shakespearean quote about hell hathing no fury, and instead goes for Chaucer, and Criseyde's claim to be: "Myn owene woman, wel at ese" (my own woman, well at ease).

Not a feminist, my ass. Those who critique Didion's gender politics should take a look at these early articles, in which Didion is not merely her own woman but encouraging other women to be their own women, well at ease, not hindered by jealousy, driven by self-respect.

All three of these early *Vogue* articles are essentially self-help pieces sprinkled with doses of personal testimony, psychoanalytical theory, and literary allusions. Given the prompts ("Take no for an answer"?!), Didion did the best she could: She managed to turn that essay into an argument for women saying, as opposed to accepting, "no." The "pull yourself together" tone of these columns reads ironically, in retrospect, given how transparently she would soon, within a few years, write about her various neuroses, breakdowns, and ailments. There are hints of the troubled person beneath the determined demeanor: references to migraines, phenobarbital, sickbeds. Her words of encouragement nonetheless found their mark. "On Self-Respect" is one of her more oft-quoted articles, especially among the kind of young women for whom Didion's words were intended in 1961. These words resonate well into the next century: "To free us from the expectations of others, to give us back to ourselves—there lies the great, the singular power of self-respect."

The fact that Didion had her first publishing experiences at women's fashion magazines is crucial to understanding both the opportunities available to women in the mid-twentieth century and the honing of her writing style. These essays taught her how you could balance a sharp wit, a head full of books, and personal experience, and speak directly to and for your audience. For several years, women's magazines were the only places that published her. She had grown up reading *Vogue*, and she knew that there were brilliant editors and writers both there and at *Mademoiselle*. But she also wrote only for them because the magazine world was extremely chauvinistic.

"It was a system set up totally on gender grounds," says the journalist and poet Calvin Trillin. While Didion was at *Vogue*, he worked at *TIME* magazine with Didion's future husband, John Gregory Dunne. "All the writers were male and all the research-ers, as they were called—most of their job was fact checking, but they were called researchers—they were all women. One of them, Johanna Davis, was so clever that her senior editor let her write stories, but she wasn't listed on the masthead as a writer." (Davis was the daughter of Herman J. Mankiewicz, who wrote *Citizen Kane*, and an alumnae of Westlake School for Girls, which Quin-tana Roo Dunne later attended. She was killed by a cab in 1974 after writing one novel.)

"The *Vogue* period is very interesting because of what she chose to write about within the framework of the assignments," says Katrina vanden Heuvel, publisher of *The Nation*. "But also the women's magazines—whether you think of *Mademoiselle* and Sylvia Plath, and *Vogue*, and *Glamour*—they have given space to women to move forward, not necessarily to stay there, and to con-tinue writing about the topics that animate them."

For example, "San Francisco Job Hunt" was a multipage re-ported feature that seemed to be intended as a self-help/travel piece for young women interested in the West Coast, but Didion turned it into an investigation of gender inequity. The writer may have later distanced herself from the women's movement, but at age twenty-five, she had no delusions about the reality of sexism.

The article quotes an editor who admits that his newspaper hasn't hired a woman in four years, except for one society editor. In advertising, "they say that raises come infrequently and transfers to non-secretarial jobs about as often as a major earthquake," Didion quips. The whole long article reads like an externalization of the writer's internal argument about why she should remain on the East Coast, rather than live closer to her roots. Still, she can't help but rhapsodize about that ocean breeze: "The feeling of the city is in its air: improbably clean, smelling of the Pacific."

Didion did eventually break through the glass ceiling of journalism, ironically at a publication known for its conservatism. The *National Review* was founded in 1955. Editor William F. Buckley Jr. had an eye for talent and was more than happy to find a young writer from California who was eager for a break and, better yet, was a fan of Republican icon Barry Goldwater. For her part, Didion was not so much drawn to the magazine's libertarian outlook as to Buckley's open door. After all, she also pitched to more progressive publications, *Commonweal* and *The Nation*. Besides, for the *Review* she wrote not about politics but about books and movies. She also wrote breezy essays rather in the style of her *Vogue* pieces—except in "I'll Take Romance" and "Marriage a la Mode," she made fun of women's magazines. It would take decades for anyone to realize that this sharp intellect could and should be used to dissect politics; in the 1980s and '90s, *New York Review of Books* editor Robert B. Silvers would send Joan Didion to political conventions and criminal trials. There she wrote some of her most important and incisive articles, this time homing in from the left.

In early 1960s NYC, Didion was getting noticed. She had a literary agent, Helen M. Strauss. She would come home from the

Graybar at night and, homesick despite her love for New York, work on a novel about Sacramento. In 1963 *Run River* was published by a small press named after its owner, Ivan Obolensky. Joan was twenty-eight.

By then, the blush was off the rose. After eight years, New York had lost its charm. In her words, in "Goodbye to All That," she had stayed "too long at the fair." Didion loved the Graybar, and the streets of Manhattan, and Central Park. But she had never truly settled. She didn't even buy furniture, floating from one person's apartment to another. When she finally alighted in a floor-through flat on East Seventy-Fifth Street, she had only a mattress and box springs, two borrowed chairs, and fifty yards of yellow silk she hung in the windows. This, from the woman whose future living spaces would become legendary: the Portuguese Bend gatehouse, the Hollywood mansion, the Trancas bungalow, the Brentwood "literary consulate," the Upper East Side condo with the restaurant-grade kitchen. The city had been a great place to be single, then to fall in love, then be heartbroken, then meet another man and marry him. But when it came time to build a home with her husband, Didion's heart took her back west.

6
Man

Abalone Cove lies at the foot of Portuguese Bend on the Palos Verdes Peninsula, one of the most beautiful and exclusive areas in Los Angeles County. The ground here shifts constantly, so much so that the utility lines run in aboveground tubes next to the coastal road, which is frequently under repair. My husband likes to take this part of Palos Verdes Drive fast, so we fly in the air over the bumps. We live just a few miles southeast of here, in the port town of San Pedro, and it is one of our favorite drives. Whales pass close to the peninsula, as do dolphins and assorted pinnipeds. Pelicans, falcons, kestrels, osprey, ravens, and gulls ride the thermals. On clear days, the mountains of Santa Catalina Island rise twenty miles offshore; on cloudy or foggy days, you would have no idea the buffalo (abandoned film extras, an LA staple) are there roaming. Across the road from Abalone is the Wayfarers Chapel, a wood and glass cathedral of the Swedenborgian faith, designed by Lloyd Wright (Frank's son).

To get to the ocean you have to walk down a fairly steep and crumbling cliff. It's a great place for tide pooling; we used to regularly spy an octopus. On low tides, if you time it right, you can pass through a cave to the other side and . . . Well, I'll let Joan Didion describe it:

"We had to be in the water at the very moment the tide was right. . . . Each time we did it I was afraid of missing the swell, hanging back, timing it wrong. John never was. You had to feel the swell change. You had to go with the change. He told me that."

Joan Didion and John Gregory Dunne lived here, above this cave, in a three-bedroom gatehouse where peacocks—exotic creatures gifted to the family that owned the estate—roamed. It was their first home in LA and possibly their most spectacular. They rented it for $400 a month, half the asking price but still about $3,500 in 2022, counting for inflation. Worth every penny, if you happened to be emerging writers who had forty thousand of them each month.

Didion's passage about the sea cave, which comes at the very end of *The Year of Magical Thinking*, encapsulates her relationship with John: They shared a sense of adventure, but he also protected and supported her. They met in New York, married in 1964, and were together until he died of a heart attack on December 30, 2003. Theirs was a storied writerly collaboration and romance, a true partnership, though not without troubles and tragedy—that famous trip to Hawai'i in lieu of a divorce, the illness of their only child. As she made clear in her first short story and novel—in all of her fictional writing, in fact—Didion did not put much stock in marriage. "Marriage seemed to me a risk venture, shadowy with shoals, uncharted sinkholes, possibilities for salvation and possibilities for insomnia, in-sickness-and-in-health-and-you-had-better-count-on-the-sickness," she wrote prophetically in the *National Review* in 1963, just a few months before she married Dunne.

But she made it work. Relating, like writing, is not something that happens, it's something you do.

"It takes two people who are willing to put in the time," she told journalist Sara Davidson. "If I sensed anything about John when I first knew him, it was that he was willing to do that."

They made it work.

Despite her professed skepticism about marriage, Didion was not aromantic. She had a definite type that Dunne, in his assertive, macho, Irish way, fit.

Joan felt the first pangs of desire in 1943. It was at a movie theater in Colorado that she "saw the walk, heard the voice," the slow, deep drawl of the screen idol who said he would build a girl a house "at the bend in the river where the cottonwoods grow." Even at eight, Didion could feel the "sexual authority" of John Wayne. The laconic star of westerns and war movies both calmed her "tendency to grow misty eyed at the dance," as she said of an ancestor in *Where I Was From*, and appealed to her Central Valley sensibilities. He embodied not so much a person as a place: "Where a man could move free, could make his own code and live by it," as she wrote in "John Wayne: A Love Song" in 1965. Wayne unleashed Didion's libido and her libertarianism.

In that *Saturday Evening Post* profile, Didion said that no man she had loved had ever taken her to that bend in the river like Wayne did. But the very year that article came out, Dunne helped take her to Portuguese Bend, a spot infinitely more beautiful than the desert town of Bakersfield, where *War of the Wildcats*, the movie in which Wayne makes the promise of cottonwoods, was filmed. Over the next four decades, Joan and John's lives became as one.

Dunne was Didion's last love, but he wasn't quite her first. Beginning with that Sacramento river party, Joan dated Robert Weidner throughout college and for a year after they graduated. They spent lengths of time apart, first while he was in the Coast Guard, then while she was in New York. Still, Bob, a bit of an old-fashioned guy, harbored hopes of marriage. True to the middle-class sexual mores of the Eisenhower Era, he says that while they fooled around, they never had sexual intercourse. What he did not know was that Joan had been bored with him for some time, as she complained to her friend Peggy LaViolette Powell in letters: "Bob and I are getting along fairly well but I want to GET AWAY from California and school and my family and Bob and make something all my own out of a few years of my life."

Didion's experiences in the big city dealt a death blow to her romance with Weidner. On a visit home she gave her college boyfriend the "dear Bob" talk. She was seeing someone else. She was "fucking" someone else, he says she told him. Ever the facts-based journalist, she provided details.

"She talked about their physical relationship and that kind of stuff," Weidner recalls painfully. "She knew how to tell a guy off in order to tell that it was over."*

The guy Joan was fucking was an infamous writer/cad-about-town named Noel E. Parmentel Jr. Parmentel definitely appealed to her John Wayne sensibilities: He was physically imposing, conservative, and talked with a Southern accent. (He was from Louisiana.) In essays for *The Nation*, the *National Review*, *Esquire*, and elsewhere, Parmentel attacked the pieties of the left, right, and center. His friend Dan Wakefield described "the tall, shambling New Orleans freelance pundit" in his book *New York in the Fifties*: "Even for his time, Noel was the most politically incorrect person imaginable. He made a fine art of the ethnic insult, and dined out on his reputation for outrageousness." Parmentel was provocative, known to start fights at dinner parties. In a world where writers liked to assert their manhood, he could make Norman Mailer look like a pansy. He styled himself a "reactionary individualist." Safe to say, he too appealed to both Didion's libido and libertarianism.

In *The Last Love Child*, Tracy Daugherty, noting that he obtained a rare interview with the aging raconteur, writes a lot about Parmentel's influence on Didion. Parmentel respected Didion's intellect and talent. He championed her writing, helping her get published in the *National Review*, for instance. Eight years

---

* Weidner, who is called Bakersfield Bob in *The Last Love Song*, although he never lived in Bakersfield, went on to become a tech entrepreneur and is a key donor to the statue and scholarship in Joan's name in Sacramento. He married Brenda Gehring in 1961; she passed in 2022. "We had an absolutely perfect marriage for sixty years," Weidner says. "Maybe Joan dropping me was the best thing that ever happened to me."

older than Didion and a veteran of the city, he was a well-informed guide to its bars and social structure. Like Didion, Parmentel was an outsider among New York liberals, and he used his difference as a strength. That undoubtedly appealed to the reserved woman from Sacramento. Handsome, well dressed, and charismatic, he was easy to fall for. Wakefield wrote of "the girls who succumbed to his Southern charms."

But Parmentel, by his own admission to Daugherty, also drank, a lot. Those Southern charms, Wakefield wrote, were "spiced with put-downs." He mocked Didion's natural melancholy, calling her "the tragic mouse" and, in a reference to *Hamlet*, "the East End Ophelia" (funny, but cruel). Far from being a stimulating influence on the young, physically fragile, and migraine-prone woman away from home, he was probably dangerous for Didion—toxically masculine, as it were. It was presumably the love affair with him that ended her love affair with New York, that made her "cry until she did not know she was even crying," as she wrote in "Goodbye to All That."

It was he, she wrote, who left a note in the back of a picture frame for her to find years later, saying, "You were wrong." (About what, she wasn't sure.) Like a stalker. Someone who can't lose an argument.

It was definitely Parmentel who threatened to sue Didion in 1977, fourteen years after the breakup, because he said the character Warren Bogart in her novel *A Book of Common Prayer* was based on him. The suit was another attempt by Parmentel to control and intimidate his former lover: The case would have had no legal standing, since the character—abusive, alcoholic, dying—

was fictional and identifiable as Parmentel only in Parmentel's eyes.

Though Bogart does send this message to his ex-wife after she finally finds the courage to leave him: "Tell Charlotte she was wrong."

It's a terrible thing—uncollegial and unprofessional—for a writer to threaten to sue another writer, especially with no legal grounds to stand on. It's beyond despicable to attempt to harm the career of a former lover, one whose success has left you far behind, years after she escaped your control.

Noel Parmentel did do a few good things for Joan: He helped her get *Run River* published by taking it to his friend Ivan Obolensky, who in 1963 published Didion's first novel. And he introduced her to another writer he was mentoring, an Irish Catholic from Connecticut who worked for *TIME* magazine, whom he told her she should marry.

Which Joan did.

She was right.

Born in 1932, John Gregory Dunne was the fourth of six children; his brother Dominick, a.k.a. Nick, also became a writer, well-known for his coverage of famous trials. Their father, a heart surgeon, died of cardiac arrest when John was fourteen. They were a large Irish Catholic family in WASPy New England and had a big, welcoming house in West Hartford, Connecticut; Parmentel called them "the Kennedys of Hartford." Didion said that the first time she visited this New England palace, shortly after the relationship with Parmentel ended, she knew she wanted to marry John. She attributed the desire to the house's order—so different from the disorder in her family home, where no one dusted and the family liked things to look old and yellowed. The New England material comforts didn't hurt either; she marveled over a closet full of tablecloths on rollers, "the way they come back from the French laundry, under tissue," she told Sara Davidson. The Didions were well off, but not private school, East Coast, ruling-class well off, like the Dunnes.

Didion said decades later in *The Center Will Not Hold* that she didn't believe in falling in love. Parmentel probably destroyed her Hollywood-bred romance for passion. Without him, she was adrift. She had known John for five years before that visit to Connecticut, but her attention had been on Noel. Maybe Dunne was her rebound relationship. It's telling that it was the comfort and stability of his family home that made her want to marry him. The attraction was at once safe and aspirational. Unlike the stereotypical short-lived rebound relationship, this one lasted until death did them part.

Like Parmentel, Dunne cut an imposing figure. He was gregarious, loud, and had a temper. He too was not above escalating a fight to blows. "I never took it that he got into a fight that was a really knock-down, drag-out fight. He may have punched somebody a couple of times," says Trillin. Dunne wrote about masturbation and getting the clap from prostitutes. This was no soft-focus glossy magazine romance. Joan was having a breakdown over her breakup with Parmentel. John was patronizing hookers in Vietnam while covering the war desk for *TIME*.

And yet, Dunne could relate to Didion's delicacy: He too had migraines, he too was terrified of snakes. His talk, and his writing, compensated for a childhood stammer. He was smart, well read, great to talk to about books and politics and people's affairs. (Dunne loved gossip though not as much as his brother Nick, who made a publishing career out of it.)

And John made Joan laugh. Despite the dust, and the migraines, the Didion families were known for their revelry. Commentators talk about the darkness in Joan's writing, but they often miss her sense of humor, her mischievous mirth and merciless satire. "She has this great laugh that is about three or four times bigger than she is," her close friend Nora Ephron said. (Admittedly that is still a comparatively small laugh.)

"John was so verbose and also hilarious," says Griffin Dunne. Nick's son adored his aunt and uncle and in 2017 made a documentary about Didion; five months after her passing, he still slips into present tense when talking about her. "Joan found him hilarious. I remember more her laughing than her being shy. She just had this laugh [Dunne switches into a high pitch] that would hit this high octave note, her lips wouldn't move, but there'd be a big smile and you'd just hear this trill coming out. Which was an intoxicating sound that as I got older, I would do whatever I could to hear over and over. That's another reason I wanted to make the doc is because she did have this, 'I'm shy, I'm a frail bird. I'm a scary, scary goddess of doom. And I write about deaths' and all that, but she's funny. And she loves to laugh."

On January 30, 1964, nine months after John Gregory Dunne first brought her to Connecticut and she fell in love with the family linen, Joan and John—Didion and Dunne—married at California's Mission San Juan Bautista. Built in 1797, the picturesque church in rolling California farmland has sustained damage from multiple fires and earthquakes but remains a mecca for the state's Catholic community and a symbol of its Spanish past. Didion wore sunglasses throughout the vows, perhaps to keep people from seeing her weep.

Joan and John initially set up house together in Manhattan. But they shared Didion's feeling that they had stayed too long at the fair. She wanted to be back in California, but maybe she had outgrown Sacramento. Dunne certainly was not going to trade NYC for Sactown. Los Angeles was neutral territory, a place they could get to know in tandem. Nick was there with his wife and children, working in the film industry, throwing fabulous Hollywood parties. That intrigued the Didion-Dunnes. (This is the nickname friends gave to the couple. Joan referred to herself as Joan Didion Dunne outside of her byline. John was always John Gregory Dunne.) Joan turned her *Vogue* job into a gig writing movie reviews; John took a leave from *TIME*, but never returned. Neither of them would ever again work an office job. They moved to Los Angeles five months after their nuptials. They rented, since they thought they might only stay a few months. They lived in California for twenty-four years.

True to its name, the Harden Gatehouse, also known as the Portuguese Point Gatehouse, sits behind a large wooden gate to an estate whose development was never completed. To get in, Didion had to get out of the car and push open the doors while her husband waited in the Corvette on the dark, winding two-lane road. (White people problems, I know.) Inside was a true Eden, complete with the occasional serpent. The outdoors was designed by the Olmsted Brothers, the sons of the designer of Central Park. If you want to see what the landscape and ocean view were like, watch the grand finale of the 1963 film *It's a Mad, Mad, Mad, Mad World*, where the contestants finally find the W that marks the treasure: It was filmed at the Gatehouse. The W was formed by palm trees leaning into each other, framing the blue expanse—a treasure indeed.

Trillin visited the Didion-Dunnes in Portuguese Bend. "We called it the writing factory because we were all working on something and then we would gather for dinner," he says. "And gossip, of course."

It's a charming picture, made possible in part by the union of two people from prosperous families. But the nickname was accurate; the writing factory was a place of industry. The product: words on paper.

A writer marrying another writer is likely to turn out one of two ways: Either they are going to find themselves competing for the scraps thrown them by the publishing world and wind up in a bitter divorce, or they are going to be each other's sounding boards and collaborators, making each other better, and more successful, writers. Given the delicate egos and precarious prospects of literary careers—not to mention my experience in my own first marriage—the first path seems to this writer the most likely. (The second time, I married a carpenter.) But in part because they learned how to steer around the potholes and pitfalls early in their marriage, the Didion-Dunnes became a true team.

In person, they complemented (and complimented) each other. He liked to talk, she liked to listen. "People always said they finished each other's sentences, but it was mostly John finishing Joan's sentences," Trillin says. "And they had the same habits. They liked to go to restaurants where they were known, and much to my dismay, those were usually really noisy restaurants. Once they got together, I almost never saw them apart."

Amazingly, they shared a column in the *Saturday Evening Post* from 1964 until the biweekly folded in 1969. Moving to Los Angeles at a time when the city was looked down on by the East Coast cultural elite, the Didion-Dunnes convinced the Philadelphia-based publication, which reached a large swath of the American public, to make them correspondents from Babylon. They alternated bylines in "Points West": One issue, Joan would write about the Getty Villa or why she hated cops, the next John would write about Portuguese Bend or why he hated snakes. There was a line illustration of the two of them at the top of the column, just their heads and shoulders—like Roman busts—staring at the viewer. Maybe "Points West" was intended to draw on the romantic allure of such Hollywood couples as Katharine Hepburn and Spencer Tracy, or the fictional Nick and Nora.

The Didion-Dunnes lived up to these roles admirably. They were each other's first readers and editors, giving copious and detailed notes on every book they wrote. Dunne typed his edits for *A Book of Common Prayer* in a list by page number. It included such picayune improvements as seafood choices: "116—Sand Dabs. No. Oysters." When Dunne died, Didion lamented that she had no one to show *Magical Thinking* to. (The book turned out just fine.)

Didion quickly became more famous and successful than Dunne. If he worried that people used him to get to his wife, he was probably right. The Farrar, Straus & Giroux editor Henry

Robbins was working with John on his first book, *Delano*, about the grape-workers' strike in California led by Cesar Chavez. In his letters to the writer, Robbins consistently asked about Joan. "Incidentally, this is highly unbusinesslike, but still—tell your lovely wife she has me in torments of anxiety waiting to hear whether she is joining you in the fold," he wrote on July 5, 1967. Didion wound up working with Robbins until his sudden death in 1979; she mourned his loss so deeply, she named her next book *After Henry*.

Many men would not tolerate being upstaged by their wife. It was certainly a plot point the Didion-Dunnes were familiar with: They did write the screenplay for the 1976 version of *A Star Is Born*, a movie about a woman who outshines her older lover. I'm guessing that becoming comfortable as a plus-one was a learning curve for Dunne, who was two years older than his wife; this is a man who once asked Dan Wakefield, the boyfriend of writer Eve Babitz, if he wrote her stories, Wakefield said. But John learned to bask in the refracted light of his wife's stardom.

"They would eat out several nights a week and John would see people at other tables craning to get a look at Joan. John would situate his chair to make it possible for them to see Joan," Griffin Dunne says.

Besides, John Gregory Dunne had considerable success of his own, most notably with the bestselling novel *True Confessions* and its movie adaptation, starring Robert De Niro. At home, they were peers and collaborators. "He was a writer who understood her work and she understood his," Griffin Dunne says. "However the outside world saw it, I think they considered each other peers and equals."

Didion and Dunne wrote screenplays together, including

Panic in Needle Park, *Play It As It Lays*, and *Up Close & Personal*. They served as screen doctors—fixing other writers' work—on additional films. This was their money gig; Joan used to always tout the importance of having Writers Guild health insurance. They were very dismissive of the Industry, as it is known in LA. "Movies are an artistic exercise only for directors. There's no way around it. That's the banal reality of it," she wrote in a 1972 letter, turning down a request to pen an article about film writing. But they loved the color of Hollywood money. As the film critic Lisa Kennedy so delicately put it in *Alta* magazine, they "were perhaps a little mercantile about the screen work."

Griffin Dunne says Joan and John used to drive their Corvette up and down the coast, crafting dialogue as they went: John would drive, Joan would write it all down. It's a ridiculously LA image: two beautiful young adults cruising the freeways past spectacular scenery in their canary-colored Corvette, writing movies.

It was a reality, but it's also a fantasy. Driving too fast around one too many curves, their marriage almost crashed and burned.

The troubles started in New York. She was in a state of collapse. "I hurt the people I cared about," she confessed in "Goodbye"; presumably, she meant John. Unable to function in Manhattan, the marriage "was a very good thing to do but badly timed." The friction continued in LA. On the long drives to Portuguese Bend, as they steered past the petrol smell and black smoke of the refineries that surround the Harbor Freeway, they quarreled. (The gardens of the gatehouse must have truly seemed like paradise after those fiery drives.) They argued a lot in those days, over everything and nothing.

In 1967 Joan took their adopted daughter Quintana Roo to

Sacramento for her first birthday. The father did not come. "My husband likes my family but is uneasy in their house," Didion explained in "On Going Home." She tried to make apologies for Dunne: "Once there I fall into their ways, which are difficult, oblique, deliberately inarticulate, not my husband's ways." Still, she was distraught. "Marriage is the classic betrayal." In her first column for *Life*, in 1969, Didion—now a well-known writer—wrote of "kicked-down doors, hospitalized psychotics . . . chronic anxieties and packed suitcases."

A few years later in Malibu, after John shouted at Quintana, Joan told her daughter they could go away if she wanted—but the child wouldn't leave her father. Instead, Dunne left. He spent days driving around the Southwest, and finally six months in Las Vegas, writing his first novel, *Vegas*—about a man having a midlife crisis in the City of Sin.

In her memoir *Miss Aluminum*, the actor and writer Susanna Moore recalls Dunne getting irate one night and storming out of a restaurant. Joan begged her friend to stay, "making me promise that I would not leave her alone with him."

In *The Center Will Not Hold*, Didion admits Dunne had a "horrible temper. . . . Everything would set him off."

In a 2022 article for *The Atlantic*, writer Caitlin Flanagan, citing some of the above evidence, calls this "abuse."

It is chilling to think of Joan Didion as a victim of spousal abuse. It's chilling to think of anyone as a victim of abuse, of course. But for many of us, Didion personifies a kind of mental and emotional strength, despite bodily limitations. She was beyond petite, barely more than five feet tall, and never weighed much more than one hundred pounds. "She was such a skeletal little woman," the writer Gay Talese says. "Her bones went right through her clothing."

Seemingly delicate women tend to attract two types of men. Some men want to make them victims, others want to protect them. And sometimes, in a third type, the two impulses entwine.

In a letter that she may never have sent, Eve Babitz accused her friend Didion of hiding behind her corporeal frailty and failing to stand up for other women—full-bodied, and thereby more threatening and sexualized, women—like Babitz. I completely agree that Didion needed some feminist consciousness raising. But Babitz was also wrong. In fact, Didion's body made her a target of abuse as well. All women are targets of abuse; that's one of the main points of feminism.

Didion may have looked like a mouse but she had the courage of a lion, and she was not one to tuck herself away out of harm. She made her path through the world like a woman twice her size, traveling alone, going into war zones, interviewing rock stars, taking on politicians. Like any woman does, she had her own war stories. When she was twenty, she traveled across country alone by train. She was sitting on the grass in the Boston Public Garden when a man came up to her and "started saying the most perverted things imaginable," she wrote in a letter to her friend Peggy. She told him to go away, and he put his hand on her arm. "Won't you please go away?" Joan said. This time he did. The next day, she took the overnight train to Montreal. She woke up to a man "making passes at me." She shouted, "STOP IT!" and pushed him off her. He came back later and tried to convince her to spend the weekend with him.

In college, her boyfriend Bob followed her as she walked home after a fight, trying to get her into his car. The police pulled him over, mistaking him for a stranger. After all, a ninety-pound young woman walking home alone in the mid-1950s was clearly a potential victim. Decades later, the recently widowed writer walked through a cafeteria at UCLA medical center, where her daughter was being treated, and a deranged man followed her, shouting vulgar names at her, so close that his spit landed on her.

And then there was Parmentel.

Didion was drawn to the type of man who would protect her from creeps like these. She wanted a John Wayne: someone strong but tender. Weidner might not have been worldly enough. Parmentel seemed to hurt her more than help her. When Dunne raged—and rage he did—did she worry that he too ultimately wanted not to support, but to dominate her?

I'm guessing she did. I suspect she worried enough that she sought Moore's protection one evening, that she considered a divorce.

No one I interviewed thinks that Dunne was physically abusive.

"He had just a volcanic temper that was scary to receive and to even witness, and he was a big yeller," Griffin Dunne says. "But I don't think he ever laid a hand on Joan. I just think he was really fucking scary when he was angry, and I think both she and Q had moments of cowering under his Irish rage over whatever set it off."

Anger can cause emotional trauma, can cause terror. I have been around men with anger issues; they are not pleasant. They should not be tolerated. But their issues can be addressed, and as with any emotional disorder, they can get better. With time, and patience, and probably some therapy.

I don't think Didion was the kind to be intimidated. She had her own neuroses, her own psychoses, that were undoubtedly not easy for John to live with.

Trillin says people misunderstand Didion's diminutive demeanor. "Someone called me at some point from the *Times*, I think, and said, 'Joan was not doing well,' because she seemed very frail. I said, 'She's tougher than she looks.' Actually anybody's tougher than *she* looks. But she's tough. If I'm not mistaken, Joan was president of her co-op."

"Joan was the strong one, in her kind of frailty she was very strong of mind and purpose," Katrina vanden Heuvel says. "I think she was the stronger one, even in the marriage."

"I often wondered about their marriage, because Joan was who she was, and it wasn't that John wasn't a good writer or admired, but she was on this pedestal on her own," says Julia Armstrong-Totten, Didion's cousin. "They very much depended on each other. They really had a symbiotic relationship. But I think in some ways, she survived better without him than he might have survived without her, even though he wouldn't admit it."

In *The Center Will Not Hold*, Didion admits that John was her defender: "He was the baffle between me and the world at large."

Didion told Davidson that in the beginning, she and Dunne argued half the time. By the end, they argued one-tenth of the time, but they were inseparable. "In the early years, you fight because you don't understand each other. In later years, you fight because you do."

In lieu of a divorce, they worked it out.

In the fucking Royal Hawaiian Hotel.

In Hawai'i, they "began a life of total togetherness that was nearly unparalleled in modern marriage," Nick Dunne wrote after his brother died.

By the time they moved to their final home, an apartment on New York's Upper East Side, their lives were in sync. They walked in Central Park in the morning (whether or not Dunne had controlled his temper, he had apparently learned to manage his fear of snakes). They had breakfast either at the 3 Guys Restaurant or the Carlyle Hotel. (They loved to eat out and had expensive tastes.) They worked in their adjoining offices, sharing news, asking for help if they were stuck on a piece of writing.

Joan Didion was a strong, self-made woman who wrote frequently about divorce and failed families but who devoted her own life to her nuclear unit. "I do not always think he is right nor does he always think I am right but we are each the person the other trusts," she wrote in *The Year of Magical Thinking.* "There is no separation between our interests and investments in any given situation."

"What I came to love later was different from what I loved in the beginning," Didion said after her partner of forty years passed. "Later we had so much history, we had a life together and we were the only people in it."

Stingray

The heroine of *Play It As It Lays* has starred in two films, both directed by her now-estranged husband. Their young daughter has been institutionalized, and Maria ("that is pronounced Mar-*eye*-ah," she explains at the outset) is pregnant with another man's child. The novel tells, from multiple points of view, the tale of her unraveling. Maria spends her mornings driving the LA freeway system, finding peace of mind and freedom in the mobility and isolation of her Corvette Stingray. In one of Joan Didion's most famous passages, the writer describes a maneuver that resonates with anyone who has driven these infamous roads: "Again and again she returned to an intricate stretch just south of the interchange where successful passage from the Hollywood onto the Harbor required a diagonal move across four lanes of traffic.

On the afternoon she finally did it without once braking or once losing the beat on the radio she was exhilarated, and that night slept dreamlessly."

Didion described negotiating a four-lane highway alone as telegraphically as she described navigating an ocean cave with Dunne. She wrote about movement and she wrote about place, and often, they entwined.

Among the perils of the Pacific are the creatures that burrow beneath the sand. A true coastal dweller knows to shuffle her feet as she wades, or else she might wind up with the toxic barb that gives the stingray its name embedded in her flesh. Joan was an adventurer who stepped wisely.

Didion liked fast cars as well as beautiful homes; she owned a 1969 Daytona-yellow Corvette Stingray and lived in a Hollywood mansion, just like Maria. No one wrote about driving in Los Angeles better than Joan Didion (though English architecture critic Reyner Banham came close). She captured the essence of the city as defined by its mode of transportation without condescension. In fact she celebrated it. "The freeway experience . . . is the only secular communion Los Angeles has," she wrote in *The White Album*. "Mere driving on the freeway is in no way the same as participating in it. Anyone can 'drive' on the freeway, and many people with no vocation for it do, hesitating here and resisting there, losing the rhythm of the lane change, thinking about where they came from and where they are going. Actual participation requires total surrender, a concentration so intense as to seem a kind of narcosis, a rapture-of-the-freeway. The mind goes clean. The rhythm takes over."

Notice the way the rhythm takes over this passage: The string of gerunds in the predicate accelerates, then she brakes for two four-word declarative sentences. This is a writer who has her hand firmly on the wheel. Note also that Joan always calls it the freeway, not the highway. Didion's love affair with the auto marked her as a California writer. Julian Wasser's photographs of her with that Corvette are even more widely shared than images of her with her typewriter. Again, the marriage of woman and machine.

But in Didion's universe, every silver lining has a cloud. LA's car culture and modernist homes are two of the city's best features, and two of the worst. Millions of people driving alone to their private air-conditioned abodes not only give the city its deadly smog, but also contribute to the existential malaise that Didion also wrote about better than anyone: atomization. The breakdown of the social contract that she laments in *Slouching* is at the center of almost all of her work—the center that "is not holding," as she put it. Maria drives all morning, but she is going nowhere.

Play It As It Lays is Didion's second novel, published in 1970. Along with *Slouching Towards Bethlehem*, the collection of her articles published in 1968, it established its author as a major new player in American literature. The *New York Times*, in its review of *Slouching*, called it "a rich display of some of the best prose written today in this country." The *Los Angeles Times* named Didion a woman of the year. Following in the footsteps of John's brother Dominick, in LA the Didion-Dunnes hobnobbed with Hollywood royalty: actors, directors, producers, movie moguls. They were *becoming* Hollywood royalty; with Nick, they produced their first film, an adaptation of the novel *The Panic in Needle Park*, with the screenplay written by Joan and John. Kitty Winn won the award for best actress at the Cannes Film Festival for her portrayal of a young woman from middle America driven to sex work by her addiction to heroin. *Needle Park* also marked the debut of a young actor from the South Bronx, Al Pacino, as a hustler-dealer. For this modern-day *Romeo and Juliet,* Joan and John spent months back in Manhattan, staying at a run-down hotel, hanging with junkies. The film, directed by Jerry Schatzberg, is unflinching in its depiction of people shooting up and overdosing.

Didion and Dunne went on to write several films together, including their 1972 adaptation of *Play It As It Lays.* Some of those scripts were never produced, and they made major bank—six figures a week—doctoring others' screenplays. It was this work, more than the journalism and novels, that funded the houses and sports car.

On the one hand, Didion was doing research by hanging with heavy drug users in sketchy New York neighborhoods. On the other hand, she was the woman with the Corvette consorting with rock stars, living the fast-paced LA lifestyle—a bit of a celebrity herself.

The Didion-Dunnes took to LA like school kids released on summer vacation. They had to move from Portuguese Bend shortly after they adopted Quintana in 1965 because they shared the gatehouse with the owner and his wife, and adding a child and a babysitter went against the lease. They eventually rented a large, two-story house on Franklin Avenue, a block south of Runyon Canyon Park and north of Hollywood Boulevard: between coyotes and runaways. At the time the home, like the Hollywood neighborhood, was a bit wrecked. That didn't stop the Didion-Dunnes from turning it into an epicenter of swinging sixties glamour.

Joan may have seemed shy, but she and her husband loved to

socialize: to go out to shows and restaurants, to see and be seen. They also loved to entertain. Griffin Dunne vividly remembers a 1968 happening at Franklin Avenue, thrown for the release of Tom Wolfe's book *The Electric Kool-Aid Acid Test*, a classic tome of New Journalism. Dunne was only thirteen, but his idol Janis Joplin was going to be there, so his parents brought him. After all, Nick and Lenny Dunne had been famous Hollywood hosts for years, though they were beginning to be outdone by the Didion-Dunnes. Decades later, Griffin made a short film based on that night. *Duke of Groove* is so clearly the model for *Almost Famous*, Cameron Crowe should be paying Dunne royalties. The party, as portrayed in Dunne's movie, was basically everything you would expect at a sixties Hollywood bacchanal for a book about acid: sex, drugs, rock stars, and movie directors, in every candlelit room (Didion loved hurricane lamps). Janis did come, though after Griffin had left. Instead, he met a tripping Otto Preminger; the adolescent mistook the German film director for the actor who played Colonel Klink in the TV Nazi comedy *Hogan's Heroes*.

Most of the Didion-Dunne parties were smaller, dinner affairs. These were coveted invitations, as their circle of friends included filmmakers (Richard Leacock, Frank Pierson), actors (Harrison Ford, Warren Beatty—who was smitten with Joan), artists (Francesco Clemente, Eve Babitz), and writers (Christopher Isherwood, Nora Ephron, Jean Stein). Earl McGrath, a gallery owner who became manager of the Rolling Stones' record label, was one of her best friends; his photographer wife Camilla documented many of these gatherings. A guest might be seated between politician Jerry Brown and a drag queen, TV producer Norman Lear and journalist Narda Zacchino. According to her cousin, Joan's parents once realized that they were dining next to sex workers whom John had met in Las Vegas. The Didion-Dunnes moved farther from the nightlife action when they bought the Malibu house in 1971, but they found a beach community: writer Brian Moore and his wife Jean, actor Katharine Ross and cinematographer Conrad Hall. Their parties were worth the drive.

Gay Talese was at one of those Trancas dinners. "I had a very wonderful evening," the fellow inventor of literary journalism says. "They had other people there—not surprisingly, Hollywood people. Not surprisingly I can't remember them. But I do remember how carefully she cooked dinner. This was a very large living room that looked upon the beach and she was at the kitchen cooking. She was very, very meticulous, and also very charming."

In 1972 photographer Henry Clarke shot the Didion-Dunnes in their Trancas house for *Vogue* magazine. There's a photo of Didion wearing two pigtails in the kitchen, prepping a meal. One of her big orange Le Creuset pots is next to her on the pink tiled counter, and jars of spices are meticulously stacked. Fruits hang in wire baskets over pots of planted herbs. This is the space of someone who loves cuisine, a food chapel worthy of Julia Child, M. F. K. Fisher, or Alice Waters. (Cookbooks and Fisher's *The Art of Eating* were among Didion's tomes that were sold for thousands of dollars in the 2022 estate auction.) The photo is one of the rare shots where Didion smiles at the camera.

Though she wrote about many things, in her thirties Didion was in part becoming a chronicler of the rich and famous: the titans of the film industry, Newport socialites, singers Joan Baez (who ate potato salad with her fingers) and Jim Morrison (Didion watched him lower a lit match to the fly of his black vinyl pants).

Dunne too was writing about Hollywood (in his book *The Studio* and later *Monster*), and for Hollywood.

In 1960s and '70s LA, Didion found a freedom that she had previously known swimming the American River, or walking the streets of Manhattan. She boarded airplanes barefoot. She shopped in supermarkets in her bikini. This is the Joan we see so often in photographs, looking effortlessly cool in comfortable clothes, almost always with a cigarette between her right second and middle fingers. In the photos by Wasser, she leans on or sits in her Stingray in a long-sleeved, full-length dress, looking straight at the camera. Often, all of her body is covered, except for her face and feet; she was more a tunicked goddess than a sexy go-go girl. She wasn't necessarily smiling. But that didn't mean she wasn't having a good time.

"I don't like to take pictures of smiling people," Wasser said. "It looks real phony. She was very natural."

Didion had a strong style of writing and she loved writing about style. One of the hallmarks of her prose is her specificity. In *The New Journalism*, Wolfe called these "status life details": morsels of information that speak volumes. In part because she did often write about women, and celebrities, and she *was* a woman, who got her start at *Vogue* and *Mademoiselle*, a lot of Didion's details are about fashion: cut, color, fabric, brand. To call these descriptions superficial or materialistic (as some critics have) is to miss the point of descriptive writing—and to reveal one's gender biases. Criticizing Didion for writing about clothes is akin to complaining about Hemingway writing about fishing.

Didion's training in the world of magazines taught her that the devils (and sometimes angels) are in the details. The wedding dress she bought at Ransohoff's, a San Francisco department store. The layette from Saks for Quintana when she was born. The black wool challis dress from Henri Bendel when Q was four. The "dirty crepe-de-Chine wrapper" a woman was wearing at a hotel in Delaware. Photos of Q at age five, wearing a cashmere turtle-neck sweater or "cutoff jeans and a denim Levi jacket with metal studs." The "black silk dress" Joan wore the night she met Henry Robbins. The Christian Louboutin shoes Q wore at her wedding: "Pale satin with bright red soles." Eduene's mother loved to give her granddaughter clothes, and that granddaughter clearly in turn dressed up her own daughter.

The Central Valley of Didion's childhood was not exactly an epicenter of cool, but the wonderful world of magazines brought style to Sactown. Joan caught the publishing bug early. As a child, she and her cousin Brenda ogled the outfits in *Vogue*. They also played a game where they made believe they boarded an elevator at I. Magnin department store, only to have the ghostly operator intone, "There is only room for one more" before the lift plunged to the bottom. (In 1970, she would in fact go to I. Magnin in Beverly Hills to buy Charles Manson associate Linda Kasabian a dress to wear at her testimony for the trial for the Manson family murders.) At age six, Didion had fantasies of being in Argentina getting a divorce in a black silk mantilla and dark glasses. (Here's a girl who fantasized about divorce, not marriage.) She told these stories in *Vogue* magazine herself, in 2011.

In college, she edited special fashion issues for the campus newspaper. When she moved to New York and actually worked for *Vogue*, she complained she couldn't afford the outfits staffers were expected to wear, including hats every day. She was trying to live off her own income, without assistance from her parents (who by this time could have afforded to help her); hence, the borrowed furniture. But the would-be thespian had a certain artistic flair: the three-quarters-length coat she made for the Nob Hill photo session, those yards of yellow fabric hanging out her Manhattan window.

As an adult, Didion's tastes were chic but simple, comfort oriented. Her "To Pack and Wear" list is all about ease and space: "2 skirts, 2 jerseys or leotards, 1 pullover sweater, 2 pair shoes, stockings, etc." This is the uniform of a working writer: easy to assemble, carry, wash, and wear. Not having to think about what to wear frees a woman to think about what to write.

Small wonder Didion became a thinking woman's fashion icon, her image pinned to dorm walls and, now, Instagram accounts for going on a half century. In 1989, she and Quintana Roo were featured in a Gap ad campaign, mother and daughter in black turtlenecks, photo by Annie Leibovitz. In 2015, the eighty-year-old icon was the star of an ad for the very chic, very expensive Céline brand. She wore black in that photo too; apparently, once she moved back to New York, she adopted the city's color code. A giant pair of sunglasses covers half her face, and her rose lips are shut tight—not just not smiling, but unsmiling. The photo, by Juergen Teller, is rather grim. But social media loved it. "The fashion Internet quivered in a way it hasn't at least since Kim Kardashian stripped nude for *Paper* magazine two months ago," said the *New York Times*.

Joan Didion undoubtedly liked nice things. French perfume. Tablecloths on rollers. I. Magnin. By the time she moved to Trancas, she used good silver every day. "Well every day is all there is," she explained to the *New York Times*. (Now there is a perfect Didion sentence for you.)

To some readers, all this designer name-dropping is off-putting. Didion has understandably been accused of glamorizing consumption, fetishizing possessions—the "English chintzes, the chinoiserie toile" in their Brentwood home (both of which I had to look up). The luxury chic that is associated with Didion reached its absurdist apotheosis on November 16, 2022, when items formerly owned by Didion and Dunne were auctioned off at that estate sale whose physical location was Stair Galleries in Hudson, New York, but whose primary transactions took place all over the World Wide Web thanks to online bidding. Two hundred and twenty-four lots of Didion-Dunne furniture, plates, cookware, artwork, books, hurricane lamps, sunglasses, and even shells—the kind you can get at any beachy tourist shop—sold for a minimum of $1,100 each, generally ten times the preauction estimate. Twenty-three linen napkins with JDD embroidered on them: $14,000. Thirteen blank—that's right, blank—notebooks: $11,000. The silver flatware: $5,500. One pair of faux tortoiseshell Céline sunglasses: $27,000. The most expensive item, $110,000, was a portrait of Didion painted by an obscure, troubled admirer from an author photo and given to Didion.

As Julia Armstrong-Totten said to me the next day in an email, about her cousin: "I can see her rolling her eyes about all the attention, but at the same time loving it!"

The proceeds from the sale went to a fund for Parkinson's research and a scholarship at Sacramento City College. But the one-day display of materialistic idolatry was hard to watch, even for a Didion fan.

The value in these pieces came mostly from their association with their deceased owner: "relics" of "Saint Joan," as her cousin wrote me. On their own, they would have been worth a fraction of the price. Many of these were well-worn items that had been passed down for generations in the Didion-Dunne family, or artworks gifted by their creators to their friends, or just paperback books. These were talismans, not jewels—treasured keepsakes, not the products of a ridiculously conspicuous consumption.

They revealed much about their owner's aesthetic: a reverence for fine old objects such as multiple sets of porcelain dishes; an appreciation for conceptual and abstract art by such twentieth-century masters as Ed Ruscha, Willard Dixon, and Brice Marden; a mix of practical (Le Creuset cookware) and sentimental (an adorable painting of a sleeping kitten gifted to Didion by Earl McGrath), of naturalism (a photo of the ocean's wash by Quintana) and urbanism (a photo of a midcentury Palm Springs building by Q).

Armstrong-Totten remembers the weight of the Le Creuset pans; she didn't know how her cousin could lift them.

Lynn Nesbit, Didion's agent, says Joan did not have a luxury problem. "She didn't spend much on clothes. . . . I don't mean they were hurting but they never seemed to live a very luxurious lifestyle. She never dressed up in fancy dresses. Even a fancy cocktail dress: I've never seen her wear anything like that. She always had skirts, sweaters or some basic little dress that probably cost a few hundred dollars."

In Manhattan, wealth is relative.

The chronicler of empire knew that the emperors wore lots

of clothes. Glossy magazines were obsessed with the rich and famous, after all; the reporters infiltrated in camouflage: Didion in her linen dresses and miniskirts, Tom Wolfe and Truman Capote in their suits and hats. In the sixties, literary journalists were up there with rock stars and movie directors as cultural royalty. One of Wolfe's greatest articles was "These Radical Chic Evenings," about a party thrown by Leonard Bernstein for the Black Panthers. Didion begins her piece "Good Citizens" thus: "I was once invited to a civil rights meeting at Sammy Davis, Jr.'s house, in the hills above the Sunset Strip."

"Style is character."

So wrote Joan Didion in a 1976 essay about the painter Georgia O'Keeffe. The italics are hers, not mine. She understood that decisions about form are decisions about content. Ornamentation is a statement. O'Keeffe's flowers were not just flowers; they were "astonishingly aggressive" fuck-yous to the men who didn't understand the artist, who tried to limit her, who judged her. I see many connections between Didion and O'Keeffe: Both grew up in agrarian areas, both fought to be understood in New York, both relocated out West so they could see the horizon again, both found inspiration and comfort in Hawai'i, both had a morbid streak (morgues, cow skulls), both loved flowers. O'Keeffe, in Joan's words, "seems to have been equipped early with an immutable sense of who she was and a fairly clear understanding that she would be required to prove it." The writer could be describing herself. Both, in their own ways, were "successful guerrillas in the war between the sexes."

I see these connections between Patti Smith and Didion too, who were friendly. The musician and poet is also an O'Keeffe fan. She performed at the memorials for both Quintana and Joan. She too has waged a sort of guerrilla war for decades.

Two photos that Smith had given Didion, of Hermann Hesse's typewriter and of Easter bunnies, sold for $29,000 and $16,000 at the estate auction. "To Joan with sympathy," Patti wrote beneath the rabbits.

Joan understood the importance of style, not just in wardrobe and furnishings, but in art, and music, and most importantly, writing. Her journalistic mission was to expose the way that style—rhetoric—could also be a masquerade: the stories that are lies. From the minute she put pencil to notebook, she began crafting her own style. At Berkeley, she analyzed the art of beautiful writing in Henry James's work. She learned to polish her style in the boot camp at *Vogue*, and would keep polishing it for the rest of her life. This is the nature of literary journalism: the merging of deep information with belletrist form.

"In interviews over the years, she has consistently emphasized her own attention to the control that certain sentences exert over content, spoken of the importance of the rhythms and echoes created at the level of syntax, and reflected on her own process of revising and editing at the sentence level," writes Kathleen M. Vandenberg in *Joan Didion: Substance and Style*. Vandenberg, a senior lecturer in rhetoric at Boston University, puts style at the center of Didion's impact, as the book's title indicates. "Style is her formal means of achieving persuasion . . . with it, she, among other things, makes her arguments present and memorable, foregrounds and emphasizes her major claims, and creates rapport with her readers."

Literary journalism—the name given to 1960s New Journalism after it stopped being new—usually borrows devices from fiction, poetry, and theater. Didion certainly was well versed in these literatures and incorporated their elements in her nonfiction writing. Maybe this is my personal bias, but I think that music was arguably an even more important influence on her style. Joan Didion wrote like a composer: concerned with rhythm, with hitting the right notes, with creating melodies and hooks (those repeated refrains), with overall song structure. I'm not the only one to say this. "Many of Didion's sentences resemble my favorite music, music no one should dance to," Myriam Gurba writes. Joan clearly listened to music, and in her work I can hear the sounds of the times that played on the radio during the transition from the Hollywood to the Harbor Freeway.

Early on, Joan's articles and novels paralleled pop and jazz standards: tuneful, bursting with hooks and riffs, formal in their structure, like songs by Carole King and Gerry Goffin, Jerry Leiber and Mike Stoller, Ira and George Gershwin. In the 1960s and '70s, she experimented with dissonance, improvisation, abstraction: Think the Doors, Jimi Hendrix, Laura Nyro. In the 1980s and '90s, she composed new musical symphonies, fusing classical music, harmolodic jazz, and stage musicals: Joni Mitchell, Stephen Sondheim, Charles Mingus, Leonard Bernstein. Her journalistic magnum opus, "New York: Sentimental Journeys," offers political commentary as spoken narrative: It's Gil Scott-Heron, Public Enemy. In the 2000s, with her memoirs, she became a confessional singer-songwriter with a raw, postpunk edge: Patti Smith, PJ Harvey, Kurt Cobain. In 2023, I listen to Kendrick Lamar and I hear Joan Didion. Both rely on the confessional voice, both offer incisive social discourse, California belonged to both of them—and they to it.

Reducing Didion's life's work to a pair of $27,000 sunglasses is distracting and disturbing. She wore big frames not just because they exuded movie-star cool and compensated for her small face, but also because she had eyes that tended to water and migraines triggered by light. She lived in California, where sunglasses are not just fashionable, they can be medically necessary. Style is character, but Céline is not Didion.

Still, I like the idea of an octogenarian fashion icon, sitting in an armchair with a lone orchid behind her and dressed all in black. Joan was goth!

Julian Wasser hated the way the Céline ad's lighting exaggerates Didion's age and frailty. Teller made "her look like an old hag . . . She looks one thousand years old," Wasser said. He preferred the Joan of his own romanticized youth: "When I shot her, she was a hot-looking girl."

Wasser photographed many famous people: Martin Luther King Jr., the Beatles, the Rolling Stones, Donna Summer, Robert Kennedy at the Ambassador Hotel, Jack Nicklaus, etc. But the photos that get circulated the most are two very different shots of two good friends: Eve Babitz, naked, playing chess with Marcel Duchamp, and Didion, covered from ankle to wrist, in front of her Corvette. The contradictions in those two shots are brilliant and hilarious: the brainy nude, the Mennonite speed racer.

Didion's framed prints of Wasser's Stingray photographs sold for $24,000 and $26,000 in the auction. The photographer sold a lot of these photos, and of other shots he took of Didion: with Quintana in her lap, with John and Q.

"Every upwardly mobile young woman in Europe and America wants those pictures," said Wasser of his iconic shots of Joan. "You get all these girls that they're regarded as bimbos, and they can relate to her because she's a class act. An intellectual-type class act."

When Joan Didion worked at *Vogue*, she often went to photo shoots. She soon learned that the key to a successful session was not for the subject to be herself (it was always women being photographed) but to be "whoever and whatever it was that the photographer wanted to see in the lens," as she later wrote in a book of Robert Mapplethorpe's work. Interestingly, her boyfriend Bob Weidner was an amateur photographer. It's clear from looking at the many iconic images of Didion that she learned how to pose for the camera in ways that pleased the photographer but also were true to herself. The quiet subject mastered the gaze, whether staring directly back at it—as she does in every Wasser photograph—or hiding her face behind her black turtleneck sweater, as she did in a famous shot by Brigitte Lacombe. Indeed, few writers are almost as well known for the photos of them—by Annie Leibovitz, by John Bryson, by Quintana Roo Dunne—as for the books by them, in the way that Didion is.

"She's very aware of herself as an icon of style and culture," says writer David L. Ulin. "There's something fascinating about the way that she navigates the artificiality of public image."

The photos are mementos of another time, souvenirs of the

dream of a golden land. Staring at them—for they command your stare—you envy the lifestyle: the potted herbs in the Trancas bungalow, the little nuclear family on their way to the beach, the writerly couple in the wooden room lined with books, the mother and daughter nose to nose on the couch.

But there's more to these images than status life details. For a shy woman, a reflective artist, a person whose bones jut through the loose fabric, Didion possesses a fascinating poise in these photographs. You're not sure if she's going to blow away or blow you away. She is beautiful, but she never comes off as objectified, or distorted, or overly made up, or underdressed, or overdressed, or dressed by anyone but herself, for herself. A writer—an intellectual—spends so much time in her head that it can be hard for her to also be present in her body. In these photos, Joan looks like she has mastered both.

Style is character.

Highball

At age eight, Joan Didion was participating in a school fire drill when blinding pain filled her head. She was taken to the army infirmary at Peterson Field in Colorado Springs, Colorado, where her father was stationed at the time. Thus began the first of what became often debilitating migraines that she suffered on an almost weekly basis, "insensible to the world around me," as she wrote in 1968.

Throughout her life, Didion battled physical and mental ailments. Some of these she inherited, some were her own struggles. Along with her groundbreaking reportage, revelatory style, and decades-long marriage, migraines, physical frailty, and mental illness—and her courage in writing openly about them—are intrinsic to Joan's story.

Migraine—a disorder in the brain that can temporarily cause immobilizing pain—ran in Didion's blood. Her great-great-great-great-grandmother Elizabeth Scott Hardin had "sick headaches," Joan wrote in *Where I Was From*. So did her paternal grandmother, Ethel Reese, who had a delicate constitution even before she died at a young age of the Spanish influenza. Ethel was "nervous" and "different," her younger sister told Joan. "I was said to have her eyes, 'Reese eyes,' eyes that reddened and watered at the first premonition of sun or primroses or raised voices, and I was also said to have some of her 'difference,' her way of being less than easy at that moment when the dancing starts," Joan wrote.

The pioneer stock that Didion talked so often about was a strength and a weakness. Frontier life could be character building, but its hardships and deprivations could also bend, and even break, spirits and minds. Joan inherited the firmness and the infirmities. "They were women, these women in my family, without much time for second thoughts, without much inclination toward equivocation, and later, when there was time or inclination, there developed a tendency, which I came to see as endemic, toward slight and major derangements, apparently eccentric pronouncements, opaque bewilderment and moves to places not quite on the schedule," Didion wrote about her ancestors, and about herself, *in Where I Was From*.

Physical as well as mental delicacy were in Joan's genes. From her paternal grandfather, she inherited her rail-thin physique, along with her taciturnity. It is one of the first things those who knew her comment on: her slight, even emaciated frame. All her life, people talked about her weight. She was "a remarkably small child," she herself admitted in *Blue Nights*. And by remarkably, she meant that "perfect strangers could always be relied upon to remark on it."

Didion faced traumatizing pressures to make her appetite conform to societal standards, pressures that are all too familiar to many of us. "My earliest memories involve being urged by my mother to gain weight, as if my failure to do so were willful, an act of rebellion," she wrote in *Blue Nights*. She could not leave the table without cleaning her plate, "a rule that led mainly to new and inventive ways of eating nothing on my plate." Her eating habits were a source of constant commentary and family tension. Her father eventually sprang to her defense, shouting at her mother: "She's not a human garbage can!" Later, Joan realized that this pressure "more or less" guaranteed "an eating disorder." I see this comment as typically Didionesque indirection from the writer who hated labels, categories, clubs, and identities, who would not come out and confess that yes, she was anorexic.

The kind of uninvited gaze and judgment that Didion experienced as a child, and for the rest of her life, can indeed be a quick ticket to body dysmorphia, to not feeling comfortable in your own skin. I was a remarkably small child too, and I know well that annoying feeling of being talked about as if you were an object, as if your body size were anyone's business but your own. This forced subjectivity is shared by big and small women, by all women really; Eve Babitz was wrong to make it a distinction between her and her friend Joan. Commentary is also counterproductive: Having so much attention paid to my physical frame made me all the more self-conscious about my consumption.

Didion admitted that at full bloom—"top height ever"—she was five feet one and three-quarters and one hundred pounds.

Her disposition worsened after she picked up paratyphoid in 1973 when traveling in Colombia for a film festival, at which point she actually *wanted* her mother to fly down and make her eat, which Eduene did. Nevertheless, Joan failed to gain weight after that illness. As she aged, she began to lose what little flesh she had.

The social pressures of a highly public life probably did not help her body esteem. In the fashion world, and in photo shoots, and at *Vogue*, skinniness is a virtue. Didion's petiteness, combined with her delicate features and soft, strawberry hair, made her a photogenic, natural blond beauty, even if she didn't smile. Her trademark big sunglasses helped compensate for the tininess of her face and allowed the introvert-extrovert to hide those Reese eyes in plain sight. Looking at pictures of Joan, with her hip bones jutting through her skirts, it's hard not to think that all that pressure did indeed guarantee an eating disorder. Didion wrote in *Blue Nights* about doctors, friends, and family who pestered her about her weight. Joan Quinn, an art collector and writer who frequently attended dinner parties that included the Didion-Dunnes, remembers Joan having a great time in the kitchen making pasta with Earl McGrath, but "she didn't eat anything. She would always poke at her food."

Didion loved the social aspect of dining together and the art of cuisine. She is almost as famous for her cooking as for her slender frame. She prepared the menus and often the food itself at the regular parties she and John threw. "She enjoyed the process of cooking—which is a very good distraction when you're writing all day—and everything to do with food," says Jean Moore, Didion's friend and neighbor in Trancas. The two women often hosted each other and friends and family for dinner. "She had to have some other activity. She would have things like tacos, and other Mexican food, and a rotating menu."

Julia Armstrong-Totten was a regular guest at the Didion-Dunne parties in Brentwood Park. She recalls smorgasbords of delicious cuisine all overseen, if not hand prepared, by her cousin. "She loved food," Armstrong-Totten says. "She loved to cook. And she ate. I dined with her many, many times. She made the most amazing fried chicken."

And yet, Didion withered. Late in her life, a dietitian tried to fatten her up with the "inevitable" protein shake, fresh eggs, vanilla ice cream from La Maison du Chocolat, and physical therapy. She loved the expensive dessert; who wouldn't want to be prescribed that? She also enjoyed the therapy. She was inspired by the fit bodies the facility seemed to produce, until one day she realized they were the New York Yankees, loosening up before a game.

Didion may have appreciated food like she did the ocean, or natural things in general: from a distance, with a certain degree of skepticism. She admitted in one interview, probably referring to the paratyphoid episode, that her anxieties and her bodily health were entwined. "One time I was sick with an infection, I was in hospital, and when I got out I'd lost a lot of weight. I was sick all summer and I couldn't eat, I was supposed to gain weight, but every time I'd look at a plate of food, the food would literally seem to reshape itself into a rattlesnake. I think that was probably having a little breakdown."

Breakdowns ran in the family. Like his father, Didion's father was slender. He too had migraines (as did her mother). And Frank Reese Didion struggled with anxieties that traced back to his mother's early death, and probably to her "way of being less than easy at that moment when the dancing starts."

When Joan was in her first year at Berkeley, her father was hospitalized under psychiatric care in San Francisco. Weekends, her mother would pick her up at the sorority house and then pick Frank up at the Presidio. They would drive out to Marin County, maybe find a baseball game somewhere to watch. On the way back, Frank would insist that he be dropped off on the north side of the Golden Gate, so he could walk back to the hospital across the bridge—with its spectacular views and its 746-foot drop to the water below. Joan wrote in *Where I Was From* that it was not until he died that she was able to face the obvious: "Those were bad walks for someone under observation for depression."

Her father's problems must have affected Didion's transition to college. She got a late start under trying circumstances. Her boyfriend doesn't recall her father's hospitalization; her cousin, Armstrong-Totten, thinks the family kept it well hidden. Robert Weidner does remember this: "The thing that bothered her was she told me that as a child, she was the apple of her father's eye, and very important in her father's life. And then she felt that when her brother was born, everything changed."

Didion admitted to being alienated from the father that she also seemed to love dearly. She recalled growing up in a house that was dark, dusty, and full of gloom. "There was about him a sadness so pervasive that it colored even those many moments when he seemed to be having a good time," Joan wrote. Frank Reese could be playing piano "and the tension he transmitted would seem so great that I would have to leave, run to my room and close the door." He always had a bourbon highball nearby. "This calls for a drink" was her father's solution "to any moment when emotion seemed likely to surface."

Bourbon was also one of the items on Didion's published packing list. A highball is often nearby in the narratives she wrote and the narrative of her life. All those parties, all those cocktails. "In retrospect we all drank more than we needed to drink but this did not occur to any of us in 1966," she wrote in *Blue Nights*.

In 1968, just as the success of *Slouching Towards Bethlehem* caused her to be named a "woman of the year" by the *Los Angeles Times*, Joan Didion suffered her own breakdown.

"The Rorschach record is interpreted as describing a personality in process of deterioration with abundant signs of failing defenses and increasing inability of the ego to mediate the world of reality and to cope with normal stress. . . . Emotionally, patient has alienated herself almost entirely from the world of other human beings. . . . It is as though she feels deeply that all human effort is foredoomed to failure, a conviction which seems to push her further into a dependent, passive withdrawal."

You need look no further than the psychiatric report that Didion published in her 1978 collection *The White Album* to understand the mental, emotional, and physical anguish the writer was in—the ancestral "major derangements." A severe attack of vertigo and nausea sent her to St. John's Hospital in Santa Monica, where Q had been born two years earlier. Didion summarized the episode with her usual wry humor a decade later: "By way of comment I offer only that an attack of vertigo and nausea does not now seem to me an inappropriate response to the summer of 1968."

Publishing the diagnosis of one's own psychosis may seem to some like narcissistic self-indulgence—TMI, as they say. But many Didion lovers appreciate her transparency as a remarkable act of bravery. We know that she survived this mental and physical collapse, and it gives us hope. She survived because she told us so and she told us how, in the opening sentence of *The White Album*: "We tell ourselves stories in order to live."

Didion had long made anxiety central to her narrative. "I know something about dread myself, and appreciate the elaborate systems with which some people manage to fill the void, appreciate all the opiates of the people," she wrote in 1967. She later described finding it "necessary to revise the circuitry of my mind." In *Slouching*'s preface, Didion, quoting Yeats, wrote about "atomization, the proof that things fall apart." She admitted to being unable to sleep and drinking gin and hot water and taking Dexedrine during the twenty to twenty-one hours a day she remained awake while writing the article "Slouching Towards Bethlehem," the centerpiece of the book.

Initially published in the *Saturday Evening Post* in 1967, "Slouching" was one of Didion's first widely read stories. At a time in her life when nothing seemed to make sense—and when her marriage was in trouble—the writer immersed herself in the countercultural ground zero of San Francisco's Haight-Ashbury. What she discovered there was not a hopeful revolt against the establishment, but people lost and adrift. This is the piece in which she struck "gold": the toddler on acid.

I take note of the irony that Didion wrote a piece that exposed the drug culture of hippies while she was out of her head on gin and speed.

It should also be noted that Didion's worst fears came true two years later, when lost children of the 1960s fell under the spell of a charismatic wannabe rock star, Charles Manson; in the summer of 1969 he and the lost children killed seven people, including the actor Sharon Tate—a member of Didion's social circle. During the trials for these murders, Joan was working on a book about Manson associate Linda Kasabian and famously bought the jailed woman a dress to wear to trial. Ultimately, Didion dropped the project over disagreements about authorial control.

I am sure there are those who thought Didion neurotic. She probably was not easy to live with. The "hospitalized psychotics" and "chronic anxieties" that she and John "refrain from mentioning" in that Royal Hawaiian hotel room where they sheltered in lieu of a divorce in *The White Album* are probably not references to Dunne's condition. In the documentary *The Center Will Not Hold*, the writer Susanna Moore recalls living with the Didion-Dunnes on Franklin. Joan would come down late in the morning, wearing her shades, and have a cold bottle of Coke and salted almonds for breakfast. Neither woman would speak, unless there were no Cokes in the fridge. "If anyone took my last Coca-Cola, we would have a scene," Didion says.

But to say that Didion's sickness was in her head is not to dismiss it. Didion demonstrated that the Cartesian philosophical split between mind and body is bunk. What was mental was physical, and vice versa, for Joan. Didion had "bad nerves," as she wrote in *The White Album*. At around the same time her ego was failing to mediate the world of reality, at age thirty-three, she was diagnosed with multiple sclerosis. "The startling fact was this: my body was offering a precise physiological equivalent to what had been going on in my mind," she wrote, in reference to her neuro-logical symptoms. Yet the ailment never manifested, and decades later, an MRI determined she did not have MS. What she had in the 1960s is a mystery; what she had in the 2000s is also vague: "Neuritis, a neuropathy, a neurological inflammation," she wrote in *Blue Nights*. In August 2007, she was diagnosed with shingles, another ailment of the nerve system, caused by the virus that also causes chicken pox. She suffered immensely for years, losing her balance, her ability to tie her shoes. *Blue Nights*, her 2011 book about Quintana Roo, is, in part, a lamentation of growing old, without a child to take care of you.

Migraine sufferers experience different stages of the attack differ-ently. One common phase is the aura. The aura can bring tingling and difficulty speaking. It can also create light flashes, spots, and blurred outlines.

Interestingly, Didion described what sounds like auras in "Why I Write." She had "pictures in my mind . . . images that shimmer around the edges." This shimmer, she noted, was the same as has been described by patients experiencing schizophrenia and people on psychedelic drugs. "I'm not a schizophrenic, nor do I take hal-lucinogens, but certain images do shimmer for me," she said. Her goal as a writer was to decipher and articulate those images in words. She described the process: "You don't talk to many people and you keep your nervous system from shorting out and you try to locate the cat in the shimmer, the grammar in the picture."

Words were this quiet woman's weapon, which she wielded against politicians and pundits, from Sacramento to El Salvador to Central Park. Writing, she said in "Why I Write," is "the tactic of a secret bully, an invasion, an imposition of the writer's sensibility on the reader's most private space."

Didion turned shimmers into grammar, weakness into strength. She used her physical difference not to play the victim but as a kind of power. Her quietness led interviewees to confess their sins, to speak of the child on acid. Because she faded into the wallpaper, like a hidden camera, subjects would forget she was there, drop their act, reveal their secrets. And Joan would write it all down.

9
Hotel

I'm staying in a high-ceilinged room at the Royal Hawaiian Hotel in Honolulu listening to an annoying man on a microphone hustling tourists in lieu of filing the book I am writing about Joan Didion. I came here because Joan came here, in fact, famously came to this hotel. I'm stalking the memory of her—and draining my bank account.

Starting at eight in the morning, the man at the Royal Hawaiian shopping center says loudly, more than once, "It's a glorious aloha Saturday morning!" I want to shout out the window: "Well, it *was* a glorious aloha Saturday morning . . ."

It was! I woke up at seven and looked out of one of the windows in my corner room to see two striking birds, all porcelain-white

except for pitch-black beaks and eyes, nestling in the tree below. I've never seen their avian kind before. Out of that window I
can also view one of the Royal's mother trees, a giant acacia, her
branches festooned with lanterns. Out the other window lies the
Royal Center, a.k.a. the mall; that's where the huckster is.

Downstairs, I am handed three complimentary banana nut
muffins and purchase the Royal Hawaiian latte: a frothy confec-
tion made with coconut and macadamia nut syrups. I promptly
become addicted. I stroll down the open-air hallway, across the
gleaming tile floors, past the lanai that has been mostly converted
into high-end boutiques, and there she is: Moananuiākea, the
Pacific Ocean. The aquamarine water and azure sky are framed
by oval arches and dotted with pink and white umbrellas. Already,
surfers are stacked at the breaks and tourists line up to get their
beachside chaise lounge for the day. Me, I grab a pink and white
striped towel off a pool chair, plunk myself and my first Waikiki
breakfast on the sand, watch the waves, then join the waves. This
is the same body of water I swim in every day in San Pedro, but
aloha, it is a lot warmer here. Overhead, more pairs of white birds
chase each other across the blue sky, darting to and fro in perfect
synchronicity. Did I wake up in paradise?

Didion spent "what seemed to many people I knew an eccentric
amount of time in Honolulu," as she wrote in *The White Album*.
She watched Robert F. Kennedy's funeral and news reports from
Vietnam from a Royal verandah. She read George Orwell. And
she wrote: about being in a room at the Royal with her husband
and daughter in lieu of filing for a divorce, about sequestering in
the room because of a tsunami warning, about the families lined
up on the sand with their lounges and umbrellas and social status

secured as guests of the Royal Hawaiian, the famous Pink Palace, one of the most beautiful hotels in the world. So named because it was built on land leased to the colonizers by the last Hawaiian queen, Princess Bernice Pauahi Bishop. Didion spent so much time at the Royal Hawaiian that it "lent me the illusion that I could any minute order from room service a revisionist theory of my own history, garnished with a vanda orchid." Joan Didion was adept at aiming her lacerating wit at herself.

The place is rather spectacular. I am a water baby. Everywhere I travel, I swim. I know beaches in New Zealand, Tahiti, Puerto Rico, Brazil, Spain, France, the Bahamas, Montauk, Newport, Michigan, Miami, and of course, California. The beach at Waikiki is a wafer-thin ribbon compared to Santa Monica or Miami Beach. But the half-moon bay creates a warm pool with a soft sand bottom dappled by sunlight. The waves break with rhythmic regularity out at the barrier reef, and then again at the mouth to the bay, and then again as they hit one reef or sand bar after another. If you are a surfer, you can choose your break, close to shore for beginners or out to the big waves for the experts.

On a Saturday in August, the water and the land are packed with people. I prefer my beaches less crowded, to not have to navigate my laps between women in inner tubes who don't understand that you have to paddle with both hands or you will go in a circle. But the festiveness of the end-of-summer frolickers is infectious. Giant catamarans plow through the crowds, surfers thread their way through the bridal party that doesn't want to get their hair wet, and in the water, the middle-class tourists staying at the Sheraton splash the Royalty next door, and for a moment you can forget the class system ensured by the roped-off rows of lounge chairs.

Inside the hotel, the women—native Hawaiians, mixed-race hapa, foreign and domestic tourists—in their long colorful dresses and flowing, flowered hair, give New Yorkers a run for their money. The men too. The patriarch of one family of three is wandering around wearing nothing but his pink and white Royal Hawaiian robe, a jet-black toupee, black rubber loafers that have big spongy thorns all over them and are undoubtedly designer shoes that cost as much as a used car, and presumably, something underneath the robe.

It is so much easier to be happy when you are in a beautiful place. It would be even easier if I were wealthy enough not to worry about sticker shock.

The birds, the white birds: I looked them up. They are manu-o-Kū, a.k.a. white terns, also known by some as fairy terns (though officially that is the designation of a different species). So named because of their deft aerial skills, that acrobatic banking alternating with sudden hovers, that tandem tango in the sky. Strikingly beautiful in their two-tone coloring, they can often be seen coupled up, canoodling in a tree or in sync in the air. Monogamous and also probably mates for life, their other nickname is love terns. They are small and bright in plumage like a parrot but agile and fierce like a seabird. On the main Hawaiian islands, manu-o-Kū can only be found in Honolulu. They began coming here in the 1960s, like the hippies, like Joan Didion, and they have increasingly flourished in the city, perhaps because they have few predators here, or because there are so many big trees and buildings in which to nest. In 2007, they were declared the city's official bird, a protected species. The pair sit below my window every day, quiet, gently grooming.

Didion spent a lot of time in hotels and motels, big and small. In addition to being a nature writer, she was a travel writer. Hence, that packing list in *The White Album*. She voyaged often for stories and books: Miami, El Salvador, Colombia, Hawai'i. In 1970 Joan and John drove around the American South. Her notes, published years later in *South and West*, include a survey of roadside motel pools. She went on promotional tours as well, signing books at stores, doing local media interviews. While living in LA, she spent a great deal of time in New York, working on *Panic in Needle Park*, her first screenplay with Dunne, among other things. When they lived in Malibu, and then later New York, they stayed at the Beverly Wilshire whenever they came to LA. She and John also loved Paris, though she never wrote about Europe; her interests were in the American hemisphere, or Pacific adjacent.

It occurs to me that as much as Didion loved to write about place, it was more often a setting, or a character, than a subject. A means to an end. In her 1984 novel *Democracy*, which is primarily set in Hawai'i, the narrator, a journalist named Joan Didion, writes, "Still: there is a certain hour between afternoon and evening when the sun strikes horizontally between the trees and that island. . . ." "That island" is an atoll where nuclear tests were conducted in the 1950s and that serves as the framing device for the tragic romance at the center of this absurdist roman à clef.

I also think Didion spent time in hotels out of choice, because she enjoyed them. They were the peripatetic writer's refuge—a place to be free of responsibilities, identities, chores, things that tie one down. Wanderlust is a tool for reinvention, a way to re-imagine yourself and your relationship to the world. In 2014 Andrew O'Hagan called Didion "the genius of what the critic Wayne Koestenbaum once called 'hotel prose.' She knows precisely how to be in an anonymous, air-conditioned space; indeed, you might say she craves them." With their daily routines—the afternoon check-in, the evening turndown service, the Do Not Disturb sign, the continental breakfast with newspaper, the morning checkout—hotels also provide a site for ritual and order. And order was something Didion desired almost as much as she feared snakes. During Q's five-week hospitalization in Los Angeles in 2004, her mother ordered the same breakfast every morning at the Beverly Wilshire: huevos rancheros with one scrambled egg.

Speaking of Beverly Hills, hotel living also appealed to the writer's expensive taste, her predilection for posh. She may have appreciated the southern motels, but when she had an option, she stayed in fancier digs: "The Lancaster and the Ritz and the Plaza Athénée in Paris. The Dorchester in London. The St. Regis and the Regency in New York." These are some of the places she lists in *Blue Nights*, hotels in which Q stayed with her, learning to order triple lamb chops from room service at a young age and to eat caviar. Didion's daughter spent so much time in hotels as a child that she called items "sundries" after "sundries" shops in resort lobbies. In later years, the Didion-Dunnes preferred the newer, chicer, more isolated Kahala Hotel over the Royal. They spent Christmas there in 1990, working on a screenplay that was never produced, their resort room with its view of the country club turned into a temporary office complete with computers and printers. Q, meanwhile, now twenty-four, was downstairs exploring; by this age, she knew the hotel—and the routine—well. "On the face of it she had no business in these hotels," Didion admitted, "she was inseparable from our working life."

Didion engaged in not just the escapism that my husband calls Greyhound therapy, but what I like to call hotel therapy: dropping yourself into the lap of luxury, with no dishes to wash or clothes to fold, even if just for one night. Long before staycations were a thing, I was known to check myself into a resort for a night or two, just to get away from my Lower East Side tenement. I even wrote an article about hotel therapy for *Travel and Leisure*, but to be honest the magazine never published it. Maybe it was *too* on the nose; I basically summed up the entire marketing principle of the luxury publication for them: spend, spend, spend. Another thing Q eventually learned was the difference between traveling "on expenses" (caviar at the Regency) and "not on expenses" (breakfast from the White Tower fast-food franchise at the Chelsea).

As always, Didion acknowledged her own neurosis while traveling. For instance, for some reason, she didn't own a watch. Apparently hotel rooms did not have clocks in the 1960s, so Joan used to call the front desk or her husband every thirty minutes to check the time. The woman "who prized control" didn't know what time it was. "This may be a parable, either of my life as a reporter during this period or of the period itself," she wrote. I'm guessing that for the clerk working the desk, or even John, it was less a parable than a pain.

She came to Hawai'i for family therapy via hotel therapy. But perhaps only Joan Didion could continue to have "bad nerves" at the Royal, to hide in her room, waiting for a tsunami.

Didion wrote that she first heard of Hawai'i on Pearl Harbor Day, when she was seven years old. Subsequently, as a child of California, staring across the Pacific, she felt the islands' pull, imagining she saw them on the horizon, "a certain shimmer in the sunset." (That shimmer again.) Americans on the West Coast vacation in Hawai'i like those on the East Coast vacation in the Caribbean: as often as they can. But after World War II, the Didions rarely left California. Joan visited Hawai'i for the first time in 1966, at age thirty-one, on assignment for the *Saturday Evening Post*. One visit and she was hooked, returning often to write and relax. She wanted to buy a place there, to retire there, but John wanted them to be in New York by then, and she gave in.

As much as she applied the balm of the islands' natural beauty to her bad nerves, she was also acutely aware of the region's fraught history. She may have stayed at the Royal, or the Kahala Hotel, or in a rented house on Kahala Avenue, a street that my friend Cathay—who grew up partly in Hawai'i—says is "like Beverly Hills and Brentwood, definitely where wealthy folks live in amazing houses with pools that open out to lawns that end in the ocean." But Didion was no conventional traveler, and she didn't write about luaus or hula dances or leis, except in disparaging comments about such phrases as "our wonderful aloha spirit." Her writing on the Royal is laced with sociological critique, much of it aimed at herself. When she deconstructs the hierarchy ensured by the even rows of lounge chairs behind the rope on the Royal beach, she implicates her own collusion by shifting into, well, the royal "we": "Anyone behind the rope will watch over our children as we will watch over theirs, will not palm room keys or smoke dope or

listen to Creedence Clearwater on a transistor when we are awaiting word from the Mainland on the prime rate." The Royal, she
wrote, "is not merely a hotel but a social idea, one of the few extant
clues to a certain kind of American life."

Didion extended this analysis to all "great hotels"; they are
"flawless mirrors to the particular societies they service. Had
there never been an Empire there would not have been a Raffles."
The Empire she refers to is the British; Raffles is the name of the
colonizer who established modern Singapore and for whom that
country's most famous hotel is named.

And yet, she fell for it. As she wrote in "Letter from Paradise,
21° 19′ N., 157° 52′ W.," "And so, now that it is on the line between
us that I lack all temperament for paradise, real or facsimile, I am
going to find it difficult to tell you precisely how and why Hawai'i moves me, touches me, saddens and troubles and engages my
imagination, what it is in the air that will linger long after I have
forgotten the smell of pikake and pineapple and the way the palms
sound in the trade winds." The urbanist had a nature-loving heart.

From the top of the extinct Pūowaina volcano you can see all of
Honolulu, from the dark rock cliffs of Diamondhead to the curve
of Waikiki to downtown's skyscrapers to the waterfront airport to
the haunted, crowded national park at Pearl Harbor to the jungly
hills with their crown of clouds—all with the ocean as backdrop.
The crater below is carpeted with green grass speckled with small
granite markers that lie flat with the land: gravestones. More than
fifty thousand soldiers, veterans, and family members are buried
here at the National Memorial Cemetery of the Pacific, including

the war correspondent Ernie Pyle, one of the first five people interred here in 1949. Another 28,788 are honored by name in the marble walls of the Honolulu Memorial: These are the people who went missing in action in World War II, the Korean War, and the Vietnam War, their remains still unrecovered at the time the memorial was erected in 1964. There are soldiers from every state and territory commemorated here. The memorial rises in five parallel rows of memorial courts to its top, where a statue of Lady Justice stands vigil. On the walls behind her are colorful tile mosaics that feature maps and descriptions of all of the Pacific battle zones of World War II.

The cemetery is rather ironically known as the Punchbowl, so named because of the shape of the crater. In 1970, Didion watched a family bury their son here, "one of 101 Americans killed that week in Vietnam." She had badly wanted to go to Vietnam in 1966 and be one of the few women to report on the war, but she didn't; she says in *Blue Nights* that it was because John was working on a book but admits that having just adopted a baby was an impediment as well. In 1969, she was in Hawai'i when news of the My Lai massacre of unarmed civilians by American soldiers in Vietnam broke. *Life* magazine had just contracted her to write a column, and this seemed to her the topic that needed to be written about. When she was able to reach her editor at home, he told her that "some of the guys are going out," and she should instead write a column introducing herself. Stewing, she typed: "I had better tell you where I am, and why. I am sitting in a high-ceilinged room in the Royal Hawaiian Hotel in Honolulu watching the long translucent curtains billow in the trade wind and trying to put my life back together."

In a crater in Hawai'i one year later, watching parents grieve,

Didion finally said what she needed to say about the Vietnam War. She describes the ten minutes it took to inter the body in plain, blunt sentences. The Punchbowl is "a place so still and private that once seen it is forever in the mind." At the end of the burial the father "stood facing Mr. Corley and me, and for a moment we looked directly at each other, but he was seeing not me, not Mr. Corley, not anyone."

Didion may have initially come to Hawai'i as a magazine writer on assignment to write a sort of thinking-woman's travel piece for the *Post*, "to play at sipping frozen daiquiris and wear flowers in my hair." Instead she saw the snakes of empire slithering beneath the umbrellas at the Pink Palace. The islands inspired some of her greatest writing, from *Slouching Towards Bethlehem* to *Democracy* to *The Year of Magical Thinking*. Hawai'i is right behind California and New York in the ranking of landscapes that shaped who she was and what she wrote. But she penned no rum-laced romance. From the beginning her subjects were the Punchbowl, the sunken ships at Pearl Harbor, the gravesites of disgraced soldiers at Schofield Barracks, the drunken sailors cruising Hotel Street looking for pleasure, and the heritage of the big families who divided up the islands like so many poker chips, just like they had in California. She perceived that beyond the chaise lounges and luaus and tiki bars, one aura "pervades Honolulu": "war."

My friend Cathay's aunt is buried in a columbarium in the Punchbowl with her soldier husband. While I wander the memorial, Cathay has a chat with the woman whose former condo we are now camped out in, my fiscal capacity for life at the Royal having been quickly tapped out. I look for family names on the walls of the Honolulu Memorial, wondering if any are distant relatives.

My uncle fought in World War II. I know he was injured when a coffee pot exploded and fragged him at Iwo Jima. But reading the mosaic description of that horrific battle, the Hamburger Hill of its day, I wonder why I never talked with Uncle Leon about what it was like to be at that battlefield.

There are birds—doves, plovers, egrets—and flowers—monkeypods, hibiscus, plumeria—everywhere. A fairy tern swoops by and then I kid you not—Cathay and her friend Lesa are my witnesses: It stops a few feet above my head and hovers, staring intensely into my face as it beats its wings. Lesa, who lives in Honolulu, says the manu-o-Kūs make her anxious because they don't build nests, they just place their eggs on branches or ledges and hope the trade winds don't knock them off. That said, if the birds lose a child, they have been known to adopt the abandoned chicks of other terns. Parents can disappear for hours at a time, flying as far as 120 miles out to sea to snatch small fish off the top of waves and then return to feed them whole—not chewed, softened, and regurgitated, like most birds—to their offspring. Because they can be found so far out to sea but reliably return home every evening, sailors use manu-o-Kū to find their way back to land.

I wonder if Joan watched the love terns. Did she see herself and John in their paired flights, Quintana in their precarious offspring? I know I am milking the metaphor of the manu-o-Kū as the Didion-Dunnes, but if Joan can have her snakes, I can have my terns.

I'm eating lunch at the Royal Hawaiian's Mai Tai Bar, reading the *New Yorker*. Then I think: What am I doing? I have a front-row seat at one of the most famous surf breaks in the world, and I'm staring at a piece of paper. I drop the magazine and watch the surfers glide up and down beneath the white foam. The manu-o-Kūs mirror their movements below the clouds.

"To sit by the Royal pool and read *The New York Review of Books* is to feel oneself an asp, disguised in a voile beach robe," Didion wrote in "In the Islands." She put the paper down, began talking to a woman next to her who was on her honeymoon, "because honeymoons at the Royal are a custom in her family, with each of her three husbands." Have I mentioned Joan's sense of humor?

This passage offers a peek into Didion's personality and methods. She has the introverted infoholic's instinct: retreat behind a screen of pages (or, in modern parlance, behind pages on a screen). But then the reporter in her surfaces: Look around, ask questions. When she writes it all down, she begins with a prepositional phrase that locates the reader in the setting ("by the Royal pool") and the action (reading). For the predicate, she chooses vivid metaphor and detail. Me, I might have written "is to feel churlish." *Churlish* is a good word, but not as good as *asp. Asp* is a great word: three letters that stretch their allotted pronunciation time. There are really two syllables in asp: "as-puh." Asp is onomatopoetic, mimicking the hissing sibilants of the signified: "asssssssssssspuh." And bonus points for Didion: snake! She finishes with another preposition, landing with a classic example of Didionesque status detail: the voile (look it up; I did) beach robe. The passage typifies the classic writer mantra that we are taught as children: Show, don't tell. Joan was the queen of show.

As I'm trying to put this chapter together, I think of another trick I have learned from Didion, a tip that she gave to Sara

Davidson, that Davidson passed on to her audience: Write down all your scenes, quotes, events, etc., on index cards, then spread them on the floor, moving cards that have connections next to each other, "like a patchwork quilt." Sadly, I didn't bring index cards to the Royal Hawaiian. Did Joan? I grab the small pad of paper for taking notes by the phone instead.

There was an incident this morning at the Surf Lanai restaurant at the Royal. I had just ordered breakfast when a man sat down at the table next to me, by the beach. Muttering to himself, he began moving all the items on the table around, taking the sweetener packets out of their container and lining them up on the table, rather like a patchwork quilt. He had an elastic bandage wrapped around one arm and his skin was damaged by the sun.

Women are taught at a young age to fear damaged men. As a small child, Quintana had nightmares about a person she called the Broken Man. The Broken Man was coming to get her, she told her mother. He said in a deep voice he would lock her in a garage. But she was going to hang on to a fence so he couldn't get her. Her daughter's nightmares traumatized Didion enough that she returns to the topic multiple times in *Blue Nights*.

At first the Royal staff treated the damaged man as a regular customer, but when he ordered two servings of pancakes and French toast, I could see the waiter and bus person look at each other. I was worried it would get ugly if he stayed; he was getting louder, more agitated, cursing. I was worried it would get ugly if the hotel tried to make him leave. The shouting would be worse, I would feel sorry for the man who clearly was not well, the police might come. That rarely ends well, as most of us know today—as Joan knew by the 1960s.

One evening on Kalakaua Avenue in Honolulu, Didion watched a car almost hit two young men in a crosswalk. During the altercation that followed, two policemen arrested one of the men, who had done nothing wrong except have hair "about as long as the average college freshman." When the small, quiet writer protested, the cops turned on her. "Both of them fixed their eyes just over my head in that gaze peculiar to police officers and troops on review. 'Move on, sister,' one of them ordered. 'I said move on.'"

In the 1968 *Points West* column in which she recounts this and other incidents, Didion writes that as a privileged white woman, she grew up believing what she had been told: The police were there to protect and serve. But then came Kalakaua. Joan realized what many people in minority and poor communities have always known: "There was the point at which 1 began to notice that every time I saw a cop stop a car on the Sunset Strip, he was stopping either a juvenile or a Mexican." She focuses her withering analysis, as usual, on rhetoric, on the way the police spoke. "It was a tone calculated—whether by deliberation or reflex—to threaten, to harass, to humiliate, to bully. I read not long ago that the police call this tone, this stance, 'aggressive prevention.' Perhaps all they are preventing is the possibility of their own credibility."

Few people know that Didion wrote an article called "On Becoming a Cop Hater" for a major American magazine as, unlike her essays on mansions and villas, it has never been anthologized. There's a direct line from this story's conclusion—"I do not go around using words like 'blue Fascism,' but it has been a very long time since I thought of a cop as a friend in blue"—to her 1991 article on the Central Park jogger attack.

I didn't want the Royal to call the police. I didn't even want them to call security. But I did have a little of that fear you learn as a small female traveling alone: that you are perceived as an easy target, that maybe you are an easy target. I was the nearest diner, and the damaged man was looking for someone to engage with. I was simultaneously thinking of a dear family member who struggles with their mental health. Anxiety and empathy sparred in my head. This was not what I was seeking this Sunday morning in paradise. I hadn't even had my latte with coconut and macadamia yet. But maybe what I needed more than my morning fix was this lesson in perspective.

Then a young man in the pressed pink shirt of the Surf Lanai walked over to the man's table and quietly started talking to him. Keenan spent at least ten minutes asking gentle questions, laughing at the man's jokes, mostly just listening. At the end, the damaged gentleman got up, shook Keenan's hand, and quietly left.

I thanked Keenan for the kindness of his approach. "I could see he was getting upset," he said. "Sometimes a person just needs to be heard for a bit. When he had calmed down, I told him it was time to move on, and he said no problem. You have to have aloha in your heart."

Aloha, Cathay explains to me, means the breath of life. To say aloha is to share the air we breathe—a particularly tricky concept in a pandemic period. Sure, it is an overused word, one that has been co-opted by tourism, by the transformation of a way of life into a commodity. But Didion was wrong to dismiss it entirely; aloha has meaning.

After breakfast I went for my morning swim. I was floating on my back when a pair of manu-o-Kūs flew low right over me. "Aloha," I called.

The Royal has changed greatly since Joan first stayed here. They built a giant Sheraton Hotel on one side, and the Royal Center on another, so the former resting place of the last king of Hawai'i is hemmed in by concrete. The Marriott company is getting all the money they can out of the acreage they lease from the native Hawaiians who still own it. The mantra now is quantity of rooms, not quality.

In the morning, before the heat and the crowds come out, the bay still charms. By afternoon the ocean is thick with frolickers floating and bobbing amid the flotsam and jetsam of old Band-Aids, straw wrappers, bits of seaweed, and stuff that I prefer not to know what it is. The descendants of the royals have asserted their authority over the property, so it is now the strangest of anomalies: a Luxury Collection Hotel that proclaims its indigenous spirit.

The island reclaims the beach in the evening. I go for a sunset swim and all the amateurs have returned to shore. Well, most of the amateurs: There's a couple clutching their fruity drinks like lifelines, but they're clearly in love with each other and the world, so I forgive them. Otherwise it's just serious swimmers and surfers now, bobbing up and down with the waves. Giving in to the flow. There are not a lot of other women out here. One decades younger than me paddles a surfboard in her bikini. She's uncertain, sticking close to shore compared to the old hands out there—though we are farther out than I have been in two days. I watch her steadfastly trying to catch a wave, not confident enough, but not giving up either. I am strictly a voyeur here, have no right to judge: I have never once tried to get up on a surfboard, though I have spent decades riding the waves with my body.

The sun has sizzled into the sea. I love watching a sunset from the water. I look up in the sky and the fairy terns are back. They weren't here in the afternoon. Either they were taking a siesta or they were far out over the Pacific, foraging.

It occurs to me that Didion was spending her "excessive amount of time" in Hawai'i when she was writing *Play It As It Lays*, when she made the protagonist of a fictional movie a former surfer. She too was a bit of a water baby: the thwarted marine scientist who thought about the sea when she felt troubled. Decades after she moved from home, it was the rivers of Sacramento she most missed—the rivers where she learned to swim, where she once, probably with Bob, got caught in a current when rafting. She explored the sea cave of Portuguese Bend with John, interviewed the lifeguards of Zuma Beach. When she journeyed in the South, she swam in motel pools. I don't know if she would have been out there with me and the surfer. There is a difference between pools and open-ocean swimming. But she must have watched the surfers. You could not not watch the surfers, especially in that pre–cell phone age; their dance with the pull of the ocean is riveting. Maybe, like me, she saw young women hanging ten and envied their communion with their bodies, and with the waves, and with the world. Their mastery of machine, the board. A couple years later, in Malibu, Quintana would spend her days at Zuma with its world-famous waves, training with the junior lifeguards, which "entailed being repeatedly taken out beyond the Zuma Beach breakers on a lifeguard boat and swimming back in." Even when the waters were so full of sharks that the lifeguards sent everyone home, Q refused to leave. When her parents decided the remote life of Malibu was not the right place for a teenage girl and moved to posh Brentwood Park, with its manicured lawns, Q was furious. The beach was her home.

I side with the willful daughter on this: I think the Didion-Dunnes should have stayed in Trancas, watching the waves.

I retract my previous suggestion: Didion didn't want to punish the film character in *Play It As It Lays* for being a surfer. She wanted to be a surfer. She wanted Q to be a surfer. In 1964—the year she moved to the Portuguese Bend house with the view of the ocean—she reviewed the movie *Ride the Wild Surf*, starring Fabian and set in Hawai'i, for *Vogue*. "I have recently fallen under the spell of teen surfing movies," she confessed. Fascinatingly, she offered a feminist critique of the "not very happy" starlets in surf movies—Maria was already taking shape in her mind. She noted "in passing the real sexlessness and extreme passivity of these girls. . . . Things would not look good for Young America from, say, Betty Friedan's point of view." Didion wanted more for the starlets, more for the surfer-girl characters, more for her daughter, more for herself. All her life she took chances, sought adventure, wanted to see where the next wave would take her. She may not have owned a watch but she could count the time between sets, she could see the crest coming, she could watch the blue wave tumble into white.

10

Girl

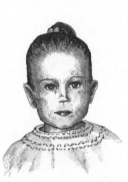

When I was seventeen and heading off to college, my grand-mother and I shared one of our last weekly meals of Kentucky Fried Chicken (Mama was born and raised in Louisville) at her apartment in a senior living facility. It was the most serious con-versation I recall ever having with this onetime seamstress who raised six children in various towns in the southern half of the country, and then Los Angeles, with her builder, World War I–veteran husband. She was an elder passing her wisdom to one of her dozens of grandchildren, at the moment of my rite of passage.

Looking back on her own life, Mama said, the worst thing that ever happened to her was not the loss of her husband, but the death via cancer of her adult daughter Louise, from whom I get my middle name. I am not sure if she was advising me to hold my own future children close or warning me not to put her only surviving daughter, my mother, through the agony she experienced. "Losing a child causes the greatest suffering of all," she told me.

As a parent myself now, I understand what Mama meant.

This is the hardest chapter to write.

Quintana Roo Dunne was born March 3, 1966, in Santa Monica. Joan Didion and John Gregory Dunne received the call from Dr. Blake Watson: "I have a beautiful baby girl at St. John's." The beautiful girl's eighteen-year-old birth mother had surrendered her. A few months earlier, after years of failed attempts to get pregnant, Joan and John had contacted the doctor about adopting. The Didion-Dunnes took the infant home to Portuguese Bend on March 6. "Once she was born I was never not afraid," Didion said in *Blue Nights*, her 2011 book about Q.

Joan had wanted a child since her *Vogue* years. In 1958, when she was twenty-three years old, she thought she was pregnant. It turned out to be a false alarm, but she became baby crazy, she wrote decades later. She dreamed about infants, pinned pictures of children clipped from magazines to the wall of her Manhattan apartment. This passion for parenting may seem strange now, in the wake of decades of feminism and given Didion's iconicity as a self-made career woman, but this was the era of what writer Betty Friedan called "the feminine mystique." Rosie the Riveter, the working woman of the 1940s, had been pushed back into the kitchen and the bedroom, to her traditional roles as wife, homemaker, mom.

I'm sure the desire to have a family was the ultimate cause of the break with Noel Parmentel, who was clearly—and by his own admission—not good father material. In John Gregory Dunne, Didion found a partner in not just writing but parenting. The father praised the daughter's championship of life in a 1977 article: "Watching her journey from infancy has always been like watching Sandy Koufax pitch or Bill Russell play basketball."

Neither Didion nor Dunne ever explained publicly why they couldn't have a biological child. The friends and family I interviewed mostly say they were never told either; I could find only one person who said Joan had explained to him the reason, and he would not go on the record. The difficulty is likely to have been on Joan's side. In *Vegas*, Dunne's 1974 memoir disguised as a novel—which is, rather alarmingly, dedicated to Parmentel (Joan may have gotten over her obsession but John was still under his charismatic spell)—he describes a doctor telling him that his sperm "won't win any races . . . but they get there." Many people who knew Didion think she was too frail to give birth. I believe that she had a health issue dating back to her early sexually active life that prevented her from getting pregnant. According to *The Last Love Song*, Dunne wrote in a 1984 letter that his wife had not worn underwear since college for "gynecological reasons" and had recently had a hysterectomy. Perhaps, it was fear or depression that she could not have a baby that made Didion want one all the more. When she thought she was pregnant in 1958, she went to the doctor who treated all *Vogue*'s young women. He warned her she might need to go to Cuba to end her pregnancy. Instead, Didion wrote, she started menstruating a few days later. She wept.

Whatever the reason, by early 1966, the Didion-Dunnes were exploring adoption, which led them to an obstetrician named

Blake Watson. At that time, abortion was illegal and private adoptions facilitated by doctors were common. Women's roles as child bearers and caregivers were a frequent subject of Didion's writing, especially in her fiction. Interestingly, Joan was one of the few of her peers to write openly about abortion. In *Play It As It Lays*, Maria has her pregnancy terminated in the bedroom of a tract house in Encino. The illicit procedure leaves the actor with disturbing memories and physical complications that temporarily impede her ability to work. These were real situations women dealt with in the 1950s and '60s, stories that needed to be told. Didion knew coworkers at *Vogue* who had abortions.

Wanting, and failing, to have a child for years, Joan and John must have been ecstatic to suddenly have this "perfect child," as Didion called Q. "She could not have been more exactly the baby I wanted," Joan wrote of the chubby-cheeked girl in *Blue Nights*.

The Didion-Dunnes doted on what would be their only child. Every year they sent out Christmas postcards with pictures of Quintana on the front, presumably because she was the greatest gift they had received. You can see the evolution of the dark-eyed towhead in these black-and-white images: the toddler with the delicate orchid over her shoulder; the five-year-old seated cross-legged wearing a polka-dotted hat; the beautiful girl in black leotards in front of a fountain. She was front and center in their personal lives and in their professional lives.

Quintana Roo Dunne grew up being photographed alone and with her famous parents. There she is, in a 1976 image by John Bryson, on the deck of the Trancas house in a polka-dot dress this time, standing next to her father, while her mother looks sideways at them, her trademark cigarette in hand. Or she is sitting

Quintana, John, and Joan in Malibu in 1976.

in Didion's lap, while Joan reads to her. Or, in a breathtakingly intimate moment of domesticity, Joan and Q are nose to nose on a couch. These are not mere poses; these are snapshots of an unusually close family, living—or so it seemed—a storybook life.

Interestingly, a Google search for images of just father and daughter yields zero results. I don't think this is because John and Q were not close; it was he who drove her to school in the mornings in Malibu. "John just worshipped Quintana," Julia Armstrong-Totten says. Rather, I think that when a woman author is photographed, she is more likely to include her child in the image, whether at her initiative or that of the photographer, because working mothers must always prove their concomitant commitment to their parenting duties. The public does not hold fathers to the same standards.

Despite the evident devotion, there is something off about these photos, about the whole picture. It begins with the name, chosen from a map. Quintana Roo is a Mexican state in the Yucatán peninsula, now popular among tourists for the Mayan ruins of Tulum and the beaches of Cancun. In 1966, "The place on the map called Quintana Roo was still terra incognita," Didion wrote. Terra incognita to white Americans, that is; well known by Mexicans, of course, and their many relatives in the United States. Quintana Roo is the kind of name that two creative people, young and in love and desirous of offspring, choose when they are traveling in Mexico in the 1960s, see the words on a map, and say to each other, "If we ever have a daughter, let's name her Quintana Roo." It's "a hippie name," in writer Richard Rodriguez's words. Joan and John didn't even pronounce it correctly: In Spanish, it is Kintana, but the Didion-Dunnes called their daughter Kwintana. Mostly, they called her Q.

Joan and John may have wanted a child, but they weren't prepared. Q entered their lives less than two months after they first met with Dr. Watson. The nine months of pregnancy that birth parents experience provides time not just to get the crib, stroller, and onesies, but to prepare mentally—and to clear schedules. The day Dr. Watson called, the Didion-Dunnes were weeks away from flying to Saigon to report on the war in Vietnam. The prospect of having a newborn did not change their plans. Instead, Joan bought a "flowered Porthault parasol to shade the baby," to match her own "Donald Brooks pastel linen dresses."

Let's just pause for a moment to consider the image of Didion in a linen dress holding a parasol over her newborn in the middle of a war zone. We appreciate her commitment to her journalistic mission above all else, but perhaps the years at *Vogue* had gone a bit to the writer's head.

Decades later, Didion made fun of her own naivete about the demands of having a child: 1966 "was not widely considered an ideal year to take an infant to Southeast Asia," she wrote with wry understatement in *Blue Nights*. And yet, she wrote, the new parents decided not to go to Hanoi not because of their infant, but because John had to finish his first book, *Delano*, about the grape-pickers' strike in California; publishing, not parenting, took precedent. "I mention Saigon at all only by way of suggesting the extent of my misconceptions about what having a child, let alone adopting one, might actually entail," Joan confessed.

Be careful what you wish for. Having a child is a seismic life change, even if you are very well prepared. The first thing the Didion-Dunnes had to do, after canceling Saigon that is, was leave the Pacific panorama and peacocks of their Portuguese Bend home, where the landlord could not, or would not, accommodate both an infant and the infant's live-in teenage babysitter. The family instead house-sat for six months for Sara Mankiewicz, widow of *Citizen Kane* screenwriter Herman, on Anita Drive in Brentwood, before renting the house on Hollywood's Franklin Avenue where they would live for four years. Q learned to walk and talk surrounded by rock stars, movie stars, writers, directors, drag queens, artists, etc.

Didion had bought a parasol, but she hadn't thought about all the things she would actually wind up needing. She must have a layette, her friend told her, so off to Saks they went. Friends and family sent clothes: sixty dresses hung in Q's closet on tiny wooden hangers, which were also a gift. In *Blue Nights*, the status details of the cashmere and silk blanket in which the baby was brought home, the layette, the dresses, the hangers, pile up like material bulwarks against charges of insufficient parenting skills, as if Didion had bought her way into Q's graces.

Didion confessed: "Only later did I see that I had been raising her as a doll."

Still, Didion's love for her daughter is palpable in her writing. After Q first's birthday party, at Didion's parents' house in Sacramento—the one that John did not attend—Joan escapes the suffocations of family to visit her sleeping child. "I kneel beside the crib and touch her face, where it is pressed against the slats, with mine," she wrote in "On Going Home."

The Didion-Dunnes included their daughter in most of their activities. They both worked at home, and Q understood, as John put it, that "our mindless staring at our respective typewriters means food on the table." They took her to meetings for books and scripts and articles; "I think she could pick an agent out of a police lineup," Dunne joked. She traveled with them, ordering kiddie cocktails from room service. It was a peripatetic lifestyle, one in which Q was often the only child in exotic and privileged circumstances.

Q was undoubtedly spoiled.

Pampered, often left to her own devices in new locations, Quintana had a strong sense of entitlement. Armstrong-Totten remembers babysitting the young girl at Didion's parents' house in Sacramento. There was a pond in the backyard, and Q insisted on going in. "She was willful," Joan's cousin says. "She wouldn't listen. I don't know if she was testing to see what she could get away with or if that's just how she was, but I kind of have a feeling that's just how she was. She was just itching to go in it. And I hated that pond, because one of my cousins had pushed me in it when I was younger, and it was dirty and swampy. But she did not want to listen to me. I can't remember how we finally got her to come back up to the house but oh, she was strong willed. She knew that her parents adored her and knew that she could push the envelope in many ways with them."

Willful, yes, but Q was also charming, engaging, creative, unusual. She had funny expressions, a unique sense of grammar for the offspring of two writers: "Where you was?" she would ask, and "Where did the morning went?"

"She was sweet," Calvin Trillin says. "She had a way of saying hello or hi when she saw you that somehow got over the idea that she hadn't seen you in too long and she just realized what a lovely person you were, and half a dozen other things. She just had a nice 'Hello.'"

"When she was five and six years old, she was just this beautiful, lovely, funny, wonderful kid," recalls her older cousin, Griffin Dunne. "Usually a teenager doesn't think hanging out with a little kid is so much fun. But she was an exception."

Even her globe-trotting journalist mother marveled at Q's bravery. "About certain threats I considered real she remained in fact fearless," Didion wrote. I don't know for sure how the daughter felt about snakes, but I suspect she did not share her parents' phobia.

It can't have been easy to be a child named Quintana Roo, the daughter of two famous parents, growing up with reporters and photographers and celebrities always around, living out of a suitcase, no siblings, often separated from anyone your age.

"Often they had their daughter with them at restaurants," Gay Talese says. "I knew the daughter to speak of, and she was a little daughter! I mean, can you imagine being the daughter of Joan and John? My own daughters have a little problem so I can identify with how she must have felt with those well-known people. People go vying for their attention all the time and you're the little daughter and you're getting no attention at all because your parents are spending their time talking to some Oscar-winning actor or some Nobel Prize–winning writer. I mean Jesus, it must be terrible."

"They adored her," Armstrong-Totten says. "They absolutely adored her, and she adored them. I don't think any of that is in question. But it must not have been easy, in certain ways, to be their child, because they were so intellectual."

Sure, Quintana's parents spent a lot of time with her, as both worked at home, or took her with them on assignments and tours. But they were *working*. There is nothing that irritates a writer more than not being able to concentrate. In Malibu a young Q made a list of her mother's favorite sayings: "Brush your teeth, brush your hair, shush I'm working."

Shush I'm working.

It's the mantra of the mother who works from home, of the writer trying to hold on to a thought. Once, Didion's mother had shushed her by giving her a notebook. Decades later, Q distracted her mother from writing.

At exactly the same time Joan Didion was starting to raise this beautiful girl she had been gifted with, her own star was rising. *Slouching Towards Bethlehem* had made her not just a journalist but "one of the least celebrated and most talented writers of my own generation," the *New York Times* raved. This was rare recognition for a female in the masculinist ranks of reporting. Joan may have canceled the trip to Saigon, but she wasn't going to take this train off the track.

It was also when Quintana was only two that Didion had the breakdown that sent her to the hospital of her daughter's birth. Perhaps not uncoincidentally, these were the years when the marriage was in trouble, when John's rage could rock the house. At fourteen Q wrote a novel about a girl named Quintana. "Her father had a bad temper, but it showed that they cared very much about their only child," the adolescent wrote.

Quintana's parents didn't always take them with her when they worked. Not even on Christmas. Not even when she was three.

"I had wanted to make this Christmas a 'nice' Christmas, for my husband and for our baby and for everyone who came to our house in Los Angeles," Didion wrote for *Life* magazine in 1969. Instead, she and Dunne were in a "bleak" hotel in New York, working on their first film together, *Panic in Needle Park.* Instead of making a creche and pomegranate jelly with the baby, as she had hoped, Joan was spending the holiday season interviewing junkies and meeting with lawyers. In "In Praise of Unhung Wreaths and Love," the mother's heartache is palpable. I don't know how Quintana Roo felt being 2,800 miles from her parents on her fourth Christmas but I'm guessing not great. I wonder what the picture on the Didion-Dunne holiday card was that year.

I think of the Didion-Dunnes' little daughter, alone with her parents in the house on the ocean cliff, trying to get their attention, having nightmares about the Broken Man. And probably, in the back of her mind or in the front of her mind, that fear of abandonment that is common to adopted children. The feeling of having lost something that you never truly had. That existential insecurity that something is wrong with you, that maybe, you could be left again.

I don't have Quintana's story from her own lips or pen. I only know what her parents said, what their friends and family say, what a couple of her old classmates recall. I look at the photos of her and the photos she took. What was going on in her head?

I was born less than two years before Quintana Roo Dunne. Didion is my inspiration but her daughter was my peer. We attended Ivy League schools at the same time, worked in New York publishing for overlapping years. We could easily have been at the same concerts, shows, openings, bars. My parents also liked to throw parties and drink. We both had working mothers of a similar age: strong, intelligent, kind, and beautiful women who sometimes seemed very far away from us, even if they were in the same room.

Had I heard her complain, as she did to her mother, on the day that her biological father sent her a letter, "On top of everything else, my father has to be a Deadhead!" I would have instantly wanted to be Quintana Roo's friend.

My sense is that Q thrived most in Trancas. She loved what she called "the seductive sea." She went to junior lifeguard camp at Zuma. She went to elementary school on a bluff by the ocean. John would drop her off and "watch her disappear down that hill, the Pacific a great big blue background, and I thought it was as beautiful as anything I've ever seen," he said in his toast at Q's wedding in 2003. He told Joan she had to see this. She watched her daughter go down the hill in her school uniform and wept.

Q met her best friend for life, Susan Traylor, now an actor and the wife of Bob Dylan's son Jesse, in kindergarten. The Didion-Dunnes had a small, close community in Malibu. It was like living in a small town.

And then they left.

In 1978 the Didion-Dunnes moved to their fifth (counting the Mankiewicz house) and final home in Los Angeles, in Brentwood Park, a posh neighborhood in Brentwood. There seem to have been multiple motivations for the move. "They were nervous that Quintana would never learn to cross the street," Katrina vanden Heuvel says, a reference to the peculiar lifestyle of Trancas, where the only road is the Pacific Coast Highway. Joan and John also felt isolated from the center of Los Angeles life, particularly the film industry, which was their bread and butter. Maybe they just wanted a house that had central heat and where snakes didn't sometimes fall from the roof of the carport. Seventeen years before the writer Mike Davis suggested that firefighters should just let Malibu burn, Joan and John acted on their own strong and not unreasonable fear of wildfires. In 2018 the house of their friend and former neighbor Jean Moore was destroyed in the Woolsey fire.

Brentwood is and was an affluent neighborhood west of UCLA and east of Santa Monica. Marilyn Monroe had lived here; OJ Simpson made Brentwood famous when he killed his ex-wife, Nicole Brown Simpson, here in 1994. The TV producer Norman Lear lived across the street from the traditional, symmetric house with the pool and gardens that Joan and John transformed into the "West Coast literary consulate," as Trillin called it.

"They had a beautiful house," says Armstrong-Totten, who dog-sat for the Didion-Dunnes. "It had a French country feel to it.

And they had a beautiful master bedroom, huge bathroom, huge wardrobe. And then there was also like a sitting room. John's office, I think of in browns, kind of masculine browns. It had tile on the floor and a ladder that you could ride around the room to get the books. There was also a TV and a couch and it was very homey. Her office was done in white, with maybe some greens and purples. Very serene, nothing on the desk."

Didion loved this house: its comfort, its geometry, its outdoor space, which she transformed into a garden. She and John entertained here often: Thursday dinners and Sunday brunches. Brentwood provided an easier existence than Malibu and was much closer to the center of cultural action. Neighborhoods like these are the secret ingredient in the LA sauce: suburban-style houses, complete with lawns, trees, and driveways, that are in the middle, not the outskirts, of the city. "Some said it was the closest facsimile of waspy Connecticut in Southern California," Stacie Stukin writes in "Brentwood Notebook" of the neighborhood where she too grew up. In that case, Dunne must have felt at home: again, the Irish Catholic surrounded by Protestants. Didion so thoroughly shed her Malibu skin that she traded in the Stingray—which always seemed to have something that needed to be fixed—for the dowdy stability of a Volvo station wagon. This, and the move in general, upset Quintana. She called Brentwood "their suburbia house."

A primary motivation for the move was the fact that Q's parents did not think she should go to high school in Malibu. "They left the Malibu house because of Quintana, because they wanted her in better schools," says Armstrong-Totten. Where they thought she should go, and where Q did go, was the Westlake School for Girls, arguably the most elite secular private school in Los Angeles, and an easy drive from Brentwood. (It has since merged with the Harvard boys school.) Classes were small, tuition high, and children of celebrities abounded: Tom Snyder, Carol Burnett, Peter Fonda. Stukin, who was two years ahead of Q, describes Westlake as "a single-sex education Shangri-La with rolling lawns, flowers, and a Maypole."

Westlake was elite but progressive. The girls-only environment made it a hotbed for feminism. Ninth graders were sent home with copies of *Our Bodies, Ourselves.* "We were marching for the ERA because we were having this phenomenal education, because we understood that women only earn seventy-nine cents to the dollar of every man," Stukin says.

But it wasn't all enlightenment at Westlake. Stukin remembers a teacher who accused Q of having her mother write one of her assignments. Parent-teacher conferences were held. Upset students stood by their classmate. Stukin, now a widely published journalist, remembers the same teacher repeatedly failing her. "It was symbolic: us as young women trying to make our way in the world, and trying to protect each other, being outraged that this teacher was picking on young women who are trying to find their voice. Women, as writers, as artists, as scientists, whatever they're trying to pursue, and she's just knocking us down."

It must have been humiliating for Q, to always be in the shadow of her mother, to not be considered good enough on her own.

And there was an underlying truth to the accusations: Quintana was not a scholar, or a writer. She undoubtedly preferred to be at Zuma than at Westlake. Her parents did spend a lot of time helping her write the applications and essays to get into Westlake, and then to Bennington College, and then to Barnard, where Q transferred after two years. "I don't think school was her thing," Armstrong-Totten says. "But it was important to them."

Ironically, Didion more than once wrote articles that criticized people who push kids into "good schools" more for the parents', than the child's, reputation. "What makes me uneasy is the sense that they are merging their children's chances with their own, demanding of a child that he make good not only for himself but for the greater glory of his father and mother," she argued in 1968, just a couple years after she and Dunne celebrated the certification of Q's adoption by bringing her with them to a coveted table at one of LA's fanciest restaurants.

At Barnard, Quintana shot photos for the school newspaper. Being able to capture the world visually, through a lens not a typewriter, turned out to be her calling. She had been surrounded by cameras as a child, small wonder Quintana grew up to be a photographer and art director.

Q took one of my favorite pictures of her mother. Didion is at a beach, palm trees silhouetted against the "seductive sea" glittering behind her. She stands barefoot in the water, her sandals in one hand, the other on her hip holding up her skirt, which is plastered by the wind against her body. This is the author photo that Christopher Lehmann-Haupt criticized in the *New York Times* for being too revealing, as Joan's body is clearly outlined through her translucent clothes. She is almost, almost smiling, but there are clouds on the horizon of this perfect frozen moment.

Quintana stayed in New York to work in publishing; her parents moved there in 1988 as well. "I was writing, doing design journalism, and I was working for *Elle Decor*, and Quintana was the photo editor," says her former classmate Stukin. "I had a couple of conversations with her and I think she had found something she really liked. And I suspect she was very good at it."

It's hard to say when Quintana's parents began to realize that their only child was troubled. In *Blue Nights*, Didion remembers Q's preschool nightmares about the Broken Man. Joan looks at photos of Q at age five taken by her cousin and sees in retrospect what she didn't see then: "The startling depths and shallows of her expressions, the quicksilver changes of mood." That was the year Quintana called the local psychiatric hospital "to find out what she needed to do if she was going crazy."

Beginning with *Play It As It Lays*, written when Q was a toddler, Didion's novels are populated with damaged daughters and distanced moms. In *Democracy*, the child is an addict who flies to Vietnam just as Americans are being evacuated; meanwhile, the mother has left the father for the older man she had been having an affair with for decades. In *A Book of Common Prayer*, Charlotte Douglas searches in vain for her fugitive terrorist child. Major derangements ran in the blood and the books.

Quintana was taken to doctors. "She was depressed. She was anxious," Didion wrote. Manic depression. OCD. Borderline personality disorder. "The names kept changing." In Brentwood, their suburbia house, she lay on the floor crying, "Let me just be in the ground."

Quintana Roo Dunne entered the world in limbo, even if she was quickly and enthusiastically claimed. Her parents had worthy intentions and were well versed on the then-current best practices for adoptive patients. Still, it was a bit like starting the race with one leg tied behind you. "Adoption, I was to learn although not immediately, is hard to get right," Didion wrote in *Blue Nights*.

Joan and John did many things correctly and well. They didn't lie to Quintana, telling her from the beginning her birth and adoption story. Dunne would always say, "Q was proudly adopted."

"John was very alert to any slurs," Trillin says. "If someone called Quintana 'his adopted daughter,' it irritated him. That was his *daughter*."

Joan and John tried to be open to the possibility that their only child would someday meet her "other mommy," as Q would call her. They said they would support her if she sought out her birth parents. As it happened (this, by the way, is one of Didion's favorite transitional phrases), bureaucratic errors revealed the mother's name to the Didion-Dunnes, and vice versa. When ten-year-old Quintana asked for it, her parents gave her that name. "We also said that if she decided to search her out, we would help her in any way we could," Dunne wrote.

Still, when they were with Q on a film shoot in Tucson, where the birth mother lived, Joan and John made a tremendous effort to conceal their presence. Everyone on the set was sworn to secrecy. Their names were kept out of newspaper stories. The Didion-Dunnes were open to the idea of a possible reunion, but they weren't necessarily going to make it easy. Didion told this story in *Blue Nights* "by way of suggesting the muddled impulses that can go hand in hand with adoption."

Quintana apparently never tried to find her birth family. But in 1998, they found her.

A letter came via Federal Express from a sister. The younger woman visited Q in New York. The siblings looked like twins. That led to meeting the birth mother in Texas and a gathering of extended members of her "biological family," as Q called them. Back in New York, the mother started calling Quintana regularly, in the mornings, as she got ready for work. The situation became emotionally overwhelming for the fragile woman, who was trying to hold down her job at *Elle Decor*. When Q asked her "other mommy" for a pause, the woman abruptly cut off all communication, disconnecting her phone.

Quintana Roo had found her birth mother, only to lose her again.

She then received a letter from her birth father, the Deadhead. For some reason, that shook Quintana even more than meeting her mother.

I'm not adopted. But from what I know from the literature, and from the friends and family members I know who are adopted—or who have adopted children themselves—I can see how it would be natural to fantasize about who your biological parents might be, to imagine them to have the qualities that your adoptive parents lack. Unfortunately, the truth is often far more complicated than the hope.

Finding "her biological family was the beginning of the problem," Griffin Dunne says of his cousin. "When she did connect, things started to fall apart. When you don't know where you're from, and then you do know, and you're disappointed, that's going to do a number. You lose the 'what if.'"

"I guess when she found her original family or biological family, nothing good came of that," says Trillin. "Sometimes it works out very well. And sometimes it doesn't."

By this point, it was clear that Quintana had a serious issue of her own. "As she got older, I would see her in New York. And I'd watch her struggle with alcohol," Dunne says. "Q had given AA a try a couple of times. You know, being an alcoholic is not terribly unusual in our family. And so she had some support, but it was still a tough thing."

There is a strong genetic component to alcoholism. This could have been part of the hand that the beautiful baby girl was dealt on the day she was delivered at Santa Monica Hospital, a bad card that she wouldn't even know she had. But her addiction became apparent over time. Still, for all her transparency, for all her self-investigation and revelation, Didion had a hard time admitting that drinking was one of Q's main issues—not to mention one of the central themes of Joan's own life narrative, and of Dunne's. Independent of any possible biological predisposition, Quintana grew up in a house where drinks were often at hand. Booze was the lubricant that kept the Didion-Dunne parties roaring, and most likely sharpened Dunne's temper. Didion herself grew up suffering from the environment created by her father's alcoholism. And yet even after her daughter's death, while filming the documentary about her own life, *The Center Will Not Hold*, the mother had to be pushed to admit that the daughter had an alcohol problem. "I was concerned because she was drinking too much," the mother admits, after some prodding. "That was the first concern."

"It was a tough thing for her to talk about," Griffin Dunne says. "Because as a mother, as a parent, of a child with a drinking problem, your first feeling is guilt. Not what's wrong with my kid, it's what's wrong with *me* that I did that to my kid."

Didion calls Q's addiction "self-medicating" in *Blue Nights*. She, incredibly, extols alcohol as "the most effective anti-anxiety agent yet known." But for Q, alcohol was neither agent nor medication. It was poison.

On July 26, 2003, at age thirty-seven, Quintana Roo Dunne was wed in the Cathedral of St. John the Divine in New York. She had met a man she loved, Gerry Michael, and it seemed a promising step toward stability and happiness for the woman who had known little of either. The fact that her groom was a bartender certainly raised alarms for many of the people who cared about her. But John made his toast, watercress sandwiches were served, and Q wore flowers in her hair. "Wasn't that just about perfect," the bride said when she called her parents later that evening.

The wedding seemed like a new beginning. In fact, it was the beginning of the end. "I was at her wedding, it was just an incredibly happy day," says Griffin Dunne. "And I watched everything fall apart. It was a horrible thing to see."

On Christmas Day 2003, Quintana was admitted to Beth Israel North Hospital in New York. What she had thought was a flu or strep throat was in fact pneumonia, and then septic shock. Thus began a series of medical conditions that would see the thirty-seven-year-old hospitalized, often unconscious, for most of the next twenty months. In *The Year of Magical Thinking* and *Blue*

Nights, Didion documents in characteristically precise detail the horrific and hard to fathom turn of events that would leave her a childless mother—and a widow. But there is no simple answer to the question, "What did Quintana Roo Dunne die of?" There was pneumonia. There was sepsis. There was a fall or a collapse on the tarmac in Los Angeles—drinking may or may not have been involved—which was either the result or the cause of a brain bleed. There were brief moments of recovery, followed by more calamity: paralysis, pancreatitis, coma.

A person of Q's age could not have been in good health to have her body fail so catastrophically. Alcoholism is a leading cause of pancreatitis. "I think they were probably intertwined," Traylor told *New York* magazine in 2011, speaking of her friend's depression, addiction, illnesses, and demise.

Quintana Roo Dunne died August 26, 2005, at age thirty-nine.

Was Joan a good mother?

It's the question you probably want to ask me. It's the question many have asked me. It's the question I have been asking myself. It's the question Joan asked herself. It's the question Joan asked Quintana.

"I think you were a good parent, but maybe a little remote," the daughter answered.

No one asks, Was John a good father?

I believe both Joan and John loved their only child intensely. They wanted to involve her in their lives as thoroughly as they were involved in each other's. Maybe that was the problem: Maybe three was a crowd in the Didion-Dunne household. Her parents bragged about how they involved Q in their work. But was that what the lonely girl wanted? On Christmas Day 1990, the family flew to Honolulu for a month. Sounds great, sure, but Joan and John were there to work intensively on a screenplay. Quintana "would be getting an unexpected holiday in the sun," Dunne wrote in his book *Monster*. But here was the daily schedule he described: "A sunrise swim, breakfast, then four hours' work in the suite; an hour for lunch, then two more hours' work in the afternoon; another swim, then three more hours' work before a late dinner with Quintana. After dinner, we went over the days' pages, then printed out a schedule of scenes for the next day."

Q was twenty-four at this time, an adult who, as Didion wrote, knew the Kahala Hilton well and could entertain herself there. She was also already a troubled woman who had perhaps become a little too adept at passing the time alone on holidays in the sun. The schedule was undoubtedly invigorating and productive for the Didion-Dunnes, who completed their writing in just eleven days. But the studio hated what they turned in. It was a project they had taken on for purely mercenary reasons—particularly to keep their screenwriters' guild bona fides intact so they could maintain their health insurance, in the face of John's growing heart problems. Fair enough, but perhaps two writers of their tremendous success could have prioritized a real holiday in the sun with their only child, as opposed to dinners squeezed between writing sessions for a project that quickly went bust.

As the daughter of the writer Jean Stein, one of Didion's closest friends, and a close friend of Quintana's cousin Dominique, Katrina vanden Heuvel had a unique perspective on Joan's family and work life. The journalist and publisher of *The Nation* recalls the Didion-Dunnes hosting a party in Trancas one night in 1973. Katrina's mom left her home with a babysitter, who happened to be a Hell's Angel. When Stein arrived sans child, "Joan said 'go back and get her, what are you thinking, Jean?'" vanden Heuvel says. "Here's Joan, who's not a natural mother. But she did have a maternal instinct, which comes through in her last book, but also in her being with Quintana as best she could, the best she could be a mother."

"There are some couples who are so tight it feels hard to bring in a child," says vanden Heuvel. "They loved Quintana, but it's almost as if there wasn't space. They wanted to make space, and in the photos, in some of the great photos, they're making space, but I think it was hard and I think the writing reflects that. I think they were good parents, as good as they could be. But she had a tough time being a mother."

In *Blue Nights* Didion repeatedly questions her own failings: "Did I all her life keep a baffle between us?" "Was I the problem? Was I always the problem?" But she also defends herself: "I do not know many people who think they have succeeded as parents," she writes, then launches into an attack on helicopter parenting. Actually, for their time, the Didion-Dunnes may have erred on the side of attentiveness. Traylor was jealous of how tightly Q's parents were involved in her life, and she remained close to Didion until Joan's death. Authoritarian parents can have troubled kids; so can laissez-faire latchkey parents.

"It could have been a very strict family, and there was no drinking, and it could have moved in the same direction," says vanden Heuvel. "I do think they raised Quintana with a lot of love and didn't hide things from her; I mean it wasn't like she was tucked away and not permitted to come out. And I think that's a healthier way of raising a kid. But they were in their writing and in their minds, and it was hard to find a place sometimes."

"The best she could be a mother." Joan Didion was not a conventional June Cleaver maternal figure, but she was the kind of mom so many women like myself strive to be, balancing commitment to our offspring with the freedom to be ourselves. Most of us, even Joan, would probably agree that she was a better writer than parent. The thing is, society systemically makes it hard for women to be both. Study after study shows that six decades after the women's liberation movement and five decades since Title IX, even as parental leave policies support stay-at-home dads and women become Supreme Court justices and vice presidents (but not presidents), women still do much more of the labor of child and household care than men.

Write the bestsellers, pose with your daughter for the photographers, laugh at your husband's jokes, make the fried chicken for the dinner party, plant your garden, be a good mom.

No wonder Joan was so quiet. She was exhausted.

Joan made her choices. She wanted a child, and she wanted a career. We like to think women—like men—are not supposed to have to choose between the two, that we can have both. But choices are made. They are made by men too, but society judges these choices differently. The judgments were even more skewed in the 1960s, when both of Didion's callings—family and writing—took off simultaneously. This makes her decisions even more remarkable in retrospect. She may have been baby crazy at age twenty-three, she may have found herself crying alone on Christmas 1969, but she was full of self-pity, not regret. "Watching an AP wire in an empty office is precisely what I want to be doing: Women do not end up in empty offices and Blimpy Burgers by accident, any more than three-year-olds and their mothers need to make pomegranate jelly together to learn about family love . . ." she wrote in *Life*. "We design our lives as best we can. The baby will know something about family love on Christmas because she knows something about it today, and she will also know something about its complexities."

I have not found any essay by John Gregory Dunne about being away from his only child at Christmas, or her first birthday, because he had to work.

I believe many of us admire Joan because she *didn't* try to be a perfect mom, because she taught us all something about love's complexities.

The life of Quintana Roo Dunne was celebrated at the Dominican Church of St. Vincent Ferrer in New York. The musician and poet Patti Smith performed. Trillin talked about Q's way of saying hello. Her remains were interred in a vault at St. John the Divine beside those of Eduene Jerrett Didion and John Gregory Dunne. Still not in the ground.

"Losing a child causes the greatest suffering of all," Mama told me.

"I will be sad always," Didion wrote in 2011.

Jogger

I'm enclosing just a few pages on which I had some comments for you to consider. You dealt with so much of what I earlier sent, there isn't much left. It is a terrific piece.

—Robert B. Silvers, letter to Joan Didion, November 23, 1990

In 1973 Joan Didion met a man who would change her life. Her bona fides as an intrepid reporter, original thinker, and elegant writer were already established. But in the deeply inequitable world of news reporting, even a thirty-eight-year-old woman of Didion's skills slammed into closed doors and glass ceilings. *Life* magazine, for instance, had hired her to write a column, but that gig went quickly down the tubes beginning the moment they wouldn't let her go to Saigon. But Robert B. Silvers saw her skills and her scope. Over twenty-four years they built the kind of productive, fraught, stimulating, nurturing, challenging, life-changing, and life-affirming relationship that every writer hopes to have with an editor—and vice versa. In this legendary magazine publisher, she found a literary mentor and partner who took her talents and intellect seriously. Silvers allowed—encouraged—her to write about the major issues and figures of her time. For the semimonthly newsprint magazine the *New York Review of Books*, which he founded with Barbara Epstein in 1963, Didion wrote investigative journalism, book reviews, philosophical essays, and war reportage that transformed her from a celebrity chronicler of pop culture, counterculture, and subcultures into one of the leading social and political commentators of her time. She visited mass graveyards in El Salvador. She bivouacked in Miami, documenting the city's transformation into a sometimes dangerous and corrupt but always interesting Latin American capital. She covered presidential campaigns, conventions, and calamities. She exposed then vice president Dick Cheney as one of the most soulless, megalomaniacal politicians America had known.

And most importantly, she wrote about the trial of five teenage Black and Hispanic males accused of the brutal rape of a white woman jogger in New York's Central Park—about the trial that took place in a Manhattan courtroom, but more crucially, the trial that took place in the court of public opinion, led by entrenched media and sensationalizing politicians. Meticulously researched, lacerating but not sensational in its analysis, relentless in its exposure of legal, activist, and journalistic snakes, "New York: Sentimental Journeys" exonerated the defendants and convicted the city of centuries of systemic racism and moral failure. In 2002, the convicted rapists' sentences were voided after another man confessed to the attack on Trisha Meili. Ten years later, and twenty-one years after "Sentimental Journeys," in the documentary *The*

Central Park Five, filmmakers Ken and Sarah Burns exposed the many ways the minors were railroaded by an inept and prejudiced legal system and guilty until proven innocent in the eyes of the press.

Once again, Joan Didion was ahead of her time.

Robert Silvers was not Didion's first great editor. In the mid-1960s, Farrar, Straus & Giroux editor Henry Robbins courted Didion obsessively. He sent her messages through her husband. He came to LA and wined and dined both writers. Joan was flattered, interested, convinced; she signed. But, busy with her newborn baby and her column for the *Saturday Evening Post*, she couldn't come up with much more than a name for the promised novel. That was okay; her deal with FSG included an option for a nonfiction book, based on and titled after her essay on Haight-Ashbury. *Slouching Towards Bethlehem* gathered several of her previously published articles and was published to great acclaim in 1968. For the next eight years, Didion wrote books only for Robbins, following him when he moved to publisher Simon and Schuster—much to her regret, as his time there was tumultuous and short. When her beloved editor died suddenly of a heart attack in 1979, she named her next anthology *After Henry*.

Women also played crucial roles in Joan Didion's career, particularly her agents Helen M. Strauss, followed by Lois Wallace, and then Lynn Nesbit. They procured and negotiated the book deals that brought Didion's writing to a wider, international audience. Her final book editor was Shelley Wanger at Knopf; Wanger began her career in 1975 as an assistant to Silvers.

But it was primarily Silvers who nurtured Didion's journalism in the second act of her life, cultivating in it a scope and gravitas that placed her alongside the leading intellects of her time.

Joan Didion's writing for *NYRB* did not immediately take her into new territory. Her first article, in 1973, was "Hollywood," a portrait of the "industry town" that she had refused to write just one year earlier, when both Robert Strozier of *Audience* magazine and Ted Solotaroff of *New American Review* had solicited her. (Perhaps she was turned off by Strozier because he called her "Miss Didion"; her "no thank you" note stated: "John's book *The Studio* involved much the same material, and nobody wants to write someone else's book. Particularly if the book is your husband's." She signed the note "With thanks, Joan Didion [Mrs. John Gregory Dunne].") She was still living in California and others still saw the culture there as her beat, as did she. Her queries to Silvers stuck to this script: In 1976, she wrote that she "would still like to do a piece about the music business," prompted by *The Rolling Stone Illustrated History of Rock & Roll*; the year before Silvers had sent her Greil Marcus's seminal tome *Mystery Train*. Oh how the rock critic in me wishes this article had transpired! What would Didion have said about Ellen Willis's great essay on Janis Joplin? Would decades of bloated prose from Marcus and Willis wannabes to come been circumvented by her laser wit and scalpel?

Despite Silvers's encouragement, Didion took six years to write a second piece for him, on Woody Allen. She was not kind to the filmmaker or his fans. Slowly, the writing became steadier and steadier, until in the 1980s *NYRB* was the primary outlet for her book reviews and also long-form reported narrative pieces. (Didion also wrote a column for the *New Yorker* and contributed

to the *New York Times, Los Angeles Times, Vogue,* and elsewhere.)
Under Silvers's guidance, Joan took on a range of topics, including
many of the most pressing issues and subjects of the time: Ronald
Reagan, Bill Clinton, the court case of comatose Theresa Schi-
avo, Martha Stewart, Republican House Speaker Newt Gingrich.
Many of these were think pieces, essays that were anchored to
new books or movies or current events but that ranged widely in
their sources, evidence of Didion's extensive lifelong reading habit.
These were big-picture stories, such as the growing influence of
religion on politics—another prescient subject. Her writing frequently and purposely cut across the grain of established opinion;
she attacked Robert Woodward for his questionable ethics toward
sources and wooden writing style decades before his reporting on
President Trump came under fire. "What they have in Mr. Woodward is a widely trusted reporter, even an American icon, who
can be relied upon to present a Washington in which problematic
or questionable matters will be definitively resolved by the discovery, or by the demonstration that there has been no discovery,
of 'the smoking gun,' 'the evidence,'" she wrote in her signature
blend of imperious and scathing prose in "Political Pornography."
"Should such narrowly defined 'evidence' be found, he can then be
relied upon to demonstrate, 'fairly,' that the only fingerprints on
the smoking gun are those of the one bad apple in the barrel, the
single rogue agent in the tapestry of decent intentions."

Didion did not see Washington, or politics in general, as a tapestry of decent intentions.

For *NYRB* she took deep dives into locations that were key loci
of social change and political conflict, honing her skill at ground-
ing narratives in places and her capacity for both prodigious

background and on-the-ground research. These long-form pieces did necessitate interviewing numerous sources, famous and infamous. But Didion knew that formal questioning often produced nothing but scripted answers. Her preferred technique was to quietly insert herself into her environment, seeping under its skin, observing its textures and smells and conversations—and contrasting the view from the ground with the rhetoric from above. Those extended stories became short books, *Miami* and *Salvador*, that allowed her to cultivate her discourse on the American empire: its corruption, ineptness, cruelty, lies.

Didion didn't make it to Vietnam in 1966 or '69, but in June 1982, she and Dunne traveled to El Salvador. These were dangerous times in the Central American nation. El Salvador was embroiled in a brutal civil war that was being partially funded by the US government. No one was safe. Two years before, Archbishop Óscar Romero had been assassinated while celebrating mass. Less than a year later, four American nuns were murdered. Six months before Didion's arrival, the entire town of El Mozote—more than 811 people, including women and children—were massacred. Just before the Didion-Dunnes arrived, four Dutch journalists were killed. TV news anchor Tom Brokaw told Joan and John that of all the war zones he had reported from, El Salvador was the place where he was most truly scared. That's when they decided to go.

Didion was forty-seven years old, a petite, pale woman. The mostly male press pool knew who she was and was skeptical of her short-term presence in this war zone. She was, as they say in the journalism trade, "parachuting" in, while many of them were long haulers, or at least veteran combat correspondents. But Didion wasn't there on an adrenaline trip or to sightsee. As part of her gradual political transformation, the former Goldwater supporter was increasingly outraged by America's meddling in foreign countries. She saw how the manifest destiny of the West that was her Moby-Dick—the ideological American icon she labored to harpoon—was connected to America's continuing southern adventures. This is why she traveled in Louisiana, Mississippi, and Alabama in 1970 and to Mexico and Central America multiple times. She is one of the few writers who connected the dots between Sacramento, New Orleans, Miami, Colombia, and El Salvador and on to Hawai'i, Vietnam, Kuala Lumpur. She loved Paris, but she basically never wrote about Europe. Yet she felt called to write about a small country whose devastation her government had an outsize role in, in the name of fighting communism.

"I'm not sure that I have a social conscience," she told *The Guardian*. "It's more an insistence that people tell the truth. The decision to go to El Salvador came one morning at the breakfast table. I was reading the newspaper and it just didn't make sense."

Didion didn't shrink from the horrors of war. She trekked past armed guards to mass burial sites. She took cabs through riverbeds in search of the front line. She interviewed El Salvador's president. She experienced the deadly earthquake of 1982. True to Rather's words, she had never known fear like she experienced in El Salvador. "Terror is the given of the place," she wrote. She admitted that even her lifelong skill at noting the telling detail seemed null and void in the context of El Salvador, that "I was no longer much interested in this kind of irony, that this was a story that would not be illuminated by such details, that this was a story that would perhaps not be illuminated at all."

Her stay there was short, just two weeks. But the resulting

articles, published the following year as the book *Salvador*, brought the American-taxpayer-funded atrocities in El Salvador to a larger public in a way that other correspondents could not. The best of those writers were appreciative of the light she shone on their world. Poet Carolyn Forché, who documented her own seven visits in two years to El Salvador in verse and later a memoir, was grateful for Didion's work raising awareness of Reagan's policies to a level that poems could never achieve. (When an El Salvadoran farmer had shown up at her door in San Diego begging her to come witness the war in his country, Forché initially told him to find a journalist.) The great *New Yorker* Central American correspondent Alma Guillermoprieto considered her sister in arms a hero. "Joan Didion walked the world like a cat through broken glass," the author of *The Heart That Bleeds* wrote. "She brought to the 21st century an anti-macho, parsimonious, meticulous, ironic and self-conscious style of delicate, black humor. Modern feminism transformed her environment: today half of any newsroom is made up of women."

In Miami a few years later, Didion embedded herself in the Cuban exile community, the dominant Hispanic population in a city that was becoming a minority-majority metropolis of international importance. She saw cadavers at the coroner's office, talked to failed soldiers of the Bay of Pigs, interviewed the literal architects of the city's transforming skyline. Mitchell Kaplan, owner of the Coral Gables–based bookstore chain Books & Books, drove Didion around for a day when she was doing reconnaissance. "Miami was just emerging as a city that was on anyone's radar," he says. "I took her to South Beach, which was just evolving, and Downtown, and to the Doral Hotel. We spent an afternoon in my car, basically, and she was quiet but really lovely and really engaging, asking questions. But mostly she was observing." Kaplan admits he fell for her old trick of being so silent, her subjects would fill the void with their words.

David Rieff referred Didion to Kaplan. He was living in Miami at the time, and his own book *Going to Miami: Tourists, Exiles, and Refugees in the New America* came out the same year as Joan's. "She got something very fundamental," the author says of *Miami*. "I don't know exactly how she did it. It's a very slight book, and yet she captures something. Miami is kind of the anti Los Angeles. It's the same thing—the global South, moving in and transforming—but on a completely different principle. She saw that very well."

I moved to Miami Beach in 2001, fourteen years after *Miami* was published as a book. I bought my paperback copy at Kaplan's Books & Books, which Didion used to frequent. Miami had changed greatly since she had written about it. But her writing was so perceptive of the changes taking place in the mid-1980s that I could see my colleagues at the *Miami Herald* and I were still catching up to her observations. We were an English-language newspaper in an increasingly Spanish-speaking city—though wisely, the publisher had launched *El Nuevo Herald*. One realization we shared with Didion: Miami was a great news town, a city of gold. Bombings, cocaine, celebrities, coups, shootouts, alligators, gunrunners, disco—great dramas and tragedies were enacted, and simultaneously denied, under the relentless tropical heat. "To spend time in Miami is to acquire a certain fluency in cognitive dissonance," Didion wrote.

"She was always ahead of her time and so she wrote about Miami way before Miami was really on anyone's map," Kaplan says. "The other thing that she saw was that Miami was a microcosm or could be a microcosm for other places in the country to come—the whole idea of immigration, of the clash of cultures that was being played out."

Beginning in the 1980s Joan Didion did for *NYRB* what women reporters had rarely been allowed to do when she began her career decades earlier, when they were confined to fashion magazines or research departments: She covered campaigns and conventions, presidents and vice presidents. In 1968, she had written about Ronald Reagan's wife Nancy, back when he was governor of California, and in 1977, her topic was the empty mansion he built on the outskirts of Sacramento. In 1989, she took on the president himself.

The Reagan article, "Life at Court," is a think piece reflecting on the legacy of his two terms based on recent books. But the year prior, Didion did weeks of leg work, not just brain work, covering the presidential primary in California and the Democratic and Republican conventions in Atlanta and New Orleans. Her resulting article, "Insider Baseball," analyzed the deep disconnect she experienced between both parties and the people they are supposed to represent. The candidates, she wrote—she barely deigned to speak George Bush's and Michael Dukakis's names—"tend to speak a language common in Washington but not specifically shared by the rest of us."

Robert Scheer traveled with Didion as part of the press crew on these campaigns. At the time he was a reporter for the *Los Angeles Times*, and an outspoken, contrarian journalist himself. He found his colleague to be a fierce and fearless road warrior. "The times that I was alone with Joan traveling, I didn't think of her as frail," he says. "I thought of her as quite feisty and capable of surviving quite well and having a sharp eye and also keeping up the schedule that was even more exhausting at times than I wanted to do. What I loved about Joan was she had none of the pain in the ass qualities— the know it all, I can figure this out in 15 minutes arrogance—that a lot of journalists have. She always felt there was a lot to learn."

Didion critiqued not just the two political parties but the entire system of political discourse, including policy advisors, pollsters, media consultants, and columnists: "That handful of insiders who invent, year in and year out, the narrative of public life." Didion had a name for these invented narratives, which became the title of her 2001 collection: *Political Fictions*. "Insider Baseball" and its companion pieces don't offer the sex, drugs, and rock 'n' roll stimulation of Joan's 1960s and 1970s writing, but they are equally insightful and arguably more important. *Political Fictions* won the prestigious George Polk Book Award for "investigative work that is original, requires digging and resourcefulness, and brings results."

In her book *Joan Didion: Substance and Style*, the scholar Kathleen M. Vandenberg examines Didion's later writings, beginning with *Salvador*, and argues that far from reifying and representing the ruling class, as other critics have charged, Didion sounded some of the earliest warnings of the Trumpocalypse to come. "She has, in both subject matter and approach, been amazingly prescient about the future of political and cultural discourse and the ways in which patterns of thinking and narratives of 'fact' are rhetorically constructed, and grounded both in the past and in the adherence to regional traditions and values," Vandenberg writes.

Joan warned us.

Didion's writing style changed with the increasing complexity of her subjects. Her articles for *NYRB* were much denser, less full of the "white space" she extolled in "Why I Write," more linear rather than fragmented, and deeply, even maniacally, researched. Rather than giving in to the widening gyre, she was now determined to make sense of the world. She had a profound understanding of the importance of narrative, of finding order in disorder. "I mean total control has always been the reason I wrote anything at all," she said in the 1972 letter to Solotaroff.

Some of the change in Didion's writing was mechanistic. Her switch to word processing programs allowed Didion to cut and paste passages in more complex and seamless ways than her old habit of arranging note cards on the floor. She wrote longer, in bigger paragraphs. She also turned less often to first-person narrative. She was now the well-informed expert offering her take on current events—finally, a female authority figure. These articles— "In the Realm of the Fisher King," "Times Mirror Square," "The West Wing of Oz," etc.—don't offer the same lyrical, conversational prose of the pieces gathered in *Slouching* and *The White Album*. They provide a different kind of pleasure: The thrill of a thorough, precise, relentless, and often unexpected interrogation. ("We are in an interrogation room, and I am interrogating Officer Gerrans," Didion wrote in "Slouching Towards Bethlehem.") And every now and then, she still gets in a jab so clever and/or ironic, it makes you laugh out loud, such as this one at Reagan in "The West Wing of Oz": "Two hours before his 1981 inauguration, according to Michael Deaver, he was still sleeping. Deaver did not actually find this extraordinary, nor would anyone else who had witnessed Reagan's performance as governor of California."

Poet Michelle Bitting draws frequently on Didion's prose for its weaving of incisiveness and insight. "There's so much in it, and yet it never feels laborious to read, you never zone out on all of the information that she's giving you," she says. "I think she knows how to press into the facts and then pull back to the personal. And all the tangents, but it never feels like, 'Oh I'm lost.' There's a music to it. But it's so clear too."

Didion wrote with the kind of authority historically allowed mostly to men. But she brought additional insights that the men could not, shaped by gender and her upbringing in Sacramento. "Clinton Agonistes," an article about President Bill Clinton's sex scandals and impeachment hearing, opens thus: "No one who ever passed through an American public high school could have watched William Jefferson Clinton running for office in 1992 and failed to recognize the familiar predatory sexuality of the provincial adolescent." As someone who attended a provincial American public high school and watched Clinton shake hands at a New York rally in 1992, I can only respond, "Exactly."

The bravery of Didion's genre innovations throughout her career created whole new ways of writing; without them, untold numbers of readers might not have become writers. David L. Ulin is an author, professor at the University of Southern California, former book editor at the *Los Angeles Times*, and editor of the Library of America editions of Joan Didion's work. "There's a real present tense quality to that writing in the sense that I always have the notion, even when I reread it now, of her in the moment trying to figure it out," Ulin says. "It's polished but I almost feel like I'm watching the movement of her thinking. That was really, really powerful for me as a young wannabe writer. I don't think I had ever been specifically aware of that idea of a piece of writing as a kind of living expression of a moment, of a writer wrestling with stuff. But in her case I'm always aware of her uncertainty, of what she doesn't know as much as what she does know."

Nowhere is Joan Didion's dedication to extensive research and re-portage, skeptical and pragmatic analysis, and withering cultural criticism more trenchant than in "Sentimental Journeys." Didion saw the Central Park case as an exemplar of everything that was wrong with the city to which she had, in 1964, said goodbye, then returned to in 1988. In the three years since she had been back in Manhattan (which were also my first three years living in NYC), the chronicler of empire had clearly trained her gimlet eye on the defining metropolis of the Empire State, on a city where the always extreme divide between very rich and very poor, between Black and white, had reached the point of blatant obscenity. This was a time of horrific poverty, friction, and violence in the city. Buildings in whole swaths of the Bronx and Brooklyn were des-olate and abandoned, yet 25,000 individuals and 11,000 families lived without shelter. In 1986, a white mob attacked three Black men whose car broke down in Howard Beach, Queens; one of the men was hit by a car and killed as he attempted to escape. In 1988, police tried to clear unhoused people who were living in Tompkins Square Park, on the Lower East Side; video footage of the resultant riot showed officers assaulting numerous people, including a videographer. Four months after the assault on the jogger in Central Park, a sixteen-year-old Black male was mur-dered by another white mob, this time in Bensonhurst, Brooklyn. And yet, Joan wrote, the mythmakers of Manhattan continued to spread, as they had for centuries, "the insistent sentimental-ization of experience . . . 8 million stories and all the same story, each devised to obscure not only the city's actual tensions of race and class but also, more significantly, the civic and commercial arrangements that rendered those tensions irreconcilable."

The attack on the jogger cut close to home: Didion and Dunne lived just one block from Central Park. Central Park itself was built on a lie, she wrote, a pastoral narrative that was really "about contracts and concrete and kickbacks, about pork." Perhaps it took a pragmatic journalist from the West to reveal what all New York City's major media players got wrong in their rush to demonize a group of Black and Brown children and beatify the nameless vic-tim. "Here was a case that gave this middle class a way to transfer and express what had clearly become a growing and previously inadmissible rage with the city's disorder, with the entire range of ills and uneasy guilts that came to mind in a city where entire families slept in the discarded boxes in which new Sub-Zero re-frigerators were delivered, at 2600 per, to more affluent families."

For "Sentimental Journeys" Didion pored through criminal records and trial transcripts. She analyzed the extensive media coverage, not only in the mainstream press, but also in the Black newspapers and talk shows. And she put to use her decades spent consuming books about history, sociology, politics, and media. Fourteen years before news anchor Gwen Ifill coined the phrase "missing white woman syndrome," Didion documented the dis-parity between the attention paid to the jogger, an attractive white woman who worked at Solomon Brothers, and the less mediagenic victims of contemporaneous assaults and homicides. She also as-tutely analyzed how police, politicians, and pundits manipulated crime statistics and stories to reinforce narratives of fear, white supremacy, and economic disparity.

The Central Park five story also went through the most rigorous and sometimes painful editing of any story Didion ever worked on. Robbins sent the manuscript back to her over and over with notes that almost matched her own verbiage in length and complexity. It was a brutal process that resulted in a masterpiece of investigative, literary journalism.

There is a brilliant picture of the city in this piece. We had difficulties with some of the sections on the Central Park case, particularly on anonymity, the rape charge, the use of "metaphorical" truth by some of the people you mention, among other points. On some of these questions, as you'll see, the comments welled up or swelled up and I hope you won't think them over done. Please consider the points I've tried to raise and let's soon be in touch.

—Robert B. Silvers, letter to Joan Didion, October 22, 1990

One of the topics over which editor and writer fought vigorously was whether to identify Meili. At that time, the widespread journalistic policy was not to name rape victims. The logic was that they had suffered enough and should not be exposed to public shaming. But many feminists argued that making sexual assault different from other violent crimes gave rape precisely the kind of gendered power its perpetrators sought. "Women do not want to be raped, nor do they want to have their brains smashed, but very few mystify the difference between the two," Didion wrote.

Her discussion of the politics of naming is extremely complex, extending over seven long paragraphs in the final article. It includes citations from legal expert Susan Estrich, journalist Geneva Overholser, historian W. J. Cash, the Reverend Calvin O. Butts III, and Malcolm X. Didion had a nuanced understanding of not just the sexism but the racism inherent in the elevation of the nameless victim to "Lady Courage," as she was called. "Yet there was in this case a special emotional undertow derived in part from the deep and allusive associations and taboos attaching, in American Black history, to the idea of the rape of white women," Didion wrote. The names of the juvenile defendants had been released by police and widely published in the media, which also repeatedly referred to the group of adolescents as "a wolf pack." This imbalance of justice led many Black-led publications, activists, and journalists to in turn name Meili. Didion's sympathies clearly lay with those parties. But Silvers would not budge on this, supporting "those who did not name her: they were following a much-damaged woman's request," he wrote in a typed note in the manuscript's margins. Didion lost this battle, but now Meili's name is openly spoken, in part because she wrote a memoir in which she identified herself in 2003.

"Bob always shaped how I thought," Didion wrote in 2017, after Silvers's death. "I had no opinion I did not run by him first. 'New York: Sentimental Journeys' (1991), on the Central Park jogger case, was far and away the hardest piece I ever worked on for this reason. Bob from the beginning knew what the piece had to be—he knew before I did—and he pushed me until I got it there. He knew exactly how dangerous the subject was, and his reaction to this danger was to make it more dangerous. His idea from the first was to get it right, to make it perfect, regardless of whatever negative reaction it might elicit in the city at that moment. When I first turned it in to him, it was clearly too long. His solution was to insist I go further. This meant making it longer. If that piece succeeds at all, it succeeds because he gave me permission to finish it."

The piece succeeds. But it took a while for it to get its due.

With the hindsight of the rapist's confession, the youths' exoneration, Meili's memoir, a Ken Burns documentary, and an Ava DuVernay Netflix series, many of the points Didion made in 1991 now seem obvious. But at the time, she was one of the few white journalists writing for a major publication who saw clearly what many in the city's Black press also saw. *NYRB* readers were not pleased. Didion said later that dozens of angry letters were received. *Newsday* journalist Jim Sleeper wrote a particularly long attack that has not aged nearly as well as the article he critiqued: "Something truly terrible did happen that night in Central Park; and the young men who made the videotaped statements made it happen," he wrote.

Silvers stood by his writer. He published Sleeper's letter because Didion cited in "Journeys" a book the Black neoconservative author had written. But the editor refused to publish a complaint sent by Judge Lois G. Forer, telling her, "The *Review* has a long tradition of printing critical letters, but the claims in them should at least be based on the text we published, and I regret this is not the case in the letter you sent us."

In "Sentimental Journeys," Didion set a new bar for investigative journalism. In 1991, the media was just beginning to question its mindless regurgitation of police-department crime statistics. Steve Weinberg was one of those reporters whose practice was changed by the Central Park story. "Most of the thousands of words she wrote offered an entirely fresh approach to understanding miscarriages of justice, an approach I had never before considered," Weinberg wrote in 2022 for Harvard's Nieman Storyboard, a leading forum for journalism educators and practitioners. The former executive director of Investigative Reporters and Editors dubs Didion's method of analyzing the surrounding cultural and historical context of the crime, not just the crime itself, "Sociological Evidence." "Among other talents, Didion exhibited attributes of a masterful sociologist in much of her nonfiction . . . 'Sentimental Journeys' constituted her most memorable and outstanding accomplishment as a reporter—one that helped shape my own journalism and whose lessons I carry to this day."

Thirty-two years later, with many media outlets breathlessly reporting rising crime rates, journalists still could make use of the master class in crime reporting that is "Sentimental Journeys."

"That Central Park Five piece showed an expression of courage, taking on the orthodoxy," says Katrina vanden Heuvel. "Joan used her capital—political, literary, and other—to really take it on. That took someone who was free and didn't feel constrained by any school, any thing. . . . I think she was fearless. I would love to read Joan Didion now, on January 6 or cancel culture. I think her writing should be taught. It's not Tom Wolfe, it's not self-indulgent. There's a vigor and a sparseness and a voice that is part of her reporting, as well as her writing. She certainly had little use for labels or for being stuck in a category, and I think there was a clarity and a realism."

In 2013 the *NYRB* celebrated its fiftieth anniversary at New York's Town Hall. At Robert Silvers's urging, Joan Didion read an excerpt from "Sentimental Journeys." In her opening remarks, she mentioned Burns's *The Central Park Five*, released the previous year, then explained that she had written about the same case the year the youths were convicted. "Much that I wrote called into question the process by which the police, the prosecutors, the jury, and the white press had very indignantly assumed that the young men were guilty of a savage crime against an exemplary young woman. My article questioned these assumptions, the haste with which they were made, and the ways they were expressed and acted on. The *Review* received dozens of angry letters, the article was published in Germany as a book, and then a kind of silence seemed to surround it as the young men served years in prison. When they were set free and when the recent film about them was released, the article, so far as I have seen, was never mentioned. It ran to some 17,000 words—the longest piece, I gather, ever published in the *New York Review*. Some of the attitudes I describe in it have changed. Some have not."

Robert Silvers died March 20, 2017. Joan's greatness was her own but it took allies to give her the time, space, and platform she deserved. "When I heard that Bob had died, I felt that the bottom had dropped out of my world," Didion wrote in a special memorial edition of the paper he had edited since he cofounded it. "An editorial note from Bob would open up new possibilities both in a piece and in life itself. What could have been an empty place suddenly flooded with light and understanding."

Morgue

The corpses had already been moved from the morgue in San Salvador when Joan Didion visited one morning in 1982. The slab had been washed down; "there were many flies, and an electric fan," she wrote in *Salvador*. Five years later in Miami, two young Cuban men who had been brought to America in the Mariel boat lift were being autopsied on the day she went to the coroner's office. "Their flesh had the marbleized yellow look of the recently dead," she wrote in *Miami*.

Didion's reporting led her to where the bodies were. She wrote about her visits to morgues and mass graves in straightforward prose with little sentiment or squeamishness. "There's something very muscular about her writing that I aspire to," says journalist Stacie Stukin. "And I don't necessarily mean that it is masculine, because it's not, but it's very strong and direct. And I think it's often characterized as minimalist, but I don't think it is minimal at all."

In the third act of her life, Didion's stoicism met its greatest challenge. In the emergency room at New York Hospital, she once again looked at death, only this time it was in the face not of a stranger, but of her closest companion. "She's a pretty cool customer," the social worker said to the doctor as they prepared to tell the sixty-nine-year-old woman that John Gregory Dunne was dead.

This time her coolness wasn't Didion's legendary reserve in play. The death of her life partner left the writer in a deep, year-long shock. It also left her alone to navigate the twenty-month medical collapse of their only child, a parent's worst nightmare.

The process of mourning inspired the most widely read book of her career.

Salvador and *Miami* had demonstrated that Joan Didion was growing beyond her West Coast roots. Still, in 1988 the fifty-three-year-old California woman did something that to many of her fans was unthinkable and even unforgivable: She moved back to New York City.

There were, in fact, multiple explanations for the seemingly inexplicable. The Didion-Dunnes moved in part because they wanted a change of pace. The couple had always shared a restlessness that kept them in motion, traveling regularly and relocating periodically. Their decade in Brentwood had been their longest time in one place since they married. They were both more frequently writing for New York publications and wanted to be back in the center of the publishing world. Quintana was also in New York, starting a career in magazines after graduating from Barnard. Dunne, the Connecticut native, wanted to be back on the coast where he grew up, in the city he knew best—where you didn't have to drive everywhere.

But the main reason they moved is not so much because John was homesick, but because he was bodysick. Beginning in 1987, he suffered a series of heart events and procedures, any one of which could have proved fatal. His father, a heart surgeon, had died of cardiac arrest, and John inherited Dad's shitty ticker. Didion might have preferred they buy a place in Hawai'i, as she had tried in the 1970s. But her husband had spent two dozen years on her turf. How could she say no?

In the twenty-four years since she had left Manhattan, Didion had established herself as the preeminent chronicler of the Best Coast. "California belongs to Joan Didion," Michiko Kakutani declared, problematically, in a long *New York Times* article in 1979. Trillin, and others, dubbed the Brentwood house America's West Coast literary consulate. Hollywood had become the Didion-Dunne gravy train, as John would hilariously and in vivid detail describe in *Monster: Living Off the Big Screen.* How could the golden couple of the Golden State abandon their throne to become just more New York literati?

They didn't. Joan and John became THE New York literati. Whereas as a young woman, Didion had felt anxious and out of place in the high-octane, blue-blood atmosphere of patriarchal East Coast publishing, in her middle age, she returned triumphantly, as an acclaimed and even celebrity author. After all, a

writer returning to a former haunt is uniquely equipped to notice its changes—or lack thereof. The top NYC publications—
NYRB, the *New Yorker*, the *New York Times*—fought to publish
her essays. In their large uptown apartment, the Didion-Dunnes
threw parties that rivaled their LA happenings. They had moved
East in part because they were tired of being the big fish in LA's
small publishing pond; they quickly transitioned to being even
bigger fish in NYC's ocean of authors. And they did it on their
own terms: One of the first guests in their new condo on East
Seventy-First Street was former California governor Jerry Brown,
who was running a maverick campaign for the Democratic presidential nomination.

In a 1992 interview they both still profess their love for LA.
John says they left because "they'd spent too much time at the fair."
It's unclear if he is intentionally quoting from Didion in "Goodbye
to All That," but no one bothers to make the obvious citation.

"I didn't realize how beautiful it was until we moved," Didion
says.

"I suppose that I love Los Angeles more than any city I will
ever know," Dunne says.

The Didion-Dunnes had owned a pied-à-terre in Alwyn Court,
an ornate apartment building just south of Central Park, for a few
years before they moved. But for a fulltime residence, they needed
something bigger. They wound up returning to the neighborhood
where they had both lived in the 1960s: the swanky, WASPy Upper East Side of Manhattan. The apartment where Joan Didion
spent the last thirty-three years of her life is on the corner of

Madison Avenue and Seventy-First Street. It's a big building with polite doormen who keep strangers firmly out on the sidewalk. A heraldic seal on its northwest corner features a lion's head with what I swear is a snake, but could just be a ribbon, behind it. Their spacious, five-bedroom apartment included a professional-grade kitchen with Sub-Zero fridge (one wonders what happened to the box it came in). They converted two bedrooms into offices, one for guests (Quintana's Brentwood Park blankets covered the bed and an old family quilt hung on the wall), and one off the kitchen where sometimes an assistant stayed. There was a fireplace, and books everywhere of course. Their windows looked out on roof-tops and a church spire—no ocean, no garden. Among their en-viable collection of art—Ed Ruscha, Richard Diebenkorn, Brice Marden, Richard Serra—hung a map of Sacramento and the his-toric Didion mantilla, passed down through the generations since pioneer days. The outdoor patio furniture from Brentwood filled one room. Joan lived her last decades in New York, but she kept California in her sights.

New York had and has changed dramatically since Joan was a young woman there. It has changed dramatically since I was a young woman there, when Didion was middle aged. Skinny, sleek skyscrapers, appropriately dubbed splinters, have sprouted across Manhattan like spiky glass weeds. There are fewer homeless peo-ple living in refrigerator boxes, thankfully, but there are still too many. Construction abounds, and yet all the floors in the build-ing across from my hotel are empty and many storefronts remain shuttered post pandemic.

And yet much is the same as when Didion worked in the Gray-bar Building or lunched with Robert B. Silvers at the Knickerbocker

Club (both of those edifices still exist, for instance). The streets remain slotted in their grid arrangement, except in the oldest parts of town where they follow old settler trails. The light still filters through the skyscrapers and shoots down the streets, turning indigo on summer evenings, "and over the course of an hour or so this blue deepens, becomes more intense even as it darkens and fades," as Didion writes in *Blue Nights*. The sounds of cars braying, people yelling, and air blasting up from the subways still fill the streets at all hours, so that even at night, the rumble of the trains hundreds of feet below Lexington Avenue or the siren of an ambulance becomes soothingly familiar. In the dank heat of summer, the smells still stick to the air like paste. For every new Trumpian monstrosity there's a concrete art deco time capsule, like the Fuller Building, just around the corner from *Mademoiselle*'s old offices (now a glass box), with its three-story entryway topped by two statues of muscled men in skirts surrounding a clock that long ago lost its arms. Maybe when Joan used to walk by here on her way from work back to the Barbizon, she could tell what time it was by looking up at this vestige of early twentieth-century optimism.

I'll be honest: To me, the Upper East Side is the least interesting neighborhood in Manhattan. It's filthy with money and dull with monochromatic privilege. When I lived downtown, I only passed through these streets on my way to one of the art museums on Fifth Avenue or to Central Park. But now, as a middle-aged woman myself, I can understand why Didion chose to live out her final years here. Yes, she had a taste for the high life. She and John dined regularly at the famous Carlyle Hotel seven blocks up Madison Avenue. She also favored Sette Mezzo, more of a new-money pasta joint than the vintage Carlyle, but still dauntingly, and deliciously, high end. And of course there is Elio's, another Italian eatery and a famous hangout for writers; Joan and John had a standard table up front, where they could see and be seen. Her book covers hang on the walls. These restaurants and more were all within strolling distance of the Didion-Dunne apartment. After decades of dependency on cars, the walkability of Manhattan must have felt liberating.

The Upper East Side is safe, quiet, clean, even tranquil. That made it boring to me as a youth, but now, I appreciate its centuries-old carriage houses and brownstones. It feels very much like Paris. And of course, there's the number one reason to live uptown: Central Park. Didion may have critiqued its copycat European design and corrupt capitalist origins in "Sentimental Journeys," but she walked its paths every day. The Seventy-First Street entrance was just a block from her apartment, and from there, she would pass the pond where hobbyists race toy boats, the bronze Alice in Wonderland sculpture, the Metropolitan Museum of Art, the Great Lawn, the Turtle Pond, the boathouse on the lake filled with rented rowboats, the Delacorte Theater where she could see extraordinary actors perform Shakespeare, the zoo—and so on and so forth. When Didion could no longer walk to the park, an assistant pushed her in a wheelchair.

The Didion-Dunnes spent fifteen good years here. Silvers was keeping them both busy writing. John's 1997 account of Hollywood screenwriting, *Monster*, was a bestseller. Quintana was also making her way in New York publishing and, in 2003, got married. That fall, Joan and John traveled to Paris.

And then the first shoe dropped: On December 25, 2003, Quintana was hospitalized.

On December 30, Joan and John returned from their daily visit to their only child in the intensive care unit at Beth Israel North. What had seemed to be a bad cold or flu had turned into a septic infection much more dire; Q was in a coma. Decades of tending to their daughter's mental illnesses and instabilities, and now this.

On the ride home, and as they settled into the apartment, John was tired. He had been irritable, despondent, for some time. His heart trouble had worsened, and after numerous episodes of atrial fibrillation followed by cardioversion, doctors implanted a pacemaker in June 2003. In the cab on the way back from the ICU, either on December 29 or 30, he told Joan everything he had accomplished in his life was worthless. And now, their daughter might be dying.

"I don't think I'm up for this," he said to Didion either on December 30, or the day before.

"You don't get a choice," answered Didion, curtly.

The great author was the pragmatic caretaker now. She built a fire because the warmth of the hearth always made them feel at home. She poured them drinks, prepared dinner. And as her husband of thirty-nine years sat at the table, the surgical reparations to his broken heart proved no match for this latest emotional burden. John collapsed into his chair, and then, as the tiny Didion tried to lift him, onto the floor.

John Gregory Dunne would never again read the newspaper over breakfast with his wife Joan Didion. He would not screen phone calls for her when she had a migraine or finish her sentences when her mouth failed her. They would no longer write movie dialogue as they drove up the coast of California or give each other notes on their manuscripts. There would be no more Hawaiian hotel rooms with Quintana.

In twenty months, there would be no more Quintana.

There would just be Joan. Lone Didion.

Liminal is a word that cultural critics like to toss around. It refers to in-between or transitional states: thresholds, boundaries. Morgues are liminal spaces, where bodies are housed between life and death, between death and the grave, or the pyre.

For nine months, Joan Didion existed in a liminal state. She went into a kind of insanity, where she believed that if only she would do certain things—such as keep all John's clothes and papers and books exactly as he left them, with the dictionary left open to the precise page, the shoes still in his closet—then the mistake of his death would be corrected. He would not be dead anymore. She could reverse fate.

"I could not give away the rest of his shoes," she wrote. "I stood there for a moment, then realized why: he would need shoes if he was to return."

It was, as she said, "magical thinking."

Central to Didion's magical thinking was her belief that she needed to know the results of John's autopsy to find out precisely when and by what biological mechanism he died, so that the damage could be corrected, and he would be alive. She didn't want to just see the autopsy report; the cool customer wanted to attend the autopsy of her husband's body. "I had watched those other autopsies with John, I owed him his own, it was fixed in my mind at that moment that he would be in the room if I were on the table," she wrote. If she could somehow fix his liminal state, then she would also be freed from her own.

In the midst of her grieving, Didion was also engaged in the quite unmagical effort to keep Quintana alive—without the father's assistance, without her husband's support. When Q finally woke from her coma, Joan had to break the news of Dunne's death to their daughter. She had to do it all over again the next time Quintana awoke, because the deathly ill woman did not remember. The loss of the life partner was coupled with the mortal struggle of the only child. A struggle that Q, and Joan, lost.

This was worse than the atrocities Joan had imagined in her novels.

"Our family, particularly the Dunne side, we've got suicides and airplane crashes and murders, and Joan and John had been spared it all," notes Griffin Dunne. "And I always looked to them as like, it's not going to touch them. It's not going to touch them, thank God, it's not going to touch them. And then it's a fucking double play, and they get it all at once. I always thought that was incredibly cruel."

There were many warning signs. Didion goes over them again and again in both *Magical Thinking* and *Blue Nights*. John's repeated heart trouble. His lethargy and anxiety all fall. The teenage Quintana lying on her bedroom floor, wanting to disappear into the Earth. The adult daughter, still despairing. Perhaps it is not surprising that the epic tragedies became the source material for Didion's most successful book. Nine months after Dunne's death, Joan did what her mother first told her to do sixty-four years earlier: write. For three months, she sat at her computer in her Upper East Side office. The resulting book, *The Year of Magi-*

cal Thinking, is an intimately personal reflection and a treatise on mourning as a state of being. In many ways it marked the writer's return to her early style: confessional, episodic, lyrical, incantatory. Gone are the long locutions and paragraphs of "Sentimental Journeys." Here are the white spaces, the repetition of phrases, the gradual revelation of information, the uncertain voice of the unreliable narrator. Many of the paragraphs are one sentence long, just a few words:

"I remember a silence."

"All that and I had not even driven down there."

"Everything else has seemed normal."

Didion tells the process of her collapse and coping in overlapping layers, as if she can only handle reliving so much at one time—as if the reader can only handle having so much revealed at one time. She repeats herself, retraces her steps, builds her progress incrementally but steadily. Short sentences. Baby steps.

It's as if the complex passages packed with complicated ideas that Didion mastered for *NYRB* have splintered. *Magical Thinking* is the diary of a breakdown from the queen of cool. It is also a love story, a romance written by the woman who once called marriage the ultimate betrayal. In a sense, it is Didion's most human book, as she shares her extraordinary experience of the most ordinary thing: death. (Although I don't know how many readers can relate to the desire to attend the autopsy of one's own spouse.)

"The difficulty that she had in her life: all of that would just make most of us pack up our things and go home," says Mitchell Kaplan. "Her mind was such that she had to somehow get to the heart of it, she had to explain it, she had to live with it, she had to taste it, to roll it around in her mind. And then she was able to forge this great heart out of it which then touched so many people. She got the human condition right in a lot of ways."

Published in 2005, *Magical Thinking* was on the *New York Times* bestseller list for twenty-four weeks, has sold over a million copies, won the National Book Award for nonfiction, and was a finalist for the Pulitzer Prize and the National Book Critics Circle Award. It is widely regarded as one of the definitive portraits of the process of grieving, the book that you give to a friend who has lost someone important. During an extensive tour for the book, many people approached Didion at readings to talk about how *Magical Thinking* had helped them survive their own losses.

"She was doing these signings where people were coming up and unloading their grief stories, their stories about being widowed or losing a child or whatever," says David L. Ulin, who interviewed Didion on stage during this book tour at Vroman's Bookstore in Pasadena. "It was really profound, I think, and cathartic for a lot of people, probably for her as well as for the people she was talking to."

"We tell ourselves stories in order to live," Didion said in *The White Album*. Throughout her career, the writer found that articulation and documentation were ways for her to connect with a world from which she had a tendency to disassociate. By telling the story of her husband's death and her daughter's illness, the author broke the spell of magical thinking. Word by word, sentence by sentence, she built her escape route. When she finished the book, one year after Dunne's heart attack, she left the liminal state of grieving and began her life as a widow.

Joan still had her words. Her editor and friend Bob Silvers understood the power of narrative in her survival. "After my husband John died, when my daughter Quintana was very sick, Bob grasped my situation, and blessedly kept me writing—on the Bush administration, on euthanasia," Didion wrote in the *NYRB*. "He intuited that I would either work or I would die."

Didion finished writing *Magical Thinking* on December 31, 2004. Quintana died less than eight months later, before the book was published. When an interviewer asked her if she had considered rewriting the book to incorporate this death, Joan responded with a two-word answer that is quintessentially Didion in its simplicity and completeness:

"It's finished."

In 2007, Didion wrote a play version of *Magical Thinking*, incorporating parts of *Blue Nights*, that opened as a one-woman Broadway show at the Booth Theatre, starring her good friend Vanessa Redgrave as Didion. Joan attended every rehearsal and performance, eating dinner at a café table that the staff set up for her. She was living out her childhood fantasies of the theater, albeit as a character, not an actor. It must have been surreal for the petite writer to see herself reimagined as a statuesque movie star.

She was reliving the worst experiences of her life every performance—but she also got to spend time with John and Quintana's memories each day.

13

Diner

She liked to sit at the tables in the center rather than the banquettes along the sides, perhaps because as a short person, she preferred to be able to slide her chair up, the better to eat soft scrambled eggs with toast and read the *New York Times*. For years, she came to this diner several times a week with her husband. After that she sat alone, a small, quiet woman. "She was not shy but private," recalls John Catechisis, who has served food at 3 Guys Restaurant for decades, and on a Sunday morning less than a year after her death, he remembers regular customer Joan Didion fondly as a woman of few words. A few booths and tables are occupied by single women of a certain age on this fall day: widows, divorcées, professionals—women dining alone.

The twentieth-century author M. F. K. Fisher—mother of all foodies—wrote about the oddity and joy of enjoying a solo meal in public. It is the first letter in her *Alphabet for Gourmets*: "To dine alone is preferable to any other way for me," she writes. In her memoir *The Gastronomical Me*, Fisher describes the way her self-sufficiency on her frequent oceanic voyages upsets others: "More often than not people who see me on trains and in ships, or in restaurants, feel a kind of resentment of me since I taught myself to enjoy being alone. Women are puzzled, which they hate to be, and jealous of the way I am served, with such agreeable courtesy, and of what I'm eating and drinking, which is almost never the sort of thing they order for themselves. And men are puzzled too, in a more personal way. I anger them as males."

Musician Andrew Bird was intrigued, not angered, by the thought of Joan Didion dining alone. Two tracks on his 2022 album *Inside Problems* ("Atomized" and "Lone Didion") are inspired by the writer. "It was a confluence of things that led me to work Didion into these two songs," Bird said in an email. "For one, I was reading *The Year of Magical Thinking* and revisiting *Slouching Towards Bethlehem*. At the same time I was thinking about a story a friend, who worked in a restaurant where Joan and John were regulars, told me. It was December 2003 and Joan and John had been coming in as regulars every Saturday night for a while. My friend then noticed their absence for a month or so until Joan came in alone once and ordered their usual drinks. I was so moved by this story especially while reading *The Year of Magical Thinking*, which chronicles the loss she suffered during that absence. She talks about not being an 'idea' writer and I see the point she's making: that the facts laid out articulately and with skill can be more powerful than describing your emotions. She honors her loss by keeping it dry and matter of fact."

At age seventy, Joan Didion found herself by herself, eating, walking, reading, thinking, writing. In less than two years the fortress of the small nuclear family that had protected her for decades was destroyed. Her parents were deceased; her only sibling was thousands of miles away; she had no blood relatives nearby. The entire country separated her from her beloved California. "She told me, 'Don't move to New York,'" her cousin Julia Armstrong-Totten says. "She really regretted it. I think she felt that things were much more complicated in some ways, that basic living could be more complicated. And she had been having health issues at this point. I don't know why but she was very adamant. 'Don't,' she said, 'don't.'"

Members of John's family were close; his brother Nick and nephew Griffin in particular rallied around her after John's death. So did others: her agent, Lynn Nesbit, and friend Calvin Trillin. Having recently lost his beloved wife, Alice, Trillin understood grief. He brought Didion congee, a kind of Asian porridge— comfort food. "There's not a whole lot you can do, just be present, that's about it," he recalls. "I'm not sure there's any good way of dealing with it, you just have to go through it. I brought congee. Then one day, Joan said, 'I think I've had enough congee.'"

For the first time since her *Vogue* days, Didion was living alone. John's books and clothes, and photos of and by Quintana, were everywhere in the apartment, constant reminders of what had been, and what had been lost. But Didion prized her autonomy. All her life, she had been an introvert, someone who craved and needed solitude to work. Wherever she lived, she had her own office, where she would retreat every morning to work. When she was finishing a book, she would hole up in her old bedroom in her parents' house, or at a hideaway in Hawai'i. She had often traveled by herself, on campaign trails and book tours, when researching and writing.

After her life partner's death, Didion fought to be able to stay by herself, on her own terms—even as her body gave out on her. She called it "maintaining momentum" in *Blue Nights*. She stayed in the apartment that had been her final home with John. She lived eighteen years after his death, a single woman, but increasingly supported by a loving circle of family, friends, colleagues, aides, and her dog, Ellie—not a fancy English sheep dog, but a Wheaten terrier.

It's remarkable that Didion had her greatest success not only as a postmenopausal female—a time when society likes to put us out to pasture—but during her years of solitude. Granted, she had this success based on her writing about her family; she was a professional widow in a sense. But what could be more genius and generous than to document, interpret, and validate this experience that is lived by so many women? Didion was "A Single Woman" of a certain age, a type described by her contemporary Nina Simone (born one year before Didion) in 1993. The song, written by Simone, describes a woman who has always been "on a private cloud" but now finds herself truly alone. "There was a time . . . I can't remember when," the iconoclastic genius and Black activist sings. "The house was full of love but then again / It might have been imagination's plan / Just to help along / One single woman."

Didion modeled a kind of self-determined womanhood that is the goal of so many writers, artists, and working women who feel called to a creative life, who strive to "Do what I want, live how I wanna live," as Destiny's Child sing in "Independent Women Part 1." She voiced the desires and fears of multiple generations in the wake of the 1960s countercultural shift that she documented with skepticism even as she profited from its gains. We know through the culture at large and through our own experiences that having it all—family, career, love, Corvette—is nigh impossible, and yet Joan seemed to be the woman who had it all. Until she didn't.

The writer Caitlin Flanagan said in *The Atlantic* that "to really love Joan Didion—to have been blown over by things like the smell of jasmine and the packing list she kept by her suitcase—you have to be female." David Rieff, David L. Ulin, Hilton Als, John Leonard, and thousands of other Didion acolytes would disagree. But female readers and writers take particular inspiration and meaning from her work. "I do feel that that is sort of the gift that she has given to us, as writers, that she empowers writers, women writers, in particular, and helps us find our voice," says Steffie Nelson, editor of *Slouching Towards Los Angeles*. "She gave a new voice to the feminine experience, this unapologetic voice. She was not putting on any airs or trying to be one of the boys; it was very feminine, but it was never messy or overly emotional, but it was still revealing and even vulnerable."

Danyel Smith was attending high school in Inglewood, in Los Angeles, when a teacher introduced her to Didion's nonfiction. "I remember feeling totally intimidated by the language and feeling like I would never be able to write as well as Joan Didion," the journalist and novelist says. "But at the same time, feeling so inspired to see sentences like hers, which to me were a lot of very straightforward, declarative, evocative sentences that seemed short, clear, and to have a very deep point. And I felt like in every class, that talent was always being ascribed to Hemingway. I had gotten really tired of that. And here was Joan Didion, who was doing it."

And yet, despite her influence as a trailblazer, when it comes to being an icon for women, Joan Didion can be deeply problematic. She never called herself a feminist, but then she eschewed labels and clubs in general; she wasn't a joiner. She did write, say, do, and not write, not say, and not do things that were at best unsisterly and at worst hostile to gender-based activism and analysis. Exhibit A: "The Women's Movement," an essay she wrote in 1972 that pretty brutally knocked the way second-wave feminism had become mired in "little sophistries, wish-fulfillment, self-loathing and bitter fantasies." Didion's critique was not entirely without merit; in the 1990s, a new generation would also voice concerns about second-wave feminism's insularity. Joan could land a good punch at clichéd notions of femininity: "One is constantly struck, in the accounts of lesbian relationships which appear from time to time in movement literature, by the emphasis on the superior 'tenderness' of the relationship, the 'gentleness' of the sexual connection, as if the participants were wounded birds," she said in "The Women's Movement." But the essay was overall a mean-spirited attack on second-wave feminism that revealed more about Didion's lack of consciousness than the real growing pains of an important and necessary movement for change. It's not that she was in denial about her gender, but her definition of womanhood was rooted in a bodily determinism that, while wonderfully goth, was not exactly enlightened: "What it is like to be a woman, the reconcilable difference of it—that sense of living one's deepest life underwater, that dark involvement with blood and birth and death."

In "The Women's Movement," Didion revealed her blindered privilege. "That many women are victims of condescension and exploitation and sexual stereotyping was scarcely news, but neither was it news that other women are not: nobody forces women to buy the package," she wrote. Of course, many women—particularly those without her race and class advantages—were and are precisely forced to buy the package. #MeNot could have been Joan's hashtag.

Didion could be equally infuriating on issues of gender in her private life. It was apparently a bone of contention in her friendship with the artist and writer Eve Babitz. In a letter discovered in 2022, that was possibly never sent but was written about extensively in both *Vanity Fair* and *The Atlantic* (glossies circling the blood of a posthumous literary alleged catfight), the author of *Eve's Hollywood* attacked her friend for refusing to read *A Room of One's Own*, a pretty grievous offense for someone who loved literature as much as Joan did. We know little about the context of this 1972 missive, found in Babitz's room after her death in 2021—six days before Didion died. Babitz wrote that Joan was mad at Virginia Woolf "about her diaries," whatever that means. But the document reveals a consequential divide between the two groundbreaking writers on the burdens and responsibilities they faced as women. Much of Eve's ire was aimed at Didion's marriage. She repeatedly addressed her friend and mentor as "Mrs. Dunn" [*sic*] and accused her of playing the quiet wife protected by the dominant man and disconnected from those less fortunate or less dependent. "You prefer to be with the boys snickering at the silly women," Babitz wrote.

Didion had indeed committed herself to a rather conventional heterosexual relationship. While she was in many ways John's equal, and even his superior in terms of fame and talent, she still signed her name "Joan Didion Dunne." She let him do the talking while she made dinner. It was an arrangement that worked for her—that in fact protected and enabled her. But it scarcely represented the overthrow of, let alone the gentle pushback against, the feminine mystique that her peers were fomenting. Didion seemed to enjoy the frisson of what we would now call hypermasculinity: She wrote about her attraction to John Wayne and Howard Hughes, defended Ernest Hemingway and Norman Mailer. When she met him, her husband was known to get into bar brawls and brothels. One of Joan's best friends was Earl McGrath, a rather legendary scenester who worked with music-biz bad boys Ahmet Ertegun and the Rolling Stones and was manipulative and abusive toward the more vulnerable Babitz; in the 2022 *Vanity Fair* story on Babitz and Didion, writer Lili Anolik accuses McGrath of pimping Eve out to Ertegun. Scott Rudin produced the play of *Magical Thinking*; his bullying behavior was brought to public attention in 2021, but decades before #MeToo, Dunne wrote with humorous affection about the producer's notorious volatility. Given her husband's documentation of Rudin's rudeness and having worked with him on movies, Didion clearly knew the toxic side of this asshole mogul.

In Joan's defense, it was pretty impossible not to break bread with shitty men if you travailed in the culture industry, or just about anywhere in America, in the twentieth century. (And in the twenty-first century.) Joan's early aversion to the feminist movement was an example of the ways in which she was not always conscious of how her own life was shaped by power structures. It was an understanding she came to over the decades. You can easily find a more enlightened side of Didion. Just look at the work.

A few years after "The Women's Movement," Joan penned an appreciation of the painter Georgia O'Keeffe that ripples with what the writer Ellen Willis called "the feminist critique." I don't mean Didion applied some litmus test to the artist's life, work, and words (just as I am trying not to do with Joan). It means she wrote about another woman with an understanding of what it means to be in a woman's body in a world controlled by men. Where "The Women's Movement" sputters with derision and pettiness, "Georgia O'Keeffe" flows with passion and compassion: "In Texas she had her sister Claudia with her for a while, and in the late afternoons they would walk away from town and toward the horizon and watch the evening star come out."

Ever suspicious of the groupthink and self-righteousness of politics, Didion homed in on individuals. She may have had her doubts about the women's movement, but she loved women. Over and over, Joan was drawn to strong female subjects in her journalism: Joan Baez, Patty Hearst, Martha Stewart, Elizabeth Hardwick, Helen Gurley Brown. She was even sympathetic to Manson Family member Linda Kasabian (less so, however, to Nancy Reagan; sisterhood only went so far.) Her very earliest articles were driven by what can only be called feminism, even if it's not a word that Joan used. For *Mademoiselle* she wrote about the gender inequity of San Francisco media. Her second essay for *Vogue*, "On Self-Respect," has probably been pinned to some young woman's wall somewhere every day since it was published in 1961, its words still inspiring: "To have that sense of one's intrinsic worth which constitutes self-respect is potentially to have everything: the ability to discriminate, to love and to remain indifferent." R-E-S-P-E-C-T indeed.

It's interesting that Didion chose a woman who murdered her husband for her first crime story. While the portrait of the homicidal protagonist of "Some Dreamers of the Golden Dream" is unforgiving, it is not unsympathetic. "Sentimental Journeys" is primarily a takedown of entrenched racism and corruption in New York, but it also offers a critique of sexual assault coverage that relies heavily and explicitly on the work of women's rights icon Susan Brownmiller.

All of Didion's novels are centered on female protagonists. Granted, these women are not typically heroic or even admirable. Rather they are antiheroes, fallible beings who are neither lionized nor villainized—neither Madonnas nor whores. Joan wrote about women as she saw them, and as she saw herself (Joan Didion is the name of the author in *Democracy*, a character personifying the concept of the unreliable narrator), not as she wanted them to be. Maria, Lily, Elena, Charlotte, and Inez struggle: to control their destinies, to express themselves, to parent, to be. What is feminism about if not women's struggle?

In her screenwriting, Didion also pushed back against the gender stereotypes of the trade. In a fax to Jon Avnet, director of *Up Close and Personal*, for which the Didion-Dunnes were writing the screenplay, the couple wrote: "JDD says this is deeply offensive to her, reinforcing the notion that women who are 'successful' at what they do 'don't want children,' i.e., are selfish, self-centered, and thwart the nurturing wishes of the men with whom they are involved." Undoubtedly, these portrayals felt personal to Joan.

The piece in which Didion most explicitly addressed her feelings about gender roles and restrictions was the speech she delivered for the Friends of the Bancroft Library at the University of California, Berkeley, in 1978. "The California Woman" begins with Joan regretting the title as "the worst kind of meaningless generalization. . . . As if California had one woman." Having thus summed up her disdain for the boxes of identity politics, Didion went on to deliver a speech in praise of several specific California women (all white), including the architect Julia Morgan, economist Jessica Blanche Peixotto, writer Gertrude Stein, dancer Isadora Duncan, and Joan's own ancestors. (Parts of this speech later appeared in *Where I Was From.*) Didion celebrates something I noticed as soon as I moved from New York to San Francisco in the early 1990s: that women were able to do far more interesting and important work on the Best Coast than on the seaboard that was still tied to traditional, European values. California, after all, is the state that gave the country the first female Speaker of the House and vice president.

On the one hand, Didion jokes about the ways in which even the California women she admires fell into gender essentialism: "She was immensely eclectic—adaptable to a fault—she would construct whatever fantasy the client seemed to require—which is perhaps the only distinctively feminine aspect to her career," she says of Morgan. But, echoing her criticism of the women's movement, she praises refusals to see gender as an obstacle. She falls so in love with a quote from the writer Mina Curtiss that she types it in all caps: "I HAVE FOLLOWED MY INSTINCTS AND TRIED TO USE COMMON SENSE IN MY BEHAVIOR." She could see this manifesto of gut plus pragmatism being carved on her gravestone, she says.

It did not become her epitaph, but it is a line worth repeating: "I have followed my instincts and tried to use common sense in my behavior."

The talk, available as a typed manuscript at the Bancroft Library, is a kind of lodestone key to/summation of Didion's world. Here is her great subject, the American empire: Visiting London and Paris the fall prior, "it seemed to me then that all of America was very far away—I FELT IT VISCERALLY AS THE NEW WORLD." Flying back to Los Angeles, "the enormity of that empty space between our own coasts struck me as it had not in years. We are still different here. We are still looking to the Orient rather than to Europe." Here is her disillusionment with the frontier myth of the Golden State and her own family's role in it, "which was in no way revisionist—but simply a more detailed version of the Wagons West panel in the textbook illustrations." Here is her Western disdain for Atlantic snobbery: "In the presence of certain high Eastern accents I fall so helplessly into the Okie diction of the Sacramento Valley as to be unintelligible."

And then there is this statement of purpose, a 180-degree reversal from the talk's opening dismissal of its title: "As I thought about it I realized that I have been writing about the California woman all my adult life, that what it means to be a California woman has been a great question to me—the California woman has been—if not exactly my subject—at least quite certainly my material."

Being a woman in a long line of mothers of courage, in community with other women, and a link in a chain to future women was intrinsic to Joan Didion's identity. She looked back to her great-great-

great-grandmothers and beyond, and she looked forward for her daughter and nieces and cousins and friends. For proof of her maternal capacity, consider the many women she supported in her life. She helped Babitz publish her first book (Babitz dedicated it in part to Joan and John "for having to be who I'm not"). The writer Susanna Moore lived at times with the Didion-Dunnes in the Franklin house. "Her silence was a refuge which I often preferred to conversation," the author of *In the Cut* said at Didion's memorial. Joan's younger cousin Julia Armstrong-Totten, an art historian, house- and dog-sat in Brentwood and would often stay at the Didion-Dunne pied-à-terre at Alwyn Court. "They kind of took me under their wing," Armstrong-Totten says. "That's how I saw it." Didion mentored the writer Sara Davidson, who in turn has passed on in her own books and articles much of the advice Joan gave her. Didion championed and befriended the writer Maxine Hong Kingston, petitioning the American Academy and Institute of Arts and Letters to give her a Livings award, saying "her two books published to date seem to me strange & wonderful and entirely original."

And of course there was Q. In "The California Woman," the writer whose vocation was launched when her mother gave her a notebook says that she plans to pass the quilt made by her great-great-grandmother on to either her daughter or her brother's oldest daughter because: "Daughters carry these souvenirs, and they also carry down the narrative, which is perhaps why women figure very large in the narration."

And there is a statement of feminist literary criticism and historiography if there ever was one.

Orchid

When Joan Didion gave a book as a present, she would some-times press a flower between its pages. She also gave gifts of plants notated by specimen (truth) and framed as art (beauty), flattening petals and pistils between Lucite, handwriting the sci-entific names and jotting the date in the corner. In one picture given to Ellen Beatriz Griffin Dunne, and now owned by her son Griffin Dunne, there are two phalaenopsis orchids, a wood fern, and a yellow marguerite daisy. The tight cursive annotating each flora is clearly Joan's, including the note at the bottom: "Pressed by Q.R.D. for E.G.D. January 28, 1973." Apparently Joan and Quintana Roo Dunne, then six, made this gift together.

Whatever her feelings about Haight-Ashbury hippies, Joan Didion was a flower child herself.

Blossoms bloom throughout her books, as prevalent—but less commented on—as snakes. The green Post-its I use to mark the floral mentions match the red snake warnings, transforming my Didion library into a string of Christmas lights. Didion's references are very specific; she knew her horticulture. "White phalaenopsis and cymbidium orchids" fill the rooms "In Hollywood." There are "sprays of vanda orchids" at the Star Market in the Kahala Mall. Nancy Reagan clips rhododendrons for the camera. On the first page of *Democracy*, the air of the Pacific atoll where Jack Lovett watches the A-bomb test smells like gardenias. In *The Last Thing He Wanted*, there is a long list of flowers in Elena's spiral-bound notebook, including Cecile Brunner roses, Henri Martin roses, Paulii roses, Chicago Peace roses, Scarlet Fire roses—and those are just the roses. There are also fresh roses in the bathrooms in a hotel in "In Bogota."

Just as her fear of snakes was real, so was Didion's passion for plants more than a metaphor. It's possible her anthophilia predates her herpetophobia; at age nine she would miss the bus so that she could walk home from school and buy a "nickel pansy" at a greenhouse. In *Blue Nights*, Didion repeatedly notes the stephanotis braided into Quintana's hair at her wedding and wonders if her daughter has chosen the small white flowers because they grew outside the terrace doors at the Brentwood house. There were also "beds of lavender" as well as mint on Chadbourne Avenue. In fact, Didion planted an extensive Renaissance-style herb garden when they bought their "suburbia house"; it was her favorite thing about that home. Flowers could render the pragmatist giddy and whimsical. One night, when throwing a party in Brentwood Park, Joan decided to decorate the swimming pool with floating candles and gardenias. Already dressed with an hour to spare, she carefully set the flowers and votives afloat. But she did not think to turn off the filter system. In moments, the flames had been doused, and the candles bounced against the drains, already clogged with blossoms.

In the 1970s, when Didion sought a tranquil place to ruminate alone, she drove down the Pacific Coast Highway from Trancas. At the exit to Zuma Beach, she took not a right toward the ocean but a left into the hills. A few miles down a bumpy back road, nestled in one of the canyons that lead from the mountains to the sea, she found paradise. Not the fantasy tabula rasa of frontier myth but a haven of nature created by man, with "the most aqueous filtered light, the softest tropical air, the most silent clouds of flowers." The Arthur Freed greenhouses where "arcs of white phalaenopsis trembled overhead" were tended by a Mexican Adam, Amado Vazquez, "one of a handful of truly great orchid breeders in the world." Vazquez won a place in Didion's pantheon of mortals by fulfilling a lifelong wish of hers: He let Didion wander in "the primeval silence" of the greenhouses filled with her great love: orchids, the plant that more than any other perfumed her places and her pages.

This was paradise controlled, contained, and carefully curated. It was always 72 degrees in the greenhouses. The humidity was kept at 60 percent. The exquisitely colorful and delicate hothouse flowers could last a century and cost hundreds of thousands of dollars—a far cry from nickel pansies.

In Vazquez, Didion found a kindred spirit, a muse, a subject she would do her best not to sell out. Her portrait of the orchid king, in "Quiet Days in Malibu," is precise and poetic. "Amado Vazquez is a Mexican national who has lived in Los Angeles County as a resident alien since 1947," it begins. She wryly notes how the spelling of his surname is "mysteriously altered by everyone at Arthur Freed except the Vazquezes themselves." He is one of twenty master orchid growers in the world, and she prefers to talk to him rather than to the bosses who own the greenhouses (prior to Amado founding his own place, Zuma Canyon Orchids). Vazquez filled Joan's arms with cattleyas, the queen of orchids. He spoke with her of his loves: country (Mexico), family, and orchids. "It seemed to me that day that I had never talked to anyone so direct and unembarrassed about the things he loved," she wrote in *The White Album*.

Orchids are the ultimate hothouse flower, exquisite and delicate blossoms that require careful tending and copious moisture—not exactly typical California conditions, except in shaded crevices like Zuma Canyon. Amado Vazquez was an orchid alchemist. He created new species through careful breeding conducted under a full moon at high tide, not for romantic reasons but for scientific ones: He found the conditions for fertilization most propitious then. (Is it wrong that I wonder if Joan and John tried this?) The greenhouses were largely stud farms; every time Joan would try to take a plant home, he would shake his head: "For breeding, not for sale today." In 1982, at Zuma Canyon, Vazquez crossed two *Phalaenopses*, or moth orchids: Music, a white flower ribbed with fuchsia, and Hugo Freed, named after the author, founder of the Malibu Orchid Society, and brother of the Hollywood musical producer Alan Freed, owner of the greenhouse where Vazquez worked. He dubbed the hybrid Joan Didion. Vazquez also crossed *Phal. James McPherson*, a white orchid with lighter purple veins than Music, and *Phal. stuartina*, white petals and sepals with a yellow and red labellum, to create *Phal. Quintana Roo Dunne.*

Country. Family. Orchids.

Georgia O'Keeffe was asked why she so often chose flowers as her subject. Didion quotes the answer in her 1976 essay on the painter: "A flower touches almost everyone's heart."

We know a lot about Joan Didion the intellectual, the ironist, the goth, the grieving widow and mother. But we don't know as much about this Joan, the woman who gave pressed flowers as gifts, who wrote warm thank you notes to old and new friends, who touched hearts. Contrary to public perception, the writer actually was often a happy, loving human being. "Joan's really a rather cheerful person who drives a bright yellow Corvette," her husband pointed out to a reporter from New York who was looking for "the Kafka of Brentwood Park."

Interviewing people about Didion—those who knew her well and those who didn't know her at all—and reading what people have said about her, I sometimes feel like she can be a Rorschach test: Everyone sees in her what they want to see; she is a screen on which we project ourselves. You could say this about any subject, of course; it's the parable of the elephant and the blind men. But I think there is something about Joan—maybe her soft-spokenness, her small frame, her femininity—that, despite the concreteness of her prose, lends itself to projection. Julia Armstrong-Totten agrees: "She could be so different with everyone she encountered, even I think with those who considered themselves to be among her closest friends," her cousin says. "Joan was pretty cryptic when she spoke, and I think somehow it must have influenced how her friends processed what she said."

This shape-shifting quality was apparent at the public memorial held for Didion on September 21, 2022, at St. John the Divine in New York. The respectful service, held nine months after her death because of the coronavirus pandemic, was organized by Shelley Wanger, Joan's editor at Knopf. The lineup offered a who's who of prominent writers, editors, musicians, actors, and politicians, including Jerry Brown, Justice Anthony M. Kennedy, Griffin Dunne, Calvin Trillin, Patti Smith, Hilton Als, Jia Tolentino, and David Remnick. The crowd was similarly sprinkled with luminaries and literati: Fran Lebowitz, Annie Leibovitz, Anjelica Huston, Greta Gerwig, Liam Neeson, Lynn Nesbit, Katrina vanden Heuvel, Carl Bernstein. Fans, lesser-known associates, and Columbia University students filled the back half of the church.

St. John is an Episcopal cathedral. "As it was in the beginning, is now, and ever shall be, world without end." These words from the Episcopal doxology comforted Joan Didion, who was raised Episcopalian, her whole life. She became someone who believed in the power of narrative, the primacy of family, the joy of cooking, Buddhist philosophy, and the California sky more than in any deity. But she still found solace in this mantra and in the gothic beauty of the Cathedral of St. John, where her daughter married, her husband's memorial was held, and the family's remains are now entombed.

Eulogies focused on Didion's public persona, on her writing. Only one relative—Dunne—spoke. There had been a small family service in the spring; it was then that Joan's ashes were placed in the cathedral's columbarium. Still, most of the speakers had personal relationships with the deceased. Two women who knew Didion intimately offered portraits of their friend that captured her as a human and a thinker in very different ways—speeches that reflected the speakers as well as the subject. Susanna Moore recalled the terse but memorable advice given to her over the decades by this woman who wrote intensely but spoke little, including "Write it again," "Crazy is never interesting," and "Evil is the absence of seriousness." Susan Traylor, who met Quintana Roo Dunne when they were both four and became best friends forever, told funny, charming stories of how Joan became a kind of second mother to her, stricter than her own but a reliable pillar on which to lean in hard times. Tales of a mom who served chocolate soufflé to children because she didn't know how to make a birthday cake and sang silly songs about mice way past their age-appropriateness revealed the fabled skeptic as a warm, awkward human being. "Malibu was out there in those days, but we all had each other," Traylor said.

The public discourse about Didion's legacy has also varied, provoking sometimes polar responses. Since *Slouching Towards Bethlehem*, Didion has largely been accepted by the public and the publishing establishment as a preeminent voice of her generation, particularly as a journalist and essayist. In the second half of her life Didion was given the George Polk Award, a National Book Award, the Medal for Distinguished Contribution to American Letters, and the National Humanities Medal by Barack Obama. But it's important to point out that she never won a Pulitzer, Guggenheim, MacArthur, or other honors that often anoint (and finance) authors of her talent and status.

As happens, the intense praise that accrued to her work over the decades fostered backlash. Some critics have attacked the very precision of her writing, wanting there to be cracks in the facade of the "archpriestess of cool," as writer Daphne Merkin dubbed her. Others have complained that she is too depressing. I tend to think of such comments as the lit crit equivalent of "Smile baby!" catcalls. Women can't win: We're either too emotional or not emotional enough. Didion definitely wrote in a wry, meticulous fashion. Understanding and controlling narrative and style was one of her main subjects and points; she practiced what she preached. She could also be hysterically funny, extremely personal, and intensely moral.

Often Didion is attacked because of what others have said about her as opposed to what she herself said—the backlash against "the cult of Saint Joan" (another Merkin phrase). I refuse to resent any woman for being successful. Besides, no one could be more dismissive of sycophancy than the saint herself. Griffin Dunne recalls moderating an event with his aunt after his documentary about her was released. "When it got to the fans' questions, if she got a question she didn't like or she thought was stupid, her look chilled the entire auditorium," he recalls.

Idolatry can also be dangerous. Didion had a stalker, who would wait for her outside the Brentwood house and leave letters in her mailbox, says Armstrong-Totten. This might have influenced the move to a building with a doorman in New York.

One of the more famous praises that turned around to bite Joan in the ass was book critic Michiko Kakutani's statement about

California belonging to Didion. Understandably, this offended the many other gifted poets, playwrights, novelists, and journalists who had for decades been crafting their own narratives about this region. The sentence also rings with colonizing overtones. "The white literary establishment handed her California but I propose we wrest it away from her," the Mexican American writer Myriam Gurba wrote in 2020.

Joan Didion knew that California didn't belong to her. Much of *Where I Was From* explores others' literary depictions of the Golden State, and she publicly and privately championed such Californian writers as Eve Babitz, Robert Scheer, and Maxine Hong Kingston. But she was a California woman who proudly described the state to the rest of the world in ways that were more complicated and representational than many of her peers and predecessors. Author Danyel Smith first read "Some Dreamers of the Golden Dream" while she was a student at Didion's alma mater, UC Berkeley. "I just could not, I could not believe how good it was," she recalls. "I'm a Black Californian, I am a California girl. I was weary at that time of people not writing about Black California, I was weary at that time, and remain so frankly, of the narrative of California being beachy and Hollywoody, and that being just the narrative of my home state. And so here Joan Didion was, for her set at least, telling it like it is, writing about a California that I was familiar with."

Responses to that seminal article alone—the one that lured Smith, and Steffie Nelson, and myself—show the myriad ways in which Didion can be understood and misunderstood. In a *Los Angeles Times* column published after Joan's death, writer Susan Straight, who was born and raised by an immigrant Swiss mother not far from where convicted murderer Lucille Miller's husband died in the burning VW, writes about the "absolute classism" she felt rereading "Some Dreamers of the Golden Dream" after Didion's death—about the way Didion generalized about the residents of the Inland Empire: "My people are not Didion's people," Straight said.

On the other hand, if there is anyone who should be upset by the way Didion wrote about the convicted murderer specifically, let alone the Lucille Millers of the world, it would be Lucille's daughter, Debra Miller. In an essay she wrote for the *LA Times* after Didion's death, Debra admitted that she had "cycled through many emotions" about "Some Dreamers." For years she hated it, felt the article shamed her family. Then in 1991, the schoolteacher read it once again. Her mother had died of breast cancer in 1986, estranged from her children. With the distance of decades, Debra Miller realized that Didion was right. "She was able, by focusing on my mother, to rip apart the tissue of lies that California newcomers tell themselves about how life will be better, different, happier here," she said in the *Times*.

Debra Miller met Joan Didion in 1997. The "cool customer" hugged her, introduced her to Dunne, "then tucked her arm in mine and escorted me into the auditorium and sat me down beside her," Miller wrote. "When an excerpt of the essay was read, focusing on the moment my father burned to death, she grabbed my arm and gave it a hug. Years of mortification melted away."

Didion's triumph against the naysayers that would keep her down on the Sacramento farm inspires those of us who keep turning to her diverse and divergent work, always discovering new ideas, phrases, syntaxes. We are grateful that she showed us we don't have to be a privileged white man to take on politicians, rock stars, criminals, and criminal lawyers. As the novelist Zadie Smith wrote in the *New Yorker* after Didion's death, "When women writers of my generation speak in awed tones of Didion's 'style,' I don't think it's the shift dresses or the sunglasses, the cigarettes or commas or even the em dashes that we revere, even though all those things were fabulous. It was the authority. The authority of tone. There is much in Didion one might disagree with personally, politically, aesthetically. I will never love the Doors. But I remain grateful for the day I picked up *Slouching Towards Bethlehem* and realized that a woman could speak without hedging her bets, without hemming and hawing, without making nice, without poeticisms, without sounding pleasant or sweet, without deference, and even without doubt."

The *New Yorker*'s Hilton Als wrote several important pieces about Didion and, with Hammer Museum curator Connie Butler, created an exhibit based on her writings called "What She Means" that opened at the Hammer in Los Angeles in October 2022. The show illustrated Didion's words with an eclectic selection of artwork as well as photos, articles, newsreels, and memorabilia. At the opening, Als was nervous, perspiring, emotional, and enthusiastic as he walked the press through the chronologically arranged exhibit. Gesturing to photographs of Huey P. Newton and Angela Davis, he recalled how Didion tried to get Newton to stop spewing rhetoric and speak directly when she interviewed him in the late 1960s. Als spoke about the importance of the overlooked *Where I Was From.* And in the final corner of the show, in front of a photo of Central Park, the Black, queer writer spoke about what Didion called her most important article, "Sentimental Journeys," where she was the first prominent writer to understand that the trial of five youths was about the historic relationship of Black men and white women in America.

In his memorial to Didion, spoken at St. John and published in the *New York Review of Books*, Als cites Didion as one of the three writers (along with Elizabeth Bishop and James Baldwin) he returns to over and over again, because she taught him "that family is always part of the story, along with place, and how the writer's job is to face the terror, beauty, banality, and truth inherent in being a citizen of both."

In my conversations with writers, booksellers, artists, family, and friends, I have found that Didion affected people on aesthetic, intellectual, moral, and emotional levels. Those who knew her personally admire the work and the woman who created it.

Repeatedly, people talk about Didion's kindness. "She was a very good friend when she was alive and at the height of her powers," says her agent, Lynn Nesbit. "She wasn't some cold, cut-off person. You felt her warmth and her interest in your life, in other people's kids and their grandchildren."

After driving Didion around Miami, Mitchell Kaplan wound up presenting her several times at the Miami Book Fair, which he founded. "She would always be really warm and open," he says. "She was never difficult to work with, she was always amenable to doing anything that you wanted, but there was always a kind of frailness to her. I wanted to do anything I could for Joan. She had a very gentle beautiful way about her. She was so lovely, so appreciative of what a bookseller did."

David Rieff was good friends with Joan and John. *Swimming in a Sea of Death*, his book about the passing of his mother, Susan Sontag, refers frequently to Didion's words. He disagrees with those who see her books as depressing. "The work doesn't give in to the despair that it notes," Rieff says. "She's an American writer, she's not a Russian writer. One could have written *Democracy* in a very different way, which would have been much more desperate. Instead Joan's despair is lyrical. And that's very original. I mean, with how many great writers could you say their despair was lyrical."

Truth and beauty. The north and south poles of art. From Haight-Ashbury to Hawai'i to Central Park to DC, Didion relentlessly sought to perform that classic journalistic function: speak truth to power. But she interrogated narrative (and narrated interrogations) because she wanted to speak like Amado Vazquez: direct and unembarrassed about the things she loved. She was as committed to the enjoyment of beauty as to the pursuit of truth. She wrote about Vanda orchids, Mexican chicken, the light over the Pacific Ocean, the smell of jasmine and gardenias, and the stephanotis in Quintana's hair because these things brought her pleasure, as beautiful things do. And because one day, they no longer would. She could have been prophesizing her own career in her final exam for Cal, when she wrote about Henry James: "For James was ultimately interested in beauty, in the perception and organization of beauty, in art—and this seems to me the end toward which all his writing is directed."

In 1978 a brush fire swept down from the Santa Monica

Mountains, using the canyons as roads to the Pacific Ocean, as Southern California wildfires do. When it was over, Joan Didion drove to Zuma Canyon. The place she had once wandered "was now a range not of orchids but of shattered glass and melted metal and the imploded shards of the thousands of chemical beakers that had held the Freed seedlings, the new crosses." Three years of Amado Vazquez's work was destroyed in a matter of days. Fortunately, he was already moving to his new nursery, which had survived. Then in 2018, the Woolsey fire destroyed some of those buildings. By then Vazquez had sold Zuma Canyon Orchids; he died not long after.

You can still turn east off the Pacific Coast Highway at Zuma Beach and drive to the business that Vazquez founded. The dirt road is rutted and narrow, running between fields and vineyards, with some trees still charred. The ocean is in the rearview, the mountains rise above the dash; you're in California for sure. Some of Amado's greenhouses stand in ruin, but a couple still house a cornucopia of exotic, brightly colored plants under climate-controlled conditions. Orchids are no longer created under the full moon at high tide here; they are imported from Asia. In one room, a worker carefully places moss and flowers together in a grand arrangement. She shakes her head at a reporter's questions; she doesn't know anything about Joan Didion or Amado Vazquez.

I am sure one of the reasons Didion loved Hawai'i is because orchids thrive in its tropical climate (although there too most varieties are imports). They are one of the common ingredients for leis, the ceremonial garlands that are both a tourist cliché and a Polynesian tradition. Leis are given as gifts of greeting and of farewell. They are the symbol of what she once mocked as the "wonderful aloha spirit."

On Christmas 2004, almost one year after her husband died, Joan Didion walked into the columbarium at St. John the Divine and hung a Hawaiian lei on a brass rod that held the marble plate with John Gregory Dunne's name on it. Afterward, she thought about how ocean travelers used to throw leis into the water as they left Hawai'i, "a promise that the traveler would return. The leis would get caught in the wake and go bruised and brown, the way the gardenias in the pool filter at the house in Brentwood Park had gone bruised and brown."

On September 21, 2022, I walked into the columbarium at St. John. Esteemed writers, editors, actors, and politicians had just shared their versions of Joan Didion with a building full of mourners. They were in the vestibule hugging, shaking hands, having their pictures taken. Only a handful of people were in the small chapel. Even the reverend who spoke at the memorial didn't know exactly where the deceased's remains were, until the violinist Alexi Kenney, who had silenced the hall with a Bach sonata minutes earlier, showed him. There was Joan, and John, and Quintana, and Eduene, all their names and dates of birth and death chiseled into one swirling autumn-red marble square. There were only a few flowers in the whole chapel, and no leis. Why hadn't I brought a lei?

"Leis go brown," Didion wrote in *Magical Thinking*. "Tectonic plates shift, deep currents move, islands vanish, rooms get forgotten."

Words survive.

Joan Didion in 2000.

ACKNOWLEDGMENTS

A number of people who either knew Joan Didion personally or had deep appreciation of her literary and historical importance shared their insights and time with me. I am indebted to Griffin Dunne, Julia Armstrong-Totten, Robert Weidner, Jeanne Didion Huggins, John Didion, Maurice Read, Katrina vanden Heuvel, Calvin Trillin, Jean Moore, Mitchell Kaplan, David L. Ulin, David Rieff, Michelle Bitting, Stacie Stukin, Steffie Nelson, Julian Wasser, Danyel Smith, Lisa Reinertson, Lynn Nesbit, Richard Rodriguez, Gay Talese, Joan Quinn, Katrina van der Lip, Narda Zacchino, and Robert Scheer.

I conducted archival research at the Bancroft Library in Berkeley; New York Public Library (NYPL); University of California, Los Angeles, Library; University of California, Santa Barbara, Library; and the Center for Sacramento History. I am grateful to the staff at each of these institutions. Loyola Marymount University (LMU) librarian John Jackson also helped me find my way to these and other resources.

Two LMU students provided invaluable research assistance. Tyler Roland poked around the internet and found all sorts of obscure Didion nuggets. He also helped me wade through the boxes of papers at the NYPL, and he fact-checked and copyedited the manuscript. Maude Bascome-Duong got this party started with preliminary research before commencing on her own postcollege endeavors. These are both Didions of the future! Thank you to all of my students in the last year, who have put up with my endless talk about Joan.

Several girl groups helped me get through the last few years, and even decades. First and foremost, the Fictionaires: Vivien Goldman and Jana Martin. The artivists of Turn It Up! put words into praxis. Denise Lopez, Laurie Steelink, and Heidi Tinsman are my Pedro pod. Colleagues Julia Lee, Robin Mizcolske, Alex Neel, Kate Picket, and Tara Pixley are my text-thread lifeline. My dear friend Cathay Che and her friend Lesa Griffith showed me their beloved Hawai'i. Susie Horgan is my sounding board for life; Laurie Steelink, my swim sister. Neighbors Tor and Tammi provided great design advice and wine. Thank you to Robbin Crabtree for giving me the time to write this.

Thank you to my family, always: Karlie, Kenda, Cole, Shine, Brett, Paul, Bettie, Bob, Kelly, Babette, Brian, Mike, and Peggy, and all my Harrod cousins.

Anne Muntges drew the exquisite illustrations for this book, visualizing the objects in my head and Didion's words. Designer Elina Cohen brought all the elements together. Thanks also to Catharine Strong at Aevitas Creative Management, Ghjulia Romiti at HarperOne, and Mina Hamedi at Janklow & Nesbit for their assistance—rising queens of publishing. I'm grateful to many folks at HarperCollins, including Judith Curr, Gideon Weil, Louise Braverman, Aly Mostel, Crissie Molina, and Laina Adler.

One Saturday, just a few hours after I had emailed the address I found for him online, Julian Wasser called me. He was somewhat crabby and impatient with this journalist who didn't have a recorder at the ready, but he answered my questions with grace and insight. Afterward I had that dazed feeling one gets from talking to a legend. I was saddened the next time I tried to reach him to find out he had suffered a stroke. Several weeks later, I learned he had passed. I'm honored to have one of his classic images of "the hot-looking girl" on the dust-jacket cover of this book.

The World According to Joan Didion simply wouldn't exist without three people: HarperOne editor Elizabeth Mitchell had a vision for a guide to Joan Didion that helped shape and channel these words from the conception to completion; she is my Robert B. Silvers.

My longtime agent, Sarah Lazin, brought Biz and me together. I am so fortunate to have these powerhouse women in my corner.

I needed a room of my own to make this book happen. My husband, Bud, built me a studio a writer can only dream about: a Gehry-esque wheelhouse perched on a hill with a panoramic view of the ocean. It's my golden dream. We call it Joan's ark.

SOURCES

I interviewed more than two dozen people for this book (see acknowledgments). I have cited those interviews directly in the text. In addition to Joan Didion's books and collections, I read numerous articles in newspapers, magazines, journals, and books by and about Joan Didion. There is no shortage of great writing about her! The following books were particularly helpful.

Hilton Als, *Joan Didion: What She Means.* New York: DelMonico Books, 2022.

Tracy Daugherty, *The Last Love Song: A Biography of Joan Didion.* New York: St. Martin's Press, 2015.

Sara Davidson, *Joan: Forty Years of Life, Loss, and Friendship with Joan Didion.* Byliner, Inc., 2011.

John Gregory Dunne, *Monster: Living off the Big Screen.* New York: Random House, 1997.

John Gregory Dunne, *Regards: The Selected Nonfiction of John Gregory Dunne.* New York: Thunder's Mouth Press, 2006.

SOURCES

Steffie Nelson, editor, *Slouching Towards Los Angeles: Living and Writing by Joan Didion's Light.* Los Angeles: Rare Bird Books, 2020.

Kathleen M. Vandenberg, *Joan Didion: Substance and Style.* Albany: State University of New York Press, 2021.

Marc Weingarten, *The Gang That Wouldn't Write Straight: Wolfe, Thompson, Didion, and the New Journalism Revolution.* New York: Crown Publishers, 2006.

Mark Royden Winchell, *Joan Didion.* Boston: Twayne Publishers, 1989.

Griffin Dunne's 2017 documentary *Joan Didion: The Center Will Not Hold* offers an intimate portrait of the filmmaker's aunt. Including interviews with Didion and many of her friends, family members, and associates, it birthed a new generation of her stans.

Mostly, I went straight to the source. Joan Didion's books and articles are available in a number of different ways. The Library of America has been grouping them by decades: *The 1960s & 70s* and *The 1980s & 90s.* Everyman's Library offers her nonfiction books up through *Where I Was From* in one handy hardcover, *We Tell Ourselves Stories in Order to Live.*

Below are her novels, collections, and nonfiction books in the order in which they were published. These are available in various editions, so I am noting them only by title and year. I recommend them all. They are nonfiction unless noted otherwise.

1963: *Run River* (novel)
1968: *Slouching Towards Bethlehem*
1970: *Play It As It Lays* (novel)

SOURCES

1977: *A Book of Common Prayer* (novel)

1979: *The White Album*

1983: *Salvador*

1984: *Democracy* (novel)

1987: *Miami*

1991: *After Henry*

1996: *The Last Thing He Wanted* (novel)

2001: *Political Fictions*

2003: *Where I Was From*

2003: *Fixed Ideas: America Since 9/11*

2005: *The Year of Magical Thinking*

2011: *Blue Nights*

2017: *South and West: From a Notebook*

2021: *Let Me Tell You What I Mean*

SCREENPLAYS (ALL WITH JOHN GREGORY DUNNE)

1971: *The Panic in Needle Park*

1972: *Play It As It Lays*

1976: *A Star Is Born*

1981: *True Confessions*

1996: *Up Close & Personal*

PLAY

2007: *The Year of Magical Thinking*

ABOUT THE AUTHOR

EVELYN MCDONNELL is the author of *Queens of Noise: The Real Story of the Runaways*; *Mamarama: A Memoir of Sex, Kids, and Rock 'n' Roll*; and *Army of She: Icelandic, Iconoclastic, Irrepressible Bjork*. She coedited the anthologies *Women Who Rock* and *Rock She Wrote*. She has been the pop culture writer at the *Miami Herald* and senior editor at the *Village Voice*. Evelyn's writing on music, feminism, nature, and culture has appeared in numerous publications and anthologies, including the *New York Times*, *Los Angeles Times*, and *Billboard*. A journalism professor at Loyola Marymount University, McDonnell lives in San Pedro, California, with her husband, son, cats, dog, and a fantastic view of the ocean.

ANNE MUNTGES is an accomplished Brooklyn-based artist and obsessive line maker who illustrates books when the content feels brilliant. Learn more at her website http://www.annemuntges.com.